Spiritualism and Phenomenology

The Things Themselves

The "return to the things themselves" is not only the imperative of phenomenology but also a way of writing and thinking. A genuine author delves into the lived experience of things and cannot be content with merely recounting the history of philosophy or using words devoid of any connection to the past. We can only think by drawing from others and through others. The Things Themselves series will demonstrate this conviction, for it is in the triple confrontation with oneself, with others, and even with God that true reflection is born.

With its dual roots in phenomenology and philosophy of religion, as well as in spiritualism and contemporary metaphysical debates, this series of books will diligently pursue its course "in the long run." No thought without a detour, no action without reflection. We will be able to think anew when we take up the challenge.

Hence, authors will be looked upon to manifest the imprint of their own rapport with the world in their writing, even if they do not make absolute commitments. The act of philosophizing is born of the relationship between the human and the world. And it is by drawing on our own experience as human beings that we will be able to think.

SERIES EDITOR
Emmanuel Falque

Spiritualism and Phenomenology

THE CASE OF MAINE DE BIRAN

Emmanuel Falque

TRANSLATED BY
Sarah Horton

CASCADE *Books* • Eugene, Oregon

SPIRITUALISM AND PHENOMENOLOGY
The Case of Maine de Biran

The Things Themselves

Copyright © 2025 Emmanuel Falque. All rights reserved. Except for brief quotations in critical publications or reviews, no part of this book may be reproduced in any manner without prior written permission from the publisher. Write: Permissions, Wipf and Stock Publishers, 199 W. 8th Ave., Suite 3, Eugene, OR 97401.

Cascade Books
An Imprint of Wipf and Stock Publishers
199 W. 8th Ave., Suite 3
Eugene, OR 97401

www.wipfandstock.com

PAPERBACK ISBN: 979-8-3852-3552-0
HARDCOVER ISBN: 979-8-3852-3553-7
EBOOK ISBN: 979-8-3852-3554-4

Cataloguing-in-Publication data:

Names: Falque, Emmanuel, 1963– [author]. | Horton, Sarah [translator].

Title: Spiritualism and phenomenology : the case of Maine de Biran / by Emmanuel Falque ; translated by Sarah Horton.

Description: Eugene, OR: Cascade Books, 2025 | Series: The Things Themselves | Includes bibliographical references and index.

Identifiers: ISBN 979-8-3852-3552-0 (paperback) | ISBN 979-8-3852-3553-7 (hardcover) | ISBN 979-8-3852-3554-4 (ebook)

Subjects: LCSH: Maine de Biran, Pierre, 1766–1824. | Phenomenology. | Phenomenological theology. | Spiritualism. | Philosophy of religion—France—History—18th century. | Philosophy and religion—France—History—19th century.

Classification: B2327 F35 2025 (paperback) | B2327 (ebook)

VERSION NUMBER 06/04/25

Unless otherwise noted, scripture quotations are from the ESV®Bible (The Holy Bible, English Standard Version®), copyright© 2001 by Crossway Bibles, a publishing ministry of Good News Publishers. Used by permission. All rights reserved.

Spiritualisme et phénoménologie. Le "cas" Maine de Biran © Presses Universitaires de France / Humensis, 2024.

To Jean Greisch

> There I glimpse an *abyss*,
> a *chaos* that *no inner light can penetrate*.
>
> Maine de Biran, *Dernière philosophie*

Contents

Translator's Preface | ix
Foreword | xi
Acknowledgments | xiii

Opening: The "Columbus of Metaphysics" | xv

Introduction: The Case of Maine de Biran | 1

Chapter 1: The Constitution of the *Myself* | 17
    A Conflict of Interpretations   17
    §1. Maine de Biran's Spiritualism   20
    §2. Standing by Oneself   32
    §3. The Reduction to the *Myself*   41

Chapter 2: The Resistance of the Body | 49
    The Reply of the Soul and of the Body   49
    §4. Maine de Biran's Phenomenology   52
    §5. The Man-Statue   60
    §6. "It Will Therefore be Rose-Odor"   68
    §7. The Exception of Touch   75

Chapter 3: In Search of the Flesh | 87
  Flesh and Body   87
  §8. Maine de Biran's Hermeneutics   89
  §9. Affected Man   102
  §10. I am Rose-Odor   109

Chapter 4: A Counter-History of Madness | 125
  Concrete Man in His Entirety   125
  §11. Maine de Biran's Psychiatric Phenomenology   130
  §12. The Outside   141
  §13. The Organic Unconscious   148

Chapter 5: The Foreign Body | 155
  The Double Absolute   155
  §14. Alienated Man   159
  §15. The Foreign Outside Myself   167

Chapter 6: Effortless Life | 190
  The Method *ab Absurdo*   190
  §16. The Sense of Effort   191
  §17. The Foreign to Myself   201

Conclusion: Three Lives in One | 219

Bibliography | 227
Index | 237

Translator's Preface

SARAH HORTON

HAVING WRITTEN ON MEDIEVAL philosophy, philosophy of religion, and psychoanalysis, Emmanuel Falque now turns to the late eighteenth and early nineteenth centuries with a book on Maine de Biran (1766–1824), who remains a largely neglected figure despite his considerable influence on French phenomenology via Maurice Merleau-Ponty, Paul Ricœur, and especially Michel Henry. Falque therefore is not departing from phenomenology, even as he finds in Maine de Biran a crucial source for his efforts to think phenomenology's limits. Further developing the notions of the spread body (presented in *The Wedding Feast of the Lamb* and elaborated on in "Toward an Ethics of the Spread Body") and of extra-phenomenality (the topic of *Hors phénomène*, to appear in English as *The Extra-Phenomenal*, and already introduced in English in "The Resistance of Presence," "God Extra-Phenomenal," and the interview "A Turning Point?," conducted by João Paulo Costa), he reads Maine de Biran, the great thinker of effort and of the sense of the *myself*, to discover what happens when effort and the *myself* break down.

Certainly, it is unusual in English to refer to "the *myself*," but I have chosen this translation for *le moi* (literally "the me" or "the myself," but often translated as "the self") because it bears emphasizing that, in the limit-experiences of which Biran and Falque write, what breaks down is not simply an abstract *self* but *my self* and the very possibility of *mineness*: as Falque repeatedly emphasizes, there is something worse than death as "my ownmost possibility," and that is the collapse of possibilities for me and indeed of any *me* for whom possibilities could exist. Yet the possibility of the annihilation of one's possibilities cannot be separated from the possibility of having possibilities, and for both Falque and Biran, the possibility of the worst, with which they ceaselessly wrestle, is not a reason to regret our humanity or the conscious effort that also constitutes it; far from it. That effort and the possibility of alienation go hand in hand underscores both the vulnerability of our humanity and the importance of the struggle whereby that humanity may each day continue.

Given Biran's emphasis on effort, which always involves a force and a resistance, this book is a natural continuation of Falque's thought, which has already been exploring force, the breakdown of our forces, and resistance, yet without having previously thematized effort or what he will call "effortless life" to the extent that his reading of Biran now enables him to do. At the same time, though, this book serves as a potential point of entry into the work of Falque, Biran, or both. Indeed, Falque's 2023 Gilson lecture series at the Institut Catholique de Paris, which became this book, was my first prolonged encounter with Maine de Biran, and I here express my gratitude to Emmanuel Falque for introducing me to this often-overlooked philosopher. It is my hope that the availability of *Spiritualism and Phenomenology: The Case of Maine de Biran* for an Anglophone audience will contribute to a resurgence in the study of Biran's thought.

Finally, I thank my mother, Joanna Horton, for carefully proofreading every page of this translation. Any errors or infelicities that remain are of course mine alone.

Foreword

CERTAIN DESCENTS INTO ONESELF are made within the intimacy of oneself. And there are places where one stays in one's stove-heated room, far indeed from every agitation and preoccupation. What could be better than writing in the heart of the Périgord a work about this man who was a subprefect in Bergerac and then a deputy of Dordogne? So close, so far—or, rather, about a stone's throw away, a distance that could be travelled by stagecoach in less than three hours. Each one has his or her Grateloup—Maine de Biran's noble house: mine is called Grange d'Ans. Having taken refuge there for many years, one can stay and abide there to think. As it was for Maine de Biran two centuries earlier, life is a diastole-systole movement between the province and Paris. There is no going without returning, no *Iliad* without an *Odyssey*. It is certainly with desire that one leaves the self when returning to worldly affairs, but one also knows that it is with happiness, yet also in pain, that it will be necessary to come back—and also sometimes to dare "to enter into solitude," there where every veritable work of thought is accomplished and where, in addition, all spirituality is nourished:

> March 12, 1815—A rainy day. I was tranquilly settled in my solitary study, rereading my metaphysical manuscripts, when I was interrupted at three o'clock by the reception of the Paris mail. I finish a note that I had begun, and I then open a letter that informs me that Bonaparte is in France, that the Chambers are convoked, and that I must return at once to my post. Instantly there is a revolution in my whole being. I pass rapidly from the profoundest calm to the liveliest agitation: my head

spins, my stomach clenches; I dine in haste, and I organize my preparations for tomorrow.[1]

Granges d'Ans, January 28, 2023

---

[1]. Maine de Biran, *Journal* I, 44, entry dated March 12, 1815. The *Journal* will henceforth be abbreviated J. followed by the indication of the volume number as a Roman numeral, referring here to the numbering established by Henri Gouhier (I–III), and not to the number of the *Journal* itself (I–IV).

Acknowledgments

WITH TREMENDOUS GRATITUDE TO Jérôme Alexandre and Florence Quillet for their reading of the manuscript, as well as to Grégory Solari and Philippe Richard for their reading of the proofs.

Opening

The "Columbus of Metaphysics"

"Who knows all that concentrated reflection can do, and whether there is not a *new internal world* that could one day be discovered by some *Columbus of metaphysics*?"[1] This annotation from Maine de Biran's *Journal*, dated July 23, 1816, "in the margin and in another ink," perhaps tells us everything about the thinker from Bergerac's thirst for adventure. Reading Maine de Biran *today* is being initiated into traveling or throwing oneself into a long "excursion"—*excursus* understood here not as a "digression" but rather in the etymological sense of an "*ex-cursum*": "I run" (*curro*) or "run out of (*ex*)," "exit from," "propose an outing," or even "enter suddenly into an unexpected and unhabitual domain." In short, it is certainly an "excursion" outside the current interpretations of Maine de Biran but also an "excursion" or an *excursus outside oneself*, triggering a sort of new "incursion"—that is, an incursion on a ground that is less trodden or that is more foreign to the "Biranian subjectivity of the flesh" that is usually all that is remembered.

Indeed, let us make no mistake here. The discovery of this "New World" by Maine de Biran, as the "Columbus of metaphysics," consists, in my view, less in the mere "inner sentiment of oneself" that is ceaselessly rehashed than in the "resistance in counter-relief" to which it gives rise. Indeed, labels never suit their authors, and still less do the trends with which one saddles them. What is true of every thinker—who, for

---

1. J. I, 176 (entry dated July 23, 1816, emphasis in original). [Unless otherwise noted, all translations of citations are my own. –Trans.]

example, is always surprised when he is asked if he is (still) a phenomenologist or not, or even if he has (rightly or wrongly) become a metaphysician—is still more true of the case of Maine de Biran. The "new America" is not necessarily the continent that has been taken for it, and it is therefore by venturing "elsewhere," or even "otherwise," that we will discover new countries.

For the thinker of Grateloup—the noble abode where he resided in that Dordogne whose deputy he was—is a case for us who follow him, as he was yesterday for his contemporaries. Rarely in the history of thought has there been one who is so "unclassifiable," even so "outside the categories" in every sense of the term: one who cannot be inventoried or assigned a place not only because he does not enter into the norms that we had previously determined, but also because he refuses the categories, because he thinks "outside" the categories, even "outside" the subject himself, which can but surprise in light of the interpretations that have consecrated him as "the" champion of subjectivity. I will return to this, but it is right to state it from the beginning, for here lies the certainly-paradoxical thesis that I will defend: *far from seeing in the figure of Maine de Biran only a return, or even the invention, of the hearth of autoaffection as of the lived or proper body* [corps propre],[2] *in reality the thinker from Bergerac wants to confront being "outside oneself"*[3] *and taking stock of an "improper body"* [corps impropre]—*which only makes him exist all the more.*

Let us make this clear from the start, and we will, of course, have to return to the point to insist on it: exteriority—"outside oneself"—here does not mean independence or pure objectivity. That would amount to having never read Maine de Biran and misunderstanding his debate with or, better, his combat against Locke's empiricism and Condillac's sensualism, or to having read him but without understanding him. Exteriority signifies rather the externalization of oneself to oneself, the "deterritorialization," as Gilles Deleuze would say, but I will not here

---

2. [The French term *le corps propre* is usually translated as *the lived body*; I have occasionally employed the literal translation *the proper body* because Falque plays with this literal sense when he refers also to *le corps impropre* (literally *the improper body*, the body that is in some sense not proper to me, that is irreducible to the lived body or to the flesh). –Trans.]

3. [The French expression *hors de soi*, literally "out of oneself" or "outside oneself," corresponds to the English "beside oneself." I have maintained a literal translation because of the theme of exteriority; Falque is playing on both the literal meaning and the figurative meaning that in English is typically expressed with "beside oneself." –Trans.]

follow his "rhizomes" and other *Thousand Plateaus*. Better, whereas his reference was spatial (from the center to the periphery),[4] my reference will rather be subjective, or internal to the subject, in what I here name *extra*-phenomenality. In other words, there is, on my view, a sort of "uncanny" (*Unheimlich*) in Maine de Biran, the very uncanny that, Freud emphasizes, is not far from me, as if set at "a distance *from* myself," but is very close, as a "distance *in* oneself": "in reality nothing new or foreign, but something familiar to psychic life from time immemorial and that has become foreign to it only by the process of repression."[5] In French we could say *étrangèreté* (foreignerness) rather than *étrangeté* (weirdness),[6] at least to take away its mysterious character—the *myself*[7] is sometimes, according to Maine de Biran verbatim, "*outside itself* and *foreign to itself*" or, in other words, "alienated" or "*alienus*," to refer here to the Prolegomena of the *Nouvelles considérations sur les rapports du physique et du*

---

4. Deleuze and Guattari, *Thousand Plateaus*, 53: "*Nomadic waves* or *flows of deterritorialization* go from the *central layer* to the *periphery*, then from the *new center* to the *new periphery*, falling back to the old center and launching forth to the new" (emphasis added).

5. Freud, *Uncanny*, 394. [Translation modified to follow more closely the French translation that Falque cites. –Trans.]

6. [*Étrangèreté*, a noun coined by the psychoanalyst Jean Laplanche, derives from *étranger*, which as a noun means "stranger" or "foreigner" and which as an adjective means "strange" or "foreign." *Étrangeté* can mean "strangeness" but carries a connotation of "bizarreness" or "weirdness" that Falque wishes to avoid here. *Étrangèreté* could be, and has been, translated as "strangerness"; in this case, because of the relation Falque indicates between *étrangèreté* and *aliénation* (alienation), and because the notions of the foreign and the alien are so closely linked in English, I have translated *étrangèreté* as *foreignerness* and have also translated *étranger* as *foreign*. This translation has the advantage of being consistent with the translation of *corps étranger* as *foreign body*, since a key theme will be that my body can in fact be a foreign body: not a bizarre, weird, or mysterious body, but rather a body that is in some sense external to myself. –Trans.]

7. [The French *moi* can mean "me" or "myself." Because "the myself" is not a typical expression in English, *le moi* is typically translated as "the self" or, especially in psychoanalytic contexts, "the ego." I have avoided the latter translation (though I certainly employ it to translate *l'égo*), since if Biran in some ways anticipates psychoanalysis, the movement still postdates him, and its concepts are not identical to his. The few existing English translations of Biran do not distinguish between *le moi* and *le soi* ("the self"; *soi* is a third-person pronoun that often translates as "oneself"), rendering both as "the self." In many contexts, the distinction has sufficiently little importance that this solution is acceptable. In this book, however, there are passages in which it is necessary to distinguish *le moi* from *le soi* in some way. I have therefore translated *le moi* as "the *myself*" (while rendering *le soi* as "the self"), and I have maintained this translation throughout for the sake of consistency. –Trans.]

moral de l'homme [*New Considerations on the Relationship Between the Physical and the Moral in Man*] (1820):

> Thus it is very justly said in common language that in such a state [when a being of our species, having the external form of a man, neither knows nor possesses himself and does not exist for himself] man is *outside himself* and *foreign to himself* (*alienus*), whence the very fittingly coined word *alienation*, to which can be attributed a greater degree of generalization than it has in the ordinary sense of biologists and doctors. This term [alienation] would indeed be very well suited to all the states particular [*propres*] to [or all the irregular states of, *sic*] the soul and the organized body that carry with them a *complete absence*, momentary or permanent, *of the sentiment of the* myself, although the vital and sensitive functions experience no interruption.[8]

The passage is sufficiently important that we will have to return to it later (chapter 5). For extra-phenomenality ("man *outside himself* and *foreign to himself*") is not just defined there but is also explicitly formulated and explicated. That the exception (the soul's "particular" or "irregular states") should become the rule (alienation as the "complete absence of the sentiment of the *myself*") or that to "*so much exception* should correspond *so much modification*"[9]—this is, in reality, what Maine de Biran sees, what he seeks, but also what he flees. Certain limit-situations of alienation or of becoming "other *to* oneself," including for the thinker from Bergerac (sleep, sleepwalking, dreaming, madness, drugs, etc., and no longer only illness, separation, the death of a child, natural disasters, and pandemics),[10] interrupt or, better, produce this "complete absence of the sentiment of the *myself*," even as I am yet, at least organically and physiologically, still living, or "although the vital and sensitive functions experience no interruption." One could not say it any better. Maine de Biran has already seen that there is something worse than being a "living one who is not yet dead" (waiting for or being anxious over death), and it is being a "living dead one"[11] (living as if I were dead)—in other words, "no longer having the sentiment of oneself," having become for oneself like a stone or an object,

---

8. Maine de Biran, *Nouvelles considérations*, 5 (emphasis partly in original).

9. See my work in Falque, *Hors phénomène*, 299–307.

10. Falque, *Hors phénomène*, 29–61. ["Separation" refers here to the breakdown of a relationship with a spouse or partner. –Trans.]

11. [The French *mort vivant*, literally "living dead [one]," is also French for "zombie." –Trans.]

still being *there* when I should or would like no longer to be *yet there*—in short, a "surviving one," an "over-living one."[12]

There are, therefore, limit-situations that the thinker of Grateloup has uniquely analyzed in which the subject does not recognize, or no longer recognizes, himself, or, rather, in which he no longer has access to any "himself" whatsoever: absolutely "outside" affection, even outside "autoaffection," incapable not only of "saying *himself*" but also of "experiencing *himself*" in his psyche (the extra-phenomenal) as also in his corporeality (the spread body). Such a man is said to be "outside himself" or "foreign to himself" (*alienus*) by Maine de Biran himself. One could certainly believe and think that there is indeed an attempt at usurpation in order to "take all the credit," so thoroughly does the French expression *hors de lui* (outside or beside himself) tend toward "*extra-phenomenality*" and put to rest all the interpretations of the thinker from Bergerac that have become commonplace, or nearly so: namely, a Maine de Biran drawn wholly to the side of interiority and of intimacy more than to exteriority or extimacy (spiritualism), or else a Maine de Biran interpreted wholly on the basis of the "body that is a subject for itself" or the "lived or proper body" more than of the "body that is an object in itself" or the "improper body" (phenomenology).

It remains that the philosopher, in the whole of his work, says this, and even ceaselessly puts it into practice: only a confrontation with multiple "foreign bodies" (not only himself but also other disciplines) can make thought advance. Even having withdrawn to Grateloup in his isolated abode at the heart of the Dordogne, Maine de Biran knew and sensed that it is only by *lovingly debating* with alterity that one can truly think and progress—hence the incessant references to other authors, which testify to his most radical honesty. The "backlash" of so many subjects that were studied in his era by a single man—and that fight "as if in a duel" in his work (psychology, anthropology, metaphysics, medicine, religion, etc.)—is so great that the solitary thinker, who also, however, belonged to high society by virtue of his "comings and goings" between Grateloup and Paris, cannot be viewed as a philosopher who was closed off or solipsistic in his thought; far from it.

The totality of Biran's oeuvre, published in eighteen volumes (by Vrin)—from his *Écrits de jeunesse* [*Youthful Writings*] (vol. 1) to his

---

12. [The French *survivre* (to survive) literally means "to over-live"; the prefix *sur-*, like the English *over-*, can refer to excess, understood here not at all as the excess of the saturated phenomenon but rather as the excess of "outliving oneself." –Trans.]

Dernière philosophie [*Late Philosophy*] (vol. 10), including and especially *Existence et anthropologie* [*Existence and Anthropology*] (vol. 10.2), after *Morale et religion* [*Morality and Religion*] (vol. 10.1)—indeed requires us today to see and read the whole of his corpus otherwise. I will be far from sticking only to the *Mémoire sur la décomposition de la pensée* [*Decomposition of Thought*][13] (1804) and the *Essai sur les fondements de la psychologie* [*Essay on the Foundations of Psychology*] (1812)—although, without denying its ingenious character, the reading of them could have been wholly other—it is, therefore, not "against" [*contre*] (for one always remains "very close" [*tout contre*]) but "otherwise" than Michel Henry's *Philosophy and Phenomenology of the Body*—written in 1948–1949, but published as a "separate book" (1965) after *The Essence of Manifestation* (1963), whose first part it should, however, have been—that I wish here to decipher and decrypt Maine de Biran's thought. And here this means doing so in light of the "extra-phenomenal" and the "spread body" rather than of "autoaffection" and the "lived body."[14]

13. ["Decomposition" refers here to the breaking down of thought into its constituent parts. –Trans.]

14. Michel Henry's work *Philosophy and Phenomenology of the Body*, written, therefore, in 1947–1948 and published in 1965, refers principally to the *Mémoire sur la décomposition de la pensée* [*Treatise on the Decomposition of Thought*] (vols. 3–4 of the Tisserand edition), and to the *Essai sur les fondements de la psychologie* (vols. 8–9 of the same edition). To which is added, of course, Henri Gouhier's anthology *Maine de Biran: Œuvres choisies*. One is thus far from the *Œuvres de Maine de Biran* published over the course of a decade by Vrin in eighteen volumes from 1987 through 1997 (under the direction of a team of researchers from the *Centre national de la recherche scientific* [CNRS], the "National Center for Academic Research"). The treatises were not all available in the same state in the period after the war and hence were less consulted or less consultable—in particular, the *Discours à la société médicale de Bergerac* ("Speeches at the Bergerac Medical Society"), *The Relationship Between the Physical and the Moral in Man* (with, in addition, the *Nouvelles considérations sur le rapport . . .* ["New considerations on the Relationship . . ."]), and of course the *Dernière philosophie* ("Late Philosophy") understood as *Existence et anthropologie* ("Existence and Anthropology"). A "partial" knowledge of the texts can therefore, to a certain degree, account for a "partial" (biased) interpretation. It remains that *this* reading of Maine de Biran via the "sentiment of effort" interpreted as autoaffection can and should be read as "the" veritable (and perhaps also the unique) source of the whole of Michel Henry's oeuvre, which constitutes his particular genius. On this necessary "distancing" relative to Henry's interpretation, without, however, denying its originality, see Devarieux, *L'intériorité réciproque*, esp. 54–55: "Whereas Biran exposes the *existential reasons* of the distraction from oneself that is proper to the ego, Henry makes this forgetting an *ontological condition*, a *condition of the essence* of the mute coming to oneself of the Self of life" (emphasis added).

In counter-relief, therefore, and no longer *in relief*,[15] that is, in my view, how we must now, in an original way, read Biran's oeuvre—in the resistances to the sentiment of oneself that he sets forth and analyzes with care (sleep, sleepwalking, dreams, madness, drugs, etc.) more than in the statements that make the "primitive fact" the summit of our appropriation (autoaffection). Man indeed is "double"; the future deputy of Dordogne ceaselessly repeats this—and I will return to the point often—as soon as his "psychology" (*Essai sur les fondements de la psychologie*) explicitly becomes an "anthropology" (*Nouvelles considérations sur les rapports du physique et du moral de l'homme*, 1820, and *Nouveaux essais d'anthropologie* [*New Anthropological Essays*], 1823). Indeed, we cannot content ourselves with the *simplex* when we are always *duplex*, nor, therefore, can we attach ourselves only to the "*homo in intellectualitate*" (man in his thought) without first referring to the "*homo in vitalitate*" (man in his animality).[16] Maine de Biran's philosophy is a "science of the mixed"—we will return to this point (in the opening of chapter 4)—in the irreducible consistency of the "mixture" that makes it so every "bracketing" of the world or of objectivity, in order to come back to or to reach the "sentiment of the self," can certainly be wished for but in reality can never be realized. Maurice Merleau-Ponty's statement in the Preface of *The Phenomenology of Perception* (1945), in opposition to Husserl but retrospectively also to Michel Henry, also holds for Maine de Biran, so long as he is read otherwise: "The most important lesson of the reduction is the *impossibility of a complete reduction*."[17]

---

15. [The imagery here comes from sculpture: a sculpture "in relief" remains attached to a background but rises out of it, having been formed through the cutting away of the stone that forms that background, whereas a sculpture "in counter-relief" is carved into the stone: the resulting hollowed-out figures lie deeper than the surface. Thus a reading "in relief" is a reading that takes at face value the explicit meaning of a text, while a reading "in counter-relief" seeks what is implicit in the text. I have chosen to translate these phrases literally to preserve the striking imagery. –Trans.]

16. On this question of the "mixture," see the excellent report by Azouvi, *Maine de Biran*, 139–206. See also Ricœur's commentary (although it is not directly focused on Maine de Biran) in *Fallible Man*, 91–105 (with thanks to Professor Jean Greisch for having reminded me of the reference).

17. Merleau-Ponty, *Phenomenology of Perception*, lxxvii (emphasis added). I thus adhere, at least in part, to Bernard Baertschi's accurate intuition: "Maine de Biran, just like Husserl, *begins with a phenomenology of consciousness*; it is, in Biran, the philosophy of the primitive fact that would be subject to the reduction. But whereas Husserl moves toward a transcendental idealism, Maine de Biran *opts for an empirical realism* because for him, just as for Merleau-Ponty, 'the most important lesson of the reduction is the impossibility of the complete reduction' [*sic*.] For Biran, what escapes the

Properly speaking "offside" [*hors je(u)*]—in the double sense of being outside or beside oneself and out of play[18]—pushing the Biranian subject to the extreme sometimes makes it no longer be one: no longer, that is, a "subject" or, quite simply, a "self." The reading *in counter-relief* of his work does not consecrate the refuge of the self but rather points to exile outside oneself. I no longer inhabit myself, for perhaps I was never made first to inhabit myself or to inhabit in myself, even though humanity has apparently always first been defined in classical philosophy as interiority. If there is a *Journal* for Maine de Biran—and I will frequently return to it—it is, in my view, a matter less of an "intimate diary," as Ernest Naville would categorize it when drawing up the list of the manuscripts found in the attic of Grateloup (and inheriting from his father, François Naville, the first crates of manuscripts that had been sent to him), than, rather, of an "extimate diary" of an explorer, a conqueror, or a veritable "Columbus of metaphysics" who was, as I have said, a discoverer of "new Americas": "One can doubtless speak of a 'journal' or 'diary,'" Michel Tournier rightly notes regarding his own "life notes" that he will thus entitle *Journal extime* [*Extimate Diary*], "but it will be the contrary of an 'intimate diary.' I have forged, to define it, the word 'extimate'"—which means, no longer *imploring* understood as "a sniveling retreat into our 'little stacks of miserable secrets,' as André Malraux said," but the *exploring* that "corresponds to a centrifugal movement of discoveries and conquests."[19]

---

reduction is *the absolute existence of the real*" ("L'idéologie subjective," 118, emphasis added). It remains that the extra-phenomenality of which I will speak here has nothing to do with "reality." That would be drawing Biran to Bergson's side, which could not be the case from the point of view of an "effortless life" [*infra*, ch. 6].

18. [*Hors jeu* is the French term for *offside*, a penalty in most football codes and some other sports. It is defined differently in each code in which it exists, but, in short, a player who commits an offside penalty has entered an area of the field that he is not allowed to be in or (as in soccer) in which he is not allowed to receive the ball from a teammate, and in this sense, he is "out of play" or "out of the game (*jeu*)." *Je*, the French word for *I*, is pronounced almost identically to *jeu* (game). Falque is thus making a pun by writing *hors je(u)* in order to convey both the sense "out of play" and also the notion of being unable to think oneself as an *I*, so much is one beside oneself, or *hors de soi* (see Opening, note 4). The pun is not, unfortunately, particularly suited to translation into English; writing "off*s*ide" with the *i* italicized, as I have done, at least suggests that some play on the word *I* is meant. I have not capitalized the *i*, as, although capitalization might be more suggestive of such a pun, it could too easily be taken to imply a presence of the *I* rather than an absence so fundamental that it is not even sensed as an absence. –Trans.]

19. Tournier, *Journal extime*, 11–12.

Let us say this frankly—and it should be taken here not as an opinion piece but rather as a turn in my own thought. I have had my fill of interiority—which signifies here, according to the idiom, "being full to the point of no longer feeling like swallowing anything," "not being able to hold anything more," "no longer being able to endure it," "losing all interest," "being tired of or over it," or even, more simply, "having had it up to here." From Descartes through a certain form of phenomenology (which does not signify that thinking "the outside in oneself" or the "extra-phenomenal" is necessarily leaving phenomenology, nor does it signify turning toward some sort of "existentialism" of a Sartrean type), everything is only internal—rightly, certainly, against the external if it is understood as mere objectivity (the natural attitude), but which should not signify only the intimacy of the lived experiences of consciousness, even in a form of transcendence within immanence (*epoché*). One can "reduce the reduction" unto autoaffection (Henry), but one can also posit and discover *in oneself* resistance to the reduction via the inassimilable that is trauma, resistance to thought in the figure of the unthinkable, and the opposition to the lived experience of the flesh via the thickness and the materiality of the body (my own perspective.) This is not to deny the merits of phenomenology, nor is it to no longer belong to phenomenology, but it is shifting phenomenology by thinking, this time, a form of exteriority or even of objectivity within subjectivity itself: seeing one's body as no longer being one's own (the spread body) and being stunned by thoughts or ideas that crush me and that are impossible to appropriate for myself (the extra-phenomenal). "Thinking does not depend on a beautiful interiority that would reunite the visible and the articulable," writes Gilles Deleuze, this time, quite rightly, referring to Foucault as well as to Blanchot, "but occurs through the *intrusion of an outside* that eats into the interval and forces or dismembers the internal."[20]

What is most surprising, then, is that it is precisely in Maine de Biran, as a thinker of interiority and of the intimacy of oneself, in the sense of the "sentiment of effort" that is always (or almost always) experienced, that one finds at the same time, by way of a counterpoint, this so-great distance from oneself to oneself or this "outside in oneself" that is impossible to contain. Let it suffice here to cite the important, in my view, outline for the Copenhagen treatise of 1811 (*The Relationship Between the Physical and the Moral in Man*), certainly crowned with success but never published in

---

20. Deleuze, *Foucault*, 87 (emphasis added). [Translation modified. –Trans.]

his lifetime, like most of his works, in fact. It can indeed happen, according to the thinker from Bergerac, and it even does happen, that—under the influence of "narcotics" or "alcoholic wines," certainly, but also in that most ordinary phenomenon of "sleep"—there occurs what he names, properly speaking, an "obscuration" or "the total eclipse of the sentiment of the *myself*"—that is, precisely what we are seeking in the subject that is "offside" [*hors je(u)*] or in the "extra-phenomenal":

> I shall point out with respect to this successive invasion of the phenomena of *sleep* how *delirium* or *mental alteration* are, as it were, only a degree or circumstance of the same *essential condition* on which this state depends, namely the *progressive suspension of the exercise of will and of effort*, and as a direct result *the obscuration and total eclipse of the sentiment of the* myself, and of all that is strictly intellectual, etc.[21]

A "progressive suspension of the exercise of will and of effort" that brings about "the obscuration and total eclipse of the sentiment of the *myself*," as a function of a condition that is here said to be "essential," and therefore constitutive of our nature, and not solely by a simple contingency or accident: this is the nub, the core, or even the "hole" [*trou*] of our existence that is traumatic (or, rather, "troumatic")[22] from its origin, which means that the "obscuration of the sentiment of the *myself*" becomes constitutive of a *myself* [*moi*] that can no longer say "I" or "me" (*moi*). There is nothing partial about this *eclipse of the sentiment of the* myself. It is "total," according to Maine de Biran's very word. It is an eclipse that plunges us into the "black night"—the night where "everything has disappeared," the "*other* night [that] does not welcome, does not open," to say it with Maurice Blanchot:[23] not obscurity as a waiting for light, but shadow unto the forgetting of all luminosity. Worse than the "night of phenomenology" (the possibility of impossibility) is the "phenomenology of the night" (the impossibility of possibility). The subject itself, that is, the "*myself*," then becomes precisely *outside itself* or offside [*hors je(u)*]—in the double sense in which the ego sometimes stands at once both "outside itself" and

---

21. Maine de Biran, *Relationship Between the Physical and the Moral*, 124 (emphasis added).[Translation modified. –Trans.]

22. [*Troumatisme*, a neologism coined by Lacan, is a play on *trou* (hole) and *traumatisme* (trauma). As there is no way to translate this play on words into English, *troumatisme* is rendered as *troumatism*, and *troumatique*, the corresponding adjective, as *troumatic*. –Trans.]

23. Blanchot, *Space of Literature*, 162–63.

"out of play."²⁴ There is no need for narcotics or alcohol to forget oneself; it suffices to sleep—but in such a deep sleep that it is also dying.

This will be clarified, however. The "total eclipse of the sentiment of oneself" is here not the forgetting of oneself or the complete proximity of oneself with oneself in the pure life of autoaffection (a sort of quasi-divine return to the immediacy of animal life) but is on the contrary the distance from oneself to oneself that means that one weighs on oneself in non-recognition and even in the impossible "experience of the *myself*." Not autoaffected, the traumatic subject is hetero-affected or, rather, "outside affection." For it is indeed the "*sentiment* of the *myself*" that is here suspended, or even annihilated, and therefore also the *affect itself* that would be capable of relating itself to itself—and not simply the intellectual life of man ("*homo in intellectualitate*") in a return to animal life or to the animal life in man ("*homo in vitalitate*"). Indeed, it does not suffice to say that the *myself* has disappeared and that sentiment or affect remains, even to belong to an anonymous life that I precisely could not designate as mine. For in a purely animal or sensitive state, man, precisely because he is man, according to Maine de Biran, suddenly stands in an "outside" or an "outside myself" that is of the order of trauma or of the "non-man." *Alienation* or becoming "other *to* oneself" (*alienus*), as I will show (chapter 5), is not a mode of humanity degraded toward animality, or of thought toward sensing, or even of thought as a mode of sensing. On the contrary, only an "exception" to the sentiment of the *myself*, which is neither wanted nor hoped for, can bring about such "modifications" of sensation, concerning which one does not know if one will be able to come back from them and even one day "sense" again. What would here seem to be psychosis and even schizophrenia is in reality also a possible modality of life in extreme situations that Maine de Biran is determined to analyze: sleep, sleepwalking, dreams, madness, drugs, etc.

The "Columbus of metaphysics" will not, therefore, cease surprising us and making us travel—casting us the invitation to cross borders, to visit other countries, and making us discover new worlds. A "country not of our birth," to take up Emmanuel Levinas's expression²⁵—not that it is rooted in an immemorial past that is definitively closed for us, but on the contrary because it projects me onto an island that is forbidden for me,

24. Cf. Falque, *Hors phénomène*, 61–64, 230–41.
25. Levinas, *Totality and Infinity*, 33–34: "The metaphysical desire does not long to return, for it is *desire for a country not of our birth*, for a country foreign to every nature, which has not been our fatherland and to which we shall never betake ourselves" (emphasis added). [Translation modified. –Trans.]

filled with trauma and with dangers, but on which I myself could well also run aground. The philosopher of Grateloup will not put "new wine into old wineskins" (Luke 5:37), nor will he "multiply loaves of bread" except by starting from bread (Luke 9:10–17). *For new wine, new wineskins*, certainly—but always while cultivating the *old vines* of the metaphysical tradition as such; I will return to this (§13a). Nothing is more contrary to the thought of the thinker from Bergerac than "throwing everything overboard" to "tack" anew, to follow here, once again, the metaphor of the navigator or the "Columbus of metaphysics." It is therefore to revolutionizing the whole of thought, but "from the inside," that Maine de Biran has applied himself: whence the luster and the fascination of those who have made the effort to regularly visit him in the original texts, Michel Henry in particular.

Will one, then, still speak of "phenomenology" with regard to the philosopher of Grateloup? Perhaps, and even certainly; I will return to this in particular, starting from the question of the "flesh," even also of the "body" (§4), but only to the degree that one understands and accepts, with Maurice Merleau-Ponty, that there is something of the "non-phenomenological" in phenomenology, and extends phenomenology itself that far: "What *resists* phenomenology within us—natural being, the 'barbarous' source Schelling spoke of—cannot remain *outside phenomenology* and should have its place *within it*. The philosopher must bear his shadow, which is not simply the factual absence of future light."[26]

Will one, then, say that there is still "spiritualism" in Maine de Biran? This, too, must not be doubted, as I will show (§1), but it is, again, at the price of a complete reworking of the concept of the soul or the spirit, understood paradoxically as being "outside oneself," or as "exteriority," and no longer as the "moist gastric intimacy" from which it is not certain that mere Husserlian intentionality has succeeded in liberating us: "I've been asked to talk about the body, so I'm going to talk about the soul," declares Jean-Luc Nancy, accurately but also against the current, in *Corpus*.

> In saying "of the soul," I simply wanted to indicate this: "*of the soul*" or "*of the body outside the self*." If the body isn't mass, if it isn't closed in on itself and penetrated by itself, it is *outside itself*. It is *being outside itself*. And this is what is at stake with the word *soul*. It in no way involves hearing, behind this word, an *ineffable interiority*. . . . If we wish to keep the word *matter*, then we should say that it is the impenetrability of what is form—in

26. Merleau-Ponty, *Signs*, 178 (emphasis added).

other words, relation, articulation, and therefore, yet again, the relation between *sensing, sensing oneself, being sensed, and sensing something* as *from the outside*.[27]

---

27. Nancy, *Corpus*, 125–27 (emphasis added). [Translation modified. –Trans.] And there is the allusion to the "gastric intimacy of the *myself*" that Husserl's intentionality would attempt to break, according to Jean-Paul Sartre, but one could doubt that Husserl's intentionality has really accomplished this, at least in view of the development of phenomenology in France, which has been wholly concentrated on an ego—invoked (Levinas), autoaffected (Henry), deposed (Marion), called (Chrétien), or stretched toward the *eschaton* (Lacoste), but never truly "destroyed" or, at the very least, "exteriorized" with regard to itself. Cf. Sartre, "Intentionality," 4: "To know is to 'burst toward,' *to tear oneself out of the moist gastric intimacy*, veering out there *beyond oneself*, towards what *is not oneself*" (emphasis added). [Translation modified. –Trans.] There is, however, this difference that existentialism thinks an "outside consciousness" before which one stumbles and that leads to the sentiment of the absurd (the "root" for Antoine Roquentin in *Nausea*, for example), whereas the "outside oneself," understood here as "extra-phenomenal" or the subject that is "offside, out of the I, out of play" [*Hors je(u)*] arises rather from a trauma of consciousness that destroys everything, unto "sentiment" itself, and that leaves the subject simply "stunned or cornered"—without any other judgment (the absurd, for example) than that of being still-there (the crisis), and without any other possible exit (commitment, for example) than discovering oneself as always modified (hyper-transformation). On this relation, at once "successful" and "failed," between Sartre and Maine de Biran, see pages 184–86.

Introduction

The "Case" of Maine de Biran

It is right, phenomenologically, to sense man in order to think him and think his thought. For, at least for Maine de Biran, it is by sensing, or at the very least by experiencing, that one thinks. Better, thought itself is a mode of the sensed or the autoaffected—and, precisely, one falls with the other (thought and affect), from the moment that limit-experiences lead me "outside myself" or that man discovers himself as sometimes "outside himself" or "alienated" in the "total eclipse of the sentiment of the *myself*." No one could doubt that Maine de Biran is, then, a "case" in every sense of the word—at once an *exception* and a *strangeness* in the ordinary course of things and of beings.

A "Case" *ad Extra* and *ad Intra*

He is a "case" *ad extra*, first, in his life as a royalist and antirevolutionary, which today can certainly surprise and even shock, but which in his era—the Revolution being taken as a parenthesis, if certainly a bloody one, between royalty on the one hand and the Empire and the Restoration on the other—could have led him to think that he was rather on the right side. So long as life, and his own life, was safe (one can imagine Maine de Biran taking refuge in Grateloup the day of the execution of Louis XVI on January 21, 1793), let us just say that the course of events, after the insurrection and its sequels in the Terror (from the storming of the Bastille in 1789 to Robespierre's execution in 1794), indeed lead one to believe that a public figure in a province was rather better off than a permanent resident of Paris—all the more so since the Empire and the Restoration did, in a sense, prove him right in his time, even though the history and establishment of the republic would definitively take their place.

Born, then, in Bergerac on November 29, 1766, under the monarchy of Louis XV, then defending Louis XVI against the revolutionaries shortly after the storming of the Bastille on July 14, 1789, when he stood, at the age of twenty-three, to protect the king with the king's guards behind the gates of Versailles (legend tells that he was wounded there), Maine de Biran died on July 20, 1824, in Paris at the height of the monarchy's glory—since at that time it had been "restored" since 1814, after the Empire and the naming of Napoleon Bonaparte as First Consul (in 1800). It was, therefore, now at the sides of Louis XVIII, the new king of France initiating the Restoration, that Maine de Biran was elected quaestor (member of the parliamentary Assembly) in June 1814, ennobled by royal degree in September 1814, and elected deputy of Dordogne in 1817, after having been named, from 1802 onwards, to the general counsel of Dordogne, then subprefect of Bergerac in 1806, and even designated by the Senate to sit in the *Corps législatif d'État* (a part of the French legislature) in Paris from 1810 onwards.

One sees, and one even senses, when one leafs through page after page of the three volumes of his *Journal*, that Maine de Biran was in no way a "hidden thinker," only secluded in his chateau, or rather his manor, in Grateloup—as if in his burrow, and shut away in the depths of Dordogne, a stone's throw from Bergerac (hardly ten kilometers), far from the affairs of the world. On the contrary, he lived in tension, between the province and Paris, and his stagecoach never stopped crossing, and crossing again, the route that binds Grateloup to the capital. And it was in this back-and-forth between solitude and society that the thread of his thought was formed and, at the same time, that his thought became more fruitful. For that matter, these lines, which are highly extraordinary, probably because they were lived and shared, testify to this; and it is through them that I myself first met Maine de Biran, whose sharing of his life, or of certain points of his life, also warrants that one should try to do the same for one's thought and for oneself:

> Entry dated August 25, 1814 [Maine de Biran is in Paris, and Louis XVIII has just been restored to his kingly seat]. I would be better disposed for work if I did not let myself be ceaselessly diverted. An insignificant correspondence, purely a courtesy,

> consumes all my mornings, and then I am wholly devoted to external life.... On the 28, I wanted to remain tranquilly at home. Our president Laîné came to distract me by proposing to me that we go to the Château, where I remained, ill at ease, until after one o'clock.... The 19 was the day of the *party thrown by the King* in the city of Paris. The sky was clear and serene, the air cool: nature also was throwing a party. The whole population of Paris was on foot, from the Louis XVI Bridge to the Hôtel de Ville.... After I arrived without difficulty at the Hôtel de Ville, it took me a long time to find the room to which my ticket called me: turned away everywhere, *I wandered in an immense crowd*, and distress and ennui immediately took hold of me. *I was in that party like a galley slave in forced labor, suffering without being able to leave.*... *A party is a beautiful thing when one has returned from it.*[1]

Ad intra, next, the thinker of Grateloup is of a rather fearful, even melancholic, temperament, as he admits himself, and of a delicate, weak constitution: "Grateloup, May 1, 1815: the *fearful* state, when I am in society, is my habitual state. This disposition is not changing as I advance in age."[2]

> March 17, 1816: the temperature has been hot for the season since the 10; there were a few fine days interrupted by rain; the river remains at a considerable height. The discussion of the budget began on March 14. I assiduously attended the sessions from noon to 5 o'clock. My attention has slackened. I am there as if at a *spectacle* whose content is of little interest and where *emotions are expected*. I have very lively emotions when there are attacks and movements that recall our revolutionary assemblies too much. I am not made to live *in the midst of men's passions*; nature has given me a *delicate, weak constitution*: I sense the constant need of support and goodwill.[3]

By Reading His *Journal*

But it is above all through his *Journal* and the story of the publication of Maine de Biran's works (today, eighteen volumes in French; that is, more

---

1. J. I, 14–15 (entry dated August 25–29, 1814, emphasis partly in original).
2. J. I, 72 (entry dated May 1, 1815, emphasis in original).
3. J. I, 113 (entry dated March 17, 1816, emphasis partly in original).

than seven thousand pages, not counting the *Journal* in three volumes of about three hundred pages each) that one knows and senses to what extent this man was indifferent to his posterity and to the traces that he could leave of himself. "Maine de Biran is the man of a single book, which he never wrote," as Henri Gouhier marvelously emphasizes in the opening of *Les Conversions de Maine de Biran* [*The Conversions of Maine de Biran*].[4] And we can but state this and imagine the unimaginable. How could this man have only published scarcely three pieces in his lifetime—a work entitled *The Influence of Habit on the Faculty of Thinking* (1802), a short essay that was an *Examen des leçons de philosophie de M. Laromiguière* [*Examination of Monsieur Laromiguière's Lessons in Philosophy*] (1817), and an article on the "Exposition de la doctrine philosophique de Leibniz" ["Exposition of Leibniz's Philosophical Doctrine"] in Michaud's *Biographie universelle* [*Universal Biography*] (1819)[5]—while he had, to his credit, more than ten complete, or nearly complete, works (which related to all the disciplines: psychology, physiology, anthropology, medicine, religion, etc.), an infinite number of speeches and notes, very numerous public and also political texts, in-depth commentaries and *marginalia* concerning all the authors of the seventeenth, eighteenth, and nineteenth centuries (one volume per century), and even a considerable correspondence of more than fifteen hundred pages (three volumes), not counting the famous *Journal* of approximately nine hundred pages (also in three volumes)? In short, he published scarcely five hundred pages in his entire life, compared to more than ten thousand pages that were ready, or nearly ready, for publication (counting the *Journal*).

This is because the solitary man of Grateloup, who, however, also belonged to society, did not write for others: he wrote solely and principally *for himself*. Did he rest from time to time? Did he sometimes at night blow out his candle or his gas lamp (which had only just become widespread, while petrol lamps did not yet exist, and neither, of course, did electric lamps)? How did he live so that he could resist the cold and hold his pen always within reach of the inkwell, writing in a hand that is certainly difficult to decipher? No one knows. But his thought never

---

4. Gouhier, *Les Conversions*, 6.

5. Henri Gouhier attests to "four," and not "three," texts published in Maine de Biran's lifetime (see "Histoire des manuscrits," in J. I, xi). The publication of the *Œuvres de Maine de Biran* by Vrin completes, or rather clarifies, this statement: "Exposition de la doctrine philosophique de Leibniz" is the text published in Michaud's *Biographie universelle* and should not, therefore, be counted as a separate work (*Écrits de jeunesse*, viii).

ceased to race ahead and to leap over obstacles, like a galloping horse that cannot be stopped—after the fashion of a reason that, as he wrote himself, "is not often asleep": "It seems that I should be more master of myself than anyone else," we read in the first note that was found written in his hand, excerpted from the "old notebook" and dated May 17, 1794 (when he was twenty-eight)—aside from a few youthful writings dated 1792—when Robespierre had just taken the leadership of the Committee of Public Safety and our philosopher had already, some time earlier, taken refuge in Grateloup.

> However, whether by an effect of *my poor constitution*, or whether *man is made thus*, I pass successively through *a thousand varied states* in one day; *a thousand thoughts, a thousand ideas* that I would like to reject, that I do not seek, that even arouse pity in me, pass through my spirit; my reason *is not often asleep*: it sees all this, it moans, it blames, or it approves; and those are its only functions.[6]

By Telling a Story

But it is above all and even more *the story of his manuscripts*, their diffusion and their publication, that lends itself to surprise and even to stupefaction. The thinker of Grateloup must, certainly, have been preoccupied with the publication of his writings and with the notoriety that such texts could have conferred on him. He does not, on the whole, seem to have been so indifferent to society life, considering how many political positions he held (subprefect, deputy, quaestor, etc.), which made him a man of "high society." That he wanted to leave a "trace of his passage upon this earth" through philosophy is indeed understandable—even though he knew this, in order to live it, and according to a motto that I myself, for my part, am not far from adhering to: no one writes to stand out, but one writes first to "auto-surpass" oneself:

> October 16–22, 1814: everything contributes to drawing me outside and making me into a most ordinary man, whereas by remaining quiet in my study *I could leave some useful trace of*

---

6. J. III, 6 (the first note in the "old notebook," dated May 27, 1794, emphasis added; Maine de Biran was then twenty-eight years old).

my passage upon the earth. I am an *out-of-place* and *failed* man: I find that I am not in harmony either with things or with myself.⁷

And yet nothing is less sure. Or, at the very least, the notable from Grateloup (we will call him this because he was ennobled by Louis XVIII in 1815 when he came to power) did nothing to leave traces, and he even did everything to "efface the traces," that is, of the whole of his work. We know of the bundles of little papers and notes that would give us Pascal's *Pensées*. But they, at least, were duly inventoried or, at any rate, neatly packed away in a trunk. Aside from the *Memorial*, which, certainly, was found by chance in the folds of his coat, the rest is a work of which no one was supposed to be unaware. We are also aware of Maurice Blanchot's taste for effacing himself, in the proper sense of the term, and even of refusing all the (photographical) snapshots [*clichés*] that could have immortalized him. But whether it is a question of Pascal or Blanchot, it is mere "child's play" to compare them to Maine de Biran.

There indeed is, first, in the very strange figure of the thinker of Grateloup, this impossibility of finishing and therefore of publishing. Our man is frail and sickly, even depressed; he says so himself, and of himself: "*I habitually sense my wretchedness*, that is, the *bad state of the sensory machine*, which most often inclines to despondency and sadness."⁸ And this is what suffices to make him what we will name, properly speaking, an "eternally dissatisfied one," or a "dissatisfied seeker," with regard to his books, certainly (which he therefore would not finish), but also his life (about which he in reality would never stop complaining). A *profound melancholic*: that is what the "savants of the psyche"—psychiatrists and other psychoanalysts—would say today. And yet—and perhaps this is the (positive) other side of the coin—this "melancholy" doubled by a "dissatisfaction" will also raise him up as an extraordinary creator, in the manner of a Søren Kierkegaard, who was just barely a contemporary of Maine de Biran (Kierkegaard was born in 1813, and Biran died in 1824). The philosopher must also go to search "in the depths of his pain" for a life, or a survival, at least to express if not to exhume.

Maine de Biran says it himself *of* himself: at the same time *about* himself and *starting from* himself. And it suffices to read him to notice this and report on the experience of it. The *Journal* is in no way inferior to the psychoanalyst's couch. For it is indeed a question of a near-descent

---

7. J. I, 23 (entry dated October 16–22, 1814, emphasis added).
8. J. II, 197 (entry dated December 28, 1818, emphasis partly in original).

into a "psychology of the depths" (of oneself with oneself), covering more than nine hundred pages and more than twenty-five years of life—although the "cure" itself, if one can call it that, would not last more than a decade, which is already a great deal, if one sticks only to the beginning and the continuation of the notebooks (from February 1814 through May 17, 1824). I mean the movement that goes from the *Journal*'s first sentence (Maine de Biran was forty-eight, but his own notes date back to when he was twenty-eight years old), finally signaling the return of the monarchy and Louis XVIII's ascension to power—"Nothing is more necessary for a prince than being loved by the people whom he governs" (February 1814)[9]—to the last line in his hand, dated May 17, 1824, that is, just two months before his death on July 20, 1824, in Paris: "I have the intimate sentiment of the wretched dependence [of the soul on this organic and indeterminate part of which we are speaking]; a *supernatural influence* is necessary for things to be otherwise."[10]

Maine de Biran, a creator like no other: this is the leitmotif—which means that hidden in him there is not only something of Kierkegaard but also of Nietzsche (§16c), even though Grateloup is not Sils Maria, and that is an understatement! The thinker from Bergerac thus does not finish or rarely finishes (his books) and is never satisfied (if not with what he thinks, in any case with what he writes). We would be satisfied with less, in view of his genius and the whole of his work. . . . And so he would make this confession, consumed and worn down by a deeply rooted *insatiability* that never stopped invading him and engulfing him. This "man of a single book, which he never wrote," as I have emphasized, following Henri Gouhier, in reality never stopped censuring himself, did not want to expose himself as a philosopher, sorely felt that "sentiment of an imperfection" that constantly gnawed at him, always believing that later things would go better, or that it would be better, as soon as he showed more maturity.

His confession is indeed striking when he states, on the date of November 25, 1816 (a day of "dry and biting cold"), the reasons for which he *will not, in the end, publish*, in addition to his other two essays, his Copenhagen treatise of 1811 (*The Relationship Between the Physical and the Moral in Man*)—which I have, however, considered, since my opening, as the pivotal text and even the precursor of the future entrance of Maine

9. J. I, 3 (entry dated February 1814).
10. J. II, 426 (emphasis added).

de Biran into the second period of his work, which saw him pass from psychology to anthropology (*Nouvelles considérations sur les rapports du physique et du moral de l'homme* [*New Considerations on the Relationship Between the Physical and the Moral in Man*], 1820):

> Thinking about it better and more carefully, I exercised a *severe censure* on this premature production, and the painful sentiment, the *sort of modesty* that I attach to it, as to everything that gives us a proof, *the sentiment of an imperfection prevented me from publishing*, since then, three other treatises, crowned since by scholarly societies [the Institute and the academies of Berlin and Copenhagen], always waiting for *one more degree of perfection and maturity* in a system of ideas whose great incompleteness I still sensed.[11]

In reality, the notable from Grateloup did not procrastinate, as one could have supposed at first glance (since he never put off until tomorrow what he could have done today); nor did he become discouraged (for even though he complains that writing is painful, all the same he never stops sitting down at his writing desk); and he did not divide himself from himself in an artificial division of tasks (as if he no longer wrote when he was in Paris and kept the exercise of thought for Grateloup alone—when, in fact, he organized philosophical meetings in the capital, as we know thanks to the testimony of François Naville, his friend and posthumous editor, who participated in these meetings that were duly named "Maine de Biran's Fridays"—as Gabriel Marcel would later do in Meudon). Let us rather say of Maine de Biran that he was not only "eternally dissatisfied" but also a "perfectionist"—the one being only the flip side of the other—that is, he was of that type of temperament that always gives priority to *dissatisfaction* because the "perfect" does not exist and never will. The wait for a book that would be perfectly finished, as if it were the summit and the last word, belongs to the mythology of every author, who should, however, know to renounce it (that false absolute perfection that is so highly sought after). The text that is perfectly and definitively integrated into an architectonics that has been issued and established once and for all does not exist: to wit, that famous "system of ideas whose great incompleteness I still sensed" of course never will be—that is, will never be complete and perfect.

---

11. J. I, 239 (entry dated November 23, 1816, emphasis added).

A Fantastical Reception

The question, which is existential, not to say "providential," at least for we who are the readers, then remains of knowing how this monumental work, with its thousands of pages and its incredible commentaries on the history of thought as such (Descartes, Leibniz, Locke, Condillac, Bossuet, Fénelon, and many others) *managed to reach us*—referring to what was certainly a "fantastical reception" as a new guest at the "banquet of philosophers," but also and above all to the manner in which the notable of Grateloup was discovered and received *yesterday*, to our great good fortune *today*. To put it another way, and anew, in order to interrogate the man, since there is no thought without lived experience, and since every thought is also a lived experience, especially for Maine de Biran: how could the will *to do nothing*, or rather to *leave everything to be done* with regard to his own heritage, have, without his knowledge, "turned," through the curiosity of a known and recognized professor at the Sorbonne (Victor Cousin) and the perseverance of an unknown admirer (the Genevan pastor François Naville, and then his son Ernest Naville), into a veritable "rescue" that was as unhoped-for as it was unexpected?[12] In that there is for the French something of Arsène Lupin, that "gentleman burglar" who disappears as quickly as he appears, or, for the English, something of Sherlock Holmes, another fictional character, British this time, a private detective with an uncommon memory from whom no trace of a crime can escape, so greatly has he developed the habit of tracking them down.

For it could have happened, and it even should have been the case, that nothing, or almost nothing, reached us from this monumental—as much from a qualitative point of view as a quantitative one—work by the philosopher of Grateloup, who both was solitary and belonged to society. Maine de Biran's negligence with regard to his traces—those that he could leave to posterity—extends to his whole life to the point of seeming pathological. The famous secret demand for a "radical effacing" of the so-called

12. Here the "rescue" of Maine de Biran's manuscripts (scattered in attics and other rooms and in unsuspected cabinets) by the philosopher Victor Cousin and the pastor François Naville can profitably be compared to the "rescue" of Husserl's manuscripts (threatened by the Nazi state) by the Franciscan Leo van Breda at the height of the Second World War (on this subject, see Bégout, *Le Sauvetage*). In addition, I warmly thank Mr. Philippe Boris, the current owner of Grateloup (Dordogne) and a worthy heir of Maine de Biran, for having welcomed me for a complete and private tour of the writer's abode, without which this book would never have gained the savor of a shared existentiality.

"Blanchotians," or "elocutionary disappearance" as the Mallarméan impossible dream, is soundly beaten here—while those who claim, even today, to follow Blanchot do not fail, with a certain "snobbery" about the author's absolute distance from his work, to follow, out of the corners of their eyes, the fate of manuscripts concerning which they fear, more than anything else, that they will be forgotten and never published.[13] Such a "forced" or at least "claimed characteristic," as a literary posture, does not appear in the thinker from Bergerac. For it is a not question of "literature" (in a prose made to be appreciated)—in Grateloup, that is—but rather of "nature" (of what makes man). This is so, and it cannot be otherwise, because Biran is, paradoxically, all the more worldly in politics for being self-effacing in the philosophical domain.

The thinker from Bergerac indeed ended up hiding, or withdrawing, what he did not want to publish (in other words, almost everything), not in a distance that he took with respect to his text but, on the contrary, and in an almost pathological manner, as I have said, on account of his great proximity and his hyperattachment to that very text—that is, to writing *by* oneself as writing *of* oneself—from which he could not distance himself and which he could not abandon. We would be wrong to praise to the skies and to regard as a virtue the detachment that he seems to evince with regard to his own writings, while, in fact, most often, these thousands of hidden or abandoned pages express only the malaise of an even greater attachment. In reality, Maine de Biran feared but one thing: namely, being misunderstood or misinterpreted—hence the fact that he gave up, in an unhealthy or at least systematic way, on publishing his books. To put the matter in a way that is slightly trivial but that will make it perfectly clear, the author of these eighteen volumes published in French today scarcely offered a crumb of them to his future readers, and not because the "newborn was perfect"—we know how authors care as much for their books as for their own progeny—but on the contrary because it appeared ever and always in his eyes as "deformed,"

---

13. On this point, see Maxime Decout's instructive chapter, "Maurice Blanchot," 115: an accusation of a "snobbery" of detachment or of tearing away applies, certainly not to Blanchot himself, but at least to those called "Blanchotians": "Blanchot's prose is thus a *prose of the tearing away* that fights against words and that exhibits its own instruments, the eye and the voice. The *dream of doing away with every organ of emission* refers back to the *chimera* that *Blanchot's literary criticism* cultivates: that of the nudity of the word, of its mad autonomy, in the manner in which the eye and the mouth can be autonomous" (emphasis added).

even "monstrous," or as if he had engendered a "monster"—like the fetuses in bowls that are dying of never being brought to term.

Certainly, and I do acknowledge this, I may be exaggerating here. The hearths of Grateloup never welcomed the crates of manuscripts for them to be burned, nor did Maine de Biran ever detach himself from everything to the point of sinking into that "false modesty" that consists in never citing or referencing oneself; quite the contrary (the *Journal* in reality never speaks of *anything but himself*, serving both as preliminary notes for his thoughts and as a collection of all the sentiments that he could have experienced as "material" for philosophizing). It is therefore solely through a *constitutive negligence*, and not a *voluntary malevolence*, that our notable who was a writer does not ever seem to have concerned himself with the future of that which had, however, overrun him in his thoughts—from the most abstract of philosophical discussions to the most personal, even the most existential, of confessions in the notes and notebooks. The only mention recorded by his notary on the subject of what Maine de Biran allegedly said about his own writings leaves us dumbfounded, especially as he leaves the responsibility for them to a certain Mr. Laîné—a politician from Bordeaux who, according to Henry Gouhier, "had neither the time nor the competence that the examination of these papers and the decisions to be taken concerning them would have required." This is the statement written up by the notary: "Maine de Biran made no mention of his manuscripts in his will, contenting himself with designating verbally, and in a general way, Mr. Laîné, his friend, as the executor of his will."[14]

One can then conduct the investigation and see to what an extent Maine de Biran's thought was thus "saved" from its planned disappearance. It is first to Victor Cousin, therefore, a celebrated professor at the Sorbonne, to whom the paternity of "spiritualism" is sometimes attributed—but should rather be credited to Paul Janet, a point to which I will return (§1)—that we own the rescue, or rather the avoidance of shipwreck. Exactly one year after Maine de Biran's death (on July 20, 1824), that is, during the summer of 1825, Cousin went to Grateloup, if not for a vacation, at least to take stock of those famous manuscripts of which people had heard even without their being published. And there he was, in the company of Félix, the son who was Maine de Biran's heir but who

---

14. Cited and commented on by Gouhier in J. I, ix. In what follows, I will refer to the totality of these introductory pages from the first volume of the *Journal* with regard to the "history of the manuscripts" (ix–xii).

understood nothing of the matter, faced with "three piles" on the table, among pages duly sorted and classified by the professor at the Sorbonne: "The first containing the political writings of Mr. Biran; ... the second, his philosophical writing; the third, his notebooks of memories."[15]

But we will not stop there—first because Victor Cousin only inherited the philosophical manuscripts, and second because the decision had been made to entrust Mr. Laîné, the only legal executor of the will, with the care of keeping the precious booty. We know now that at least a portion of the "pages" was sent to Bordeaux to respect both the principal (Biran) and the agent (Laîné). A portion of the manuscripts remained, however, at Grateloup, until the "entirety of the notes" returned at last to the master's abode upon Laîné's death, as his family knew neither *what* to do nor what to do *with them* (like Maine de Biran himself in his lifetime, for that matter). Aside from the philosophical portion selected by Victor Cousin—in particular the *Essai sur les fondements de la psychologie* [*Essay on the Foundations of Psychology*] of 1812—the entirety of the manuscripts in question, certain works and treatises, certainly, but also the fifteen hundred pages of the *Journal* with the *notebooks* (called the "notebooks of memories"), could then have remained "a dead letter" in a forgotten corner of Grateloup and fallen definitively into oblivion. All that would have remained would have been the figure of the philosopher of *disputations* (with Descartes, Leibniz, Locke, and Condillac), who was perfectly brought to light by Cousin, and which is already a great deal, but neither the interaction with his personal life revealed by the *Journal* nor the "anthropological" turn taken in the 1820s.

It was therefore necessary to wait until 1843, or almost twenty years after Maine de Biran's death, for a sort of "awakening" to occur in a Genevan pastor by the name of François Naville, who in his youth had attended the last philosophical meetings that the Dordogne deputy had organized in Paris when he was sitting in the Assembly, and for him to make up his mind to send a letter to Maine de Biran's son, Félix, to find out if there might not still be a few forgotten manuscripts at Grateloup (perhaps he had heard of the two piles, historical and personal, that Cousin had not been able to, or did not want to, take away). What a surprise it is, then, to read and to hear, since François Naville himself recorded the reception of the package, that he received by stagecoach in Geneva "*two cases of manuscripts*, in December 1843 and September 1844: *the first, weighing*

---

15. J. I, x.

16 kg, containing the papers preserved by the family of Laîné, who died in 1835; *the second, weighing 14 kg*, those that the philosopher's son had found in Grateloup, the Birans' residence in Périgord."[16]

We could then suppose that the story was finished, and we can but be honored by the fact that François Naville was able, so many years later, to get his hands on what Victor Cousin had abandoned, or what had been forbidden to him. But of course this "fantastical reception" (of the manuscripts, that is) does not end there. Everything being a matter of generation, the son of the Genevan pastor, this time in the person of Ernest Naville, hastened to Grateloup some three years later (in September 1847—twenty-three years after Maine de Biran's death) to see, with the authorization of the master of the house, if there might not still be a few stray manuscripts, or manuscripts that Félix had neglected to send. La Valette-Monbrun, in his *Essai de biographie historique et psychologique: Maine de Biran, 1766-1824* [*Historical and Psychological Biographical Essay: Maine de Biran, 1766-1824*], thus retraces the story of Ernest Naville's almost-minor discovery, with the support and the good care of Félix de Biran: "As he left the hospitable abode of Grateloup five days later, what Ernest Naville took with him was *a whole trunk of papers*, written in Maine de Biran's hand, and philosophical works that had belonged to him or were annotated by him.... He congratulated himself on having gotten his hands on three planners."[17]

A "*trunk of papers*, written in Maine de Biran's hand," for the son (Ernest Naville), two "cases of manuscripts," "the first weighing 16 kg" and "the second weighing 14 kg," for the father (François Naville), an enormous "pile" of manuscripts for Victor Cousin—the story had therefore begun and would then ceaselessly continue, in a posterity that grows without ceasing, commensurate to the profundity of the thought that was brought to light: "a master to us all," exclaimed Royer-Collard, and "he is our Kant" (which will become "the French Kant"), declared Jules Lachelier. Nothing could be less certain than that the French Arsène Lupin has finished his work as a burglar or that the English Sherlock Holmes has finished his work as an investigator. For it does not suffice to receive a gift, be it a treasure or a booty whose existence no one had ever before suspected—because of its *quantity*, certainly (more than twenty volumes if one counts the edition of the *Œuvres* [*Works*] and of the *Journal*), but

---

16. J. I, x (emphasis added).
17. Cited in J. I, xi (emphasis added).

also because of its surprising *quality* (a sort of Descartes whom no one expected and who did nothing less than overturn everything by definitively tying the psychic to the organic, or the "moral" to the "physical," to say it in Maine de Biran's very terms). One cannot but remain stunned, even dumbstruck, before such a manna which has come from "providence," whatever may be the sense one attributes here to the word—pure chance, *fatum* or destiny, or a divine decree.

No one can thus read an author independently of the conditions of the reception of his thought. What is true of the tradition, and perhaps even more of Catholicism, which is scarcely inclined to any "pure discourse," be it demythologized (Rudolf Bultmann) or "dehellenized" (Hans Küng), then applies, perhaps even more, to Maine de Biran. It is not that we should not return to the text itself—quite the contrary—but that the conditions of his reception, in particular in the domain of the spiritualism of Victor Cousin and later of Boutroux and Lachelier, even Bergson himself, have drawn Biran's work to the side of consciousness and freedom in the "primitive fact of effort," which perhaps was not the only reading of it that could be made. Returning to the flesh and to autoaffection, Michel Henry then called, starting in the opening of *Philosophy and Phenomenology of the Body*, and with the sharpness for which he is known, for a complete distancing from the spiritualist interpretation of Maine de Biran, preferring to it, even imposing on it, his phenomenological version:

> [Maine de Biran] has been customarily situated at the source of a current of thought which would continue through Lachelier, Boutroux, Ravaisson, Lagneau, to Bergson—a current of "spiritualist" thought which would be characterized by its attention paid to the "interior life," by an "introspective tendency." This has constituted a *serious misconstruing* of his contribution.[18]

Whether or not there is a "misconstruing" in the spiritualist interpretation of Maine de Biran—I will return to this (§1)—is not, for the moment, the question. Better, the "backlash of spiritualism on phenomenology," although not acknowledged as such, is perhaps what led the phenomenologist Michel Henry, at the end of his existence, onto another path or a new path, inasmuch as the opening to the divine also attested to by Maine de Biran in his old age (see the conclusion, "Three Lives in One") could shed a new light on the entirety of the work of Michel Henry himself,

---

18. Henry, *Philosophy and Phenomenology*, 9 (emphasis added).

including in his most philosophical considerations. Maine de Biran also at the end of his life (November 1823), like Michel Henry later on (*I Am the Truth*, 1996), commented in his *Journal* on the prologue of John's Gospel,[19] and we will return to this at the end of our excursion.

The thinker from Bergerac is therefore at the beginning for the phenomenologist (*Philosophy and Phenomenology of the Body*, written in 1948–1949, though published only in 1965), but also at the end (he will be massively present in 2000 in §26 of *Incarnation*), and between the two there is no, or almost no, mention of him. At the dawn of being born (to his thought) and of dying (to thought), "encounters" are essential. The encounter with Maine de Biran was essential for Michel Henry, and it will be essential for me as well—although in a wholly other sense: on the side, this time, no longer of autoaffection or the lived body but of extra-phenomenality and the spread body. But here we will read Biran *in counter-relief* and no longer *in relief*, according to an interpretation that is, if not opposed to, at least different from Michel Henry's—inasmuch as the works studied and the concepts will not be the same, or at the very least I will not conclude that there are contradictions in Maine de Biran the moment the interpretation no longer seems to fit.[20] To the *refuge in interiority* (the "phenomenal *myself*" and the "lived body," so many terms invented or at least employed by Maine de Biran himself), I will oppose the case of a *possible exteriority*, or rather of an "outside in myself," from the moment that the sentiment of the *myself*, as I announced in the opening, comes, in limit-situations, to be "totally eclipsed" (sleep, sleepwalking, dreams, madness, drugs, etc.).

The history of this *fantastical reception* of the manuscripts now being finished, we will at least have been convinced that "no one should get up in the morning without reading the newspaper [*journal*]," to take up Karl Marx's famous remark, reported by his (French) son-in-law and collaborator Paul Lafargue:

> In spite of the late hour at which Marx went to bed he was always up between eight and nine in the morning, had some black coffee, *read through his newspapers* and then went to his study, where he worked till two or three in the morning.[21]

---

19. J. II, 412–17 (entry dated November, 1823).

20. Chapter 6 in Henry, *Philosophy and Phenomenology*, which categorically refuses the heterogeneous as a sort of "metaphysical residue" in Maine de Biran's thought that it is necessary to be rid of (§12).

21. Lafargue, "Reminiscences of Karl Marx," 34 (emphasis added). [The French word *journal* can mean a newspaper or a personal journal or diary. –Trans.]

But when it comes to "journals," here there will be no question of the "daily"—for nothing is worse than losing oneself in the ephemeral when thought must first adhere to the imperishable, or at the very least to the durable. It is indeed the *Journal* of the inner movements of the thinker of Grateloup that will here let us enter into his thought, according to the "story of a life" that in reality he never ceased to conceptualize philosophically. Never so much as in the "case" of Maine de Biran has it been possible to say, "I am *myself* the matter of my book" (Montaigne)[22]—not here in some sort of autobiography but in an intellectual and spiritual combat of oneself with oneself that means thought always remains that "silent inner dialogue of the soul with itself" (Plato).[23]

Alea jacta est—"the die is cast." This was Caesar's motto at the moment of "crossing the Rubicon." The march forward in the wake of Maine de Biran in terms of *extra-phenomenality* and *corporeality envisioned otherwise* can therefore begin, or rather continue, if it is not a forced march. But it remains necessary to agree, and even to want, to humbly put on the "mantle of philosophy"—the very one that Maine de Biran, according to an entry in his *Journal* dated December 4–12, 1814 (in days when "the temperature was constantly humid and warm"), had always and only desired to wear, knowing, nevertheless, how hard it also is, in solitude, to withdraw: "I must henceforth learn to do without public considerations, without renown, and *cover myself with the mantle of philosophy*, taking as a motto: *qui bene latuit bene vixit*—'he lives well who keeps himself well hidden' (Ovid)."[24]

---

22. Montaigne, *Essays*, 13: "I want to appear in my simple, natural, and everyday dress, without strain or artifice, *for it is myself that I am painting*. . . . So, reader, I am *myself* the matter of my book" (emphasis added). [Translation modified. –Trans.]

23. Plato, *Theaetetus* 189e: "[By thinking I mean] *a talk which the soul has with itself* about the objects under its consideration" (emphasis added); Plato, *Sophist* 263e: "Aren't thought and speech the same, except that what we call thought is speech that occurs without the voice, *inside the soul in conversation with itself?*" (emphasis added).

24. J. I, 31 (entry dated December 4–12, 1814, emphasis added).

1

The Constitution of the *Myself*

> Trying to objectify the *myself* or to grasp it from outside is like wanting to go to a window to see oneself go by.
>
> MAINE DE BIRAN, *DERNIÈRE PHILOSOPHIE*

A Conflict of Interpretations

HENRY BERGSON HAS CERTAINLY commented on Maine de Biran (spiritualism of life); so has Michel Henry (phenomenology of interiority); and Maurice Merleau-Ponty has as well, albeit in a wholly other sense (phenomenology of opacity). Indeed, what applies to spiritualism for "consciousness" also applies to phenomenology for the "body." If the reading of the latter (phenomenology) is directly opposed to the former (spiritualism), this is because phenomenology, to say it with Maurice Merleau-Ponty, has ceased to place "the body into the world" and "the one who sees (the seer) into the body" as in a complete and definitive interlocking structure. This "chiasm" or "reciprocal insertion" of the visible body and the seeing body also reveals itself as Biranian, so long as one does not confine the "primitive fact of effort" to subjectivity alone: "We have to reject the age-old assumptions that put the body in the world and the seer in the body, or, conversely, the world and the body in the seer *as in a box*," noted the author in the posthumously published manuscript of *The Visible and the Invisible* (1964). "My body as a visible thing is contained within the full spectacle. But my seeing body subtends this visible body, and all the visibles with it. There is reciprocal insertion and intertwining of one in the other."[1]

It is thus, surprisingly, to Maine de Biran himself and to his *Essai sur les fondements de la psychologie* that Merleau-Ponty also refers to find this first origin of a chiasm in the process of being constituted. In 1947–1948, the date when Biran appeared on the program of the *agrégation*[2] in philosophy—whence the renewed interest in Maine de Biran by Michel Henry, who during the same period was drafting *Philosophy and Phenomenology of the Body*, or Henri Gouhier, who published *Les Conversions de Maine de Biran*[3]—the author of *The Phenomenology of Perception* was then teaching an *agrégation* course on the thinker from Bergerac in Lyon's department of letters and at the École Normale Supérieure de Paris (in 1948, therefore), which would later be transcribed under the title *Malebranche, Biran, and Bergson on the Unity of Body and Soul* (first published posthumously in 1978). And what did he see, or rather what did he read, in the *Essai sur les fondements de la psychologie*, despite little-developed remarks? Not at all a "sentiment of the *myself*" as a place of pure interiority, or even of autoaffection, but on the contrary the end of the experience of the internal, to return to a certain form of opacity—whether it is irreducible or not will be for us to decide. As he was by Michel Henry, and in exactly the same era, then (1948), Maine de Biran was also anointed by Maurice Merleau-Ponty as the "precursor of phenomenology," but this time outside of any interiority that would have the unique prerogative of being able to constitute itself by itself:

> There is no longer [in Maine de Biran] any *privileging of the experience of the inner*: inner experience must be an effort to grasp again *an interiority which is at first opaque*. A text such as this

---

1. Merleau-Ponty, *Visible and the Invisible*, 138 (emphasis added).

2. [The *agrégation* is a competitive examination that French students in most fields must pass in order to teach at the secondary or tertiary level. It is generally, though not necessarily, taken after one's second and final year in a master's program. The texts on which one will be examined for the *agrégation* in philosophy are different each year, and institutes of higher education offer courses focusing on these texts for students preparing to take the exam. –Trans.]

3. One can find the complete program of the *agrégation* in philosophy in France (at least with regard to Bergson) as an appendix to Bianco, *Après Bergson*, 360–64. Maine de Biran indeed, therefore, featured on the program in 1948, with the *Essai sur les fondements de la psychologie* ("Introduction générale" [general introduction], Part I, first and second sections, chapters 1–2: "Détermination du fait primitif du sens intime" [determination of the primitive fact of the intimate sense]), a text reproduced in its entirety in Henri Gouhier's anthology, published a few years earlier during the war.

[*L'Essai sur les fondements de la psychologie*] is beyond empiricism: *anticipating phenomenology*, Biran seems in this work to move toward a philosophy which is *indifferent to the distinction between interior and exterior*.[4]

That there is a great distance between the Merleau-Pontyian interpretation of Maine de Biran (with some remarks about his "irreducible opacity") and his Henryian signification in terms of the primitive fact of effort as "autoaffection" is, to say the least, obvious. The *conflict of interpretation* is, moreover, so great that it is surprising that it is not more often noticed and even studied—with Michel Henry usually left the privilege of being the sole author or phenomenologist to discuss it. The first arrow was, however, loosed quite plainly by Michel Henry himself in *Incarnation* (2000), in the very place where he develops "the analytic of the 'I can,'" based precisely on Maine de Biran (but without explicitly citing Merleau-Ponty, whom everyone who knows how to read can nonetheless see). The divorce is consummated without truly being made explicit. There is certainly no question here of putting it on trial, but we must at least recognize that a single one of the parties (Michel Henry) cannot take the sole truth of the Biranian "primitive fact" away with him: "Where and how is every power's *immanence to itself* accomplished?" wonders, then, much later, the author of *Incarnation* as he takes up, point by point, the Biranian critique of the Condillacian statue, to which we will return. "In Life, in the way Life comes with pathos in itself," insists the advocate of autoaffection.

> If corporeity is the entire set of our powers, it is in *flesh* and as *flesh* that this corporeity is possible. *The flesh is not the result of the touching/touched chiasma and cannot be correctly described by it*. The flesh comes *before the chiasma* as the condition of the power-to-touch and thus of touching as such.[5]

Better, and thereby signifying that the breach is far from being closed, there is at least one reference in Maurice Merleau-Ponty's course that leads us to think that the originality of the thinker from Bergerac lies rather in the gap between oneself and oneself, and no longer at all in the proximity of oneself to oneself. A distance between the subject and itself is drawn more from the "chiasm of the flesh" for the author of *The*

---

4. Merleau-Ponty, *Incarnate Subject*, 68 (emphasis added). [Translation modified. –Trans.]

5. Henry, *Incarnation*, 137 (emphasis added).

Phenomenology of Perception than in the "irreducibility of trauma," as is my own perspective in *The Extra-Phenomenal*.⁶ Regardless, in the one case (chiasm) as in the other (trauma), Maine de Biran's thought cannot be reduced only to the pathos without distance of suffering and of enjoying, even if, indeed, he was reportedly the first to discover it. It is necessary to choose between a distance between oneself and oneself with the other in oneself (Merleau-Ponty) and the proximity of oneself to oneself in the pathos of itself (Henry)—and on the basis of the interpretation of the same author: "Everything in Biran's work is based on this *antithetical view*," Merleau-Ponty decisively emphasizes in his own interpretation of the *Essai sur les fondements de la psychologie*. "What is henceforth embedded at the heart of philosophy is no longer the recognition of the *I by the I*, but the relationship of the *I to what is not itself*."⁷

There is no question, certainly, of now conducting an "intraphenomenological" struggle regarding the right and correct interpretation of Maine de Biran (the struggle, and let us hope it is a "loving" one, between Michel Henry and Maurice Merleau-Ponty) at the very moment when it is necessary to distinguish the contours of spiritualism on the one hand in its insistence on the "sentiment of the *myself*" (in relation to consciousness) and of phenomenology on the other hand with regard to its primary focus on the "primitive fact of effort" (in relation to the body). But if the two—the "sentiment of the *myself*" and the "primitive fact of effort"—cannot be separated, perhaps it is, to be frank, because spiritualism and phenomenology are not so very distant from each other as is believed and said, often wrongly.

§1. Maine de Biran's Spiritualism

If it is now necessary to return to "Maine de Biran's spiritualism," or rather to the so-called "spiritualist" interpretation of the thinker from Bergerac, this is because it is right to understand it, or at least to set it forth, before too immediately contesting it. Michel Henry's previously-cited phrase (p. 14)—according to which it "has constituted a *serious misconstruing*" to "situat[e]" Maine de Biran "in a current of 'spiritualist' thought"—does not

6. [At the time of this translation, Falque's *Hors phénomène* is still forthcoming in English, but since it will appear under the title *The Extra-Phenomenal* (trans. Nikolaas Cassidy-Deketelaere), I use that title when it is referenced in the body of the text. –Trans.]

7. Merleau-Ponty, *Incarnate Subject*, 65 (emphasis added).

do justice to the "domain of consciousness" that, in my view, also appears in a major way in the philosophy of the thinker from Bergerac.

Thus—I have just articulated this, but it is necessary to insist on it—it is faced with the "primitive fact of the sentiment of the *myself*," primarily deployed in the *spiritualist interpretation* of Maine de Biran, that the "subject that is offside" or "alienated" will, on my view, be "outside consciousness" (an outside that is within, and not an exteriority of the objectivist type, as I have said in the opening of this work). And it is also faced with the "sentiment of effort" and the "resistance of the organic," from which the "lived or proper body" is born, including *in phenomenology*, that the very idea of an "improper body," or even a "spread body," can be developed, since the appropriation of our own body is not always realized for us, according to Maine de Biran (sleep, sleepwalking, dreams, madness, drugs, etc.). The "backlash of spiritualism on phenomenology," instead of letting "metaphysics" and the "descriptive interpretation of phenomena" stare stonily at each other, as if in an irreducible opposition, will then come about via a *transformation of oneself by the other*, outside of any arbitrary exclusion, and as a condition of progress in thought: "The conflict between spiritualism and phenomenology will no longer take place," as we must recall here. Better, it is in their encounter and their *backlash* that a new fruitfulness for thought will play out.

a) A Strange Label

We will note from the start that Maine de Biran was not, and could not have been, familiar with the term "spiritualism" as a current of thought because it was forged "after him" precisely in order that he, among others, should be saddled with it: "Let us note that 'spiritualism' began to be spoken of when the spirit no longer appeared as the third person of the Holy Trinity (the Holy Spirit) or even as the divine Logos," notes Jean-Louis Vieillard-Baron as early as the opening of his impressive "summa" entitled *Le Spiritualisme français* (*French spiritualism*).

> The term "spiritualism" was not in common usage before 1850 [let us recall that Maine de Biran died in 1824], while "materialism" was used as early as the beginning of the eighteenth century, for example in Leibniz, who opposed the *idealists* to the *materialists*, as Plato opposed the Friends of the Ideas and the Friends of the Earth.... The term "spiritualism" was established only after Cousin, in particular with Paul Janet (1823–99)....

> Despite its late recognition as a distinct philosophical current of thought, spiritualism was established as *the common philosophy* over the course of the nineteenth century.[8]

The matter is therefore clear, at least historically speaking. Maine de Biran is not and cannot be called a "spiritualist," a title with which he has been adorned but that he could never have claimed—no more, of course, than he was some sort of "phenomenologist," even if Michel Henry on the one hand emphasizes in *Philosophy and Phenomenology of the Body* that the thinker from Bergerac is "one of the true founders of a phenomenological science of human reality,"[9] and Maurice Merleau-Ponty on the other hand emphasizes in *The Incarnate Subject* that he "anticipat[es] phenomenology."[10] Applying the label of "spiritualism" to Maine de Biran would be about the same as believing that Aristotle really wrote a work entitled *Metaphysics*. In either case, the attribution is false, or at the very least "not authentic"—without denying, however, that it makes sense [*sens*] (or is a misinterpretation [*contresens*]) in the history of the reception of each of these thoughts: *meta* as "after" or "beyond" in Aristotle (we know how Martin Heidegger feasted on this amphibology to denounce metaphysics as such in its entirety); or the *spiritus* as "spirit" or *pneuma*, or even (Platonic) *noûs*, but in no way the "soul" or *psyché* as one will find it in a significant way in Aristotle. Whoever says *spiritualism* says an "opening to" a form of transcendence, since this is the sense of spirit the moment one refers to *noûs* or *pneuma*, more than to *psyché* in its opposition to *soma*. We are far, truth be told, from any finitude closed upon itself, particularly as in *Being and Time*, whose unsurpassability (at least for me) is known.

In other words, if there is "spiritualism," in Maine de Biran, certainly, but also in my own work, it will always be "after the fact" and not "before the fact." This is not a secondariness that would make spiritualism itself secondary in relation to a phenomenology of finitude, for example, but is precisely because only the Absolute itself produces *in us* the openness to the absolute (in accord on this point, moreover, with Henri de Lubac). Within the framework of the aforementioned "spiritualism," the *spiritus* or the *noûs* will be inscribed in the *psyché* only in that we will recognize something "more" in man, or a sort of "supplement

---

8. Vieillard-Baron, *Spiritualisme français*, 13 (emphasis partly in original).
9. Henry, *Philosophy and Phenomenology*, 8.
10. Merleau-Ponty, *Incarnate Subject*, 68.

of soul" (Bergson) that can be perceived or required not independently of but rather by transforming a "finitude whose future is closed and whose foundation is null" (Heidegger).[11] I will therefore accept, for my part, being called "spiritualist" as I will also lay claim to being a phenomenologist. But "spiritualist" here has only the sense in which the "spiritual" will no longer play the easy role of the overcoming of man in himself but will rather be inscribed in a "meta-physics," understood, on my view, not as the "overcoming of *physis*," (*meta* in the sense of "beyond") but as the "traversal of *physis*" (*meta* as "through"). "Overcoming the overcoming" [*Dépasser le dépassement*]—of metaphysics: I have already established this imperative as also this leitmotif.[12]

The backlash of spiritualism on phenomenology that is to be accomplished today, starting from the "case" of Maine de Biran, demands not only a return toward metaphysics but also a rethinking of *physis*. The "traversal of physics" (*meta-physis*) indeed opens, in my own perspective, onto two "abysses," one *below* and the other *above*, precisely seen by Biran himself in the duality of the absolute or of what is separated. There are, according to the thinker from Bergerac, two forms of absolute that lead toward an "outside in oneself": the absolute or the separated from oneself through trauma, and the absolute or the separated from oneself in God himself. In the two cases, from *below* (trauma) or from *above* (God), the subject abandons himself to what is not himself and definitively leaves the primitive fact of the "sentiment of the *myself*" to rejoin, or confront, the "foreign" that is not oneself. Thus we will find in Maine de Biran himself, and in particular at the end of his life—I will return to this (Conclusion)—a form of "spiritualism" that is the other side of the "extra-phenomenal," such that, on my view, a figure of "God extra-phenomenal" will also respond to *extra-phenomenality*.[13]

b) Which Is Not So Unsuited to Him

This having been said—specifically, that Maine de Biran could never himself have figured among the "spiritualists"—this label is not so unsuited to him, and even suits him rather well, in particular in his taking up and transforming of Descartes in the act of the *cogitatio*, as I will show

---

11. See Falque, *Metamorphosis of Finitude*, 95–111.
12. See Falque, *Crossing the Rubicon*, 133–34, 134–36.
13. See Falque, *Chair de Dieu*, 123–58.

(§3), or in his direct continuation by Louis Lavelle or René Le Senne.[14] For whoever says "French spiritualism," as Jean-Louis Vieillard-Baron also justly emphasizes, says not only an "opening to the divine" but also and rather a *secularization* of the values of Christianity:

> Most of the spiritualists [Maine de Biran, Victor Cousin, Lachelier, Ravaisson, even also Boutroux, Lagneau and Bergson, etc.—I have added this list myself] are *secular*. There are indeed several levels of secularism: *secularism-hostility*, which took the forms of political and social anticlericalism; *secularism-neutrality*, which takes the form of religious indifference, neutrality signifying vacuousness and insignificance; and *secularism-tolerance*, in other words, the welcome of religions in their diversity. Spiritualism, working on the basis of a metaphysics of religion in general, is an "altruistic" philosophy of the welcome of the other.[15]

There can be no doubt that if Maine de Biran belongs to one of these three forms of secularism (hostile, neutral, or tolerant), it is indeed with the third (tolerant) that he must be counted—even though his fierce opposition to the Revolution, as a royalist, could have led him to greater radicality. In any case—and to take up these three forms of "secularism" that thus define "spiritualism" as a philosophical, and not a religious, current of thought—anyone who *today* lives in France, is born in France, and closely observes France knows and experiences the validity of that strange form of secularism (here called "tolerant")—which is most often regarded from afar, or from elsewhere, as an aversion to religion (secularism-hostility) or a mere indifference (secularism-neutrality), whereas it can also become a space where the religious, at least in its aspirations, is inscribed within the human as such, even in society (secularism-tolerance). The motto of the French Republic—*Liberty, Equality, Fraternity*—is not only the standard inherited from the Revolution but also incarnates the secularization of certain Christian values, probably more rightly than wrongly, that are still implicitly present in society. Incomprehensible *from the outside* (where it is often seen as a bastion against religion), secularism can and must be lived otherwise *from the inside* (where it remains, in counter-relief, a societal presence of religious values).

French spiritualism has, then, contributed to this to a considerable degree—that is the least one can say—and we would be wrong to ignore it in order to invalidate it too rapidly. For despite the reproach that has

14. See Canullo, *Coscienza e libertà*.
15. Vieillard-Baron, *Spiritualisme français*, 14 (emphasis added).

often been (wrongly) addressed to these nineteenth-century thinkers for working within the most institutional French society, they transformed it *ad intra*, or at the very least inhabited it: Maine de Biran, a subprefect of Bergerac; Victor Cousin, a councilor of state; Lachelier, a school inspector; Ravaisson, an inspector general of libraries, etc. In short, and even before the separation of church and state (in 1905), when, certainly, secularism could have changed in meaning (becoming at times more hostile or neutral than tolerant), spiritualism contributed to a "pacified and open space" in society. But the stakes of French spiritualism were not only political or academic. They were first intellectual and philosophical, even spiritual. Spiritualism indeed worked to introduce *in philosophy* a third term—spirit (*pneuma*) between the soul (*psyché*) and the body (*soma*)—in order to not condemn all reflection to a duality of soul and body that could only have ruined it.

With spiritualism—and this will be even truer with Maine de Biran at the end of his life (see the conclusion "Three Lives in One") as, moreover, for Michel Henry, also in his final trilogy (*I Am the Truth*; *Incarnation*; *Words of Christ*)—it is in a sense *the Bible that enters into philosophy*, in the manner of Emmanuel Levinas—but not only through the Old, or rather First, Testament (Judaism), but crossing this time via the New, or the Second, Testament (Christianity). The secularization of the Paulinian *pneuma* in a tripartite biblical anthropology—"Now may the God of peace himself sanctify you completely, and may your whole *spirit* [*pneuma*] and *soul* [*psyché*] and *body* [*soma*] be kept blameless at the coming of our Lord Jesus Christ" (1 Thess 5:23)—this is what definitively closes any bipartite Greek anthropology of the soul (*psyché*) and the body (*soma*).[16]

Neither the spiritualist nor the phenomenologist can any longer "fight each other in a duel"—hence the hypothesis of a "backlash of spiritualism on phenomenology" that is developed in the present essay. For both seek together, although in different or differentiated ways, to exit from the pair of "soul" and "body" as mere separate substances: spiritualism by introducing the *spirit*, understood as *pneuma* or *spiritus*, as a medium or aspiration of the soul and the body, and phenomenology by substituting the

16. On the theological deployment of this "tripartite anthropology that French spiritualism *philosophically* inherits," see Irenaeus, *Against Heresies* 6.6.1: "The perfect man [*perfectus homo*], consists in the commingling and the union of the soul [*commixtio et adunitio animae*] receiving the spirit of the Father [*assumentis Spiritum Patris*] and the admixture of that fleshly nature [*et admixtae ei carni*] which was moulded after the image of God." See also my commentary in *God, the Flesh, and the Other*, 129–32.

philosophemes of *Leib* and *Körper* for the so-called metaphysical concepts of *psyché* and *soma*. Do the "flesh" (*Leib*) and the "body" (*Körper*) suffice, then, for replacing the "soul" (*psyché*) and the "body" (*soma*)? Nothing is less certain. It remains that the attempt is the same *in* spiritualism as *in* phenomenology—namely, the attempt to renew the very act of thought such that the phenomenologist will not have all to himself the privilege, if not of truth, at least of originality.[17]

I indicate, following Jean-Louis Vieillard-Baron, "that 'spiritualism' began to be spoken of when the spirit *no longer appeared* as the third person of the Holy Trinity (the Holy Spirit) or even as the divine Logos," in order not to deplore it but to rejoice over it. Contrary to an opinion that is false, or that is wrongly popular, the "(French) secularization of the Holy Spirit," if I may express myself thus, is not *only* a catastrophe for the Holy Spirit, or for God himself, or even for believers. Certainly, the explicit is better than the implicit, at least for those who believe in it (in God) and claim "to have faith." But the aforementioned "spiritualists"—from Maine de Biran to Bergson by way of Cousin, Lachelier, Ravaisson, and even Boutroux and Lagneau—will also have taught us that man's *spirit* is worthwhile as such and that we can neither insist on it as immediately being or coming from the divine Spirit nor reduce it to the mere "understanding and its categories," as the Neo-Kantians of the same era wished to demand (think only of the virulent debate between Léon Brunschvicg and Maurice Blondel, on the occasion of the latter's defense of *Action* in 1893, concerning the famous "supernatural" that is at once "necessary but inaccessible").

That the *pneuma* (the spirit) should become the site of a philosophy or a current of thought, in addition to the *psyché* (the soul) and the *soma* (body), can but lead to recognizing in man something other than himself in himself—in just the manner, albeit in another tradition that did not last (except in Plotinus), of the *noûs*, regarding which Plato indicates in the *Timaeus* that the demiurge first installed "intelligence [*noûs*] in the soul [*psyché*]," then "the soul [*psyché*] in the body [*soma*]."[18] *Noûs* (intelligence), *psyché* (soul), and *soma* (body) in the Platonic Greek tradition (*Timaeus*) and *pneuma* (spirit), *psyché* (soul),

---

17. On this impossible "forgetting of the soul," including in philosophy today, see my work *Chair de Dieu*, 264–82.

18. Plato, *Timaeus* 30b: "Guided by this reasoning, [the god] put intelligence [*noûs*] in soul [*psyché*], and soul [*psyché*] in body [*soma*], and so he constructed the universe. He wanted to produce a piece of work that would be as excellent and supreme as its nature would allow."

and *soma* (body) in the Paulinian biblical tradition (1 Thess 5:23): there is in man something like a "supplement of soul," as Bergson has taught us,[19] and perhaps it first fell to Maine de Biran, as I will show, to reveal this, or at the very least to indicate it.

c) A Claimed Spiritualism

That Maine de Biran would perhaps not have so easily claimed the label of "spiritualism" if it had been affixed to him in his own time probably goes without saying, for anyone who knows how to read him according to his strictest literalness: "Did Maine de Biran himself call himself a spiritualist?" rightly asks Anne Devarieux.

> No, so much does Biran refuse and reject at once both *materialism* and *spiritualism*, giving preference to neither. The true representative of spiritualism is indeed, in Biran's view, G. W. Leibniz, who gave spiritualism its model by choosing *force* as a principle: "Thus the real *model* of *spiritualism* is found in the doctrine of Leibniz, which has the notion of *force* for a principle; the model of *materialism* is wholly in the doctrine of Spinoza, which hinges on the notion of *substance* as its sole pivotal point."[20]

This spiritualism (Leibniz), then, is not a materialism (Spinoza), and it is not an idealism (Berkeley) either. If such categories can certainly seem amusing today—particularly when it comes to saddling Leibniz with the title of "spiritualist," when today we retain from him only the monadology or the theodicy, and Spinoza with the label of "materialist," when he now appears more as the thinker of immanence—the mention of this phrase from Maine de Biran has, in short, the merit of indicating that the word "spiritualist" existed, including in his era and in his work, even if it required a wholly other sense: that is, a *force of spirit* capable of animating things and beings (Leibniz) without being confined to the pure materiality or substantiality of their existence (Spinoza) or to a form of ideality

---

19. Bergson, *Two Sources*, 310: "So let us not merely say, as we did above, that the mystical calls for the mechanical. We must add that the body, now larger, awaits a *supplement of soul*, and that the mechanical would require the mystical" (emphasis added). [Translation modified. –Trans.]

20. Devarieux, "Au principe du spiritualisme?," 60. The reference to Maine de Biran is indicated in a footnote but not reproduced in the text (and I have added it to the citation reproduced here): Maine de Biran, *Commentaires et marginalia: XIXe siècle*, 253 (emphasis partly in original).

with no consistency other than what we can think of it (Berkeley). We will return to this (§16). There is in Biran, at least faced with and against Spinoza, a force of the Leibnizian model—which became the "primitive fact of effort"—that will not be satisfied either with what it attains (the impossible total proximity of oneself to oneself) or with what it could assimilate, even devour (in the manner of Spinoza's *conatus*). The "spiritualism of force" in Maine de Biran, far from sticking only to the mere active and universal substance of the world in the manner of Leibniz, is transformed into this "effort in us," and solely "in us," by which we attain, or become conscious of, our own interiority.

What thus constitutes Maine de Biran's great originality, to judge by reading Félix Ravaisson's *French Philosophy in the Nineteenth Century* (1867), is having made it possible "to rediscover *activity*—beneath the passivity of sensations," that is to say, "spirit itself"; it is he who "noticed that the operation by which we know . . . is activity, effort, will"—thereby "reveal[ing] the crucial fact."[21] Nothing could be clearer. If there is "spirit" in Maine de Biran, or if a certain form of "spiritualism" can be conferred on him (whereby he could, then, have claimed it), it is on the one hand because there is *activity* in man and not only pure passivity as the autoaffection of oneself by oneself, and on the other hand because the *spirit*, far from designating some part that would be abstract or separated from the body, is from the start integrated in and tied to the body in order to move it. Whereas phenomenology could have wrongly believed that spiritualism was content to speak of "only man's spirit," as in Maine de Biran, and that it missed his body—this is the hypothesis of Michel Henry, speaking of the "serious misconstruing" that consisted in classifying the thinker from Bergerac among the so-called "spiritualist" currents of thought (the Introduction to *Philosophy and Phenomenology of the Body*)—we must say, on the contrary, that the *spiritus* of spiritualism, if we stick to the texts of the thinker of Grateloup, under the name of the "primitive fact of effort," designates very precisely the impetus or the freedom of a consciousness that experiences itself in its body through

---

21. Ravaisson, *French Philosophy*, 27: "Maine de Biran noticed that the operation by which we know, which Kant attributed to what he called intellectual spontaneity, is *activity, effort, will*. . . . Our knowledge, our thoughts, according to Maine de Biran, are thus, *like the movements that we enact in our limbs*, effects of our will, as is everything that belongs to us. . . . Maine de Biran revealed *the crucial fact* that reveals us to ourselves as an existence situated beyond the course of nature—a fact that, *through us*, makes us understand that such is any veritable existence" (emphasis added). [Translation modified. –Trans.]

its will and is therefore not confined only to the passive autoaffection of subjectivity (§16). There is a "vital force" in Biran, inherited from Leibniz (in the definition of substance as "force"; I will return to this [§16c]), such that the subject experiencing itself "in itself" (*conscium*) is also the "master of itself" (*compos sui*) and by virtue of this *is* a man. If man is *duplex* and not only *simplex*, according to the thinker from Bergerac, as I said in the opening, it is because the *homo in intellectualitate* (man in his thought) also counterbalances the *homo in vitalitate* (man in his animality). The "sentiment of myself" draws me out of pure sensibility from the moment that there is experienced for consciousness the possibility that this "I"—"*I am* rose-odor" (§10)—would arise that does not belong to animality and that even, to follow here the "spiritualist" vein, makes man leave animality.

The thinker from Bergerac is certainly one of the first thinkers of "force" as such, albeit by situating it exclusively within subjectivity—that is, this time, as the "internal effort from oneself to oneself," the principle of inner freedom and not the unique producer of "reality" in general: hence its name of "effort," which certainly applies only *for* oneself and *in* oneself but is not closed in *on itself*. This is—I will return to this point (§16)—neither Spinoza's *conatus* that is inherent in all living things, the larger of which devour the smaller ones, nor the Nietzschean force that exercises its power only by creating, nor the Bergsonian force as the ever-increasing vital thrust, but rather the effort in itself and for itself of an inhabited body that certainly exists by auto-experiencing itself, though according to a mode of the will that is also a freedom that we must not forget. The "*I am* rose-odor" in Maine de Biran that takes the baton from Condillac's "*it will therefore be* rose-odor"—but while distorting the phrase, as we will see (§10a)—makes clear to what extent subjectivity also, from the start, has to be freely expressed and not only sensed or auto-experienced, for which reason its "becoming conscious" as the "primitive fact" also refers to what is specific to humanity.

Properly speaking, therefore, if one wants to distinguish the spiritualist interpretation and the phenomenological interpretation of Maine de Biran, it will be necessary to indicate that the difference lies less in a relation to spirit on the one hand (spiritualism) and to the body on the other (phenomenology) than in the *signification* and the *orientation* that must be given to this unique and indissoluble unity of the soul and the body. Whereas spiritualism will see in it the movement toward an other than and elsewhere than oneself in the dynamism of the effort that is wholly stretched toward the spiritualization of man in general (in consciousness), phenomenology will adhere more to the appropriation of the body whose particularity consists less in exhibiting itself than in being recognized as one's own or in autoaffecting itself (the lived body). It is therefore the *sense* or, better, the *direction* that changes—oriented rather toward consciousness (spiritualism) or turned more toward the body (phenomenology). The human being is ever and always "spirit and body"—or "soul and body" endowed with a "spirit"—in an indissoluble unity, either in a "dynamic of the spirit" that sweeps the body along with it in the case of spiritualism, or in an "appropriation of the body" that is simply one with the spirit, or even with pathos or autoaffection, in the case of phenomenology.

How will it then go *for us*, that is, on our side, if we also hold to the hypothesis, which in my view is a major one, of an "extra-phenomenality of consciousness" and an "improperness of the body," including in Maine de Biran, in the experiences or, rather, the limit-situations of non-dynamization (spiritualism) and non-appropriation (phenomenology)—sleep, sleepwalking, dreams, madness, drugs, etc.? It will then be a matter of a new and other schema or, rather, of a mode of thought that one cannot so easily make one's own, at the very least insofar as the "outside oneself" (in itself) is always more difficult to approach than an "inside" (for itself) and that the relay of extimacy destroys, as it were, all the soft pretentions of intimacy. Whether the body is raised ever more toward consciousness to unfold consciousness in its humanity (spiritualism) or consciousness is lowered or comes ever closer to the body to be identified with it in its ordeal of itself (phenomenology), it is indeed a question, in this double movement of *anabasis* (ascent) or *catabasis* (descent), of always starting from, and holding to, the originary unity of the spirit and the body. But that there should be an "outside the spirit" (the outside-the-phenomenon)[22] and even an "outside the body" (spread body)—this is what is harder to think, and what Maine de Biran will not,

---

22. [Falque's phrase *le hors phénomène* is typically translated as "the extra-phenomenal" (which also translates *l'extra-phénoménal*), a convention that I have for the most part followed in this translation. Literally, it translates as "the outside phenomenon," which is unacceptable as an English rendering because it suggests a phenomenon of outsideness, whereas the *hors phénomène* is neither spatial nor phenomenally experienced. On a few occasions when it seems useful to mark linguistically the connection between *le hors phénomène* and other phrases including the word *hors* ("outside" or "out"; it can also mean "except" or "excluding"), I have translated it as "the outside-the-phenomenon." –Trans.]

however, hesitate to touch upon in an "outside to oneself" or, rather, "in oneself" that certain limit-experiences give us, if not to experience, at least to know there as existing and as being impossible to bypass.

Reascending to the source, and studying now, as precisely as possible, how the subject constitutes itself in Maine de Biran, be it in order then and by default to witness its deconstruction into phenomena that it could not have appropriated for itself—this is the task that is now incumbent upon us in order to attain the "being outside oneself" that has been so sought-after. It is indeed truly necessary that the subject recognize itself first "in itself" and "appropriated for itself" in order then to discover it or, rather, to note it, in extreme cases, as "outside itself and foreign to itself," in other words as "alienated" or *alienus*, as I have already remarked in the opening (p. xvii). And this returns us here—I was then referencing the prolegomena of the *Nouvelles considérations sur les rapports du physique et du moral de l'homme*—to "the states particular to [or irregular states of, *sic*] the soul and the organized body that carry with them a *complete absence*, momentary or permanent, *of the sentiment of the* myself, although the vital and sensitive functions experience no interruption."[23] There are moments in our lives when everything tips over—in sleep, certainly, but also in sleepwalking, dreams, madness, the effects of drugs—"holes" in existence where, as I quoted (p. xxiv), relying that time on *The Relationship Between the Physical and the Moral in Man*, called the "Copenhagen treatise," "*the obscuration* and *total eclipse* of the sentiment of the *myself*" are such that one is no longer even able to say "I" or "me."

In this "constitution of the *myself*" through consciousness or, rather, through the "primitive fact of the intimate sense," Descartes then becomes the privileged interlocutor—so we await the debate with Condillac to examine in what the "resistance of the body" (chapter 2) and the "search for the flesh" (chapter 3) consist, before there arise the limit-experiences of a "counter-history of madness" (chapter 4), of the "foreign body" (chapter 5), and of the "effortless life" (chapter 6). There is, therefore, an obligatory crossing via Descartes, that "French horseman who took off at such a good pace," as Péguy put it,[24] and from whom the thinker from Bergerac will certainly borrow the approach (in the act of the *cogitatio*) but not the final point (in the *cogito*): "What genius

---

23. Maine de Biran, *Nouvelles considérations*, 5 (emphasis added).
24. Péguy, "Note conjointe sur M. Descartes," 80.

other than that of Descartes," exclaims Biran at the heart of his *Nouvelles considérations sur les rapports du physique et du moral de l'homme*, "the father of all our modern metaphysics, could have conceived of the real founding of all human science on the primitive fact of consciousness or the existence of the thinking *myself*, as on its unique basis, the only true and solid one; who else could have recognized the characteristic of self-evidence, that *criterion* of all certainty, in a small number of primary, elementary, and simple ideas, given to the human soul as a light that first enlightens it about itself, before revealing other existences to it?"[25]

§2. Standing by Oneself

a) A Confession

A confession in the *Journal*, dated November 25, 1817, after an evening spent in Paris at the home of the Abbé Morellet, an Encyclopedist who was renowned at the time, suffices to make clear, and to make known (at least only for the eyes of Maine de Biran, of course, since none of all this was published) that the search for the *myself* is not so obvious:

> On November 25, I spent the evening at the Abbé Morellet's. Psychological conversation. My "old friend" [sic] brusquely asked me: *what is the* myself? I could not answer. One must place oneself *in the intimate point of view of consciousness*, and then having present this unity that judges all phenomena while remaining invariable, one *apperceives* this *myself*; one no longer asks *what it is.*[26]

This unique declaration, recorded as if in passing and just before adding to the following note—"from [November] 25 to 29, a mild temperature, good weather"[27]—suffices to say that the "myself" *is* not. Or, rather, the confession of being unable to answer—"I could not answer"—determines the conditions of the answer. For, if it is necessary to say it phenomenologically—and this is indeed what was, rightly, so blindingly obvious to Michel Henry—it is in the "mode of the reduction" (*epoché*) and not according to the natural attitude (objectivity) that Maine de Biran thinks and writes. He did not know how to answer the Abbé Morellet's question

---

25. Maine de Biran, *Nouvelles considérations*, 108.
26. J. II, 95 (entry dated November 25, 1817, emphasis in original).
27. J. II, 95 (entry dated November 25, 1817).

"*What is* the *myself*?" not because he did not know the answer but because there is no answer to such a badly posed question. The *myself* itself indeed cannot bend itself to a question of the form "what?"—just like phenomenology, which would later be said to not answer the "'what' of the objects of philosophical research," to take up the famous Heideggerian definition of phenomenology in its "concept of method," but "the 'how.'"[28]

The *quomodo* in its modes of givenness, and no longer the *quid* in its objectivity. One already finds there the new phenomenal quest of egoity, here initiated in a unique and original way by Maine de Biran. How the *myself* "appears to me," we read ("one *apperceives* this *myself*"), and no longer "*what* the *myself is*" ("one no longer asks *what it is*")—this is what truly makes the *myself* or, rather, delivers the correct point of view on the *myself*: "One must place oneself *in the intimate point of view of consciousness*." One certainly cannot but be surprised by the philosophical profundity of this remark, set down in a notebook or journal for no one, or almost no one, and which, however, even before any determination of phenomenology (the *epoché* in Husserl or the definition of phenomenology in Heidegger), already anticipates its method.

b) The Experience of the *Myself*

But that is not all. For if the thinker of Grateloup did not know how to answer the Abbé Morellet, that is first because oneself's access to oneself is a matter of experience or, rather, of a "sentiment" (of its own existence), and formulating it is already distancing oneself from it and therefore, in a certain manner, objectivating it. After the author of the *Essai sur les fondements de la psychologie*—his masterwork of 1812 (which he never stopped reworking until 1822, without, of course, ever publishing it either)—deconstructs, step by step (we will come to this), the Cartesian *cogito*, it is to a question of *testing* (*épreuve*), *experience*, or *experimentation* that he submits the *cogito* as he convokes it anew. Once again, the future deputy of Dordogne here aims perfectly accurately and establishes himself as a pioneer of that which will be best in the search for phenomenality. The *Meditations*, despite the absolute "genius" of Descartes as "the father of all our modern metaphysics," as I have

28. Heidegger, *Being and Time*, 24 (s. 27): "The expression 'phenomenology' signifies primarily a *concept of method*. It does not characterize the 'what' of the objects of philosophical research in terms of their content but the 'how' of such research" (emphasis in original).

emphasized, goes nowhere, or in nothing, as Husserl also would see very clearly in opposing intentionality—"all consciousness is consciousness of something"—to the mere apperception of oneself by oneself: "Descartes was often asked," Maine de Biran, a bit irritated, acknowledges and admits, "what he meant by *substantial thought that is one and void of any representation*, and on the basis of *what fact* or *what sort of experience* he admitted the reality of such a thought ... and he was never able to answer this pressing question."[29]

A "fact" (which he then calls the "primitive fact" qua pure and simple given) or an "experience" (of oneself by oneself, but in a sentiment or an affect rather than a thought) can alone found my *myself*. For what constitutes the "absolute sentiment of existence," with, of course, all its Rousseauist roots, is not that I exist, but that I sense *myself* or experience *myself* as existing (rather than as a simple "existence," or even a *res cogitans*, that I could objectivate). What indeed surprises Maine de Biran "is not so much that there is being, or that I am a being [*être*], but the fact that I *sense myself* existing. I *sense that I sense*."[30] "I sense that I sense [*sens*] (or that I feel [*ressens*]),"[31] rather than "I think that 'I sense myself'" or "I think that 'I think myself sensing." For if sensing, be it a matter of sensation or affection (*sentiens*), belongs to thought, according to the second of Descartes' *Meditations*—"a thing that imagines and that senses"—it is as the "thinking thing" or *res cogitans* that I discover myself sensing. In

---

29. Maine de Biran, *Essai sur les fondements*, 175 (115–16 in the Vrin ed.) (emphasis added). For the *Essai sur les fondements de la psychologie*, I refer first to the Tisserand edition, which by not rearranging the texts makes it possible to identify them more easily. I will give the reference to the complete Vrin edition if necessary.

30. On this "absolute sentiment of existence," see Bégout's anthology *Maine de Biran*, 20–25 (cit. 20, emphasis added).

31. [*Sentir*, which I have translated throughout as "to sense," means "to sense" or "to feel" (or "to smell," depending on the context), usually though not necessarily in the sense of sensing or feeling something external. *Se sentir* typically means "to feel" in the sense of feeling one's own physical or emotional state (well, ill, awake, tired, happy, sad, etc.), but it can also mean—and in this philosophical context does mean—"to sense oneself." (Note that, for example, the phrase *je me sens*, translated as "I sense myself," contains a conjugation of *se sentir*: because *se sentir* is a reflexive verb, the object pronoun forms part of the verb and always matches the subject.) *Ressentir* means "to feel" in the sense of having an internal, subjective awareness or experience; it often connotes an intense feeling or inner experience. Unfortunately, there is no English translation of *ressentir* that makes clear the etymological connection to *sentir*; I have translated it as "to feel," but the reader should bear this connection in mind whenever any form of the words "feel" or "feeling" (*ressenti*) appears. At a few points when it seems particularly useful to remind the reader of this connection, I have included the French in brackets. –Trans.]

THE CONSTITUTION OF THE *MYSELF*

other words, the false or incorrect question posed by the Abbé Morellet to Maine de Biran one evening in November 1817 in Paris—"*what is the myself?*"—is the very question that Descartes poses to himself in his second *Meditation*, which invalidates his *cogito* from the start by introducing into it something of the "thing" or of the *"res" cogitans*:

> But *what then* am I (*sed quid igitur sum*)? A *thing that thinks* (*res cogitans*). What is that (*quid est hoc*)? A thing that doubts, conceives, affirms, denies, wills, refuses, and that also imagines and senses.[32]

We will therefore no longer "reascend," according to Biran in his *Essai sur les fondements de la psychologie*—who saw well before Husserl in his *Cartesian Meditations* (1929) "Descartes's failure to make the transcendental turn" as a result of committing the "fateful change whereby the ego becomes a *substantia cogitans*" ("transcendental realism, an absurd position")[33]—from the *cogito* to the *res cogitans*, at the risk of "substantifying" the thinking thing. But we will "descend," on the contrary, into the heart of our incessant *cogitationes*, not to grasp a finally-stabilized subject (and we know how truly the host of Grateloup would never be stabilized, including for himself), but to attain that "primitive thought," that "sentiment," or that "primitive fact" by which I sense or feel my *myself*, or, rather, I feel *myself* as myself: "To proceed in a regular fashion to this analysis" (of the sentiment of the *myself*), continues, therefore, Maine de Biran, attempting this time to reach *the experience of the cogitatio*, "I take up Descartes's principle *I think, I exist*, and *descending into myself*, I seek to characterize more expressly what is that *primitive substantial thought* that is supposed to constitute my whole individual existence, and I find it identified in its source with the *sentiment of an action* or of a *willed effort*. This effort will therefore be for me the *primitive fact*, or the fundamental mode that I am seeking, and whose characters or signs I am called to analyze."[34]

---

32. Descartes, *Meditations*, 66 (AT VII, 22) (emphasis added). [Translation modified. –Trans.]

33. Husserl, *Cartesian Meditations*, 24: "Unfortunately these prejudices were at work when Descartes introduced the apparently insignificant but *actually fateful change* whereby the ego becomes a *substantia cogitans*, a separate human '*mens sive animus*,' and the point of departure for inferences according to the principle of causality—in short, the change by virtue of which Descartes became *the father of transcendental realism, an absurd position*" (emphasis added).

34. Maine de Biran, *Essai sur les fondements*, 117.

c) The Sentiment of the *Myself*

Let us leave aside, for the moment, the *action* in the "sentiment of an action" or the *effort* in the "willed effort," since the body alone and its own resistance in itself will deliver the key to it, in a carnal and no longer solely affective ordeal of oneself, by which the body, therefore, or, rather, the "flesh" if one speaks as a phenomenologist, will be fully committed (chapter 3). All that matters, at the point where we are, is this "primitive substantial thought" that thus constitutes what we are—this "sentiment of oneself by oneself" or this "primitive fact" of a fundamental given that I can neither bypass nor obstruct. It is a "primitive fact" of the self that therefore takes as primary the *sentiment of the self* (and not the thought of oneself) and that we will be very careful not to understand in the sense of some empirical fact as a subjective experience given for itself, following the type, or the model, of an objective experience outside oneself. I do not notice myself sensing, or sensing myself, by looking at myself "from outside" or "via the outside." As Maine de Biran will emphasize much later, in a remarkable fashion, in his *Nouveaux essais d'anthropologie* shortly before his death,

> The sentiment of the *myself* is not and cannot be that of the very *substance* of the soul or of the sensing or thinking thing. . . . Trying to objectify the *myself* or to grasp it from outside is like wanting to go to a window to see oneself go by.[35]

We will therefore understand the "primitive fact of the sentiment of the *myself*" in the most common sense in French of "being abreast of the fact of" [*être au fait de*][36]—not just in the sense of "being in the know" or

---

35. Maine de Biran, *Dernière philosophie*, 91 (emphasis added). An "impossibility of going to the window to see oneself go by" could take the baton, starting from Maine de Biran this time, from the accurate confrontation of the man on the balcony watching "hats" and "coats" go by in Descartes (second *Meditation*) and the passerby in the street who wonders if the man on the balcony "placed himself there in order to see me" in Pascal (L 688/B 323). On this confrontation between Descartes and Pascal, see Marion's analysis in *On Descartes' Metaphysical Prism*, 322–33, esp. 322–24.

36. This is Romeyer-Dherbey's accurate suggestion in *Maine de Biran*, 195 (in the entry "*fait*" of the lexicon). [*Être au fait de* is an idiomatic French expression; while there are English equivalents, the word "fact" is not an essential part of any of them (one could, and ordinarily would, write simply "being abreast of"), but *fait* is essential to the expression *être au fait de*. Moreover, as Falque's subsequent discussion indicates, one can be *au fait de* some event without "knowing all the facts" of it; one may, that is, be aware of the fact of the event without being fully informed of all the facts or details concerning it. To clarify the point, it is useful to cite a portion of the passage from

"being informed," as if the *myself* could, even for a few minutes, escape itself to become uninformed about itself (although, and I will show this, it is the whole object of an extra-phenomenality in myself that escapes the sentiment of the *myself*), but in the sense of an "event that takes place" or an "existing situation" from which it is impossible for me to withdraw myself. One can indeed "be abreast of the fact" of something that one learned through hearsay or from a third party (a love, a divorce, or a resignation), and "being abreast of the fact," one cannot rid oneself of it or detach oneself from it, especially if it is not known to others (who are not "abreast of the fact") and scarcely known to myself (who does not know "the facts"). In short, the *primitive fact* has to do not with the empirical but with the "there" that is undetachable from me because it is me. There is the *myself* who knows, or rather who senses, and the thing that I know, or rather that I feel [*ressens*]—but this indissoluble link between me and the thing is felt *in myself*, like a fundamental given that is inseparable from myself. Far from being an "immediate given of consciousness" that still belongs to the consciousness in which emotion is inscribed (duration, for example), it is the emotion itself, or rather the affect, that becomes the fundamental site of the self in which things manifest themselves, in a sort of noetico-noematic correlation that is closer, in this regard, to Husserl than to Bergson: "There is a *primitive fact for us* only insofar as we have the *sentiment of our individual existence* and the *sentiment of some thing, object or modification* that coincides with that existence and is distinct or separate from it."[37]

Better, continues the thinker from Bergerac in his ascertaining of the "primitive fact," "without this sentiment of individual existence that in psychology we call *consciousness* (*conscium sui, compo sui*), there is no fact that can be said to be *known*, no knowledge of any sort; for a fact is nothing if it is not *known*."[38] The matter is important enough to be emphasized. Here, starting from the general introduction of the *Essai sur les fondements de la psychologie* (§II. "Détermination du fait primitif du sens intime" ["Determination of the Primitive Fact of the Intimate Sense"]), what is ordinarily, and also rightly, named the "spiritualist"

Romeyer-Dherbey to which Falque refers: "By 'fact,' one commonly designates the positivity of things; by 'fact,' Biran certainly designates a positivity, but one that is essentially distinct from that of things: that of the power of apperception, which implies in its content the givenness of a world" (Romeyer-Dherbey, *Maine de Biran*, 195–96). –Trans.]

37. Maine de Biran, *Essai sur les fondements*, 15.
38. Maine de Biran, *Essai sur les fondements*, 15.

interpretation of Maine de Biran is fully justified: that is, a philosophy of "self-consciousness" (*conscium sui*), even of "self-mastery" (*compo sui*), even though this access of oneself to oneself occurs according to the mode of affect (the sentiment of oneself) rather than the mode of thought (reflection about oneself). Far from the "serious misconstruing" that would consist in associating Maine de Biran with a "current of 'spiritualist' thought," we will recognize, therefore, inversely, in the backlash of spiritualism on phenomenology, that the sentiment of the *myself* is also a *mode of consciousness*—albeit expanded from thought to the body and to affect (as it is, moreover, but in another way, when "Adam *knew* his wife Eve" in Genesis 4:1).

The footnote in the same passage specifies this, moreover, and confirms it remarkably. Being "abreast of the fact of this fact" is indeed the task proper to the "thinking thing" (and therefore to the man who is conscious of himself) because he not only senses, and senses that he senses (and therefore feels [*ressent*]), but he makes this "re-sensing" [*re(s)-sentir*][39] the very site of apperception—that is, here following Leibniz, to whom we will return ("little perceptions"), the act by which the human subject, *qua man*, apperceives himself [*s'aperçoit*] that he perceives, or rather perceives *himself* by perceiving:

> Not only are foreign existences facts for us, but in addition proper and individual existence is *a fact for the thinking thing exclusively* among all animated beings. This admirable faculty that he has of *knowing himself* or of *apperceiving himself*, as a *fact of which he becomes aware* [*dont il se rend compte*] is an essential, characteristic attribute from which the philosopher must begin in order to deduce everything, as the thinking subject necessarily begins from it in order to know everything.[40]

---

39. [The previously discussed sense of *ressentir* as internal awareness or experience (see note 31 in chapter 1) remains relevant in this passage. By writing *re(s)-sentir* here, however, Falque plays on the resemblance (and etymological relationship) of *ressentir* to *re-sentir*, "to sense again," thus emphasizing that sensing oneself sensing is a reflexive action, or a return of the self to itself: one does not only sense but also, in the same movement, senses oneself sensing. A remark by Romeyer-Dherbey about the sense of Biranian reflection may help clarify the play on words, even though Falque does not explicitly reference reflection: "In 'reflection,' the prefix *re* designates not the opening of a gap but a movement of return, not a return upon oneself, but a return *to oneself*; reflection returns us to ourselves, and that is why the word 'simple' is often, in Biran, associated with the word 'reflection'" (*Maine de Biran*, 202). –Trans.]

40. Maine de Biran, *Essai sur les fondements*, 15n1.

d) A Pure Given

Knowing oneself is not "thinking oneself" (Descartes) but "becoming aware of oneself" as a "fact" or as a pure given. Certainly, there is no deduction (which Descartes always opposed also), but there is no intuition either. Here there is no "immediate seeing," which would still belong too much to the order of intellection or of an act of the understanding. It is rather an apperception of oneself through sensation (I feel myself, a point to which we will return with the paradigm of the statue) at the same time as through affection (I auto-experience myself in the inner sentiment of myself). "Apperceiving" oneself "that one perceives," in the manner of Leibniz in apperception—this is what constitutes the human who not only senses, senses that he senses, and therefore feels [*ressentir*], but also *knows* that he senses with a knowledge that makes him gain access to a consciousness of himself. Not only does man "sense" or "have a sensation," like other animate beings, to say it in Maine de Biran's language, but he "perceives" in the sense that he "senses" and "himself apperceives himself" in this sensation. It is therefore verbatim in the "sensing [of] the sensation"—here one could believe that one was reading Merleau-Ponty and his famous paradigm of the "touching-touched," taken up from Husserl—that the human is born, but with this one difference, and not a minor one at that: this sensing of the sensation makes consciousness, or gains access to consciousness. The reading here is not solely phenomenological (the descent into the flesh of the touching-touched), it is also spiritualist (access to consciousness through the apperception of oneself): "*Sensing* or *having a sensation*," emphasizes this same footnote in the *Essai sur les fondements de la psychologie*, with an exceptional modernity for us today, "is not the same thing as *perceiving* or, as one of our philosophers has said, *sensing the sensation*: the former (sensing or having a sensation) expresses an *external fact* that an intelligent being can recognize by certain signs in the organic beings that move themselves or are moved in a certain manner; the latter phrase (perceiving or sensing the sensation) expresses *a wholly internal fact* for which the individual who *senses and perceives* is both the *witness* and the *actor*."[41]

By virtue of a surprising contemporaneity that we, therefore, cannot but note here, one could believe that one was reading Maurice Merleau-Ponty and the famous example of the "touching-touched" that he took up from Husserl. One could believe, that is, that one was reading of the

---

41. Maine de Biran, *Essai sur les fondements*, 15n1.

"reversibility of sensing" in *The Visible and the Invisible*, which means that "we no longer know *which sees* and *which is seen*" because when one touches or, rather, when one "touches oneself" (sensing the sensation, as Maine de Biran would say), one no longer knows "*which is touching and which is touched*"—and that is what is called the "flesh":

> If one wants metaphors, it would be better to say that *the sensed body* and *the sensing body* are as the obverse and the reverse, or again, as two segments of one sole circular course . . . so that the seer and the visible reciprocate one another and we no longer know *which sees* and *which is seen*. It is this Visibility, this generality of the Sensible in itself, this anonymity innate to Myself that we have previously called *flesh*.[42]

Before any *phenomenological interpretation*—it is only with the example of the "statue" that it will take shape [*prendre corps*], and that is the least one can say—we will indeed, therefore, hold first to a *spiritualist interpretation* of Maine de Biran regarding this consciousness of oneself or, rather, this "sentiment of oneself." For "perceiving" or "sensing the sensation" is indeed a *fact of the consciousness* or, rather, *the spirit that appears to itself*. Man becomes man not through thought but through "touch," and in this Maine de Biran agrees entirely with the philosopher who said so before him (namely Condillac); but it is a touch that is an internal autoimpression rather than an external impression, a point to which we will return at length in the example of the "marble statue" (chapters 2–3). I sense myself sensing by feeling myself from the inside (Biranian subjectivism); I do not sense myself sensing by sensing a self received or noted from outside (Condillacian sensualism). Going from "myself to myself" by suspending the world, which one will perhaps have considerable difficulty finding in Maine de Biran, as in Michel Henry later—this is the operation of a phenomenological reduction at the heart of sensation that will definitively invalidate the Cartesian passage from the *cogito* to the *res cogitans* and will make precisely this suspension into the site of a "fundamental sentiment," even of an "inner tingling," as the thinker from Bergerac will say in his treatise *Influence de l'habitude sur la faculté de penser*, of which we cannot be rid and that properly constitutes us.[43]

---

42. Merleau-Ponty, *Visible and the Invisible*, 138–39 (emphasis added). [Translation modified. –Trans.]

43. Maine de Biran, *Influence de l'habitude*, 54–55: "These variable modes of the *sentiment of our existence*, although they are almost always conflated with the impressions of external senses or their images, can nevertheless *leave their obscurity*, either *by*

§3. The Reduction to the *Myself*

a) The Impossible Substantification of the *Myself*

> The Biranian critique of the enthymeme [a logical consequence from "I think" to "I am"] does not bear on the immediate grasping of the *Myself*, and Michel Henry is right to highlight the fundamental agreement of the two great thinkers (Descartes and Biran), but bears on the *hypostasis* or the *substantialization* of existence.[44]

This statement by Xavier Tilliette in his "Nouvelles réflexions sur le *cogito* biranien" ["New Reflections on the Biranian *cogito*"] suffices to explain the Cartesian deconstruction carried out by Maine de Biran and its relevance for phenomenology—if indeed intentionality in Husserl (followed by all phenomenologists, including Emmanuel Levinas first and foremost) has no other aim than to exit from a definition of consciousness as a thing, even a thinking one (*res cogitans*), to posit it as an act. This critique or, better, this severe rejection of the "substantification of the Cartesian self" by Maine de Biran is efficiently carried out as soon, or nearly so, as the opening of the first part of the *Essai sur les fondements de la psychologie* ("Système de Descartes" [Descartes's System]). Rarely have any pages been so accurate and so pertinent, including for our modernity—and probably it is not without reason that the jury for the *agrégation* in philosophy in France therefore put on the program for the 1948 oral exam, just after the war, this first section of the *Essai* (on Descartes, Leibniz, and Kant), in addition to the "Introduction" (with the determining of the "primitive fact"). One understands the enthusiasm, if not of the students taking the *agrégation* themselves, at least of the professors who had to teach it, Michel Henry and Maurice Merleau-Ponty included.[45]

---

the particular attention that we give them by examining them in this connection or *by taking on by themselves striking characteristics* that no longer permit us to misunderstand them and refer them to foreign causes; thus it is that in these states of hilarity, of an *inner tingling* that results from a perfect harmony among all the parts of the system, it is impossible not to sense that *the cause of this bliss is in ourselves*" (emphasis added). [This passage comes from the first version of Biran's *Influence de l'habitude sur la faculté de penser* and is thus not found in the English translation, *The Influence of Habit on the Faculty of Thinking*, which is based on the second version. –Trans.]

44. Tilliette, "Nouvelles réflexions," 437 (emphasis added).

45. For the program of the *agrégation* in philosophy, I refer anew to Bianco, *Après Bergson*, but this time specifying very precisely the texts given to be studied for the oral exam (cited on p. 360): Maine de Biran, *Essai sur les fondements de la psychologie*: "Introduction générale," §2, "Détermination du fait primitif du sens intime"); Part I

As I have indicated (p. 35), Descartes "fail[ed] to make the transcendental turn" in Husserl's view by making the "fateful change whereby the ego becomes a *substantia cogitans*" that is, "the absurd position" that is "transcendental realism." Wrongly passing from the *cogito* to the *res cogitans* and continuing to think (including thought) in the mode of a thing or of objectivity—this is the great "misfiring" of Cartesian philosophy according to phenomenology, which it is therefore appropriate to not reiterate. The objection concerning the "solipsism" of the *cogitatio* (the *oneself* alone) is hardly anything compared to the reification of consciousness in the *res cogitans* (the thinking thing). If the first launch certainly missed the subject's alterity, the second missed the activity of consciousness. By posing the question "what?" (*quid*) about the *myself* or the thinking thing, as I have insisted (p. 33), one avoids the question of the "how?" (*quomodo*) of the subject as it appears to itself. Better, in order for such an activity of consciousness to not be empty, it remains necessary to link the *cogito* to its *cogitatum* without ever ridding it of the *cogitatum*, in a correlation of the noema and the noesis that will later be named intentionality. Maine de Biran showed this too, well before everyone else. It is enough to make one believe that he was being read "in secret" while everyone, or nearly everyone, pretended ignorance of him—and even though he did not confine himself to this pure subjectivity, since the subject, in trauma or the limit-experience, is as though extra-territorialized.

b) The Phenomenal Subject and the Real Subject

In this classic passage, entitled "Système de Descartes," in the first chapter of the first section of the *Essai sur les fondements de la psychologie*, Maine de Biran, as a pioneer, makes this fully visible and also known. "In Descartes's phrase, 'I think, therefore I am,'" he writes, very explicitly and altogether pertinently, "this subject 'I' in the conclusion: *I exist* is certainly not identical to what is expressed by the same sign in the major premise: *I think*. Here, it is a *phenomenal subject*; there, it is a *real subject*."[46] The phrase is perfect and even anticipatory. In the manner of

---

("Analyse des faits primitifs de sens intime"), first section, chapters 1–2: systems of Descartes, Leibniz, Kant, then Bacon, Locke, and Condillac; and second section, chapters 1–2 (effort as the "primitive fact").

46. Maine de Biran, *Essai sur les fondements*, 123–31 (for the whole of the chapter entitled "Système de Descartes"); cit. 125. The same passage, but cut to reestablish the

Descartes's "fateful change" that is the confusion of a "transcendental realism," the thinker of Grateloup thus denounces, as if in advance, the non-distinction between the "phenomenal subject" and the "real subject": phenomenological terms in French that are surprisingly used by Maine de Biran himself, as will also be the case for "lived body," as I will show (chapter 3). It is a question here of an "enthymeme in Descartes's phrase," Biran emphasizes very precisely, "to the degree that the premise (I think) already contains the conclusion (I am), but in another sense of 'I.'"[47]

It is fitting, in consequence, to separate the "I" of the act of thinking of the *cogitatio* (*the phenomenal subject*) and the "I" of existence (*the real subject*). For existing, at least as a man or an act of consciousness, is apperceiving or sensing one's existence according to a continuous flux and is not deducing from the *myself* that thinks (I think) a being that thinks (I am) or even a thing that thinks (thinking thing). Indeed, and still following Maine de Biran's exact wording (while one could believe that one was reading Husserl verbatim):

> The mere proposition *I think* [phenomenal subject], identical to this proposition: *I exist for myself*, states the primitive fact, the phenomenal liaison between the *myself* and the thought or the apperception, such that the subject begins and continues to exist for itself only insofar as it begins and continues to *apperceive* or to *sense its existence*, that is, to think.[48]

This says everything, at least with regard to the phenomenality of the subject that apperceives itself or, rather, to what this phenomenality will be once the "thing in itself" of the *myself* is definitively abandoned in favor of its apperception, or its auto-apparition, for myself: "Having consciousness of oneself is existing *for oneself*," specifies the text, "but being a thing or a substance *in itself* is not *existing for itself* or *sensing itself existing*."[49]

c) A Reduction to the *Myself*

There is, then, no better way to put it. The thinker from Bergerac carries out, perhaps without knowing it because he does not have the word for it

---

order of the Vrin edition, is found in *Œuvres*, 7:77–81. Unless stated otherwise, I am following the Tisserand edition in order to rely on the complete text.

47. Maine de Biran, *Essai sur les fondements*, 124.
48. Maine de Biran, *Essai sur les fondements*, 124.
49. Maine de Biran, *Essai sur les fondements*, 123.

even as he espouses its reality, what can, properly speaking, be named a reduction or *epoché*—definitively ridding himself of the natural attitude or of the position of a *myself* as an "existing" or "thinking thing" in favor of the apperception of oneself by oneself in the sentiment (rather than the thought) of experiencing oneself. Becoming both the "actor" and the "witness" of its own existence (p. 40), "apperceiving itself internally" in the sentiment of oneself as the primitive fact, and definitively leaving behind any questioning in the form of the *quid* (what?) as well as any answer that would demand a *res* (a thing or a "state of a thing"): this is what causes the ego or, rather, the "myself" to be this time truly *reduced to itself* and *liberated from any reification* that would be an obstacle to its auto-grasping of itself by itself or to its apperception in act. A striking phrase from this same passage of the *Essai sur les fondements de la psychologie* says so, by way of a "metaphysical counter-meditation" or, rather, to definitively renounce Descartes:

> I am for myself *not a thing* or an *object* whose existence I affirm by giving it thought for an attribute but a subject that *recognizes itself* and *affirms to itself* its existence, insofar as it *apperceives itself internally* and thinks.... The phrase "I am a thinking thing" therefore implies a *contradiction* with the primitive fact.[50]

Descartes's absurd position, later deplored by Husserl, is therefore already set forth by Maine de Biran via this explicit "contradiction" between the thinking thing and the primitive fact. As does the father of phenomenology, the thinker from Bergerac "expressly puts forth doubts" regarding the legitimacy of the passage from the *cogito* to the *res cogitans* in Descartes, with the author of the *Meditations* totally missing, on his own terms, the distinction between the "phenomenal subject" and the "real subject"—that is, between the *myself* that "senses itself" and "feels itself" (I think) and the subject that exists ("I am"): "I note that Descartes, by abruptly crossing the whole interval that separates the *fact of personal existence from the sentiment of myself* and the *absolute notion of a thinking thing*, opens the door to all *doubts about the objective nature of this thing that is not the myself*."[51]

The "reduction of the natural attitude," for which Biran does not have the word but does possess the notion, is then named the "danger of absolutization" in the etymological sense of *ab-solutus*, that is, of what is

---

50. Maine de Biran, *Essai sur les fondements*, 126–27 (emphasis partly in original).
51. Maine de Biran, *Essai sur les fondements*, 127 (emphasis added).

separated that could make an objectivity of the thinking *myself* (thinking thing) exist by itself independently of the act of thinking or, rather, of sensing or, better, of "re-sensing [*re-sentir*]." The "sentiment of the *myself*" is here named the "fact of personal existence," not at all in the empirical sense of a fact or assessment that is external to oneself, as I have said, but in the sense of being "abreast of the fact of oneself" insofar as one cannot detach oneself from oneself—at least when one "knows oneself" or, rather, when one "senses oneself."

If a gap must certainly be maintained between Maine de Biran and Edmund Husserl insofar as the former paradoxically and retrospectively radicalizes the latter by reducing the reduction itself to pure "autoaffection" understood as the "sentiment of the *myself*"—and it is all to the credit of Michel Henry that he showed this and took inspiration from it—we will first of all recognize that the thinker from Bergerac did not miss the "transcendental orientation," to put it in the terms of the father of phenomenology, thus attaining, as if in advance, the "reduction to the pure *myself*" that was so much hoped for. There is no question in Maine de Biran, any more than in Husserl, of "naturalism" (the natural self) or of "psychologism" (psychic life) of the ego because the *myself* is in each case constituting rather than constituted: "By phenomenological epoché," indicates the founder of phenomenology in the *Cartesian Meditations*, thereby rewriting, as it were, "otherwise" and "without knowing it" the *Essai sur les fondements de la psychologie* of the thinker from Bergerac, "I *reduce* my *natural human Ego and my psychic life—*the realm of my *psychological self-experience—*to my *transcendental-phenomenological Ego.* . . . The *Objective world*, the world that exists for me, that always has and always will exist for me, the only world that ever can exist for me—this world, with all its Objects, I said, *derives* its whole sense and its existential status, which it has for me, *from me myself, from me as the transcendental Ego,* the Ego who comes to the fore only with transcendental-phenomenological epoché."[52]

d) I Do Not Always Think

Are we then always in this flow of thought of the autoaffected subject—such that if I cannot "always think" (Descartes), it is indeed necessary that I always "sense" or, rather, sense *myself* or feel *myself,* including as

---

52. Husserl, *Cartesian Meditations,* 26 (emphasis partly in original).

thinking (Henry)? "*Affectivity is the essence of autoaffection*," we read by way of an answer to the question at the heart of *The Essence of Manifestation* (1963)—a work concerning which we must repeat that "everything" comes from a "certain" reading of Maine de Biran, and about which we know, besides, that *Philosophy and Phenomenology of the Body*, published later (1965) but written earlier (1947–1948) constituted the first part.

> [Affectivity] is the manner in which the essence receives itself, senses itself, in such a way that this "sensing itself" as "sensing itself by itself," presupposed by the essence and constituting it, discovers itself in it, in affectivity. . . . This is what constitutes the essence of sentiment, the essence of affectivity as such: sensing oneself by oneself, in such a way that sentiment is not something which senses itself by itself, this or that sentiment, one at this time, at another that one, but precisely the fact of sensing oneself by oneself considered in itself in the effectiveness of its phenomenological realization, namely, in its reality . . . affectivity is the original essence of revelation.[53]

The "sentiment," the "sensing oneself by oneself" that is not *this* or *that* sentiment but the "*fact* of sensing oneself by oneself," by making affectivity the center of the personality—here one could believe that one was reading Maine de Biran, but it is indeed Michel Henry, and not in a peripheral way but of course at the heart of his thesis, namely, *The Essence of Manifestation*. And this is the case for at least three reasons (but this is not all there is to it, since Biran, according to my "own interpretation" and in certain "limit-situations," will also be the thinker of the improper, of heteroaffection, and of the spread body). There are three reasons, then, stated as follows, and that are common to the two thinkers: because affectivity is absolutely fundamental, because there is nothing outside autoaffection, and because no subject can constitute itself without remaining adhered to this affectivity that experiences itself. *Videre videor*: "It seems to me that I see." This is what is really irreducible in Descartes's second *Meditation*, masterfully deployed by Henry in *The Genealogy of Psychoanalysis* (1985). Neither "I see" nor "I think I see," but whether I sleep or wake, it "seems to me" (*videor*) that "I see" (*videre*). "Seeming" paradoxically becomes the highest degree of certainty because *pathos*—suffering and enjoying—is indeed the irreducible of which I cannot rid myself and by which I am autoaffected.[54]

53. Henry, *Essence of Manifestation*, 462–63. [Translation modified. –Trans.]
54. Henry, *Genealogy of Psychoanalysis*, 11–40 (esp. 17: "The cogito's ultimate

But "does one, however, always think," or, rather, "does one always sense oneself," or "does one always experience oneself"? This is the crucial question that we must ask ourselves—according to the hypothesis that the subject can indeed become "foreign to itself" (chapter 5) after "the *myself* has been constituted" (the present chapter). For the exception proves the rule, and this will be the entire stake of extra-phenomenality—in my own eyes, certainly, but also in the eyes of Maine de Biran, for whoever simply knows how to read, and to follow step by step, this same passage of the critique of Descartes in the *Essai sur les fondements de la psychologie*. It can indeed happen, emphasizes and confirms the thinker from Bergerac, as a good doctor of the soul who was so close to the medical world (a point to which we will return; he was the founder and president of the Bergerac Medical Society [*Société médicale de Bergerac*]), that in certain *extreme experiences* that he very precisely names "complete sleep" but also "cases of malfunction" about which one can imagine anything (illness, separation, death of a child, natural disaster, pandemic), I *no longer sense myself sensing* or even *being autoaffected*, to the point of losing the "very sentiment that I exist" (and not solely the thought of myself). Outside thought, I am also "outside affection" and "outside autoaffection" in the case of trauma understood not only as a blockage of my affectivity but perhaps also as a manner of being of the "myself" that can "no longer say 'myself'" and that I would never have suspected of being able to "come to this." "I exist insofar as I think, or for as long as I think," emphasizes Maine de Biran, taking up Descartes verbatim in his second *Meditation*. But this is in order to immediately add—fundamentally, in my view, and as a perfect illustration of my leitmotif, "So much exception, so much modification," in *The Extra-Phenomenal*—"Yet I *do not always think* (in *complete sleep*, in *cases of malfunction*), or I *do not always* have *the sentiment that I exist*: therefore the individual who is called myself is not only a thinking thing whose essence is solely and exclusively thought."[55]

What, then, is going on in this "complete" (or deep) "sleep" or in these "cases of malfunction" in which I precisely do not, or "not always," have the "sentiment that I exist"? This is in reality what I, *here*, that is

---

formulation is the proposition *videre videor*: it seems to me that I see" [Translation modified. –Trans.]).We will thus maintain Descartes's *videre videor* (second *Meditation*) and the "sentiment of oneself" and the "primitive sense of effort" in Biran as the two major philosophical sources of Michel Henry, to which one can, of course, add, from a theological point of view, Meister Eckhart's *Sermons* (the *Sermon on Detachment* in particular) and the Gospel According to St. John (the prologue in particular).

55. Maine de Biran, *Essai sur les fondements*, 125.

to say in this work, am seeking to understand. I am not seeking a mere illustration or confirmation of the "extra-phenomenal"—the inner and personal experience of trauma should suffice to convince us of this: for if we are not all "traumatized," at least we are all "traumatizable." What is true of the *psyché*—the "subject that is off*side*" or detached from itself in limit-experiences—will then be even more true of the *body* in the incredible debate that opposed Maine de Biran to Condillac regarding the "marble statue" that suddenly sets itself in motion, senses "a rose-odor" and "touches itself." In this touching-touched a certain form of egoity or, rather, of ipseity will certainly be expressed, at least for Condillac—but to which Biran will oppose the pure internal and muscular effort of the hand to justify an "I sense" or, better, an "I feel myself" independently of any exteriority.

Rather than separating out "sensualism" on the one hand (Condillac) and "subjectivism" on the other (Maine de Biran), we will rid ourselves of these labels that always make us read authors incorrectly. Condillac indeed is often seen *only* as the adversary to whom Maine de Biran addresses himself, and the *Treatise on the Sensations* is almost always read as the "foil" to the *Essai sur les fondements de la psychologie*. But that is getting things the wrong way round and always preferring the "inside" (Biran) to the "outside" (Condillac), as if that went without saying. Before the "search for the flesh" via the invention of the lived body by Maine de Biran (chapter 3) there stands the "resistance of the body" given at the origin, at least in Condillac, and of which it is hardly certain that we can so easily be rid (chapter 2). For the real difficulty, and the most crucial question, as Husserl posed it, though without resolving it, in a posthumous manuscript of 1921, is not the question of incarnation or the "becoming-flesh" (*Verleiblichkeit*) but rather the question of embodiment or the "being-a-body" (*Körperlichkeit*). For it is not the "inside" beginning with oneself that in reality poses a problem but rather the possibility of reaching an "outside" that is not oneself. To the "lived or proper body" (flesh) there is opposed the "improper body" (body), or the body that I cannot so easily appropriate for myself. And this is in reality the Gordian knot that is to be undone and which it is indeed necessary, if not to untie, then at least to dare to think: "Thus it is a *fundamental problem* to think through and clearly define *how flesh is also constituted as physical flesh*."[56]

56. Husserl, *Zur Phänomenologie der Intersubjektivität*, 77, cited in Franck, *Flesh and Body*, 83 (emphasis partly in original). On this point, see my commentary in *Loving Struggle*, 164–73.

2

The Resistance of the Body

> Thus I forewarn the reader that it is very important to put himself *exactly in the place* of the statue we are going to observe.... In short, he must be *only* what it is.
>
> CONDILLAC, *TREATISE ON THE SENSATIONS*

The Reply of the Soul and of the Body

ONCE THE "*MYSELF* IS constituted" (chapter 1), there now comes the "resistance of the body" (chapter 2). To the "reply of sentiment" responds, then, the "reply of resistance," in such a contemporaneity that the "phenomenal *myself*" auto-appears in the "lived body"—two "phenomenological" terms rigorously set down on paper, even invented (we will come to that), by Maine de Biran himself. Hence this word "reply" is chosen in order not to forget that it is *in one and the same movement* that the "sentiment of the *myself*" and the "primitive fact of effort" come to encounter each other: "It is by a 'reply of resistance,'" we read in a footnote of the *Mémoire sur la décomposition de la pensée*, not published, of course, and written just after the treatise *The Influence of Habit on the Faculty of Thinking*, "and not only 'the reply of sentiment' that the extent of the *lived body* manifests itself inwardly and is circumscribed," or nearly so.[1]

---

1. Maine de Biran, *Mémoire sur la décomposition*, 439n (emphasis added).

We will therefore turn to the "lived body," a term from Maine de Biran himself, not by virtue of the objective or even mechanical movement of my soul on my body, as if to drive it, but through the doubling, subjective in itself, but from the point of view of the body this time, of the sentiment of oneself experienced through affect. From the "I sense myself" insofar as I "feel myself" or experience myself in the *sentiment of the myself* (chapter 1), we now cross to the "I sense myself" insofar as "I sense that I sense" in *the muscular effort of my body*, or even in the *resistance* that could be opposed to it (chapter 2). And by reason of this double usage, and of the same usage, of the "reply" to say the "myself" (reply of sentiment) and the "body" (reply of resistance), we are not passing successively from consciousness understood as "affect" to the flesh aimed at as the "lived body," but rather it is therefore in "one single moment" that *affect* and the *flesh* (*Befindlichkeit* and *Leib*, as phenomenology would say) answer each other. Contrary to a simple parallelism of soul and body as two attributes of a single substance in the power of the *conatus* (Spinoza), here there is rather an "inner primitive duality between two 'distinct and not separated terms' that are a force called 'hyperorganic' and the inner resistance of the 'lived body' in what is called the 'primitive fact of effort.'"[2]

Biranian effort indeed differs from the "power of persevering in its being" (*conatus*) in that, on the one hand, there is never any question of persevering, growing, or diminishing but rather of "remaining" (in oneself) and, on the other hand, it directs itself not toward other beings (to devour) but rather toward itself to sense *itself* (or to autoaffect *itself*). The term "reply of resistance," after the fashion of the "reply of sentiment," is here perfectly chosen. For anyone who says "reply" says not only repetition, as if only the initial event counted for judging it (the repetition of a misdeed) or the concluding event for establishing it (the repetition of chant), but the absolute recommencement and the response to which repetition leads. There is a "reply" when everything begins again as it had begun (the reply of an earthquake or a volcano)[3] and when the one's phrase is always the response to the other (the reply of an actor).

If, therefore, there is a "reply" in Maine de Biran between the soul and the body, it is not because what is carried out in the soul also occurs in the body, as if there were a causal interaction between two attributes

---

2. This excellent definition of Biranian effort is issued by Devarieux, "Michel Henry et Maine de Biran," 122.

3. [In French, the term for "aftershock" is *réplique* or *réplique sismique* ("reply" or "seismic reply"). –Trans.]

of a single substance, be it nature or God (Spinoza). There is a reply because there is a "reply *to* the reply" or, rather, a "reply *of* the reply." In other words, it is because what occurs in sentiment was already a "reply" (I who feel myself by myself in the affect of my sentiment of existence) of what happens in the body or, rather, in my flesh, which is also a "reply" (I who sense myself by myself or in myself, in my internal muscular effort, for example). The *reply of resistance* in effort (internal to the body) then designates, properly speaking, the "*lived body*" and justifies the explicit use of the term, so important for today, at least within the framework of phenomenology (§4)—as with the Biranian distinction between the "phenomenal *myself*" and the "real *myself*," concerning which we have also seen to what an extent it was able to ground contemporary philosophy in an apperception of oneself, independently of any thingification or reification (§2).

If "the most important lesson of the reduction is the *impossibility of a complete reduction*," as I have said following Maurice Merleau-Ponty in the Preface to the *Phenomenology of Perception*, and if it is difficult to stake everything on the "flesh" (*Leib*) without also seeing in it the resistance of the "body" (*Körper*) in an "impossible embodiment," including in Husserl in his *Manuscripts* (see §3d), this *double resistance*—to the *reduction* that is *finished* or even suppressed in autoaffection and to the *lived experience of the flesh* that would have entirely forgotten the thickness of the body—will then be read, remarkably, in the lively debate between Condillac and Maine de Biran about the man-statue. It is indeed not certain, as I have emphasized, that the one (Condillac) can serve only as a "foil" to the other (Biran), and it is by letting each one "be himself" that we will discover there an "outside oneself" or an "outside": in the limits that are external to the body for the one (Condillac) and in the resisting terminus for the other (Biran). We will then cross from the "resistance of the body" in Condillac to the "search for the flesh" in Maine de Biran (chapter 3), not only to measure the gap between them but also to make clear how, and to what an extent, the debate between "flesh" and "body" has already played out in the past—and that interrogating it today on the basis of this "source-corpus" that has already been worked on (Henry, Merleau-Ponty) now becomes another and a new manner of orienting thought or, at the very least, phenomenology itself.

§4. Maine de Biran's Phenomenology

a) The Invention of the Lived Body

After spiritualism taught us how to "stand by oneself" in the "sentiment of the *myself*" (§2c) and phenomenology taught us how to "reduce" oneself "to the *myself*" in a pure subjectivity of the "phenomenal *myself*" (§3), there now comes the specificity or, rather, the absolute originality of Maine de Biran (§4)—that for which he is known, for which he is praised, for which he is so often returned to today, at least on the part of phenomenologists: namely, the "lived body." If there is an "invention of the myself" by Pascal in the seventeenth century,[4] there is an "invention of the lived body [*corps propre*]" by Maine de Biran at the crossroads of the eighteenth and nineteenth centuries.[5] The opinion is unanimous, and it is important to insist on it before advancing further. Michel Henry states it first in *Philosophy and Phenomenology of the Body* (published in 1963 but written in 1948): "The first and actually the only philosopher who, in the long history of human reflection, saw the necessity for originally determining our body as *a subjective body* is Maine de Biran."[6] Maurice Merleau-Ponty takes it up next in *The Incarnate Subject* (published in 1968 but on the basis of a course also given in 1947–48): "Biran . . . displaces the notion of evidence again. He takes as his point of departure *the experience of the body and of its motility*."[7] Finally, Paul Ricœur acknowledges it in *Oneself as Another* (1990): "I should like, at the start of this brief overview, to give proper credit to the one who opened up this field of investigation of the lived body, namely Maine de Biran. . . . Maine de Biran is therefore the first philosopher to have introduced the lived body into the region of nonrepresentative certainty."[8]

---

4. Carraud, *L'Invention du moi*: "This book analyzes what permitted the invention of the *myself*, immediately occluded by Leibniz's individual and Locke's self, and brings to light what it inaugurated: for the first question posed to the *myself*, by Pascal as by Descartes, is not the question of knowing what it is but the existential question of knowing *who* it is" (back cover copy).

5. This is according to Devarieux's accurate suggestion in "Maine de Biran et l'invention du corps propre," 30: "In other words, just as before Pascal—as Vincent Carraud has shown—no philosopher substantivated 'the myself,' before Biran no philosopher spoke of '*the* lived body.'"

6. Henry, *Philosophy and Phenomenology*, 8.

7. Merleau-Ponty, *Incarnate Subject*, 51 (emphasis added). [Translation modified. –Trans.]

8. Ricœur, *Oneself as Another*, 320–21. [Translation modified. –Trans.]

What is thus an obvious assessment for numerous phenomenologists, and important ones at that (including Paul Ricœur), is thus textually established in the Biranian corpus. Though the phrase "*corps propre*" already appears under the pen of Leibniz (but only to signify the monad and not the appropriation of the human body as such), and though it finds its veritable genealogy in a certain Abbé Joseph-Adrien Lelarge de Lignac,[9] it is, properly speaking, in the work of the thinker from Bergerac that the phrase acquires, *stricto sensu*, its patent of nobility and even its conceptualization.[10]

All this would, certainly, be of little importance if the phenomenologist's *eureka* did not here find at the same time the place of its greatest surprise and of its perfect contentment. One imagines Maurice Merleau-Ponty, who, in 1945, had just published *The Phenomenology of Perception* while ceaselessly translating the Husserlian *Leib* by "flesh" [*chair*] but also by "lived body" [*corps propre*]—and finding it again everywhere, or almost everywhere, all through his Biranian reading (to which the references in *The Incarnate Subject* go from the *Mémoire sur la décomposition de la pensée* and the *Essai sur les fondements de la psychologie* to the *Note sur l'idée d'existence* [Note on the idea of existence]).[11] One sees Michel Henry as well, in the same era, in his study, also rereading Husserl in Emmanuel Levinas's translation of the *Cartesian Meditations* and discovering in it the "flesh" or, rather, the "lived body" as the site of the distinction between *Körper* and *Leib*. And one indeed glimpses

---

9. See Azouvi, "Genèse du corps propre," 85–107. The reference is to Leibniz, *Principles of Nature and Grace*, 637: "And each outstanding simple substance or monad... is surrounded by a mass composed of an infinity of other monads which constitute the body belonging to this central monad [*le corps propre de cette Monade centrale*]," as well as to Lelarge de Lignac, *Éléments de métaphysique*, 97: the "sense of the coexistence of our own body [*notre propre corps*]."

10. I will add, with Devarieux, that one indeed finds the expression "*corps mien*" (*corpus meum*, "my body") in Descartes and "*corps sien*" (one's body) in Condillac, but not the phrase "[*le*] *corps propre*" ([*the*] *lived body*) (substantivated) as in Maine de Biran. See "Maine de Biran et l'invention du corps propre," 31: "I will maintain, consequently, that until Biran, there was, in French-language philosophy, quite simply no determination of the lived body." She references Condillac's "*corps sien*" (one's body): see the same article 34n11: "When touch circumscribes several distinct and coexisting sensations within limits where the "myself" does not respond to itself, the statue has the idea of a *body* different from *its own* [*un corps différent du sien*]" (*Treatise on the Sensations*, 235).

11. On this point, see the highly instructive list of the "table of correspondences" between the Tisserand edition (PUF) and the Azouvi edition (Vrin) for Merleau-Ponty's references to Maine de Biran in *L'Union de l'âme et du corps*, 151–54. [This table is not reproduced in the English translation. –Trans.]

Paul Ricœur, later drafting his "A Study of Husserl's *Cartesian Meditations*" (1954), later reprinted in *À l'école de la phénoménologie* (1993) [and in *Husserl: An Analysis of His Phenomenology* (1967) in English], delighting in this obvious correspondence, not to say coincidence, between the translation of the Husserlian *Leib* by *corps propre* in French (to distinguish it from the *Körper* or "objective body" [*corps objectif*]) and in already finding this distinction at work, not only named but also conceptualized, in the Biranian corpus.[12]

Here there is, truth be told, especially for a *French person* who reads and translates German phenomenology, such a cause for stupor and satisfaction that what could have been only a mere homonymy of terms—the phrase "*corps propre*" ["lived body"] both in phenomenology and in the Biranian corpus—becomes in reality a site of encounters between the highest thoughts across the centuries. On this point, at the very least, it is beyond doubt that Maine de Biran "anticipates phenomenology" (Merleau-Ponty), "is one of the true founders of a phenomenological science of human reality" (Michel Henry), or is among those who cause the reader, whether he frequents them up close or from afar, to find himself "incontestably" in the vicinity of "Husserl's phenomenology" (Ricœur).[13]

b) Touch

A footnote by Maine de Biran, drawn from his *Mémoire sur la décomposition de la pensée*, that is, one of his first works, though of course never published, suffices to make clear what the phrase, and the notion of, "the lived body" means, insofar as he is its pioneer and first inventor. And thinking it, to follow him anew here, is "relying on the hands" as the principal organ of the senses. Indeed, and we will return to this, *it is through the hands*, or even *through the hand*, at least as a paradigm or archetypal example, that the ego will say "myself." Whether it is a question of Condillac in the statue's *external resistance* to itself (the hand that strikes the

---

12. On this genesis and this translation of *Leib* by *chair* ("flesh") in French—a decision that was not obvious and that was produced by the joint impetus of Paul Ricœur and Maurice Merleau-Ponty (but that was not Emmanuel Levinas's idea when he translated Husserl's *Cartesian Meditations* in 1931), I refer to my contribution "Turn of the Flesh," 235–62.

13. One will find a particularly well-founded panegyric about this in the introduction to Luís António Umbelino's work (in Portuguese) *Somatologia subjectiva*, 2–16. Here I wish, via this footnote, to particularly thank the author for his unfailing support and his friendship in this plunge, which is new for me, into Maine de Biran's work.

chest and senses at the same time its solidity and its impenetrability) or of Maine de Biran who feels from the inside the *internal resistance* of the body or, rather, of the flesh (the *myself* that experiences itself by and in itself on the basis of the mere muscular effort of its hand, independently of any grasped object), it is indeed first a question of "touch" (and therefore of constituting a new paradigm for the history of philosophy that is not solely the paradigm of sight) and then of "taking" or "not" (such that the hand becomes the source location through which to discover the *myself* or, rather, to discover oneself "as oneself").

Regarding "touch" first, in Aristotle and therefore also in Condillac and Maine de Biran, who are his most direct heirs (after centuries of thought had forgotten to come back to him), it is a matter not of one sense among others but of something like "the sense of all the senses" or even "the essence of sense," insofar as, as Jean-Louis Chrétien perfectly emphasizes in *The Call and the Response* (in his fourth chapter, "Body and Touch"), "I cannot touch without immediately being touched by what I touch, before any reflection, by virtue of its own tangibility. That with which I come into contact comes into contact with me."[14] This is *the reflection of sensing*, which makes it so I cannot "touch" without "being touched." But this time this is the case in every sense of the term, according to the thinker from Bergerac: "being touched" in the sense of sensing (*sensation*) but also "being touched" in the sense of feeling [*ressentir*] (*autoaffection*). There is an *amphibology of sensing* (sensation and affection) that produces precisely the "reply" of the body and the soul in Maine de Biran, as I have shown, such that sensing (the lived body) and feeling (the sentiment of the *myself*) are one and the same.

"Touching" is then not "seeing," so far removed is the proximity of the former from the distancing of the latter. For seeing does not permit seeing *oneself*, save by being mirrored in the other's pupil, which Plato analyzes so well in the *Alcibiades*.[15] Whereas "touch" necessarily requires "being touched"—whether by oneself (the touching hand and the touched hand) or by another (the caress) or even simply by an object in the world (touching the table and feeling its touchedness by analogy with the "flesh of the world" in Maurice Merleau-Ponty)—"seeing" and "hearing" always

---

14. Chrétien, *Call and the Response*, 85. [Translation modified. –Trans.]

15. Plato, *Alcibiades* 133a: "I'm sure you've noticed that when a man looks into an eye his face appears in it, like in a mirror. We call this the 'pupil', for it's a sort of miniature of the man who's looking."

require, inversely, a distance between the "sensing" and the "sensed," such that exteriority, even objectivity, always end up winning out.

The sense of touch is thus the one that is *most proper* to me because it is on the one hand *the closest* to me (I cannot set myself at a distance from it, and it cannot set itself at a distance from things) and because it is on the other hand the site of the *conservation* of myself for myself, for others, and for the world. There is no living animal that does not touch or even that does not touch *itself*, whereas the animals deprived of sight or hearing are quite numerous (Uexküll's famous "tick," for example): "While . . . it is evident that an animal cannot be without touch, the other senses are for the sake of doing well and do not belong to just any chance kind of animal—though it is necessary that they belong to some," Aristotle perfectly emphasizes in chapter 3 of the *De anima*.[16]

Hence the fact that we may rightly speak here of a "carnal hermeneutics," born with Aristotle and of which Maine de Biran, in the wake of Condillac, is one of the greatest heirs, after having long been forgotten.[17] In light of Husserl at least in his manuscripts (*Ideas II* §36), of Merleau-Ponty in the whole of his work and in particular at the end of his life (the chiasm in *The Visible and the Invisible*), and even of Levinas insofar as the caress defines eros as a new mode of knowledge (the appendix of *Totality and Infinity*), one can, then, only be surprised that Martin Heidegger, for his part, never left the "model of seeing" and therefore of distance, even though he claimed to leave the aforementioned "metaphysics" in all respects. For if there is one point that characterizes Plato's famous allegory of the cave, it is not only that it defines as if in advance the site of an "adequation of the mind to the thing," with the idea of the Good as the idea of "what is fitting," but above all that it takes as the definitive model of all philosophy that "prism of vision," even of the sun's light, which in reality the philosopher

---

16. Aristotle, *De anima* 434b20.

17. On this point, one may profitably read the collection edited by Kearney and Treanor, *Carnal Hermeneutics*, as well as Kearney, *Touch*, esp. 33–59. This is a genesis of the "touching-touched" that suffices to convince one of the possibility of an "other" philosophy—no longer based on distance or videoconference (vision) but on proximity or presence in flesh and blood (touch): "*Our existence is increasingly lived* at distance. *As we move* from flesh to image, *we are in danger* of losing touch *with each other and ourselves. How can we combine the* physical *with the* virtual, *our* embodied experience *with our* global connectivity? *How can we* come back to our senses?" (*Touch*, back cover copy, emphasis added). This is also a historical study that would gain by enriching itself from the debate between Condillac and Maine de Biran concerning the "marble statue" as a "missing link" (there is no mention of Condillac or Maine de Biran in *Touch* . . .).

from Freiburg never left behind—from truth as *a-letheia* or *unconcealing* to the *clearing of being* where the *Ereignis* manifests itself.

No one can escape this questioning that, however, does not appear, or appears so little, in the established commentators of the thought of the philosopher from Freiburg, the very ones who want, "with him," to overcome metaphysics. For how can one claim to "overcome" [*dépasser*] when that which determines metaphysics as such—namely, the model of "seeing" or of "light," or that which was thus named as early as the opening of Aristotle's *Metaphysics* and would define it from start to finish (the primacy of the sense of sight or of "visual sensations")—precisely *does not pass* [*passe*]? "All humans by nature desire to know. An indication of this is our liking for sensations. For even apart from their utility, these are liked because of themselves—and *most of all* the *visual sensations*."[18] This was not, however, the sole model and the only decision to make, including according to the Stagirite. The treatise *De anima* [*On the Soul*] would precisely substitute for it "touch" as *the most universal* of the senses, albeit touch "by the hand and with the hand" as *the most proper* to man—a new line of an "outside the metaphysics of seeing" that we would do well not to forget and of which Condillac and Maine de Biran would become the worthy heirs.

c) The Hand

Indeed, it does not suffice to confine oneself to touch and to what constitutes its primacy that was found anew beginning with Maine de Biran. It remains also necessary to pass via *the hand*, for it really is also thereby—by touching one's chest with the hand (Condillac) or by sensing the muscular effort in one's own hand (Maine de Biran)—that a new philosophical field opens, which will be reinvested within the framework of phenomenology, from Husserl through Merleau-Ponty and Levinas.

The hand is remarkable, emphasizes Aristotle anew in *De anima*, precisely because it is the "instrument of instruments"; hence the fact that the soul, said, verbatim, to be "just as the hand is," will learn from the hand to become through its intellect the "form of the senses," and through the senses the "form of sensible things."[19] One can certainly interpret

18. Aristotle, *Metaphysics* 980a (emphasis added). [Translation modified to follow the French translation that Falque cites. –Trans.]

19. Aristotle, *De anima* 432a. [Translation modified to follow the French translation that Falque cites. –Trans.]

this in the sense that the hand "can do anything" or even "be anything." Instrument of instruments, or organ of organs, it is not an instrument by itself but forges instruments that will be like continuations of its own body: "The hand would seem to be not one instrument, but many; indeed it is, as it were, an instrument for instruments," specifies and corroborates the Stagirite, this time in *Parts of Animals*. "For the hand becomes a talon, claw, horn, spear, sword, and any other weapon or instrument; it will be anything thanks to its ability to grasp and hold anything."[20] To put the matter otherwise, in the continuity given to it this time by Henri Bergson in the celebrated ending of the *Two Sources of Morality and Religion* (1958), in which the mechanical requires the mystical as its "supplement of soul," "The workman's tool is the continuation of his arm, the tool-equipment of humanity is therefore a continuation of its body."[21]

But, inversely—and perhaps it is here that we move closer to Maine de Biran—the hand that "can do anything" (with the instrument or the instrument as a "continuation" of man's body) is also the hand that "can do nothing" (apt for all instruments). Able to experience or, rather, to grasp or caress all things, it can grasp or caress nothing. And it is in this emptiness [*vide*] or, rather, in this *power of anything* when there is nothing (to be grasped or caressed) that the hand experiences *itself*. Other animals always have their horns, their claws, or their beak on them like a "ready-to-wear" and a "ready-for-use." But this is not the case for man, as is well known—here in reality Aristotle is just redeploying the myth of Prometheus, following Plato, and he recognizes that it is indeed in the void [*vide*] (of a specific organ for taking, or defending oneself, or caressing) that the fullness of the absolute potential of the hand is said: "Those who say that mankind is not well constituted, but on the contrary is the worst constituted of animals—for (they say) he is barefoot, naked, and without weapons for defence—are wrong."[22] It is not because "they have hands that human beings are most intelligent," as Anaxagoras wrongly maintains, but on the contrary it is "because they are the most intelligent [*phronimôtaton*] of animals that they have hands."[23]

It is not fullness—having one's hands full—that creates human existence but rather emptiness: having nothing "in one's hands" or

20. Aristotle, *On the Parts of Animals* 687a–b. [Translation modified to follow the French translation that Falque cites. –Trans.]
21. Bergson, *Two Sources*, 309.
22. Aristotle, *On the Parts of Animals* 687a.
23. Aristotle, *On the Parts of Animals* 687a.

"in hand." For, having *nothing* in hand or in one's hands, one can take *anything* in hand or receive *anything* in one's hand. To say it phenomenologically, it is when *Dasein* is no longer grappling with beings in the mode of the "present-at-hand" (*Vorhandenheit*) or the "ready-to-hand" (*Zuhandenheit*) that it discovers itself as "having hands" or as being able to discover or welcome anything in the world as such in a "being-there" that has no other reason but *being*—precisely *there*. It is when the hammer is missing from [the hand of] the hammerer, for the very young Martin Heidegger in his cooper father's workshop, that the world appears—or, let us say here, that the workshop itself appears, and appears as such by way of a "set of beings that are available" for hands that are empty and ready to receive them.[24]

This "hand that *can do anything* because it *is nothing*" and that is therefore first an "empty or vacant hand," to take up an expression from Jean-Louis Chrétien regarding Aristotle,[25] then becomes, in my view, precisely what surreptitiously leads us to, or back to, Maine de Biran. For if the ego accesses itself in the internal muscular effort of its own hand through which it "feels itself" and "autoaffects itself," a point to which I will return (§10b), it also remains necessary, as is proper to man, that he can have nothing in hand—neither things nor himself, unlike with the resistance of his chest struck by his own hand that will confer on him the double sentiment of "solidity" and "impenetrability" by which the man-statue will say "me" (Condillac). No longer "having hands" to "take [*prendre*] anything" (Aristotle) or to "take nothing" (Heidegger), but "being one's hand" to take oneself—not to extricate oneself [*se déprendre*] but to attach oneself to oneself as the sole "taker." This is the great thought of the Grateloup notable, which constitutes his great originality. I do not only

---

24. See Heidegger, *Being and Time*, 57 (s. 61): "Being-in-the-world, as taking care of things, is *taken in* by the world which it takes care of. In order for knowing to be possible as determining by observation what is present at hand, there must first be a *deficiency* of having to do with the world and taking care of it" (emphasis in original). [Translation modified. –Trans.] And 64 (s. 69): "Association geared to useful things which show themselves genuinely only in this association, that is, hammering with the hammer." See also Greisch's commentary, *Ontologie et temporalité*, 132: "The being of the hammer is 'known' through the fact of hammering," as well as Courtine on the usage of the hand in a Dasein that is neither "present to hand" (*vor-handen*) nor "ready to hand" (*zu-handen*) in *Heidegger et la phénoménologie*, 283–303.

25. Chrétien, *Call and the Response*, 95: "For Aristotle, the hand that matters is the prehensile hand, the hand that takes, grasps and holds, the *hand* therefore that is *empty* or *vacant*, the hand that *can do* anything because it *is nothing*, resembling in this respect the soul" (emphasis added). [Translation modified. –Trans.]

take myself by taking the world (Heidegger), but I take myself by extricating myself from everything except myself (Maine de Biran). The properness of myself, or my "lived or proper body," is here what constitutes the point of departure for my subjectivity, which means that outside my subjectivity nothing can, or nothing should, happen—aside from those limit-experiences, to which I will return, in which my own body [*propre corps*] (illness, paralysis, sleepwalking) but also my psyche (dreams, madness, drunkenness) are lived as "foreign" (chapter 5).

§5. The Man-Statue

The paradigmatic example of the statue, or the man-statue, which was so well known and so much commented upon in the eighteenth century, will make clear, in a way that is as descriptive as it is decisive, exactly what happens with this reply of resistance by which I experience myself in my body or, rather, my flesh (lived body) and feel myself in my affect (sentiment). The amphibology of "sensing oneself" [*se sentir*] in French here plays out in full: that is, there is "sensing oneself [*se sentir*] in one's sensing and sensed flesh" (sensation) and "feeling well or ill [*se sentir bien ou mal*] in one's interior state" (affection). I have said so, but this will play out in an exemplary way in the "case" of the statue. The "reply of effort" (lived body) is at the same time the "reply of sentiment" (affect), and it is in this double and simultaneous relation to oneself that the *myself* is constituted. Here is developed before our eyes, as is rarely the case in the history of thought, the greatest phenomenological variation and description over the course of time. For, in the wake of Avicenna and the hypothesis of the flying man, of Descartes imagining himself as a jug or a glass body, of Locke ceaselessly deploying Molyneux's problem of the man blind from birth recovering his sight, or of Diderot, who takes the baton in the *Letter on the Blind for the Use of Those Who Can See* by finally praising blindness as another possible form of knowledge, there now comes the example of the statue in order to resolve this problem, henceforth a classic one after Descartes (the *cogito*) and Locke (the *tabula rasa*): "What is the origin of our knowledge?"—or, better, to take up the formulation of the question as it was relayed by Condillac and then by Maine de Biran: "How can the sensible and mobile being first learn to know its own body?"[26]

---

26. Maine de Biran, *Essai sur les fondements*, 381.

a) The First Man

Who has not dreamed of being Adam—the first man, through whom everything happened (including sin, unfortunately)? And who has never wondered what it would be like to emerge in the word without possessing anything acquired or innate and, therefore, to learn everything, including what sensing, seeing, tasting, smelling, and touching could possibly signify? The hypothesis, certainly a surprising one, is not vain—and the "methodological fiction" here is not that of merely an invented evil genius but that of the existence of a man who will be surprised to be thus "brought into the world." Never will the reduction (bracketing everything) have engendered constitution (discovering oneself step by step "in the world") to such an extent to the point of ordaining a thought experiment as the best way of knowing oneself as engendered.

The fiction—of the man-statue that will progressively begin to sense, see, taste, smell, and touch—was not invented by Condillac. It is already found in Boureau-Deslandes, who was close to Malebranche, in his *Pygmalion, or the Animated Statue* (1741), which Rousseau would reproach in *Émile, or On Education* (1762) for the inanity of the hypothesis of an adult man coming into the world before even having been a child and therefore having been educated.[27] This would, however, be the position, and the situation, depicted by the Comte de Buffon in volume 3 of his *Natural History* (1749): "I imagine, therefore, a man such that one could believe that he was *the first*," suggests the naturalist or, rather, he ventures the hypothesis while giving his imagination free rein,

> that is, a man whose body and organs were perfectly formed but who would *awaken wholly new* for himself and for all that surrounds him. What would be his first movements, his first sensations, his first judgments? If this man wanted to tell us the history of his first thoughts, what would he have to say to us? What would this history be? I cannot avoid *making him speak himself*, in order to make the facts more perceptible: this philosophical account, which will be short, will not be a useless digression.[28]

The framework is therefore laid out—which will then serve as the site of the debate between Condillac and Biran, but outside all theology this time. For Buffon's originality is to see in the "man-statue" not "a" man

---

27. See Armand, "Quand le conte," 181–93.

28. Buffon, *Histoire naturelle* (1749), cited in an appendix to Condillac, *Traité des animaux*, 219 (emphasis added).

or "the man" ("Of the First Knowledge of *a Man* Limited to the Sense of Smell," chapter 1 of Condillac's *Treatise on the Sensations*) but truly the figure of a humanized, even naturalized, Adam, who emerges in Eden as an adult in whom all there is to the sensations, speech, and intelligence seems to be given at once. Far from only the enclosure of oneself on oneself in search of one's *myself*, the first man awakens to the world before knowing himself, in a sort of *Canticle of the Creatures* of the one who is surprised to arrive or to be planted in this Eden or this nature: "I open my eyes—what an excess of sensation! Light, the canopy of heaven, the earth's greenery, the crystal waters: everything occupied me, animated me, and gave me an inexpressible sentiment of pleasure."[29]

This is thus a "first man" who "awakens brand new" to the world or to the creation, that is, with nothing acquired and no innate presuppositions and who "would speak himself" about his own story. It is indeed here a question of being born to the world and to oneself, but without any preparation, not even intra-uterine or even infantile, and of conducting oneself the telling of one's own life or one's own emergence in the world. As Jakob von Uexküll would later put into practice for the first time in *A Foray into the Worlds of Animals and Humans* (1934), it no longer suffices to look at the animal world from the outside, but it is necessary to put the machine operator in the machine, or the conductor in his locomotive: "discover the *machine operator* who exists in the organs just as we exist in our own body."[30] Animals are not *things* any more than Condillac's statue is; they become for the first time the *subjects* of their own bodies, and it is thus that it is necessary to see them—from the inside.[31] The room is not the same if it is painted by Van Gogh, seen by a fly, or seen by a dog,[32] and the tick, which waits at the top of a plant's stalk for the passage of the dog

---

29. Buffon, *Histoire naturelle* (1749), cited in an appendix to Condillac, *Traité des animaux*, 219.

30. Uexküll, *Foray into the Worlds*, 42 (emphasis in original). [Translation modified. –Trans.]

31. Uexküll, *Foray into the Worlds*, 42: "Whoever still holds the view that our sensory organs serve perception and our motor organs serve the production of effects will also not see in animals simply a mechanical assemblage; they will also discover the *machine operator* who exists in the organs just as we exist in our own body. But then he will see in animals not merely things but subjects, whose essential activity consists in action and perception" (emphasis in original). [Translation modified. –Trans.]

32. Plates 2–4 in Uexküll, *Foray into the Worlds*, 90–91.

so as to exercise its "bloodsucker" on it, knows the world only by taste, smell, and touch, hardly by sight, and not at all by hearing.[33]

And although he went only step by step and "sense after sense" to constitute the ego, as would Condillac in his *Treatise on the Sensations* (1754), Buffon's *Natural History* also consecrated touch (and the hand) as the first of the senses a few years earlier, pioneeringly and therefore giving homage to Aristotle (see *supra*)—and above all as the sense in which the *myself* is rooted, where the solid part of my being lies and by which ideas take shape:

> I brought *a hand* to my head, I *touched* my forehead and eyes, I explored my body; *my hand* seemed to me then to be *the principal organ of my existence*; what I sensed in that part was so distinct and so complete, the enjoyment from it seemed so perfect in comparison to the pleasure that light and sounds had caused me, that I *attached myself* entirely to this *solid part of my being*, and I sensed that *my ideas were taking on depth and reality*.[34]

Touch and the *hand*—the Aristotelian tradition of the *De anima* can now be perpetuated, but this time in order to be subjectivized. For the knowledge of oneself by the Abbé (Condillac) is substituted for the discovery of the world by the naturalist (Buffon), to become the unique program definitively set by the thinker from Bergerac (Maine de Biran). It is no longer "sensing" (touching the world) but "sensing oneself sensing" (touching-touched), or even feeling [*ressentir*] (experiencing sensing in oneself) that becomes the path of radicalization by which the subject is born to itself, no longer as a *thinking or reflective ego* but as a *touching and carnal ego*. Touch supplants sight, taste, hearing, and smell, making the "lived body" enter, definitively this time, into the history of philosophy.

b) It will be, I am

At the moment of reading and commenting on the constitution of the world by the "marble statue" that has also suddenly come to existence by serving as a model for the birth of the subject to itself, we will then be surprised to see that Condillac is always read today through Maine

---

33. Uexküll, *Foray into the Worlds*, 45: "We ask this question: Is the tick a *machine* or a *machine operator*? Is it an *object* or a *subject*?" (emphasis added). [Translation modified. –Trans.]

34. Buffon, *Histoire naturelle* (1749), cited in an appendix to Condillac, *Traité des animaux*, 219 (emphasis added).

de Biran and the *Treatise on the Sensations* through the lens of the *Essai sur les fondements de la psychologie*. The declarations with regard to a supposed naivety on the part of Condillac or the supposed "sensualism" of his doctrine must not make us forget a genesis of man or, rather, of the subject that is surprisingly constructed and whose first lines by the Abbé with regard to the statue—"it will therefore be rose-odor"[35]—never undergo the transformation that Maine de Biran imposed on them: "I am rose-odor."[36] As Francine Markovitz-Pessel emphasizes in her work *La Statue de Condillac* [*Condillac's Statue*], but simply as a suggestion that we should now take advantage of and complete:

> There are two statements that are not equivalent: *it is* rose-odor, *I am* (a) rose-odor. Can Condillac's statue say, in the first person, as Maine de Biran writes, *I am (a) rose-odor*? One can long seek this phrase in the *Treatise on the Sensations*. Condillac's object is precisely the *disappropriation of the* myself, and it is only when touch enters onto the stage (at the end of the *Treatise*) that the statue can say *myself*. . . . It is in any case remarkable that, as he was reflecting on Condillac's statue's inability to have a *myself*, the real foundation of its modifications, Maine de Biran still makes it say: *I am* (a) rose-odor.[37]

Condillac is not, therefore, Maine de Biran, and it serves no purpose to see in the former only the preparer or the originator of the latter, as if he should be understood only through what he became or what was made of him—like the so-called "pre-Socratics" who supposedly had no other aim than that of preparing for or anticipating Socrates, so it is fitting to call them, rather, "physicists." There is more than a half-century between the *Treatise on the Sensations* and the *Essai sur les fondements de la psychologie*, and Maine de Biran was only fourteen when Condillac died (1780). Far, therefore, from seeing the former (Condillac) only in the orbit of the latter (Biran), we will let the Abbé de Condillac be read

---

35. Condillac, *Treatise on the Sensations*, 175. [Translation modified. –Trans.]

36. Maine de Biran, *Essai sur les fondements*, 16; Vrin edition, 2.

37. Markovits-Pessel, *Statue de Condillac*, 20–22 (emphasis added). This observation is particularly well spotted—Condillac never having written "I am (a) rose-odor" as Maine de Biran indicates and quotes. It remains that Maine de Biran did not write either, at least in the *Essai sur les fondements de la psychologie* (1812), "I am *a* rose-odor" but "I am rose-odor." The absence of the indefinite article—"a"—will have its importance for stating the most total "neutrality," as I will show (hence the fact that I put it in parentheses in the text). We should therefore, in my view, "correct this detail" to see this interpretation through all the way to the end.

in himself and for himself. And in this purely Condillacian formulation "it will therefore be rose-odor" (and not "I am rose-odor"), neither the statue nor the man will say "I," and they will even never say it, contrary to what Maine de Biran nonetheless said and did. At the very most, the statue or the man will say "me" in the accusative in Condillac, and never "I" in the nominative as in Biran. Better, a *neutrality of the subject* is given *at the origin* in sensation—and perhaps this is what is going on with the subject that is "offside," less in the constitution of oneself by oneself (auto-affection) than in the shock of trauma (heteroaffection or, rather, outside affection): "In the fiction of the statue, it is the experience of a *myself* conceived *in the third person*," Simone Romagnoli accurately writes, even if only to then regret it, as a Biranian, because of the dependence on the "random determinations of exteriority."[38]

c) The Double Reading

As with Maine de Biran, there are *two possible readings* of Condillac, one "in relief" and the other "in counter-relief." The one that is second historically (the reading in counter-relief of Maine de Biran) is always deciphered *downstream*, once the statue is constituted and is discovering at the same time in itself the *double resistance* of exteriority faced with the organic (§15) but also of the non-self in the limit-experience (§17). Inversely, the reading that is first originally (the reading in relief in Condillac) is described *upstream*, to constitute the statue precisely where the absence of presuppositions and of any constitution is complete and radical, including in the calling into question of an irreducible transcendental ego, be it an "I think," an "I sense," or an "I sense myself." With Condillac, the *neutrality of the subject* goes as far as possible—supposing that one agrees to read it in the aim more of the Levinasian "there is" or the Blanchotian "neuter" than simply of Condillacian sensualism.

"*It will therefore be* rose-odor," and not "*I am* rose-odor": the statue will say nothing of itself until the experience of touch in Condillac (when it will say "me" and especially not "I"), to the point that it knows neither

---

38. Romagnoli, "La décomposition," 342–43 (emphasis added): "We can observe that, in the fiction of the statue, it is the *experience of a myself conceived in the third person* and exposed to the random determinations of *exteriority* (first the olfactive sensory impressions), which is described as constitutive of the life of consciousness. Maine de Biran will criticize precisely this idea of a passive *myself* grounded on sensations that succeed and transform each other."

if it is nor *what* it is, not in a denial or a doubt applied to oneself (Descartes), nor in a total detachment of oneself from oneself (Eckhart), but in a complete neutrality of oneself as a subject that is "off*side*"—outside itself and out of play—as is the case in trauma. Paradoxically, the "there is" of the rose-odor understood as pure resistance of presence in Maine de Biran takes precedence over any supposed gift of the present or of presence as an always-presupposed or already-posited *Gegebenheit* (in the manner of Maine de Biran's "primitive fact"). If Maine de Biran's "I am rose-odor" is suitable when *everything is going well* (with the affirmation of an "I am," of an "inner sentiment," or even of an "autoaffection" or a "lived body"), it is hardly certain that it resists when *everything is going badly*, when all that remains, and all that resists, is the *there is* of the presence of a *myself* that does not know, or no longer knows, what presence means, if not the simple fact of being there. At the moment of presenting the rose to be *sensed* or *smelled* by the marble statue that for the first time begins to sense and to move—the statue that has never seen, heard, tasted, or touched anything (more by *negation* than by *privation*)—we must say, with Bernard Baertschi who rightly emphasizes this in his article on Condillac's statue,

> There are *not yet* any beings and things for the statue: there is only an odor, that is, a sensation.... Properly speaking, one cannot even say that there is a rose-odor for *it*: *there is* odor, for the statue does not know itself as a being-subject any more than it knows the world as a being-object. Here we are below the subject-object distinction, in something like an *originary neutrality*. In short, there is only a sensation and nothing more.[39]

A sort of "spread body" or body-object that will wait for a long time indeed before becoming a body-subject through touch (and before simply saying "me," never "I"), Condillac's marble statue, *read otherwise*, conjugates, in my view, both the *expansion of the body*, where the body, or at least the sick body, experiences itself as an object and no longer as a subject (in palliative care, for example), and the *expansion of the psyche*, since received ideas are also endured because they arise from "(always-)transformed sensation" (in the case of madness, for example). Reading Condillac with new eyes is not condemning him for sensualism but praising him for a sort of "transformism"—in the philosophical sense, certainly, but we know that Lamarck, who was its first

---

39. Baertschi, "Statue de Condillac," 335–36 (emphasis added).

initiator (1744–1829), was the exact contemporary of Maine de Biran (1766–1824) and in part also of Condillac, who preceded him but died before the French Revolution (1714–1780).

The method of the Abbé de Condillac is radical because nothing is presupposed, especially not the privation of our senses that the statue would or should have. Rather, therefore, than depriving the state *negatively* of the senses that we have (the method of the *tabula rasa*), it is a question of seeing it *positively* without the senses, without our senses, even "outside sense"—if one accepts the play on words that is certainly not Condillac's here: outside the senses (sensations) and outside sense (signification). Condillac indeed attains a rare *neutrality of existence*—that of a marble statue that is certainly deprived of everything (all senses and all sensations) but that is existing *otherwise* (outside senses, sensations, even significations). There is something of the "extra-phenomenal" in Condillac's marble statue, to dare to see the hypothesis through to the end, in that the neutrality that is attained, or that is presupposed at the start, requires *thinking in a new way*—no longer by subtraction but by addition, no longer by privation but by composition. It is a question not of destroying but of constructing and of accepting that by thus constructing we can live and think *otherwise*, or even live and not think *yet* (or at all), since to think it is already necessary to compare (between sensations).

"So much exception, so much modification": the leitmotif of *The Extra-Phenomenal*, already cited, here plays out in full, and I will return to this, since Condillac's statue is only "modified sensations," which we will certainly regret within the framework of a critique of sensualism where nothing is stable any longer (neither the *cogito* nor the sentiment of the *myself*), but which we will, however, recognize as essential within the perspective of the extra-phenomenal, in particular following a "trauma," in that one is *no longer the same* and *never* will be *again*. There are cases in which one becomes "foreign to oneself"—from illness to pandemic, for example (*The Extra-Phenomenal*)—*upstream* of the constitution of oneself in the statue that is both virgin and neuter in Condillac and *downstream* of being oneself in the exception to the "primitive fact of effort and the sentiment of the *myself*" in Maine de Biran (from sleep to the effects of drugs; I will return to this). In short, rather than moving too quickly in condemnation of Condillac or seeing in him only a propaedeutic to Maine de Biran's subsequent criticism, we will let him "be thus": that is, an original and originary thinker of *neutrality* and *transformation* and not only the one who is always lacking an "I am" or an "I sense" or an "I sense myself" that is always posited and presupposed.

§6. "It Will Therefore Be Rose-Odor"

a) An Apperceptive Transposition

If, therefore, the ambition of the "blank slate" fully plays out in Condillac (since the statue, as we will see, has thus far felt *nothing*), it is in another sense, or by seeing the senses otherwise. From the spirit, it extends to the body and is, as it were, universalized, even radicalized. Whereas John Locke's *tabula rasa*, like Occam's razor, though in another manner entirely, worked only on the impressions of memory (Locke) or the act of nomination and signification (Occam), it now acts on the sensations of the body itself, which have disappeared or, rather, never were. It is therefore a matter not of becoming what I am not (deprived of sensations) but on the contrary of being the one that I have never been by becoming wholly other, as if I had to begin my existence again or, rather, begin it otherwise. There is no question here of cutting away but of *imagining*, no longer of destroying (the man that I am) but of *constructing* (the man that I have never been). This is true of Condillac's marble statue as a "methodological fiction" that is still more radical than those of Boureau-Deslandes's *Pygmalion* and Buffon's *first man*, to the point of an entire work being devoted to it. "We imagined a statue internally organized like ourselves, and animated by a mind deprived of every kind of idea," attempts Condillac, therefore, in the opening of the *Treatise on the Sensations*. "We further supposed that its marble exterior did not allow it the use of any of its senses, and we reserved for ourselves the freedom to open them at will to the different impressions they are susceptible of."[40]

It is a marble statue, then, certainly like us and "organized internally like ourselves." This matters, for it is not a question of seeing a foreign body, and still less an external body, in the marble statue. We are the marble statue! Or, rather, we have to become it. The titles of each chapter of the *Treatise on the Sensations* prove this, or at least state it. It is indeed a "man" who will say *me*, and not a "statue," even though it will be a question only of a statue: "On the First Knowledge of a *Man* [and not of a statue] Limited to the Sense of Smell" (part 1, chapter 1), or "How a

---

40. Condillac, *Treatise on the Sensations*, 170.

Man [and not a statue] *Limited to Touch Discovers His Body and Learns That There Is Something External to Himself*" (part 2, chapter 5).[41] It is therefore indeed here a matter of a complete "apperceptive transposition of the other," to put it in the terms of phenomenology. But, contrary to what Husserl will say about it in the *Cartesian Meditations*,[42] this will be accomplished in a total and radical fashion: an "affective fusion" (*Einsfühlung*), as Max Scheler would say, and not mere "empathy" (*Einfühlung*), according to Edith Stein's accurate critique.[43] It is therefore a question, not only of my "myself" (*ego*) becoming an "other myself" (*alter ego*) but of there being no "other *than* myself" (*ego alter*) except this marble statue that I fully become and that successively and progressively begins to smell, hear, taste, see (by combining these senses), then touch.

The "Important Notice to the Reader" is *important* enough—this is the least one can say—to be followed and applied to the letter. The matter is indeed not only "important" but "very important." It signifies that whoever is not willing to accomplish the reduction (bracketing everything concerning oneself and one's sensations) and enter into a new and other constitution (my own body engendered according to sensations) will never know what it means to be a body and soul and perhaps, one day, to say "me." Not remaining in one's place, "dis-placing" oneself, taking the place of the other that is the place of the marble statue: this is the apperceptive transposition that we therefore cannot miss, at the risk of understanding and experiencing nothing of what is proposed: "Thus I forewarn the reader that it is *very important* to put himself *exactly in the place* of the statue we are going to observe." Better, it is not only a question of putting oneself "in the place of"—and Condillac even warns that only "readers who put themselves *exactly in its place* will have little difficulty in understanding this work," while "others who do not will put forth innumerable difficulties against me"—but in addition it is necessary to "live as if," or, rather, "to be with," or, more radically, to be only "one" with the marble statue that will progressively begin to be animate: "[The reader] should *begin to live when it does*, have *only* a single sense when it

---

41. Condillac, *Treatise on the Sensations*, 175, 232.
42. Husserl, *Cartesian Meditations*, 108–11, 117–20.
43. Scheler, *Nature of Sympathy*, 18 (the example of the acrobat on the wire as "affective fusion," *Einfühlung*), as well as Edith Stein's critique, *On the Problem of Empathy*, 16–18; "Empathy and a Feeling of Oneness." On this point, and on the gap between "affective fusion" according to Scheler (*Einsfühlung*) and "empathy" in Stein (*Einfühlung*), see my contribution "Edith Stein," 83–107.

has only one, acquire *only* those ideas that it acquires, contract *only* the habits that it contracts: in short, he must be *only what it is*."

Being "myself" only what it is, and not "it" being what I am—this is the absolute dissymmetry demanded by the *Treatise on the Sensations*: not first becoming a man (with all his sensations), but no longer being a man—like Uexküll's tick, who, as I have said, could well be reduced to only one or two senses (taste and touch, for example). And finally, it is *not us* and is never us who will judge whether it came to become "like us"—endowed with five senses—but it is *it* that will "judge like us" before we can "judge like it." The marble statue initiates and maneuvers, even if the "driver" is not, and perhaps never will be, "in the locomotive," to paraphrase Uexküll. Even though Condillac speaks of man by speaking of the statue, as I have said, it is indeed, then, first a matter of *positively constituting it* (its existence to resemble ours) rather than *negatively cutting it away* (our existence to identify us with its existence): "The statue will judge things *as we do* only when it has all the senses and all the experiences we do: and we will judge *in the same way it judges* only when we suppose ourselves deprived of everything that it lacks."[44]

It is not only everything that follows in the work but also in experience that depends, therefore, on the importance, and even the "very great importance" (the "very important" notice to the reader). And it is indeed because Maine de Biran will also accept to enter into such an apperceptive transposition of the other—although, as I will show, the ego will never truly become the statue because it is always already presupposed, according to him—that the debate will be fought every step of the way to know *which one*, the "it's me" or the "I sense that I feel [*ressens*]" is first—and *which one*, the "foreign body" or the "lived body," I must first consider.

b) Being Rose-Odor

The matter has been foreshadowed enough that it can simply be stated now. In what do the first pieces of knowledge of a "man restricted to smell" consist? The *tabula rasa* is complete here. Not only has the statue experienced nothing, it does not know what experiencing means. Ignorant of "affecting," at least in Condillac's view, it is still more ignorant of

---

44. For this passage and all of these citations, see Condillac, *Treatise on the Sensations*, 155 (emphasis added). [Translation modified. –Trans.]

"autoaffecting." Two points of view then become distinct, or rather oppose each other: the actor's point of view ("in relation to itself") and the spectator's point of view ("in relation to us"). Let us make no mistake, however. The actor's point of view—that of the statue that "senses" the rose-odor—is a point of view that is ignorant of itself. Better, we will not confuse the "actor's point of view" with the "subject's point of view." For speaking of the "subject's point of view" is already presupposing that *there is* a subject—"I am rose-odor" (Maine de Biran)—when no "I am" has been constituted in Condillac and even never will be: it is confined to an "it's me, it's me again,"[45] which is already a great deal.

Certainly, the statue "in relation to us" or seen from outside, "if we present it with a rose"—that is, if it is *already there* and if we consider that it is already capable of sensing *like us*—will be "a statue that senses a rose." Because we are already capable of sensing a rose-odor, a carnation-odor, a jasmine-odor, or a violet-odor—so many odors cited by Condillac himself—we think and will think that it senses a "rose-odor" that is not the odor of carnation, jasmine, or violet. *Already* we are for ourselves (subject), and *already* we judge concerning the thing (object), such that the distinction between the internal and the external is presupposed, which Condillac rejects, at least on this point (as regards the olfactory sense), as Biran will do just as well (only the internal, at least in a first movement, constitutes me myself). If some claim a purely phenomenological Biran via the absolute primacy of the "subjective body" or the "lived body" (Henry), that will not suffice for relying on and rejecting a Condillac who is exclusively a metaphysician, as I will show, or even a Biran still caught in the contradictions of metaphysics (see the last chapter of *Philosophy and Phenomenology of the Body*: "A Critique of the Thought of Maine de Biran: The Problem of Passivity").

In "relation to itself," on the contrary, things are wholly otherwise—from the point of view, that is, of this marble statue that is first reduced to nothing, that has never sensed anything, judged anything, or thought anything, and that does not even know what "sensing," "judging," and "thinking" mean, and still less saying "I am": "If we present it with a rose,

45. [Strictly speaking, in English this phrase should read "It's I, it's I again." French, however, cannot employ the nominative here but uses a form of the accusative (*c'est moi, c'est moi encore*), and because Falque's analysis highlights the grammar of the phrase, I have translated it in accord with the colloquial English usage that does employ the accusative. The English translation of *A Treatise on the Sensations* that I am citing renders this phrase as "This is me, this is me again" (234), but the French *c'est moi*, like the English *it's me*, is the phrase that one would typically use to identify oneself. –Trans.]

... it will be only *odor itself of this flower* [*elle ne sera que d'odeur même de cette fleur*].[46] The French, or the formulation "in French," is worth stopping over and must be emphasized. Étienne Bonnot, Abbé de Condillac, does not say here: it will be "only rose-odor" but: "it will be *only odor itself of this flower.*"[47] Indeed, saying "only rose-odor" would presuppose that there are several odors and even that one can already distinguish among odors. There would be rose-odor, then carnation-odor, then jasmine-odor, then violet-odor. But this is not the case, at least for Condillac. There are not "odors" (rose, carnation, jasmine, violet); there is "the odor" (rose or carnation or jasmine or violet), such that the statue becomes only the sole odor that it senses.

Better, to the *neutrality of a statue* that will be able to speak of itself only in the third person as a subject that is "offs*i*de" or even in the neuter—"it will be" (Condillac), and we see here how far we are from the "*I am* rose-odor" (Biran)—responds the *neutrality of the odor* itself: "odor itself of this rose" and not "rose-odor" or "*a* rose-odor." Being "only odor" is not, at least in French, being "an odor" inasmuch as the *neuter of the odor* (there is only one and there exists only one, that of the rose) prevails over the *multiplicity of odors* (a rose-odor among other odors, as one could also wrongly believe in one sense, an olfactive one, among other senses: visual, auditory, gustative, or tactile). This is not the case. The reduction is *a maxima*: the statue, in relation to itself, "will be *only odor* itself of this flower."

The phrase "it will therefore be rose-odor" thus suffices by itself to sum up the whole of Condillac's thesis, at least with regard to the opening of the first sense (smell) to the first sensation—odor: "*It will therefore be rose-odor*, carnation-odor, jasmine-odor, or violet-odor according to the objects that act on its sense organ."[48] The conclusion—"it

---

46. Condillac, *Treatise on the Sensations*, 175 (emphasis added). [Translation modified. –Trans.]

47. [The French phrase employs a form of the partitive article, a type of indefinite article that does not exist in English. Unlike the English indefinite articles (*a, an*) and definite article (*the*), the French partitive does not mark out one (specified or unspecified) thing among a class of such things. In this particular context, the point is, as Falque explains, that the statue is not "*an* odor itself of this flower," which would imply the existence of odors of other flowers, while in fact the statue has not yet discovered the existence of other odors. Entirely omitting any article conveys in English the neutrality to which Falque refers, at the price of sounding awkward given the length of the phrase. –Trans.]

48. Condillac, *Treatise on the Sensations*, 175 (emphasis added). [Translation modified. –Trans.]

will *therefore* be"—cannot here take the form of a deductive syllogism. For anyone who would say "therefore" and would draw a conclusion after having "presented the rose to the statue" would formulate it from the outside: it was nothing, and it becomes something. But from the point of view of the inside, in the "locomotive" and not "while watching the train pass," to again take up Uexküll distinguishing the animal world and the human world (the example of the tick), "being nothing" and "becoming something" is already "outside sense," understood here, this time, as "outside signification."

c) The Statue That Is "Offs*i*de"

The Condillacian statue is "offs*i*de" because it is both "outside the *I*" (outside the subject) and "out of *play*" (outside the world or out of the field), inasmuch as the very idea of the subject or the world signifies nothing for the statue itself, even though the phenomenalizing subject (that senses and that senses that it senses) and the phenomenalized horizon (the rose-odor that is not the odor of carnation, jasmine, or violet) would remain what the sensing and sensed statue would be "for us," that is, seen from outside. Let us say this anew. Extra-phenomenality or the "extra-phenomenal subject" indeed designates the state of the statue upstream of all sensation: that is, being nothing either for oneself or for the world and becoming *only what happens to me* inasmuch as it is full *of my* chaos or, rather, *what happens* inasmuch as it is full *of chaos*, since it is still too much to say that something happens "to me" or that the chaos is "mine." The statue is "*only* rose-odor" [*que d'odeur de rose*] as I am "*only* illness," "*only* separation," "*only* death of a child," "*only* natural disaster," and "*only* pandemic" in the case of trauma. There is no longer either subject or object but only the pure neutrality of a *myself* that can no longer say "myself" (neither in the nominative [I], nor in the accusative [me], nor in the dative [to me]): "it will therefore be"— what?—subjectively and from its point of view this statue to which one presents a rose to sense, while the very categories of "subject" and "point of view" do not (yet) have any sense at this stage in the constitution of the statue (upstream) and will no longer have any sense in the case of trauma (downstream). The statue will be the complete *neutrality* of a "there" that is so present in the "resistance of presence," a point to which I will return (§15a), that it cannot this time answer it in a phenomenology that is finally "without appeal": "rose-odor" or "*only* odor itself of this flower."

We are here reaching the key moment, and we are ceasing to see the "Condillacian statue" in the light of its "Biranian critique." One will certainly say, rightly and following Renaud Barbaras in Le Tournant de l'expérience [*The Turn of Experience*], that Biran leads us "to distinguish the sensation that already belongs to exteriority from the power of sensing oneself by oneself" and that he therefore differentiates "what, in the empiricist tradition, is conflated under the term *sensation*, namely the content and the state, and the sensed and its experience."[49] But, on the one hand, this is presupposing that it is necessary to enclose Condillac in what is called empiricism in opposition to "the turn of experience" later produced by the aforementioned phenomenology. The diagnostic is accurate, except that there are cases—"the extra-phenomenal"—in which the "content and the state," the "sensed and its experience," precisely are not, or no longer, distinguished because *I become* exactly that from which I am suffering and the idea of saying "I" and even of "suffering" no longer makes any sense. And, moreover, this is thinking that the "ego" always remains irreducible ("I am") and that the "lived body" presents itself to me each time as the first of bodies: "*I am* my body," rather than "*I have* a body," or even "there is body," in the manner of "*it will be only odor* itself of this very flower." The veritable point of view of the Condillacian inside in its radical reduction unto the ego itself—by putting oneself "exactly in the place of the statue," repeated twice in the "Important Notice to the Reader"—requires, just this once, seeing and thinking the Condillacian marble statue otherwise, neither to accept it unanimously nor to arbitrarily reject it, but to note a situation that is extreme and possible: that of extra-phenomenality, here given upstream of our constitution in Condillac (being "*only* rose-odor," [que d'*odeur de rose*] like "*only* illness," "*only* separation," "*only* death of a child" [que de *maladie*, que de *séparation*, que de *mort d'un enfant*] . . .), but which can also be deciphered downstream in Maine de Biran, that is, in the man who, once constituted, is, however, suddenly and because "it befalls me," devoid of all his qualities,

---

49. Barbaras, *Tournant de l'expérience*, 102. We will here be grateful to Renaud Barbaras for having introduced, perhaps for the first time in French thought, or in the wake of Maurice Merleau-Ponty, "French spiritualism" at the heart of "phenomenology" without any presupposition in favor of the legitimacy of one party rather than the other. It remains now to overcome the categories of empiricism, idealism, subjectivism, etc., if indeed extra-phenomenality permits us to interpret "otherwise" or "in counter-relief" (in the crisis) that which "in relief" still remains of the order of knowledge.

or is "a man without qualities": illness, sleep, paralysis, madness, sleepwalking, dementedness, drunkenness, drugs, etc. (§17).⁵⁰

§7. The Exception of Touch

a) The Impenetrability and Solidity of the Body

One can then certainly retrace all the stages through which the statue will pass in the *Treatise on the Sensations*: from the sole sensation of the rose-odor, to the attention that the statue will give to this impression (turning itself toward it), to the enjoyment or the suffering that it will undergo from it (a pleasant or unpleasant odor), to the preservation of the odor in its memory (the impression as such), to the comparison of odors among themselves (rose, carnation, jasmine, violet), to the judgment that it can draw from them (the rose-odor is not the odor of the carnation), to the surprise that it experiences at these diverse sensations (there is a multiplicity of odors), and to the ideas that it preserves in memory (for example, identifying the good odor as an odor called "rose" to be able to find it again and return to it). One could also show how each sense combines with the others and that it is not a matter simply of smelling, then seeing, then testing, then hearing, and finally touching to constitute a common sense but that, on the contrary, the senses respond to each other, as with Locke's "Molyneux's blind man" who suddenly has to recognize by sight what he had first identified by touch (the cube or the sphere).⁵¹ But this is not the case; rather, it will not be the case. It is not because this does not matter—quite the contrary—but because it

---

50. One will recognize here the allusion to *L'Homme sans qualités* [*The man without qualities*] by Robert Musil (published in German in 1930 and translated into French in 1957 by Philippe Jaccottet). "A man knocked down in the street in Vienna by a truck, taken by an ambulance without anyone knowing whether he is living or dead": this is the beginning of the novel—"outside the phenomenon" as such. See Musil, *L'Homme sans qualités*, 9–12: "Of which, remarkably, nothing came."

51. Locke, *Essay Concerning Human Understanding*, 271–72: "Molyneux's problem" (a variation of the man blind from birth distinguishing the cube from the sphere), which can be considered, methodologically, as the ancestor, albeit in a different way, of Condillac's "marble statue" and then of Maine de Biran: "*Suppose a Man born blind, and now adult, and taught by his touch to distinguish between a Cube, and a Sphere of the same metal, and nighly of the same bigness, so as to tell, when he felt one and t'other, which is the Cube, and which the Sphere. Suppose then the Cube and the Sphere placed on a Table, and the Blind Man to be made to see. Quære, Whether by his sight, before he touch'd them, he could now distinguish, and tell, which is the Globe, which the Cube*" (emphasis in original).

is necessary to return to the essential point and aim very exactly at the question initially posed by Condillac and Biran: "How does the sensible and mobile being first learn to know its own body?"[52]

Forging ahead in the Condillacian "constitution" (after the total "reduction" of the sensations) of the "statue limited to the sense of smell" and that "can only know odors" (*Treatise on the Sensations*, part 1, chapter 1), we therefore pass to "how a man limited to touch discovers his body and learns that there is something external to himself" (part 2, chapter 5). The turn here is no less crucial than it is radical. For it is indeed a matter here of the capacity to say "I" or, rather, "me," and therefore a matter of what modern philosophy will name the "birth of the subject." And here also a certain *neutrality* remains: not that of the absence of the subject conflated with its object (the rose-odor) but that of a subject that is born to itself able to say "it's me" or "it's me again," designating itself from the outside as a "self" or a "me"—and not an "I am" or still less an "I am rose-odor," with the presupposition of an interiority that would already be capable of constituting everything. Certainly there is here an "outside" that is not the "outside" in me as "foreign to myself" (§17) but "foreign outside myself" (§15).

But being so hasty as to say that it is only a matter of empiricism and sensualism prevents us from reading in it at the same time certain limit-situations by which sometimes *I* do not recognize myself when they happen (to me) or concern (me). When "illness" or a "natural disaster" "befall" me (the extra-phenomenal), at the very most I would say, "It's me, it's me again!" certainly in the continuity of existence and of my existence, but as if at the same time "fate" were hounding me, and as if finally "I" no longer recognized this "me" or at the very least could not decline it in the nominative (I) but only in the accusative (me). Condillacian sensualism, if one still insists on expressing oneself thus, makes "me" an object with regard to myself, as a body (impenetrability and solidity, which I will discuss) and as thought ("me" and not "I"), such that to the *spread body*—"body" (*Körper*) rather than flesh (*Leib*), for in illness, for example, there is more of the "improper or inappropriable body" than of the "lived or proper body"—*spread thought* responds this time: saying "me" and not "I" in thoughts that corner me (the extra-phenomenal) rather than overflowing me (the supra-phenomenal). "Something thinks" (Nietzsche), "I am being thought" [*on me pense*]

---

52. Maine de Biran, *Essai sur les fondements*, 381.

(Rimbaud), the "unpower of thought" (Artaud)—so many terms for saying the *psychic neutrality* (the extra-phenomenal) to which a *physical neutrality* (the spread body) also responds, as if in parallel.

Impenetrability and solidity are, then, according to Condillac in the *Treatise on the Sensations*, the two characteristics of all bodies, certainly, but of my body in particular. And it is through the bodily (rather than fleshly) resistance that my own body imposes on me that I will say "me" or, more precisely, "it's me." Touch is indeed the unique sense through which is constituted, if not egoity (I am), then at least ipseity (myself), not only because I touch myself and sense myself—the reflexivity of sensing (while I cannot smell myself, see myself, taste myself, or hear myself)—but also because bodies themselves are impenetrable (or confer on me the idea of impenetrability) and because the sensation of solidity that they send back to me causes me to come to experience them as resistant (outside myself) and therefore to say "me" on their basis and not on the basis of myself alone (as Maine de Biran will say). Condillacian resistance is like Delacroix's *Jacob Wrestling with the Angel*: it is by leaning on another resisting body, albeit here an object and not another fleshly body, that I experience myself.

"Impenetrability" will first be a "property of all bodies," emphasizes Condillac—namely, the impossibility, for different bodies, of "occupy[ing] the same place."[53] "Each one has its place in the sun," to say it more trivially, since one body cannot substitute for another, which, of course, we judge here more than we sense it. What we do, then, have the experience of, once the impenetrability of bodies and therefore the place that belongs to them is granted, is their "solidity." For when two bodies "press each other," and even before my body encounters its own body in the experience of the touching-touched, "we apperceive more perceptibly [*d'une manière plus sensible*] the resistance that they put up against each other."[54] The solidity of impenetrable bodies means that they "mutually exclude each other." They resist because the solid bodies (that exclude each other), since they are impenetrable (each one has its place), can no longer become "mine" or, rather, invade mine to such an extent that it would become impossible for me to say "me." Whereas the Condillacian marble statue "will therefore be rose-odor" by *sensing* or *smelling* the rose for the first time (it had never sensed anything before), it will not, or

---

53. Condillac, *Treatise on the Sensations*, 233.
54. Condillac, *Treatise on the Sensations*, 233. [Translation modified. –Trans.]

no longer, be "rose-touch" by touching it or, rather, by touching "itself." For as we have shown, starting from Aristotle (§4), only touch touches itself and only the hand senses itself, contrary to all the other organs that will never manage this (hearing oneself through the ears, smelling oneself through the nose, seeing oneself through the eyes, or tasting oneself through the tongue). The hand has this unique ability to be "nothing" through being capable of "anything," as I have said, following Jean-Louis Chrétien (p. 60), and from this vacuity is born our humanity as receptivity and not only as grasp.

In the *impenetrability of touch*, and precisely by virtue of the *solidity of bodies*, the statue that had not yet touched itself in what we must indeed name a "touching-touched" will not be able to say, or we will not be able to say of it, "it will be table-touch or cube-touch," as we were able to say "it will be rose-odor." Bodies exclude each other, and this is what is uniquely proper to "touch" (the last of the senses analyzed by Condillac), contrary to "smell" (which was the first). By touch, and only in touch, "I do not become the modifications" of the very thing that I sense: "Thus it is not the same thing to have a sensation of solidity as to have sensations of sound, color, and odor that a soul, not knowing its body, apperceives naturally as modifications in which it finds itself and only itself," writes Condillac, very precisely, to define the exclusivity of touch compared to all the other senses. The exclusion of bodies from each other, rather than the inclusion or absorption of bodies in me without, nevertheless, my ever being able to say "I" or "me," is what produces touch and constitutes its specificity:

> Since *what is proper to this sensation* of solidity is to represent at one and the same moment two things that *exclude each other*, the mind will not apperceive solidity as one of those modifications in which it finds only itself; it will apperceive it necessarily as a modification in which it finds *two things that are mutually exclusive* and as a result it will apperceive it *in these two things*.[55]

b) The Soul Outside Itself

Because bodies resist each other among themselves and resist me, in a resistance that could also be called a "resistance of presence" (*The*

---

55. Condillac, *Treatise on the Sensations*, 233 (emphasis added). [Translation modified. –Trans.]

Extra-Phenomenal, chapter 2), what is first is not "giving" but "resisting," which will, moreover, also be first, albeit in another sense (resistance to myself rather than to the object) in Maine de Biran. Whereas the soul has always established the myth of interiority, in philosophy (the *cogito* in Descartes) as in theology (introspection in St. Augustine), now, suddenly, with Condillac, the soul "passes from itself to outside itself," as the author of the *Treatise on the Sensations* incredibly emphasizes here. It is outside itself because it is a question of not sticking only to the self or remaining enclosed within a *myself*—which, besides, has not yet been discovered. It is not the label "sensualism" that counts here, with which we too easily condemn Condillac to save Maine de Biran by his "subjectivism," but rather the recognition of an "outside oneself" that is not oneself: "There you have then a sensation [touch] with which the soul proceeds *from itself to outside itself*.... If the hand says 'me' it does not receive the same response in turn from a solid body that resists it. Thus the statue judges *the ways of being wholly outside itself*."[56]

Let us remember my opening ("The 'Columbus of Metaphysics'"). If I have "had my fill" of interiority (p. xxiii), it is because it is only from the inside that the soul can be shut up in a box (the body), as if to judge from the outside. It becomes *itself* an "outside," not, certainly, within the framework of trauma here, for Condillac, but within the framework of sensation. Because a body whose impenetrability I have the idea of and whose sensation of solidity resists me and resists my body, my soul cannot, or can no longer, let itself be absorbed by its own modifications, be it in a neutral way (it will therefore be rose-odor); rather, it exits from itself to discover an exteriority that resists it and that makes it exist: "I've been asked to talk about the body, so I'm going to talk about the soul," as I have noted (but we will take it up again here), following Jean-Luc Nancy in his *Corpus* that, in this respect, is more Condillacian than Biranian.

> In saying "of the soul," I simply wanted to indicate this: "of the soul" or "of the body outside the self." If the body isn't mass, if it isn't closed in on itself and penetrated by itself, it's *outside itself*. It is *being outside itself*. And this is what is at stake with the word *soul*. It in no way involves hearing, behind this word, an ineffable interiority.... If we wish to keep the word *matter*, then we should say that it's the *impenetrability* of what is form—in other words, relation, articulation, and therefore, yet again, the

---

56. Condillac, *Treatise on the Sensations*, 233, 235 (emphasis added). [Translation modified. –Trans.]

relation between *sensing, sensing oneself, being sensed, and sensing something as from the outside*.[57]

c) Laying a Hand on Oneself

Having passed via the sensations of smell, hearing, taste, and sight (and their respective combinations), Condillac's "marble statue," now animate and even "very animated," does not know everything; far from it. Better, if it knows all or many of the things in the world, it knows nothing of itself and, above all, nothing of its own body, as long as it has not touched or has not touched *itself*: "It does not yet know that it is composed of parts that can move one on top of the other or onto external objects,"[58] as the *Treatise on the Sensations* highlights verbatim. "The statue has movements"[59] (a subheading of the chapter) but *does not know* which movements are its own. Far from being able to say "I *am* my body"—which will be the invention of the "lived body" in Maine de Biran, as I have said (§4)—at the very most the animate statue will admit that "I *have* a body," with that certainly-existential conviction that one day also my body will have me (be it in illness or in death) and therefore that the disappropriation or even the objectivation of oneself also constitutes the "me" that is accused or cornered in existence and not the "I" that is always appropriated for its being-there.

Everything will then be the fruit of chance, or nearly so. The machine of my own body—of this body that I cannot yet call mine and that I will perhaps never call mine—therefore moves here and there in space of itself, but without constituting space. And it encounters sensations according to luck—odors, for instance (rose, carnation, jasmine, or violet)—with which it identifies itself, in reaction to which it can produce movements or experience a certain mood (love or disgust), from which it can draw ideas and judgments by comparison, to the point of designating them (the rose-odor is not the odor of a carnation), but without ever saying "me" and still less "I": "It is *naturally, mechanically, by instinct and without being aware of it* that the statue moves," specifies Condillac to state the movements of his body that are totally ignorant of themselves, "and it remains for us to explain how it will discover, from its own

---

57. Nancy, *Corpus*, 125–27 (emphasis added). [Translation modified. –Trans.]
58. Condillac, *Treatise on the Sensations*, 232.
59. Condillac, *Treatise on the Sensations*, 232. [Translation modified. –Trans.]

movements, that it has a body, and that beyond it there are other bodies."[60] The existence of my body as an "object" (it *has* [*elle* a]) and of other bodies as objects (there are others [*il y en a d'autres*]): this is what Étienne Bonnot, Abbé de Condillac, is intentionally aiming at—which is far from any determination of the "body-subject," but which we cannot, however, reduce to a simple empiricism or sensualism, at least to describe certain limit-situations that sometimes happen to us or occur in us.

And here what is impossible, or perhaps also what is expected *for us* but not *for it*, occurs: "Now as soon as its [the statue's] movements are repeated and vary, it necessarily will happen that the statue repeatedly lays its hands *on itself* and *on objects that come close to it*."[61] There we have it. "Laying a hand on oneself," even if by chance—that is what starts up the "myself." After smell, hearing, taste, and sight—these four senses being, then, combined in order ("smell and hearing united," "taste joined to smell and hearing," "sight with smell, hearing, and taste")[62]—comes touch or, rather, the touching-touched. By the luck of its touch (or the chance of its dismembered body), not only will the statue discover that *there are* other bodies by touching them externally to itself "because it does not find itself in those that it touches," but it will also note that it *has* a body by touching itself for the first time, according to a "reflexivity of sensing" and not of "thought." Everything begins, and perhaps everything ends, with an external sensation that certainly leads to the conclusion of a body that is external but that will say "me" through the contiguity of the sensations of a touching-touched—but only and ever on the basis of the outside. Better, exteriority, or the world outside myself, will be recognized only on the basis of the limits of my body, not because I feel them from inside, but because I trace their contours by touching myself and by going round them as if from outside, in each of its parts (*partes extra partes*). Finding oneself or losing oneself, or finding oneself there (with oneself and one's body) and not finding oneself there (outside oneself and one's body): this is what traces the limit between interiority and exteriority. It is an interiority of "stumbling over" [*butée*]—as one stumbles over a body or an object—rather than of reflection and an exteriority of "pushing back," that is, of an impossible appropriation: "In laying *its hands on itself*, the statue

---

60. Condillac, *Treatise on the Sensations*, 233 (emphasis added). [Translation modified. –Trans.]

61. Condillac, *Treatise on the Sensations*, 233 (emphasis added). [Translation modified. –Trans.]

62. Condillac, *Treatise on the Sensations*, 208, 210, 220.

will only discover that it *has* a body when it distinguishes the different parts of that body and when it recognizes *itself* in each part to be the same sensing being; and it will discover that there are other bodies only because it does not find itself in those that it touches."[63]

d) It's Me, It's Me Again!

The soul projected *outside itself*, in bodies, then waits to *become itself*, in its body. And it is here that the experience of touching (bodies) becomes the experience of the touching-touched (its own body) and that the hand—the instrument of instruments, as we have seen with Aristotle—intervenes, not grasping bodies but experiencing (from outside, for Condillac), the resistance of my own body. Attaining indeed the identity of myself is ensuring a continuity of myself. It is therefore "all along the body" or *partes extra partes*, as I have said, that the touching of my body will ensure its touched to make of it a body that is mine or in which I recognize myself. And if there is a "hand," the constitution of my own body, be it from outside, will not occur "*in* the hand," as it will for Maine de Biran (muscular effort without a grasped object), but "*beneath* the hand," in the external being-sensed that it experiences from its own body. It is a "beneath the hand" that means sensing the hand or the body "by sensing that I sense it" for Condillac and, on the contrary, "feeling" [*ressentir*] it in order to sense where I myself, or the other, sense myself for Maine de Biran: "But if the statue happens to move its hand the length of its arm and, without skipping over any intermediate part, onto its chest, its head, etc.," specifies Condillac, it will sense, as it were, *beneath its hand* a *continuity of myself*: "This same hand that has brought together the formerly separated parts into a single continuum will thereby render their extension more perceptible [*sensible*]."[64]

Thus distinguishing the "outside itself" and the "itself" will therefore here be the operation of touch rather than of any other sense. For it is by "touching myself"—while I cannot smell, hear, taste, or see myself, as I have said—that the sensation of the solidity of my own body, which I feel while being unable, this time, to reduce it or assimilate it, will, as it were, bounce back *on me*. The impenetrability and the solidity of my own

---

63. Condillac, *Treatise on the Sensations*, 233. [Translation modified. –Trans.]

64. Condillac, *Treatise on the Sensations*, 234 (emphasis added). [Translation modified. –Trans.]

body for myself constitute its thickness and its consistency rather than its autoaffected or even discarnate (at least in the sense of the "true body" that is also materialized) character: "We can suppose that its [the statue's] *hand* will move naturally to some part of its body, onto the *chest* for example," as Condillac already describes it, almost phenomenologically, even though it would be a phenomenology that is closer to exteriority and the world (Heidegger and Merleau-Ponty) than to interiority and the flesh, understood as autoaffection (Husserl and Michel Henry).

> Then its *hand* and its *chest* will be distinguishable by the *sensation of solidity* that they send mutually and that places them necessarily *outside of each other*. However, in distinguishing *its chest* from *its hand*, the statue *will find its "me"* anew in each of them because it *senses itself* equally in both of them.[65]

Difference, and even differentiation, is what makes existence. This is the leitmotif of the Condillacian touching-touched, which is distinct from the Biranian touch inasmuch as bodies exclude or oppose each other from the outside to experience themselves from the inside, and not in a resistance that is so interiorized that it would thereby lose all exteriority (which, in reality, is not truly Biran's thesis, which always preserves the "resisting terminus," as I will show). From the resistance of bodies, we will pass to the "resistance of the body" or even of my own body. My "hand" is not my "chest," but it is when my hand "knocks itself against" my chest that I recognize this hand as mine and this chest as mine also. *The exclamation of the "me"*—"it's me, it's me again!"—is born of the surprised discovery that I was not me and that perhaps I never had been. For the first time, and among all the senses of sensation, there is responding, and phenomenology is not, or no longer, "without appeal [*appel*]."[66] And the response to the call [*appel*] comes not from thought (in the manner of the discarnate madman who would deny that "these hands and this body are mine," according to Descartes) or from affect (the "inner sentiment" and the "primitive fact of effort" according to Biran) but from the body itself—not the "flesh" (*Leib*) in the test [*épreuve*] of its own body (the lived body) but the "body" (*Körper*) in its extension or, rather, its "spread." Suddenly, the sensing being (the hand) and the sensed being (the chest) speak

---

65. Condillac, *Treatise on the Sensations*, 234 (emphasis added). [Translation modified. –Trans.]

66. This is the title of the conclusion of *Hors phénomène*, 453–60: "Une phénoménologie sans appel." [This title may be translated "A Phenomenology without Appeal" or "A Phenomenology without a Call." –Trans.]

to each other because they exclude each other and are differentiated from each other. The hand says to the chest: you are not me, but I sense you as a part of me. And the chest says to the hand: you are not me, but with you we will constitute my *myself* [*mon moi*] or, rather, "our *myself*" [*notre moi*] or, better, our "it's me" [*c'est moi*]—as if seen from the outside, for it is always from the outside, where, according to Condillac (or Nancy) the soul has been projected, that the *myself* apperceives itself: "As soon as it places its hand on one of the parts of its body the same sensing being responds, as it were, from the one part to the other, 'It's me.'"[67]

"It's me," and not "I am." We have said enough about this regarding the rose-odor—"it will be" (rose-odor), "I am" (rose-odor)—but here the matter repeats itself for the entire body. It is not that the statue becomes anew totally absorbed in the modified sensation (which is the case for the rose-odor) but that, conversely, it is referred back to itself by touch, though again and anew in a certain neutrality. Saying "it's me" is certainly answering a call—that of being summoned to an identity or even to a recognition that causes to exist. But saying "it's me" is also refusing to say "I am." For, since Condillac, contrary to Descartes, the "it's me" as a vision of oneself by oneself as if from the outside is better than the "I am" that will be repeated again in Maine de Biran's "inner sentiment." Despite the call or, rather, thanks to the call, a certain *neutrality* remains in Condillac. Rather than assuming an ego or seeing in it the hearth of a subjectivity ("I am," or, rather, "I sense," or even "I feel"), I remain for myself and to myself an *ego alter* or an other *than* myself—like this chest and this hand that did not belong to me so long as they had not touched each other—and that in their mutual recognition discover each other, as if by chance, as identified and composing a single body, without their having sought this: *alter ego*, or other myself.

Better, and because Condillac is not devoid of radicality either, even if this privilege is most often assigned to Maine de Biran alone, just as a *continuity of the body* (that touches itself *partes extra partes* according to a *continuum* of the gesture) is necessary, a *continuity of thought* or, better, of the word or the exclamation by which I recognize myself is necessary as well. The soul that is "outside itself" and as if forgotten in things in all its "modified sensations," except the sensations of touch, enters less "into itself" (which will be the case in Maine de Biran since, from the beginning, it never left itself) than it notices itself and "always itself" or,

---

67. Condillac, *Treatise on the Sensations*, 234. [Translation modified. –Trans.]

better, "itself again." Everything here lies in the "*again*" [*encore*]—both in the temporal sense of the reiterated rather than the continued (being surprised to find "self" or, rather, "myself" again in another touched body part—the head by the hand, for example) and in the additional sense of surplus (there is "again" and "again" *myself*, and each experience of a part of myself through touch will indeed end by constituting a "myself" in its globality). The shout of "*It's me again!*" deserves to be repeated here, reinforcing the "it's me" that has already been exclaimed twice: "Let the statue continue to touch itself, and everywhere the sensation of solidity will represent two things that are mutually exclusive and at the same time contiguous, and everywhere also the same sensing being will respond from one to the other: '*It's me, it's me again!*'"[68]

Everything then depends on the *response to the touched body*, this time in the sense of a code or an impetus that is given (like the receiver of a radar that awaits the signal that was sent and to which it will be necessary to indicate that it is, if not received, at least addressed). From the "statue that recognizes its own," we then pass to the act whereby it "discovers that there are other bodies." It is not thought but touch (the hand) that tells me and makes me see that *there is world* (in all the senses of the term) external to myself—with which I cannot totally identify myself and in which I cannot absorb myself (the rose-odor). Like Descartes, we must pass from a *first* to a *sixth Meditation*, or, for Condillac in the *Treatise on the Sensations*, from a first (smell) to a fifth (touch) chapter and therefore find again the world after a constituted "me" (but not an "I").

Let the body indeed be "foreign," understood here as "not recognized" as mine, and the statue will say nothing about it or, rather, it will say something about it as about a thing external to myself but not as about a limb that is mine that makes the "myself." But let the body emit some echo or furnish a response via touch, and it will then be said to be "mine" and will make the "myself." On the basis of the signals, like Morse code received discontinuously, it will be necessary to create a properly human language, in contact with its body, to say, "It's me." If the statue is modified "in its hand" but not "in this body that it touches" by apprehending an external body (the hand gripping a ball or a bullet, for example), it will therefore not say "me" or will not draw forth any "me" from this. But let it be both modified "in its hand" and "in this body that it touches" in the touching-touched of itself this time (the hand touching and striking the

68. Condillac, *Treatise on the Sensations*, 234 (emphasis added). [Translation modified. –Trans.]

chest), and it will cry out not only "It's me!" (in the shock of the touching of oneself) but also "It's me *again!*" in the contiguity of the hand's gesture on the body. It will, this time, be "itself" (me), on the basis of the "outside itself" (differentiating its body from other bodies):

> But if it touches a *foreign body*, the "me" that feels a modification in the hand does not feel itself modified in this body. If the hand says "me," it does *not* receive *the same response* in turn. . . . The *sensation of solidity* which gave them consistency in the one case gives it to them likewise in the other; with this difference that the "*me*" that *responded previously to itself* ceases to respond.[69]

The body thus extends itself or, rather, "spreads" itself, according to Condillac. And perhaps this time the aid of Maine de Biran will be necessary, leaning on this same example of the statue, not to find a limit to my own body, whose extension could "spread itself out" to infinity, but to discover in oneself the hearth of a "me" or, rather, of an "I" by which "*I am* rose-odor" and to which the hand will say "me" or, rather, "I" in the exclusively inner and muscular effort of the organ—independently, this time, of any grasped or expropriated object, including my own body. The "search for the flesh" (*Leib*, chapter 3) takes the baton from the "resistance of the body" (*Körper*, chapter 2), and perhaps that is the only way or, rather, the relay, for the Condillacian body's *me* to not succumb both to the surprise of not being everything and to the worry of not knowing precisely "where it is," in the sense of the "there," where it *maintains itself* in order to remain:

> When the statue comes to learn that it is something solid, I imagine that it is quite *surprised* not to find itself in *all* that it touches. It extends its arms, as if to look for itself *outside of itself*, and it cannot yet judge if it *will not indeed find* itself there anew; experience alone can instruct it. From this surprise is born the *disquiet* to know where it is and, if I may venture to express myself in this way, exactly up to what point it is.[70]

---

69. Condillac, *Treatise on the Sensations*, 234–35 (emphasis added). [Translation modified. –Trans.]

70. Condillac, *Treatise on the Sensations*, 235 (from the sections "its surprise at *not being* everything that it touches" and "*effects* of this surprise," emphasis added). [Translation modified. –Trans.]

3

In Search of the Flesh

> The *myself* cannot exist for itself without having the immediate internal apperception or sentiment of the *coexistence of the body*: that indeed is the primitive fact.
>
> MAINE DE BIRAN,
> *ESSAI SUR LES FONDEMENTS DE LA PSYCHOLOGIE*

Flesh and Body

WITH MAINE DE BIRAN, as I have emphasized (§4), there is born the invention of the *lived body* (or of the "inner extension")—not in notion only, but the phrase itself, at least in French: "It is by a 'reply of resistance' and not only 'the reply of sentiment' that the *extension of the lived body* is manifest *internally* and is circumscribed, or nearly so," already said the *Mémoire sur la décomposition de la pensée*.[1] But does it suffice to name "the extension of the lived body" to say its reality? Or, rather, does the reading of the lived body as the "subjective body," neatly thus defined within the framework of a certain phenomenology (in particular that of Michel Henry and Maurice Merleau-Ponty), resist the letter of Maine de Biran himself? There is no question here of a "Biranian orthodoxy," as others have been able to speak of a "phenomenological orthodoxy." But it is by interrogating *the things themselves* that we will

---

1. Maine de Biran, *Mémoire sur la décomposition*, 439n (emphasis added).

be able to shed light on the famous debate between "flesh" and "body" as it already played out in the eighteenth and nineteenth centuries between Condillac and Maine de Biran.

As I have shown, and as I have even insisted on at length, there can be no question of reducing Étienne Bonnot, Abbé de Condillac, only to the role and title of a "foil" for Maine de Biran. Condillac having never been studied for himself within the framework of phenomenology, at the risk of seeing in him only the error of the "objective body" faced with the correct champion of the "subjective body" or of the flesh, it was necessary, if not to restore his memory, at least to prove the possible relevance "of the consistency and the resistance of the body" as thought and posited by him. Condillac's *Treatise on the Sensations* is rich in teachings, as I have insisted and shown at length: through the "*rose-odor*" on the one hand with which the statue is identified (that is, the forgetting of oneself in things that occurs in modified sensations but that can just as well happen in the framework of a trauma or of the extra-phenomenal, in which I also experience myself as neutralized and "outside myself": "it will therefore be rose-odor") and through the *animate statue* on the other hand that ends up, "as if by chance," *touching itself* and "laying a hand on itself" (saying "me" but never "I": "It's me, it's me again!"). The idea of the impenetrability of bodies, and of their solidity, is not only characteristic of a naïve sensualism that is to be criticized and rejected but the avowal of a veritable "resistance of presence" in which what is first is no longer the act of "giving" or of "giving oneself" but the neutral *there is* of the rose-odor or of a pure existentiality: "If we present a rose to it," emphasized the *Treatise on the Sensations*, "the statue will be *only odor itself of this flower.*"

I have insisted on this. Being *only* odor is not even sensing *an* odor, just as saying, "It's me, it's me again!" is not saying "I" and never will be. The phenomenalized horizon (rose-odor) and the phenomenalizing subject (the touching-touched of the statue) will have a great deal of difficulty constituting themselves, at least in Condillac, whereas they will be directly given in Maine de Biran, on the basis of an egoity that is always delivered in advance: "*I am* rose-odor," as Maine de Biran will erroneously copy when citing the *Treatise on the Sensations*, while Condillac wrote only, and always wrote only, that "*it will* therefore *be* rose-odor." The devil hides in the details, and it is there that we must flush him out. It is not that Maine de Biran is here accused of a hermeneutic fault or even of a *lapsus calami* (having transcribed "I am" when Condillac wrote "it will be") but that the egoity that is presupposed in the one (Biran) only serves to better show the neutrality described by the other (Condillac). It is thus the entire debate about "flesh" and "body" that is here set forth as well as the possibility, or not, of returning to it and orienting it otherwise.

§8. Maine de Biran's Hermeneutics

a) An Ontology of the Flesh

We will certainly be surprised to see this chapter, entitled "In Search of the Flesh" (chapter 3), after the "constitution of the *myself*" (chapter 1) and the "resistance of the body" (chapter 2), open with "Maine de Biran's *hermeneutics*"—after "Maine de Biran's *spiritualism*" (§1) and "Maine de Biran's *phenomenology*" (§4) began the first two chapters. This must be said first: the enterprise here undertaken will not content itself with the "case" of Maine de Biran—or, rather, it studies it precisely as a "case," as I have mentioned from the introduction onward: "both an exception and a strangeness in the ordinary course of things and beings." As a counterpart, but not in opposition, to Michel Henry's *Philosophy and Phenomenology of the Body: An Essay on Biranian Ontology*,[2] *Spiritualism and Phenomenology: The Case of Maine de Biran* intends to examine and answer the contemporary interrogation of the relation of spiritualism (chapter 1) to phenomenology (chapter 2) and even to carnal hermeneutics (chapter 3), psychiatric phenomenology (chapters 4–5), and medicine in general (chapter 6).

Hence the detour via the contemporary questioning (in the manner of Maurice Merleau-Ponty, Michel Henry, and many others) is necessary, while traversing the oeuvre of the thinker from Bergerac, in order to not remain confined only to the history of philosophy. Maine de Biran certainly needs his *exegetes*—in the end rather numerous—highly competent since Henri Gouhier and after Victor Cousin, who was their first initiator. But he also requires his *interpreters*—those who do not confine themselves to *what he said* but who agree to enter onto this steep path of what he *makes us say*. Speaking now of a "carnal hermeneutics" in Maine de Biran is neither fleeing his text nor imposing a "straitjacket" on it; quite the contrary. It is seeking for today the lighting that suits him so that he can be examined in a new light.

2. [The English translation omits the subtitle. –Trans.]

It is then *hermeneutics*, for once, that we will call upon to guide us regarding the distinction between the *flesh* and the *body* (and not only solely regarding the "sense of the world or of the text")—in the last Ricœur who was its promoter at least at the end of his life via the tenth study of *Oneself as Another*, "What Ontology in View?" There is indeed a "carnal hermeneutics," perfectly named in English by Richard Kearney and Brian Treanor in *Carnal Hermeneutics*, and this amounts not simply to being satisfied with the "flesh" (*Leib*) that has always been posited by phenomenology but also to positing the primacy, or at the very least the question, of the "body" (*Körper*).[3]

If there is a "swerve of the flesh" within the framework of contemporary phenomenology,[4] this was also seen and denounced by Paul Ricœur in his late work, as (almost) a "retraction" relative to the collection of older texts compiled in *À l'école de la phénoménologie* [*At the School of Phenomenology*]: "Only as the *ontology of the flesh* breaks free as far as possible from the problematic of constitution," we read in a turning-point of the already-cited tenth study of *Oneself as Another*, "can we face the inverse paradox . . . namely, not what it means that a *body is my body*, that is, *flesh*, but that the *flesh* is also a *body among bodies*. It is here the phenomenology finds *its limit*."[5]

That a body may be not solely "my body," that is, "flesh" or "lived body," but that this same flesh can at the same time be, or even become, a "body among bodies": that is the essential question. As I have emphasized, by way of a transition between the recognition of the "resistance of the body" (chapter 2) and the "search for the flesh" (chapter 3), the real problem of phenomenology today or, rather, of its "limit," as Paul Ricœur perfectly indicates, is not the problem of its "becoming-flesh" or "incarnation" (*Verleiblichkeit*) but rather the problem of its "being-a-body" or "embodiment" (*Körperlichkeit*): "Thus it is a *fundamental problem* to think through and clearly define how flesh is also constituted as physical flesh," as I also added, following Husserl's posthumous manuscript dated 1921.[6] Descartes's sixth *Meditation* is in reality more complex or more difficult to

---

3. See Kearney, "Wager of Carnal Hermeneutics," 15, 53–54: "Before words, we are flesh, flesh becoming words for the rest of our lives. . . . I must have both an intimate body for me (*Leib*) and a physical natural body among other bodies (*Körper*). . . . This is where phenomenology reaches its limit and calls for more."

4. See my work *Wedding Feast*, 1–4.

5. Ricœur, *Oneself as Another*, 325–26 (emphasis added).

6. Husserl, *Zur Phänomenologie der Intersubjektivität*, 77, cited in Franck, *Flesh and Body*, 83 (emphasis in original). See also p. 49 above.

reach than the second one—and this is what Maine de Biran understood perfectly. It is not the *cogito* that poses a problem (be it "reflexive" for Descartes or "carnal" in Biran) but the discovery of or the reunion with the world as such, including my body aimed at as a body among bodies.

And there lies the whole paradox. For it is precisely in the very place where Paul Ricœur claims the primacy, and even a sort of revenge, of the *body* over the *flesh*, if not of my "improper body" (a thing among things) over the "lived or proper body" (confined to the "I sense" and the "I sense myself"), that he refers to Maine de Biran on the one hand and to spiritualism on the other. Everything happens as if the "backlash of spiritualism on phenomenology" that I am calling for were already playing out or beginning *ab initio* in Paul Ricœur at the end of his life and as if it is precisely this that we must continue. It is indeed a matter of doubling the "phenomenological discovery" of the proper body in Maine de Biran by its "ontological dimension," without which it cannot truly operate: "I should like, at the start of this brief overview," acknowledges the hermeneut, as if to pay a debt that was contracted long ago, "to give proper credit to the one who opened up this field of investigation of the lived body, namely Maine de Biran: he truly gave an *appropriate ontological dimension* to his *phenomenological discovery*."[7]

The Biranians are well aware of this. There is the "phenomenological Biran" (of which Michel Henry is doubtless the most eminent representative in *Philosophy and Phenomenology of the Body*), and there is the ontological Biran (the Biran of Bernard Baertschi in *L'Ontologie de Maine de Biran* [*Maine de Biran's Ontology*]). While the one (Henry) relies on the Biranian distinction between the "phenomenal subject" and the "real subject," already mentioned and studied (§3), the other (Baertschi) refers to existence, if not as a "body," then at least as a term that resists all interiority while constituting it: "The philosopher seeks *what is* [and not only what appears]. *Existence* is the goal of his words and the terminus of his meditations," writes Maine de Biran in his *Notes sur le premier problème de la philosophie* [*Notes on the First Problem of Philosophy*] (1815)—published by Henri Gouhier, before the publication of the *Œuvres de Maine de Biran*, under the title *De l'existence* [*On Existence*] (1963).[8] The controversy between "phenomenology" and "ontology" is less violent than it

---

7. Ricœur, *Oneself as Another*, 320–21 (emphasis added).

8. Maine de Biran, *Commentaires et marginalia: XIXe siècle*, 204–5 (emphasis partly in original). This phrase is at the root of Baertschi's work *L'Ontologie de Maine de Biran*, 15 (though cited incompletely). It was reprinted in Maine de Biran, *De l'existence*, previously-unpublished texts published by Henri Gouhier, 15.

seems. Perhaps it is necessary to maintain that we do not have to decide between phenomenology and ontology—"we do not have to choose because Biranism is neither a phenomenology of transparency and autodonation nor an ontology" (Montebello)[9]—and that we must also at the same time find in Biran a theory of the *phenomenon* (appearing) and a theory of the *absolute* (the external being in itself that is separated as the "terminus that resists the primitive fact of effort") (Baertschi).[10]

It remains that the "doubling" of the "phenomenological discovery" of the body by its "appropriate ontological dimension," according to Ricœur, leads the whole of Biranian interpretation in another and new direction. For Ricœur is indeed referring here to a new "ontology of the flesh" (and not only to a phenomenology of the flesh)—relating, certainly, to the phenomenological interpretations of Maine de Biran (Merleau-Ponty, Henry), but also to a so-called "spiritualist" interpretation (Gabriel Marcel): "The second point of reference, and the most important one along the path that leads from Maine de Biran's philosophy of effort to the three great philosophies of one's own body that I named earlier [Marcel, Merleau-Ponty, Henry]" refers necessarily to an "ontology of the flesh" that was already deployed by Husserl himself.[11] It is thus, by what I here name the "backlash" of spiritualism on phenomenology, of which Paul Ricœur is, as it were, the pioneer, that a sort of "metaphysical resistance" to the reduction would occur, including in Maine de Biran, for which the example of the "cast-iron cannonball" or, rather, of the irreducibility of the "solid body" will be the paradigm via the impossible negation of every form of exteriority.

---

9. Montebello, *Décomposition de la pensée*, 202–19: "Entre noumènes et phénomènes," 213.

10. Baertschi, *L'Ontologie de Maine de Biran*, 437 (emphasis added): "There remains the essential problem: why did Maine de Biran feel the need to complete his theory of the *phenomenon* with a theory of the *absolute*? . . . If Maine de Biran develops a *theory of the absolute*, it is to ensure that our knowledge is truly a knowledge of the *real*. In other words, our philosopher does not judge it sufficient to show how the *myself* constructs the totality of objects with the aid of *significations*; what he wants to know is whether the world in which he thinks and acts is *real*, that is, autonomous in relation to his seeing and grasping: 'The philosopher seeks *what is*.'"

11. Ricœur, *Oneself as Another*, 322 (on the threefold line of descent, Marcel, Merleau-Ponty, Henry, see 320; on the ontology of the flesh, see 325).

b) Backlash

I have said this, but we should recall it and return to it: the term "spiritualism" has never referred simply to a "philosophy of consciousness" in opposition to phenomenology as a "philosophy of the body or the flesh." Their real difference, as I have noted, "lies less in a relation to spirit on the one hand (spiritualism) and to the body on the other (phenomenology) than in the *signification* and the *orientation* that must be given to this unique and indissoluble unity of the soul and the body.... The human being is ever and always 'spirit and body' . . . in an indissoluble unity, either in a 'dynamic of the spirit' that sweeps the body along with it in the case of spiritualism, or in an 'appropriation of the body' that is simply one with the spirit, or even with pathos or autoaffection, in the case of phenomenology" (§1c). Paradoxically, it is perhaps more on the side of spiritualism than of phenomenology that the real "body" lies—hence the "backlash" of the former (spiritualism) on the latter (phenomenology), which Paul Ricœur already finds or, rather, discovers.

He clearly acknowledges this in his "Intellectual Autobiography" (1995), and we know that Ricœur himself came first from spiritualism (Lagneau) before crossing to phenomenology (Husserl) and finally playing the game, if not of the backlash, at least of the grafting of "hermeneutics onto phenomenology" or even, in my view, of "spiritualism onto phenomenology." It is by seeking this conciliation—I would prefer, for my part, to speak of a "boomerang effect"—between phenomenology and spiritualism, or even existential philosophy, that the Ricœurian reading of phenomenology becomes, certainly, a thought of the reduction but also an effort, or a noticing, of the resistance to the reduction. The attempt at "conciliation" between Husserl (the orthodox interpretation of phenomenology) and Gabriel Marcel (the existential tendency) leads Paul Ricœur, by his own admission, precisely toward the "resistance to the reduction" (Merleau-Ponty)—which is the very resistance that we are seeking in the erroneous and too-rapid focalization of the whole of Biranian thought onto only the "sentiment of oneself" (ego) and the "primitive fact of effort" (lived body), as if nothing could escape or thwart it:

> Carefully respecting the rights of the "realist" interpretation, I thought I could maintain *the chances of a reconciliation* between a phenomenology that was neutral with respect to the choice between realism and idealism, and the existentialist tendency of the philosophy of Marcel and Jaspers. I discovered in the preface

> that Merleau-Ponty, at the request of Émile Bréhier, had placed at the front of his *Phenomenology of Perception a resistance of the same nature to the orthodox interpretation of the phenomenological reduction*; the philosopher, whom I admired, going so far as to say that the reduction, though still necessary, was condemned *never to be completed* and perhaps *never genuinely to begin*.[12]

This idea of a "resistance to the reduction" or of a reduction that is "condemned *never to be completed* and perhaps *never genuinely to begin*" is precisely what requires not only that we not confine ourselves to the phenomenological reduction alone, as if phenomenology had by itself to "assume in our century the very role of philosophy,"[13] but also that we not condemn and exclude as *ontical* everything that would not be *phenomenology* in order to stick, in a sort of condescending attitude, only to the *ontological* as such. The false debate between metaphysics (and therefore spiritualism) and phenomenology (at least orthodox phenomenology) arises from the fact that every form of *special metaphysics* is supposedly to be excluded, if not since Husserl, who is hardly interested in the matter, at least following Heidegger, who rejects it. The Kantian division, in the *Critique of Pure Reason*, of the transcendental ideas into "**three classes**, of which the **first** contains the absolute (unconditioned) **unity** of the **thinking subject** [the soul: 'psychology'], the **second** the absolute **unity** of the **series** of **conditions of appearance** [the world: 'cosmology'], the **third** the absolute **unity** of the **condition of all objects of thought** in general [God: 'theology']" becomes, as it were, definitively invalidated in the name of a general metaphysics that deals uniquely, and more globally, with being.[14] *Dasein* certainly leads to *being qua being* (existential philosophy) but with it loses *beings* (the whole of the so-called "human" sciences). One understands this, or one would have understood it, in a time when Marxism, structuralism, and psychoanalysis were invading the field of thought, but one cannot today remain as

---

12. Ricœur, "Intellectual Autobiography," 11 (emphasis added). [Translation modified. –Trans.]

13. See Marion, *Reduction and Givenness*, 1: "In an essential way, phenomenology assumes in our century the very role of philosophy" (the first sentence of the work). This phrase was certainly true of the century in which it was written (in 1989, so in the twentieth century), but it perhaps is not, or no longer, true of the twenty-first century, in which the relationships between "metaphysics" and "phenomenology" have changed considerably, including the aforementioned question of ontotheology and of the overcoming of metaphysics.

14. See Kant, *Critique of Pure Reason*, 406 (A334/B391, boldface in original).

if "blocked" on that nascent moment. The times have changed, and so has thought—hence this "backlash" that today is needed, and of which Paul Ricœur and Maurice Merleau-Ponty were in reality the pioneers. The "human sciences" are called "human" because they also deal with man in a socio-historicized field; and metaphysics is divided into two parts called "general metaphysics" (being) and "special metaphysics" (the soul, the world, and God), of which the former should not be excluded for the benefit of the latter only on the grounds that the latter supposedly concerns thingified beings. Moreover, one can but be surprised by the *forgetting of the soul* in our days, in the name only of the "flesh" or the "body" where the soul and its "core" (*der Kern der Seele*), including in its metaphysical approach, remained an essential concept just as much in Edmund Husserl (*Ideen II*) as in Edith Stein (*Beiträge*).[15] The *backlash of spiritualism on phenomenology* thus requires us to think and to posit *a sort of "metaphysical resistance" within phenomenology*: that is to say, a program that is still to be conducted, in modes of reflection (spiritualism and phenomenology) that are less to be opposed than they are to be made to encounter each other to mutually enrich each other.

c) Metaphysical Resistance

The absolutely justified renewed interest today in the "young Paul Ricœur" thus arises less from his hermeneutic of the text, of which full use has been made in the past, in particular within the framework of theology, than from this "spiritualist" or, in other words, "metaphysical vein," in which it is a matter not of thinking systematically, of positing things' existence by itself, of going beyond phenomena and presupposing the absolute, as the majority of phenomenologists believe and think, but rather of sticking to a "real" of which Bergson would say that it is a site of existence, of resistance, and of growth of the things as such.[16] Far from any realism (of the Thomist sort, for example), Maine de Biran's spiritualism will nevertheless also stick to the "real," if we apply this "label" to him only retrospectively, inasmuch as it refers precisely to the *absolute* in the double or even triple sense of the term: whether the absolute of the separatedness of the world or of external existence

---

15. Stein, *Philosophy of Psychology*, 231. See Bouillot, *Le Noyau de l'âme*, 20.

16. See Le Roy, *Une philosophie nouvelle*, 16: "The real is noted and not constructed." See also the accurate commentary of Vasseur, "Penser le réel," 21–34.

(§15), the absolute of what is inassimilable in me (§17), the absolute of God whom one can melt into (see the conclusion, "Three Lives in One"). It is an absolute—separated external existence, inassimilable internal existence, and opening to the divine—that will certainly be said to belong to metaphysics but that phenomenology can interrogate both in the "resistance to the reduction" (of the irreducible that remains) and in the possibility of a "philosophy of religion" (not necessarily of a revealed theology converted into phenomenology but of the affirmation of a transcendent God to whom man could indeed aspire).

Hence the two, or even the three, possible faces of Maine de Biran—on the basis, moreover, of the "conversions of Maine de Biran" that were so well brought to light by Henri Gouhier and that I am redeploying here in the order of my own development: a certain form of "anthropological realism" starting in 1813 (*Rapports des sciences naturelles avec la psychologie* [*Relationship between the Natural Sciences and Psychology*]), a discourse on limits or "alienation" starting in 1820 (*Nouvelles considérations sur les rapports du physique et du moral de l'homme*), and a certain form of "religious spiritualism" starting in November 1823 (*Journal IV*, vol. 3), shortly before his death.[17] Thus there are, if one starts with the first manuscripts, not three but four readings of Maine de Biran, which are less to be opposed than to be confronted with each other: the one inherited from the *Essai sur les fondements de la psychologie* as a support for the spiritualist and phenomenological interpretations (Bergson, but also Henry relying, for his part, on the *Mémoire sur la décomposition de la pensée*); the later reading of *Note sur l'idée de l'existence* or the *Notes sur le premier problème de la philosophie* (previously placed by Henri Gouhier in the volume *De l'existence*), which carries out precisely this metaphysical resistance to pure and simple phenomenalization; the reading of the dialogue with psychiatry and medicine in general (which in reality goes from the *Discours à la Société médicale de Bergerac* [*Speeches at the Bergerac Medical Society*], pronounced between 1807 and 1810, to the *Nouvelles considérations sur les rapports du physique et du moral de l'homme* of 1820); and the spiritual reading of the end of the

---

17. Gouhier, *Les Conversions*. This is a series of conversions that nevertheless draw Biran toward "Platonism" and its "beyond," according to Gouhier ("If Biran advanced beyond Platonism, he did not go all the way to the end of Christianity"), whereas a new reading today would lead more toward a certain form of "radical and complete anthropology" or, let us say, of a study of the "science of man."

Journal and of Maine de Biran's life in the explicit affirmation of a "life of the spirit" (the three lives).

It is therefore impossible to say that *there is only* the internal or that everything *is* internal in Maine de Biran. There is also something of the external (resistance to the reduction) and of the superior (the absolute of the spirit), even though everything *comes* first and originally from the internal. The "primitive fact of the intimate sense," as I have shown (§2), and the "primitive fact of effort," which I will come to (§16), are indeed the points of departure of our whole entire being in its autoaffection and its lived body, but this latter cannot be reduced to them. The double transcendentalism of affect and the lived body (phenomenology) must coexist with the position of a world that is separated from me and that is not me (metaphysics): "It is indeed true to say that when I say '*me*,'" Biran emphasizes anew in his *Notes sur le premier problème de la philosophie*,

> I say at the same time that it is not a matter of *everything that is not me* and that I detach myself from it, as when I say, "It is not *me*," I state clearly that *I have the sentiment of two different existences*. . . . I have the sentiment of a *composed existence* or a *double existence* whose two terms are really inseparable. This is the *primitive duality* that is not analyzable and does not branch into two facts of the intimate sense; but when I say, this object that I see, that I touch is *not me*, I am indeed really separating this *foreign existence* from the one that *is proper to me*. . . . It is certain in my eyes that I exist and that there exists something *different from me*.[18]

This text by Maine de Biran from 1815—at the turning point in his thought that Michel Henry never took into account except to see in it, in a way that is, to say the least, surprising, the Cartesian remainder of a "metaphysical duality" without considering that it is in reality a matter of a "primitive duality" (the last chapter of *Philosophy and Phenomenology of the Body*, to which I will return)[19]—is important enough

---

18. Maine de Biran, *Commentaires et marginalia: XIXe siècle*, 206–7; reproduced by Henri Gouhier in his edition of Maine de Biran, *De l'existence*, 19. It is cited (only in part) and commented on by Baertschi, *L'Ontologie de Maine de Biran*, 97. This treatise is to be completed by Maine de Biran, "Note sur l'idée de l'existence," in *Dernière philosophie*, 213–19.

19. See "A Critique of the Thought of Maine de Biran: The Problem of Passivity" in Henry, *Philosophy and Phenomenology*, 154–82: "The determination to grasp the profound intuition of Biranianism and to remain faithful thereto, therefore, implies the rejection of everything which, in Biranianism, does not really belong to it, but rather belongs to philosophical positions against which it was gradually constituted without

to be commented on here. For here lies precisely that which it is indeed necessary to name not only the "backlash" of spiritualism on phenomenology but also the "metaphysical resistance" within phenomenology. The Biranian "primitive duality" indeed forbids reducing everything to autoaffection, as it forbids reducing everything to the lived body. If "the most important lesson of the reduction is the *impossibility of a complete reduction*," as I have already cited, following the Preface of Maurice Merleau-Ponty's *Phenomenology of Perception*,[20] we will therefore distinguish between the "resistance *to* the reduction" (the thesis that I maintain here and that *The Extra-Phenomenal* has ceaselessly demonstrated through the phenomenological angle of trauma) and the "reduction *of* the reduction" (the thesis advanced by Michel Henry to reach autoaffection beneath every distance as also beneath every intentionality). "Resisting" requires opposing, even if this "sentiment of resistance or of effort" comes only from oneself, whereas "reducing" and "reducing the reduction" ends by losing every contradiction to end on a monism of a pure and simple autoaffection.

Are we proceeding from *the external to the internal* (Condillac) or from *the internal to the external* (Biran)? This, then, is the real question, and not: Is there an internal (autoaffection and the lived body) that would be capable of denying everything external (affection that comes from the outside and the foreign body) so that the suspension becomes such that all exteriority is definitively lost? "The two worlds are thus given to us in an intimate connection in the *primitive fact of existence*," the *Notes sur le premier problème de la philosophie* emphasize anew, in a decisive and incisive way, to *also* claim exteriority (starting from interiority, of course), "that is, the *internal world*, the *myself* as the force that wills and produces effort, the *external world* as the *object* that resists without our being able to know them otherwise than in this fundamental relation, never in themselves: we must stop there."[21]

---

always succeeding in eliminating them completely.... The Biranian theses which stem from dualism essentially deal with instinct, sensibility, affectivity, imagination, i.e., precisely the points on which Biran speaks without any originality; it is what he borrowed from others which is false" (154–55).

20. Merleau-Ponty, *Phenomenology of Perception*, lxxvii (emphasis added).
21. Maine de Biran, *Commentaires et marginalia: XIXe siècle*, 207 (emphasis added).

d) The Cast-Iron Cannonball

As early as the *Mémoire sur la décomposition de la pensée*, Maine de Biran had already, in reality, been determined to distinguish and establish the internal and the external on the basis of the "primitive fact *of existence*"—which is not exclusively the "primitive fact *of the intimate sense*." And this could or should have not escaped Michel Henry's reading, which quotes precisely the last *Mémoire* (*sur la décomposition de la pensée*)—such that a purely phenomenological reading in terms of both "autoaffection" and "flesh" could not have been fully justified. It remains, or remained, necessary not to stick only to the "marble statue" (the only phenomenological debate that was developed) but to also turn toward exteriority or the "cast-iron cannonball."

Let us take a "cast-iron cannonball" that we will hold and grip in a hand, which Maine de Biran therefore, in the *Mémoire sur la décomposition de la pensée*, names "solid" or "the image of the solid."[22] It is a solidity that we will, moreover, remember is that by which my own body resists me and permits me to say, "It's me, it's me again!" in Condillac (§7). It is, then, necessary to distinguish, as the thinker from Bergerac indicates with precision in his *Mémoire*, two different circumstances in the exercise of the senses (and of touch in particular)—the "voluntary determination" (the *myself*) and the "perception of their results" (the non-myself):

> It is therefore here again the perceptions of touch that serve as a point of departure for us. In the complete exercise of this sense, several circumstances that it is very important to not conflate are found to be included: a *voluntary determination*, a series of movements or acts by means of which the *passivity of the sensitive organ* is placed within reach of its object.[23]

Voluntary activity (the *myself* in its interiority) and passivity of the sensitive organ (in contact with exteriority) therefore go together. If effort is always internal and muscular—a point to which I will return with the example of the statue—and if it can even experience itself without an object and independently of any object (inside the hand), this is also because an object can and must resist it: "Let us take away this object," Maine de Biran then requires in a resolute phenomenological reduction or *epoché*. "The same voluntary determination can be effected again without the

---

22. Maine de Biran, *Mémoire sur la décomposition*, 260.
23. Maine de Biran, *Mémoire sur la décomposition*, 258 (emphasis partly in original).

involvement of any external force,"[24] he specifies—which will be his thesis faced with Condillac's marble statue, since there is no need for the statue to touch itself, to sense the "impenetrability" and the "solidity" of its own body, in order to say, "It's me, it's me again!" or, rather, "I am," according to Biran. Only the *inner* and *organic* tension of the hand, as I will show (§10b) will suffice to explain it.

But we would be wrong to forget what follows in the text—which means that the "ontological" (what is) must also face "phenomenology" (what appears), or that we must indeed today think a "resistance to the reduction" ("There is" in Levinas, the brute world in Merleau-Ponty, or the "extra-phenomenal" in my own perspective), rather than a "reduction of the reduction" (according to Michel Henry).

> *Let us take away this object....* The force of resistance is no longer in it (non-myself), but the memory that relates to it and that makes it be recognized as absent still emerges from a contrast or a comparison analogous to the one that established its existence, which presupposes the memory of the first comparison.[25]

Without the existence of the (bracketed) object, there thus remains the "memory of its existence," which in reality duplicates the resistance. In other words, far from suppressing the thing, or what one could name reality (rather than the noumena), it is by relying on the *res* of the natural attitude that the never-"finished" reduction (Merleau-Ponty) is constituted, since there always remains in it a certain form of exteriority: first in sensation (the passivity of the subject that comes from the impression of the object on me) and then in imagination (the memory of this same impression in me). There is therefore something *of the irreducible in the reducible*: this is the conclusion at which we must indeed arrive—from the point of view of Maine de Biran, certainly, but also of phenomenology in general. There is no question of speaking here of "descriptive realism" or "phenomenological realism" in the sense in which "the things and the world exist independently of us and of our thought," a point to which I will return (chapter 4). For, far from denying the reduction (and therefore opposing non-phenomenology to phenomenology) and far from thinking an existence *in itself* of things (neither the primitive fact in Maine de Biran nor the extra-phenomenal in my work contest the primacy of subjectivity, although they oppose

---

24. Maine de Biran, *Mémoire sur la décomposition*, 260.
25. Maine de Biran, *Mémoire sur la décomposition*, 260 (emphasis added).

to it resistance or consistency), it is here a matter rather of recognizing that the object outside myself (objectivity) or in myself (objectness) can be totally suspended without losing the buttress that gives me access to myself, even in the absence of that object. The privation of the object (Biran) takes priority over the absence of the object (Henry), and this is why the thinker from Bergerac could therefore write: "*Let us take away this object*. . . . The force of resistance is no longer in it (non-myself), but the memory that relates to it and that makes it be recognized as absent still emerges from a contrast or a comparison analogous to the one that established its existence, which presupposes the memory of the first comparison." In other words, and this is what is essential, "something" always remains, the "solid" as resistance or its "image" as permanence, which means that I will never be able to think or live "without it," albeit in image and no longer in the mode of perception alone: "The individual [by the effacing of habit] *will represent to himself as a mass the image of the solid*, but without preserving the consciousness or the memory of the acts that necessarily contributed to giving it the current form."[26]

To take up again the example of the "cast-iron cannonball," which in reality is only the translation of this "solid" or this "body as a mass," be it perceived or imagined, in order to "hold onto the ball that drags his arm down . . . the individual will have to make an effort"—and he will remember it. Likewise, if "this object is placed on his hand that he wills to close[,] at a certain moment, the movement of his fingers will be stopped, even if he makes a very great effort."[27] Even if the effort is internal, there always remains what Maine de Biran names a "resisting terminus," a point to which I will return (§15). Once again, this is not because the world and things exist independently of me—this is certainly true, and Husserl never denied it, but it simply makes no sense for the phenomenologist (what good is a "world in itself," or even a "God in himself," if there is not first a "world for me" and a "God with me"?)—but is because the world, like others, must be able to oppose resistance "to me." As I have said, there is here something of the "struggle with the angel," including in Maine de Biran, and returning now to the example of the "marble statue," in the debate with Condillac but seen from Biran's side this time, is interrogating it otherwise and furnishing a new descriptivity for it. Regarding the point where Paul Ricœur

---

26. Maine de Biran, *Mémoire sur la décomposition*, 260.
27. Baertschi, *L'Ontologie de Maine de Biran*, 8.

insisted, in what I have named "the hermeneutics of Maine de Biran," on my flesh being not only "flesh" but also "a body among bodies"—"How am I to understand that *my flesh* is also *a body*?"[28]—it will therefore be a question of showing that the "flesh," including in Maine de Biran, is not "without body," contrary to Michel Henry and the interpretation that I have been able to conduct elsewhere.[29]

But it remains necessary to pass via "affect," for it is truly there, in reality, that the status of corporeality also, and paradoxically, is decided. For man it is indeed in the capacity to be or, better, the reality of being, affected, or even autoaffected or not, that the sense of our body is measured—"flesh" for some as a pure lived experience of the body (Husserl, Merleau-Ponty, or Henry), or "also body" for others as an irreducible consistency (carnal hermeneutics in the late Ricœur of *Oneself as Another*, the hypermateriality of the body in the early Levinas in *Time and the Other*, or the spread body in my own perspective). The determination of the "lived body" (*Leib*) depends on the modality of "affectivity" (*Befindlichkeit*)—and this is the essential lesson to draw from this Biranian reading of Michel Henry. Affected man (§9) will indeed necessarily lead to a transcendental and originary body in a pure interiority (§10b), while the outside-affection (§14) will reduce me to a pure objectivated corporeality that is, if not extended, at least "spread" (§15).

§9. Affected Man

a) A Mysterious Property

It was indeed necessary that the "shepherd's answer to the shepherdess" then be pronounced—that is to say, a repartee, according to the French expression, that certainly ends the discussion, but not without an argument (the shepherdess, as early as the seventeenth century, representing the romantic advance made to the shepherd, and not the reverse, and waiting for him to be willing to comply or even succumb). The fascinating debate between Maine de Biran and Condillac regarding the

---

28. Ricœur, *Oneself as Another*, 326 (emphasis added). It is thus toward the "ontology of the body" more than toward the "ontology of the flesh" alone that Paul Ricœur turns here to answer his guiding question: "Toward Which Ontology?" [The English translation gives the title of the tenth study as "What Ontology in View?"; "Toward Which Ontology?" is a literal translation of the French. -Trans.]

29. See Falque, *Loving Struggle*, 143–73.

marble statue—and which was, according to Michel Henry himself in *Incarnation*, "the quickly forgotten achievement of a sequence of modern thought that was as brief as it was decisive"[30]—then begins, properly speaking, with a letter addressed to Desttut de Tracy (dated April 30, 1804), just before the *Mémoire sur la décomposition de la pensée* and well before the *Essai sur les fondements de la psychologie* that will be its acme. Acknowledging having read "all of Condillac," and then incarcerated during the Terror in the abbey that was transformed into the "prison of Carmes" (which has since become the Carmes seminary of the Institut Catholique de Paris), the count Destutt de Tracy maintains the accuracy of the Condillacian interpretation of the *successively* animated "statue," against Maine de Biran who wishes to see in it a sort of *immediately* given "test [*épreuve*] of oneself." In contrast, according to Biran, and according to a well-conducted critique, everything is a matter of a "force" or "mysterious property" that in reality is always *already there* in the statue and of which Condillac is ignorant without, however, being able to deny it—perhaps today christened "autoaffection"—without which no movement, nor even any sensation, would be possible. For, without autoexperiencing *oneself* (the egoic and transcendental structure of affect), one cannot really see how the statue could experience (sensing the rose-odor, for example): "Condillac, by placing a *soul* or a *spiritual substance* [also called a "mysterious substance"] in the statue, tacitly presupposed some *mysterious property* that would be joined to pure sensation and would transform it into perception or other intellectual acts."[31]

It is indeed necessary, according to the thinker from Bergerac, that something happen *within* the statue (even to sense a rose, and all the more to say *me* in the act of touching *oneself*) for something to occur *via the outside*. In other words, although it is here a matter of turning the reproach into a merit, the marble statue could never have gone from what Biran names the "first state of the statue to the one that immediately follows" without an already-given *guaranteed continuity*. Biran is Leibnizian with regard to his conception of "force" as substance, a point to which I will return (§16c). In this sense, it is indeed necessary to posit *a priori* a *continuum* from "little perceptions" to "perception," according to Biran—even if, on the one hand, this continuity would be given, according to him, in the sensing subject autoexperiencing itself rather than in an

30. Henry, *Incarnation*, 138.
31. Maine de Biran, *Correspondance philosophique: 1766–1804*, 361 (emphasis partly in original).

already-constituted monad, and, on the other hand, the "obscure perceptions" (I will return to them also) come to resist even the "little perceptions" and require that the "portion of obscurity" in the sensing subject (§15b) not always be illuminated. In short, Condillac, who believed he had invented everything—by constituting a subject that would progressively end up saying, "It's me, it's me again!" on the basis of the experience of "touch" and of the "touching-touched"—in reality, according to Biran, discovered nothing at all, since everything was given in advance.

The judgment of this statue drawn from progressive and then simultaneous sensations (olfaction, hearing, taste, sight, with their respective combinations) unto the exclamation of "me" (through touch) is in no way synthetic, and still less is it synthetic *a priori*, to say it with Kant, but is only "analytic." The marble statue has learned nothing about itself that was not already attributed to it—and we have seen, however, the whole progressive movement that goes from the fact of "being rose-odor" to the "soul outside itself," then the statue that "lays a hand on itself" unto the "it's me, it's me again!" (§6)—such that Condillac resembles those *alchemists* who believed they had transformed metal (sensations) into gold (the discovery of the subject), while either the precious metal was already there under the trappings of a sensation that did not dare to acknowledge itself as such, or it would never be attained, such that there would be no subject. Condillac, the champion of the *acquired* in the aforementioned sensualism that he defends to the point of radicalizing Locke's empiricism, cannot not recognize, according to Biran, this absolute presence of the *innate* in the straight line that runs from Descartes to Leibniz, even if posited otherwise: "One can reproach Condillac," adds Biran, not without malice, in the letter to Tracy, "with having somewhat imitated those *alchemists* who persuaded themselves that they had made *gold* by combining or working on substances that *contained in advance* a few fragments of that metal; I do not believe, at least, that he can be entirely exculpated from the reproach that he addresses to Locke for having attributed a few *innate faculties* to the soul."[32]

---

32. Maine de Biran, *Correspondance philosophique: 1766–1804*, 361–62 (emphasis partly in original).

b) The Separated Affect

But in reality, according to the thinker from Bergerac, the dice are loaded *from the start*. For Condillac's operation amounts to separating the inseparable, cutting the uncuttable, dividing the indivisible—separating, that is, the affect from its outside and therefore thinking an "outside-affect," or an "outside-the-affective," which is just as impossible as it is unacceptable. Thus speaks Biran to Tracy—a lesson that Michel Henry will retain: "Condillac places himself in the opposite point of view [from Descartes' point of view of the *myself* and of innate ideas] and begins by *separating the affective element* from that which is not it."[33] *Separating the affective element from that which is not it*—this is therefore the error, in Biran's view. This says everything, or nearly so, and we understand Michel Henry's rightful fascination with Descartes's *videre videor* (it seems to me that I see) and Biran's "primitive fact of effort," which goes hand in hand with his condemnation of Condillac. It is not that Condillac, in the *Treatise on the Sensations*, was necessarily wrong and that we must oppose him—Michel Henry is too attentive a reader to simplify to that extent—but that it is necessary to radicalize. There is indeed a "departure" in Condillac that is never expressed—an "I sense" and an "I sense that I sense," even an "I feel *myself*"—such that Biran is only stating the condition by which the statue can become animate. Condillac's marble statue, without any sensation and even before sensing or becoming "rose-odor," is already, according this time to Henry (and Maine de Biran), a "subjectivity reduced to itself" or "pure impressions." It affects itself or, better, autoaffects itself, a condition *sine qua non* for affecting or being affected: "[Maine de Biran] was one of the first to pose explicitly the question of the knowledge of the *lived body*," we read in Michel Henry's *Incarnation*, taking the debate up again at the end of his life (2000). "To resolve it, he proceeded in a series of the most remarkable phenomenological reductions. First, he reduced our subjectivity to itself and to its pure impressions. Condillac called this reduced impressional subjectivity a statue."[34]

As we can see, Michel Henry as an interpreter of the statue straightaway takes Biran's side, if not to criticize Condillac, at least to mention the transcendental relation of oneself to oneself from the point of view of affection, without which nothing could happen to me. Better, the statue,

---

33. Maine de Biran, *Correspondance philosophique: 1766–1804*, 361 (emphasis partly in original).

34. Henry, *Incarnation*, 138 (emphasis added). [Translation modified. –Trans.]

which was "a-sensational" in Condillac (if we can thus name the *tabula rasa* before any rose-odor) becomes "impressional" in Biran, or at the very least in Michel Henry as a reader of the thinker from Bergerac. Here there is certainly a "tour de force," though in the face of it we can but yield if we confine ourselves only to Biran's "letter to Tracy" (1804) that I just cited. Autoaffection is always first, and the "deadly sin" consists on the one hand in "*separating the affective element* from that which is not it," to take up Maine de Biran verbatim, and on the other hand in thinking that one can move from the non-affected to affection, while there would be neither the sensed nor affection without autoaffection.

For there is a fundamental distinction that Maine de Biran insists on maintaining against Condillac, which is the gap that it is necessary to preserve, or even to dig, between "experiencing" and "becoming." Condillac's error, at least if we confine ourselves to Biran's letter to Tracy, arises from his wanting to introduce temporality, and even mediation and progression (the modified sensations), whereas in reality the experience of the affection of oneself by oneself is atemporal, absolutely immediate, and totally given: "If there is no *me* in the first affection," inveighs Biran while addressing himself to Tracy, "how could there be in the second, or in the passage from the one to the other, or in the combination of several?" For in such a case—that is, the Condillacian hypothesis of a progression or a learning process by the statue to the point of saying "me" through touch—one would then really be obliged to say (wrongly), not that the sensing being "experiences" ("I do not say that it *experiences*") but that it "*becomes* successively or simultaneously."[35] The decisive word has here been stated. It is a matter of "experiencing" or of "autoexperiencing" oneself" but not of "becoming." What characterizes Biran, at least when he is reread within the framework of "radical phenomenology" is the absence of becoming and even of history and temporality for a subject to whom everything is *already given*, including himself to himself. The *pathos* of suffering and enjoyment does not become: it is the experience of myself in an Archi-Revelation of affect in which there remains, and can remain, only the very act of experiencing *oneself* or of experiencing *myself*.

It is thus rightly that Michel Henry, a direct heir of this Biranian "fact of the intimate sense," is classed among the philosophers of "givenness" and therefore figures prominently among the authors of the so-called "theological turn in French phenomenology"—whatever he might

35. Maine de Biran, *Correspondance philosophique: 1766–1804*, 361 (emphasis in original).

have said or thought about this besides. Affection is autoaffection or the givenness of oneself to oneself (even if also in another rather than by another in the case of an autoaffected trinity) whereby everything is given and delivered "at once." "Sensing oneself" is the essence of the sentiment by which I sense and feel all things: "This is what constitutes the essence of sentiment, the essence of affectivity as such," as I have already noted following *The Essence of Manifestation* (1963), directly derived from *Philosophy and Phenomenology of the Body* on Maine de Biran, written in 1943, that is, more than twenty years before being published (1965):

> Sensing oneself by oneself, in such a way that sentiment is not something which senses itself by itself, this or that sentiment, one at this time, at another that one, but precisely the fact of sensing oneself by oneself considered in itself in the effectiveness of its phenomenological realization, namely, in its reality.[36]

c) Lapidary Existence

The matter is therefore clear. Michel Henry, in the wake of Maine de Biran, seeks to "radicalize" Condillac's statue rather than to simply oppose it and to reascend to auto-impressed subjectivity rather than to deny as a whole the operation of reduction that the *Treatise on the Sensations* had, for its part, carried out perfectly (by abstracting away all the senses before reintroducing them one by one and in a combined fashion). Neither Henry nor Biran contest the legitimacy of the "statue" as if we were directly born to ourselves through our five senses. In that case, Biran and Condillac could not come together regarding touch alone—not even to say "I" (on the basis of the intramuscular tension of my hand that grasps nothing) and not to say "me" (on the basis of the impact of my hand against my chest). Maine de Biran criticizes not the suspension of the senses, any more than does Michel Henry, besides, but that everything goes in only one single direction: from the "outside" toward the "inside" (the hand that strikes the chest) and not from the "inside" toward the "outside" (the hand that feels itself without anything).

It remains that we will recall the "double reading" *in counter-relief* and no longer *in relief*, including of the statue of Condillac, that I have suggested (§5b). For here a third way is traced, outside Biran's and Henry's unilateral interpretation concerning the "marble statue."

---

36. Henry, *Essence of Manifestation*, 462–63. [Translation modified. –Trans.]

Indeed, not everything should be rejected in this inanimate statue in Condillac—even if it cannot (yet) say "me" and even if it will never say "I." For what is said about "modified sensation"—about the statue that becomes "rose-odor" to the point of saying "me" through touch—can, conversely, be read in the case of trauma: not gaining sensations but losing all one's sensations, not saying "I" or "me" but discovering myself "outside myself," as if I will never, or never again, be able to name myself, identify myself, or myself appear to myself—that is, being, properly speaking, "outside the phenomenon."

Indeed, in modified sensation, as I have insisted (§7), the soul is projected "from itself outside itself," as the author of the *Treatise on the Sensations* noted verbatim: "There you have then a sensation [touch] with which the soul proceeds *from itself to outside of itself*. . . . If the hand says 'me' it does not receive the same response in turn [from a solid body that resists it]. Thus the statue judges *its ways of being wholly outside itself*."[37] There really is a "pure outside" of oneself in sensation, which means that the statue does not recognize itself ("it is *only* rose-odor") and will say "me" (and not "I") only on the basis of an "outside itself." The double neutrality of a body that is modified solely in precisely that which happens to it (the sensation or the rose-odor that "befalls it") and that will never say "I" but only just "me" (in the accusative, less in recognition than in an outside that suddenly becomes inside) will therefore try to reach the *limit-situation* of the "outside-being-affected" that is neither autoaffected nor heteroaffected—downstream through suppressed sensations (trauma) rather than upstream through constituted sensations (sensualism). Outside myself, and hardly able to say *me* in the subject that is "offside": this is, according to Condillac, what we are "at the start" before any sensation (the marble statue), and this is, in my view, what we could become "in the end" outside any sensation in trauma (becoming again a marble statue or "like a stone"—as Charlotte Delbo poignantly describes it in *None of Us Will Return* regarding Auschwitz [§15]).

Below the "human" there lies the "animal." But below the "animal" is found the "bestial." And below the "bestial," the "mineral" always molders. There is something of the *lapidary* in man, as I have already noted elsewhere (*Nothing to It*)—in the etymological sense of that which becomes "stone" (*lapis*) and not only "cutting," such that the return to the "inorganic" (*Anorganisch*) or the "lifeless" (*Leblos*) professed

---

37. Condillac, *Treatise on the Sensations*, 233, 235 (emphasis added).

by Freud in *Beyond the Pleasure Principle* (1920) in the figure of the *id* does not fail to be readable, at least in counter-relief, in that stony marble statue in the process of becoming animate.[38] Whereas the statue progresses in the transformed sensations (*Treatise on the Sensations*), it regresses and is cut off from everything, including itself, in trauma (*The Extra-Phenomenal*, according to my own perspective). But in all cases, as in these two cases, a *lapidary existence* or *existence of stone* awaits us in our existence—whether in the progression of sensations (sensualism) or in their pure and simple suppression (trauma). Learning solely *through* experience (sensualism) presupposes that there is *non*-experience or even *an*-experience rather than *in*-experience: "The worst is not that something worse can still happen to me (an illness or a war, for example), but the worst is that nothing worse or better can arise, since my capacities to suffer or to make an event have been annihilated."[39]

§10. I am Rose-Odor

"*I am* rose-odor": this will then be Maine de Biran's phrase, counterbalancing but also twisting from the inside—like the "serpent in Genesis," as we could say by exaggerating a bit[40]—Condillac's exact expression: "*It will* therefore *be* rose-odor." Whereas the one (Condillac) posits the pure neutrality of an "it will be" (in the third person), the other (Biran) straightaway affirms the identity of an "I am" (in the first person) to draw from it an ego (in the nominative). Neither calling nor called—for here there is neither giving nor given but rather resisting and resisted—the transfer from "it will be" to "I am," as I have indicated (§5), will mark one of the major turning-points for saying today

---

38. Freud, "Beyond the Pleasure Principle," 38: "If we are to take it as a truth that knows no exception that everything living dies for *internal* reasons—*becomes anorganic once again* [*ins Anorganische zurückkehrt*]—then we shall be compelled to say that 'the aim of life is death' [*das Ziel alles Lebens ist der Tod*] and, looking backwards, that the '*lifeless*' [*das Leblose*] existed before the living" (emphasis in original). Cited and commented on in my work *Nothing to It*, 72–77. [Translation modified in accord with the modifications made by the translators of *Nothing to It*, 73. –Trans.]

39. See my article "Mémorandum," 124.

40. See Yahweh's word that is distorted or twisted by the serpent as soon as he first speaks when addressing Eve. Yahweh's initial word was "You *may surely eat of every tree* of the garden, but of the tree of the knowledge of good and evil you shall not eat, for in the day that you eat of it you shall surely die" (Gen 2:26–27). The taking up of this same word, according to an interdiction that the serpent generalized, was "Did God actually say, 'You *shall not eat of any tree* in the garden?'" (Gen 3:1).

in what our corporeality consists. It is, then, with the aid of a "distorted word" (I am rose-odor), with "nothing beneath the hand," to rejoin the "primitive fact" of effort (the purely internal muscular tension), that Biran corrects, or rather deploys in another sense, Condillac's statue. In the two cases, it is indeed a matter of constituting *subjectivity* ("me" in Condillac, "I" in Biran) *on the basis of corporeality* (the "solidity of the body" in Condillac, the "lived body" or flesh in Biran)—such that, well before Nietzsche, we can rely on this debate in order to exclaim later, with Nietzsche in one of the *Unpublished Fragments* (1882), "*Der Leib philosophiert!*"—"The body philosophizes!"[41]

a) The Distorted Word

Then there comes the text or, rather, the "text to text" debate, as we also speak of "skin to skin" in the proximity of the mother and her child at birth, so close are they and also so near to separating from each other. Biran's letter to Destutt de Tracy (April 30, 1804) then reaches its summit, its acme, as I have said, in the *Essai sur les fondements de la psychologie*—in two passages in which the thinker of Grateloup takes up and refutes the Condillacian interpretation of the statue that "becomes rose-odor" on the one hand[42] and that through touch ends by exclaiming, "It's me, it's me again!" on the other.[43]

"I am rose-odor"—and no longer "it will therefore be rose-odor"; this, then, is the erroneous fashion in which the *Essai sur les fondements de la psychologie* this time cites and comments on Condillac's *Treatise on the Sensations*, which we previously studied:

> Yet, so long as the statue *is* rose-odor and nothing more, it does not exist for itself; it has no point of foundation internal to the copula *I am*; for if there were, for the statue, a real foundation anterior to the expression of this fact "*I am rose-odor*," it would no more be identified with this modification than the individual who says of himself, "I am ailing, sad, well, or ill" identifies himself with such accidental modifications that he attributes to himself as circumstantial facts of his existence, associated with it but not identical to it.[44]

41. Nietzsche, *Unpublished Fragments*, 202 (5 [32]).
42. Maine de Biran, *Essai sur les fondements*, 14–28.
43. Maine de Biran, *Essai sur les fondements*, 381–97.
44. Maine de Biran, *Essai sur les fondements*, 16.

This first gives cause for surprise, as we should remember and reiterate (§5b), following Francine Markovitz-Pessel in her work *La Statue de Condillac* (2018):

> There are two statements that are not equivalent: *it is* rose-odor, *I am* a rose-odor. Can Condillac's statue say, in the first person, as Maine de Biran writes, *I am a rose-odor*? One can long seek this phrase in the *Treatise on the Sensations*.[45]

In short, if one wanted to find the phrase of Maine de Biran citing Condillac—"I am rose-odor"—one will never find it, not only because it is not there with regard to *form* but because it cannot be there with regard to *content*. Better, the movement is reversed, and that is why we are free to relate the Condillacian "soul outside itself" to the "outside-the-phenomenon" ("outside-the-subject" and "off*side*"), while waiting to find it anew, in Maine de Biran this time, in the exception to the "primitive fact of intimate sense" (sentiment or affect) and to the "primitive fact of effort" (the lived body). Whereas on the one hand (in Biran), the movement of the statue is only the movement of "appropriation" (in an "I am" rose-odor that is always already posited in advance, even if it is sensed and felt and not only thought), on the other hand (for Condillac) it seeks and attains "dispropriation" (in an "it will be" or "it becomes" rose-odor to be totally transformed, modified, by it, and it will even be able to identify itself with it). Where everything is *given*, including the ego to itself, even if through the lived body, it turns out that even this was in reality *acquired*, or rather learned, through an alterity that ceaselessly modified me.

Was Maine de Biran therefore dealing with chimeras? How can such a critique be effective if from the start the fundamental phrase of its egoity is false: "It will therefore be rose-odor" (Condillac), "I am rose-odor" (Maine de Biran)? We know that it is in misinterpretations that the greatest philosophies, as well as the renewing of thought, are forged. For it is only when one has no ideas that one contents oneself with commenting. Michel Henry knew this—assuming his own reading of Biran, justified at least in part, and which permitted him to make great advances. We will also be right to take up the defense of the "Biranian heresies" of Michel Henry and even to blend our two authors in a common "homodoxy" (or "school of thought")—the heresies will take nothing away from the authors' "reciprocal geniuses" (Devarieux).[46] Henry is, in the end, in good

---

45. Markovits-Pessel, *Statue de Condillac*, 20.
46. Devarieux, *L'Intériorité réciproque*, 9: "Michel Henry is a heretic in

company with Biran: distorting a thought (Biran with Condillac, but also Henry with Biran) is, in the end, demonstrating an authentic fidelity—a "creative" fidelity beyond "constancy," as Gabriel Marcel would say[47]—and not solely a "reproductive" one, as so many students practice it, often emulating their "professors" or "tutors," who, we also forget, should be their "masters."[48] In "heresy" there lies the right "orthodoxy," once the interpretation of a text is also historically documented. It is because it has forgotten this that philosophy sometimes ceases to think.

Why, then, and how, does the Biranian critique of Condillac's statue make sense—at least in this first moment when the marble statue begins to become animate and senses the rose-odor? It is because, and this is clearly indicated, it is necessary from the origin or, rather, from the beginning, to anchor oneself in the Archi-Revelation of a principle, to speak like Michel Henry, or to posit a "point of foundation internal to the copula *I am*," to say it with Maine de Biran.[49] Certainly, there is no "I am" but only an "it will be" in Condillac, and therefore to identity and subjectivity in the one (Biran), we will oppose alienation and objectivation in the other (Condillac). But once this is said, mentioned, and analyzed (§5b), it remains to give the floor to the thinker from Bergerac himself and to let him speak—so that his Condillacian critique can also do its work of novelty. Seeking an "internal foundation" outside all exteriority is not indeed very original in the eighteenth century, at least in the wake of Descartes, even if it is necessary to desubstantialize him, as I have shown (§3a). It remains that if interiority is this time "affectivity" and no longer thought (the feeling [*ressenti*] of the rose-odor), and

---

phenomenological territory. My thesis is that this heresy is Biranian, that Maine de Biran is the heresy of Michel Henry, that his reading of Biran *constitutes* the essence of his heresy, not only in Biranian territory but in the philosophical and, consequently, phenomenological territory, if not in 'theological territory.' *Hairesis* designated, for the pagans, not a false or pernicious doctrine, but a *school of thought*: it was to homodoxy and not to *orthodoxy* that heterodoxy was opposed. It was Christians who introduced the new sense into pagan territory" (emphasis in original).

47. See Marcel, *Creative Fidelity*, 153: "It seems important to me to distinguish carefully between constancy and fidelity. . . . It may at once be observed, however, that constancy, construed as immutability, is not the only element entering into fidelity. Fidelity implies another factor which is far more difficult to grasp and which I shall call *presence*. . . . Here reflection reveals at the core of fidelity *something novel* which dissipates the feeling of *staleness*, of *rancidity*, which threatens to overcome us whenever we focus our attention on a virtue, on the reliability of a certain value" (emphasis partly in original).

48. I refer here to the beautiful work Léna, *Honneur aux maîtres*.

49. Maine de Biran, *Essai sur les fondements*, 16.

although it is drawn from the "lived body" rather than the objectivated body (the primitive fact of felt effort in the hand independently of any object), there is here something that is more than "brand new." It is, on the contrary, "unseen" and "unheard of." Not only does it not suffice to christen Maine de Biran the "French Kant," but one could in addition elevate him to the rank of "French father of German phenomenology"—so long, that is, as French philosophy's effrontery in relating everything back to itself is still tolerated.

From the "sensation" of the rose-odor indeed (Condillac), we pass to the "sensing oneself" or to the experience that it produces for the statue (Maine de Biran). It is no longer experience as an "empirical learning process" (*experior*) or a "traversal of oneself" (*Erfahrung*) but experience as "inner lived experience" and also "intimate lived experience" (*Erlebnis*). It is no longer the "I am rose-odor" that interests Biran when he reads Condillac, even if while twisting him. It is rather the "I am ailing, sad, well, or ill" by which he brackets or even neutralizes the rose-odor, at least qua exteriority: "For if there were, for the statue, a real foundation anterior to the expression of this fact '*I am rose-odor*,' it would no more be identified with this modification than the individual who says of himself, '*I am ailing, sad, well, or ill.*'"[50]

"I am my (lived) body" and "I am my affect" (that is mine): this is Maine de Biran's path of subjective phenomenology, which Michel Henry certainly finds again, but so do Ricœur and Merleau-Ponty. "I am rose-odor" as "I am ailing" (or enjoying). Here is found the new absolute point of departure that must be posited, and we see to what extent Michel Henry in his entirety only drifts from it. The "I am" my affect, or even the "I am" my body, straightaway takes priority over the "I have" or "I undergo" an affect (from the outside), or even the "I have" a body" (including in its matter and its objectivity): "the primitive fact," to cite again the famous definition from a bit farther in this same text of the *Essai*, whose conceptuality I have already explained (§2b), "is not sensation all alone but the idea of the sensation that takes place only insofar as *the sensible impression concurs with* [*concourt avec*] *the personal individuality of the* myself."[51]

"Concurring with the *myself*"—this is the unique object or, rather, the aim of the sensible impression: a *myself* that is not "produced" but

---

50. Maine de Biran, *Essai sur les fondements*, 16 (emphasis in original).
51. Maine de Biran, *Essai sur les fondements*, 18 (emphasis added).

"concurred with" in the sense that the *sensible impression* (the sensed and the felt [*ressenti*]) and the *personal individuality of the* myself (egoity) participate together and at the same time in a single ordeal—like "horses" competing on [*concourant à*] a single course and set up on a single starting line.[52] Maine de Biran is a "philosopher of the given" and therefore a precursor of Michel Henry and of a considerable portion of French phenomenology—inasmuch as there is always a revealed that stood "already there," whether to constitute me in my "autoaffectivity" (Henry) or to overwhelm me in the vis-à-vis with alterity (Levinas) or to depose me in the figure of the *interloqué* (Marion). In each case, as in every case, there occurs, from the origin, a sort of "deneutralization of neutrality"—like, moreover, the "deneutralization" brought about by the face in Emmanuel Levinas relative to Maurice Blanchot's "pure night."[53] Yet there always also stands there, in Condillac's mineralized marble statue, though according to "another departure" which is that of the absence of oneself to oneself or of the "pure outside in oneself," a *lapidary existence* that perhaps still has something to teach us (§9)—such that the "outside-the-phenomenon," or even the "spread body," will not, in this case, be missed or obliterated only on the grounds that it supposedly does not belong to phenomenality.

Far from opposing Maine de Biran to Condillac, or a certain path of French phenomenology (of the given) to the one that I, for my part, am trying to trace with others (the *there is* in the early Levinas or the *irreducible* in Henri Maldiney), we will on the contrary find there two different ways of thinking, such that being "only rose-odor" [*que d'odeur de rose*] will indeed designate a certain form of (traumatic) reality, as well as recognizing that "I have a body" and not only that "I am my body" (in illness, for example). The impossibility of appropriating *myself*—in my body (spread body) as in my thought (the extra-phenomenal)—also causes to be reached a form of *minerality* that always lies in wait for me in traumatic existence (being "like a stone"), and Condillac's marble statue can also help think it, so long as we do not reduce an "it will therefore be" (rose-odor) to an "I am" (rose-odor). The exception of touch in the "it's me, it's me again!" (§7d) then responds to, and highlights in Condillac himself, the total identification of the statue with the mere "it will therefore be rose-odor" (§6). What sense can then be reattributed to "touch" and the "hand" in Maine de Biran this time, of

---

52. [*Concourir* can mean "to compete" or "to concur" in the sense of "coinciding" or "tending together toward the same end." –Trans.]

53. See Falque, *Hors phénomène*, 142–45.

whom we know how much he also draws on Aristotle to again give this sense priority? This is the site of the "birth of Biranian carnal subjectivity" or of the "I am," which we should now interrogate.

b) Nothing Beneath the Hand

"The hand can do anything because it is nothing."[54] This phrase from Jean-Louis Chrétien in *The Call and the Response* has served us as a spearhead (*fer de lance*) or, rather, a launching pad (*rampe de lancement*) for this debate between Condillac and Maine de Biran concerning the sense to give the "marble statue" that is animated from the outside (Condillac) or already animated from the inside (Biran). For it is indeed in Aristotle's *De anima*, as I have shown (§4), that the double analysis of "touch" and the "hand" takes root—the function and the limb acting in the statue that touches itself (or does not) to say "me" (or "I"). Touch is the "first of the senses" for the Stagirite, and Biran, like Condillac, remembers this, first because it is the most universal, since it belongs to all animals and is even the condition for being an animal: "It is evident that an animal cannot be without touch."[55] But it is "first" also because, as I have also emphasized, it alone is reflexive: "I cannot touch without immediately being touched by what I touch, before any reflection, by virtue of its own tangibility. That with which I come into contact comes into contact with me," points out Jean-Louis Chrétien, commenting on Aristotle.[56]

As for the "hand," and this is the second Aristotelian point also at work in the "statue"—touching "by the hand" that stumbles over the chest to say "me" (Condillac), or sensing muscular effort "in one's hand" to say "I" (Biran)—it is the "instrument of instruments," which, therefore, being capable of anything (the instrument as the "prolongation of the body" and therefore of the "hand," as I have said with Bergson), can do nothing: "The hand would seem to be not *one instrument*, but *many*; indeed it is, as it were, *an instrument for instruments*," as I have specified, this time relying on Aristotle's *Parts of Animals*. "For the hand becomes a talon, claw, horn, spear, sword, and any other weapon or instrument; it will be anything thanks to its ability to *grasp and hold anything*."[57]

54. Chrétien, *Call and the Response*, 95.
55. Aristotle, *De anima* 434b20.
56. Chrétien, *Call and the Response*, 85. [Translation modified. –Trans.]
57. Aristotle, *On the Parts of Animals* 687a–b (emphasis added). [Translation

And this is precisely Biran's originality compared to Condillac—for which it is here a question of recognizing his supremacy, or at least his phenomenological supremacy. Like the Heideggerian *Dasein*, a possibility that I have also indicated (§4c), the statue becomes, in the Biranian reading of Condillac, "handless"—or, rather, outside any hold that would be *present at* hand or *ready to* hand (*sous la main*).[58] Neither *Vorhandenheit* (present-at-hand) nor *Zuhandenheit* (ready-to-hand), the hand no longer has anything "before it" (*vorhanden*) or "for it" (*zuhanden*) in order to grasp things and grasp *itself*. There is no resistance on the outside—for it is only "in the end" that the "cast-iron cannonball" or the "solid" will always resist—but only a life on the inside. It is therefore with "nothing beneath the hand" (*rien sous la main*), and that is the least one can say, that the Biranian subject knows not only that he "has" a hand or hands (which would be the case for Heidegger with a *Dasein* open to the world) but that he "is" a hand or hands. The reduction is complete, radical, and universal. If there is an "effort" (which is not "external pressure," which for Biran tells us nothing about the ego), it can be felt *only* in the hand—that is, in the pressing part (the hand), and outside the pressed part (a body or the other hand). There is no longer any object outside myself (objectivity), but there is not even any longer a *myself* that gains access to itself through the resistance of its own body (touching-touched). There remains only a "touching itself" understood as "feeling itself from the inside"—hence the duality of "what do you sense?" in French as "sensing" [*sentir*] or "feeling" [*ressentir*]—otherwise called, by Maine de Biran, the "internal immediate apperception of the lived body": "The sense of effort is *wholly internal*," masterfully writes the thinker from Bergerac in the chapter of the second part of the *Essai sur les fondements de la psychologie* that so greatly impressed Michel Henry,

> and the type of resistance that the muscles oppose to the force that contracts them cannot in any way be objectivated or represented *outside*. The *pressure* is sensed *in the hand that presses* and *in the part that is pressed*; the *effort* is sensed *only in the hand*, and the resistance in the part in which it is applied. This mode

---

modified to follow the French translation that Falque cites. –Trans.]

58. [*Sous la main*, literally "beneath the hand," is Falque's preferred French translation of Heidegger's *Zuhandenheit*, rendered in English as "ready-to-hand." The phrase "nothing beneath the hand" should thus be understood both in its literal sense (the Biranian self says "I" before having anything in or beneath its hand) and in the sense of "nothing ready-to-hand" (the Biranian self says "I" before having anything ready-to-hand). –Trans.]

of resistance is no less sufficient, as we have seen, for completing the internal immediate apperception of the *lived body*.[59]

c) THE HYPERORGANIC

Everything is therefore first *internal* but also *intramuscular* for Maine de Biran. And if there is resistance, a point to which I will return (§15a), it is not external but is nevertheless organic—even physiological and medical, when one knows how attached Biran was to studies on paralysis, as I will show, having himself founded the Bergerac Medical Society (whose opening session was on February 15, 1807). And this is what here raises a question and must be subjected to questioning. For whatever one says about it, and whatever one thinks about it, in the supposed reduction of all the thought of the philosopher from Bergerac to the flesh or the "lived body"—"this *relation of flesh to the body is intelligible only starting from flesh and not starting from the body*" (Henry)[60]—there is something of the muscular, the organic, and even the *hyperorganic* in the sentiment of oneself: "If Michel Henry is right in his interpretation," as Bernard Baertschi rightly highlights in a footnote, "it is *false* to identify the *hyperorganic* with the *spiritual*, as numerous historians of Biranian thought have done; it would be necessary to give this term another sense; it would mean that it is a matter not of the *organic body* but of the *transcendental body*."[61]

Certainly, the hyperorganic is, in Maine de Biran, that which gives birth to subjectivity and defines the human soul: "It is true to say that the apperception of the *myself* is the only essential characteristic of the *hyperorganic force* that we call the soul" (which we understand here in the sense of "force of the *myself*" or "internal force").[62] Certainly, it is necessary to distinguish "animal contractility" and "human contractility." But that which precisely constitutes the human and its hyperorganic as a redoubling of the organ or the muscle of the hand that "senses itself" and "feels itself" by itself without an object is not only its (animal) passivity but its (voluntary) activity—whereby effort produces the "me"

---

59. Maine de Biran, *Essai sur les fondements*, 9:381 (emphasis added).

60. Henry, *Incarnation*, 136 (emphasis in original) (commenting on Maine de Biran).

61. Baertschi, *L'Ontologie de Maine de Biran*, 81n13 (emphasis added).

62. Maine de Biran, *Commentaires et marginalia: XVIIe siècle*, 30n: "It seems to me that it is true to say that the *apperception of the* myself is the only essential character of the *hyperorganic force* that we call the *soul*" (emphasis partly in original).

or the "I" in the return on oneself. It is because "I sense myself" and "feel myself" (sensation and affection) in my body, which is properly independent of any external object, but in a complete coincidence of soul and body—as with Descartes, who "thinks himself" and "thinks himself thinking" (reflexivity), but this time in a complete dualism of the thinking substance and the spread substance—that the "personal *myself*" is engendered. It is thus the *voluntary hyperorganic*, insofar as it becomes conscious of itself in its motility, that constitutes man (the spiritualist interpretation), and not exclusively its pure egoity as a form of passivity (the phenomenological interpretation): "In voluntary contractility," firmly mentions Biran in a late footnote, "it is necessary to recognize a *hyperorganic force*, the idea of which cannot come from outside but from the fact of consciousness. There is a *human duality*, an *active and free* force and a force *under the empire of necessity*."⁶³

There is no exception to the organic, let alone from the hyperorganic, at least in the view of Maine de Biran himself, and therefore no "flesh" without "body"; quite the contrary. I will return to this in the exceptional situation—with the paralyzed hand or an atrophied part of the body concerning which we will ask whether or not it is an obstacle to access to egoity (§15)—but it is clear that, for the thinker from Bergerac, it is always and also the "muscular" or, rather, the "voluntary, reflected-onto-itself intramuscular," otherwise named "hyperorganic," that I could lack for saying "me" or, better, for saying "I" if I did "not feel" it. As Anne Devarieux rightly emphasizes, and perhaps this is Michel Henry's "real" heresy: "Digging upstream of Biranian effort, from the *ego* to the *Before-the-ego*, Henry transforms an *active internal experience* into a *passive test* [*épreuve*] *of oneself.*"⁶⁴ In short, if there is certainly *pathos* in Maine de Biran, its belonging to a neutral life that precedes it does not go without saying. One will find no "archi-" or pure originary in Biranian thought, be it a matter of Archi-Life or Archi-Revelation, inasmuch as nothing is given outside the resistance that is first and that presupposes not only the "lived body" (the flesh as the pure lived experience of oneself by oneself—*Leib*) but also the organic (muscular and therefore belonging to the domain of the body—*Körper*).

---

63. Maine de Biran, *Dernière philosophie*, 373 (emphasis added).

64. I am here citing Anne Devarieux's initial article, which can be read as the original core of her vast enterprise of confronting Michel Henry and Maine de Biran in her work *L'Intériorité réciproque*: "Michel Henry and Maine de Biran," 130 (emphasis added).

d) The Three Bodies

Will it then be possible any longer to maintain the Henryan interpretation according to which there are "three bodies" in Maine de Biran or three types of knowledge of the same body on the basis of the "lived body" alone? Nothing is less certain. One would, however, have to take it for granted if one stuck to the central analysis of Maine de Biran that *Philosophy and Phenomenology of the Body* delivers:

> Consequently, it is not two bodies which we must distinguish but rather three. 1) *The originary being of the subjective body*, i.e. the absolute body revealed in the internal transcendental experience of movement. . . . 2) The *organic body* is the immediate and moving terminus of the absolute movement of the subjective body, or rather it is the ensemble of the termini over which movement has a hold. . . . 3) The *objective body* which is the object of an external perception and which can become the theme of scientific research.[65]

This division is indeed surprising, for it does seem that there is an an-organic before the hyperorganic, as there is an organic before the objective. If the second division is accurate (from the organic to the objective), the first is not (from the an-organic to the hyperorganic). There is nothing more surprising than this "originary body" before any body or this "lived body" that is not simply "flesh" (*Leib*), to say it with Husserl, but *archi-flesh* as an originary source point that is so affective or autoaffected that it loses all its organicity and its corporeality. As Bernard Baertschi rightly points out in *L'Ontologie de Maine de Biran*:

> There are not, for Maine de Biran, as [there are] for Michel Henry, three bodies but two: there is no distinction between the originary lived body and the resisting organic body, and this is why, each time the philosopher from Bergerac takes up the problem of the body in relation to the different types of knowing, he distinguishes only two possible approaches to the body, internal apperception and transcendental perception.[66]

---

65. Henry, *Philosophy and Phenomenology*, 129, 132 (emphasis added). [Translation modified. –Trans.] This insistence on the first type of body (the "subjective body") as the heart and the very invention of Maine de Biran is stated as early as the introduction (8): "The first and actually the only philosopher who, in the long history of human reflection, saw the necessity for originally determining our body as *a subjective body* is Maine de Biran" (emphasis in original).

66. Baerstchi, *L'Ontologie de Maine de Biran*, 88–89.

Michel Henry's "heresy" would thus arise from this distinction, even this separation, between the transcendental movement as the affection of oneself by oneself on the one hand (the originary being of the subjective body) and the organic and internal resistance of the body in the "primitive fact of effort" on the other (the muscular contraction of the hand without any grip). Yet, for Biran, as Baertschi highlights anew, "there is no distinction between movement and organic resistance: it is the *muscle in motion* that resists the voluntary determination; the *body* in motion is the resisting content."[67]

In other words, everything happens as if, for Michel Henry, the organic body (the second body) was not organic but spiritual or, rather, transcendental—hence the superposition of a "third body" (originary or absolute), the site of the Archi-Revelation or the pure *pathos*, as *The Essence of Manifestation* would say, that is totally absent from the notion of the "lived body" that was first forged, however, by Maine de Biran himself. Reducing or totally "bracketing" the resisting and hyperorganic content of the body, even in itself, the author of *Philosophy and Phenomenology of the Body* preserves only "sensed movement as it takes place, the sentiment of effort": "The phenomenological, i.e., *original, real, and absolute,* being of the body is thus a subjective being. The *absolute immanence of the body* is affirmed at the same time."[68] Everything happens as if I felt my (fleshly) body *without* my (organic) body. Or, better, everything happens as if there were already in Maine de Biran or, rather, first in Maine de Biran—since the whole of the project of *Incarnation* arises from him, as it were, such that the first book written on Biran (1948) always remains the source of the last, or nearly the last, book written on phenomenological, but this time also theological, incarnation (2000)—a "flesh without body," as I have shown elsewhere.[69]

Resisting such an interpretation by Michel Henry, since for me the "organic body" remains, if not first, at least essential in the notion of the "spread body" (between the extended body and the lived body), is not necessarily condemning Maine de Biran but reading him *otherwise*. If I have, as it were, "saved" the man-statue in Condillac, or at the very least shown that it cannot be interpreted through a Biranian lens alone, inasmuch as the sentiment, for the soul, of being projected "outside itself" in

67. Baerstchi, *L'Ontologie de Maine de Biran,* 89 (emphasis added).

68. Henry, *Philosophy and Phenomenology,* 58 (emphasis partly in original). [Translation modified. –Trans.]

69. See Falque, *Loving Struggle,* 143–73.

sensation could also be the sentiment of trauma (the outside-the-phenomenon), it is not in order to now, in return, condemn Biran. The trivial opposition between "sensualism" and "subjectivism," like that between "spiritualism" and "phenomenology," as I have said several times, makes us lose sight of what is proper to each one: an "outside" that is external to oneself in Condillac (the resistance of the body) and an "outside" that is internal to oneself in Biran (the effortless body, or the body "outside effort," in the limit-experience of sleep, sleepwalking, dreams, madness, drugs, etc.). Better, and including in Maine de Biran, it will be necessary to think and to posit an "outside" or a "foreign *outside* oneself" (exteriority) that would not be only the "foreign *to* oneself" (limit-experience or trauma), since as the hand also "stumbles" over itself, or over the world in the case of paralysis, and thus makes clear that it is indeed necessary that there also be a world or an external "resisting terminus" for there to be a sentiment of the *myself* and a sense of effort that, although restricted to myself, is not enclosed in myself.

If Maine de Biran is the inventor of the "lived body," as I have shown (§4a), nothing indicates that he is at the same time the inventor of the "absolute or originary body" understood as a transcendental body or as pure autoaffection, independently of any real organicity, or hyperorganicity, as Michel Henry seems to suggest. It is in the literal sense that we should also understand the "organic" in Maine de Biran, that is, as "that which takes place in the organs," in particular the "hand" in the act of sensing itself and feeling itself in itself. Perhaps in this regard more Nietzschean than Husserlian, as I will show via the "virtual force" that is deployed specifically in Maine de Biran (§16), the thinker from Bergerac, the president of the Bergerac Medical Society, will never leave "muscle" or "muscles," in which the "sentiment of the *myself*" and the "primitive fact of effort" feel themselves from the inside. For Maine de Biran at the very least, the idea of a "flesh without body" is as far removed from his thought as would be the idea of a soul separated from a body: "Even if the body is a subjective being," points out Bernard Baertschi regarding Maine de Biran, against the tide but accurately, "it is also an objective being, and this from the same point of view, within the primitive fact."[70]

---

70. Baertschi, *L'Ontologie de Maine de Biran*, 88.

e) ALL WITH ONE HAND

But we will not move too quickly, however, to condemn everything in the Henryan reading of Maine de Biran, which would be neither right nor convincing. For what the author of *Philosophy and Phenomenology of the Body* saw, and what no one has so well analyzed before him, including Merleau-Ponty, is that there is no need for a "touching-touched" to discover one's subjectivity. We certainly have been able twice already to be surprised by the virulent criticism of the chiasm of the touching-touched in *Incarnation* without, however, naming the one who is here directly aimed at (Merleau-Ponty): "*The flesh is not the result of the touching/touched chiasma and cannot be correctly described by it. The flesh comes before the chiasma* as the condition of the power-to-touch and thus of touching as such."[71] But it is now understood rather than rejected. For it is with one single hand, or *all with one hand*, that the lived body is given—independently of any "touching" (of the thing) and of any "touching-touched" (of oneself).

For Biran indeed or, rather, for Henry interpreting him accurately but according to a univocal aim, not only does the statue have "nothing beneath the hand" but also needs *only* "one hand." It is not "*doing* everything with one hand" but "*being* everything with one hand." For one hand, and not two, is enough for being. While the "touching-touched" indeed depends on two organs that touch each other first in an exteriority to then discover a certain form of interiority in Condillac (the hand and the chest) and in Merleau-Ponty (the left hand touching and the right hand touched), nothing remains here any longer—except the pure *epoché* of *one* hand that will here be said to be "autoaffected" or to be experiencing its own egoity. The hand (that touches or senses itself and feels itself) is no longer an exception compared to the eye that, for its part, cannot see itself, any more than the ear can hear itself. "All with one hand" (and not two) through a single "handy" move (since it is a question of a mode of being)—this is the in-itself of the autoaffected subject:

> However, this hand that successively wanders over the different parts and that becomes the unit of measurement of a sensible surface *does not palpate itself* any more than the eye sees itself, and yet it can be known *before* being employed as an instrument of measurement.[72]

---

71. Henry, *Incarnation*, 137 (emphasis added).
72. Maine de Biran, *Essai sur les fondements*, 382 (emphasis added).

It is therefore "without yet knowing its body as an object of representation and intuition, through the exercise of tactility," Biran radically concludes, that the subject gains access to the "primitive self"—exclusively through the "lived body" (*Leib*) and not the "objective body" (*Körper*). Whence the celebrated definition of the "primitive fact," most often mentioned, starting from this very passage from the *Essai*, as the existence or arising of the *myself*, this time on the basis of the "sentiment of the coexistence of one's own body" (Biran)—rather than in the impenetrability and solidity of the body (Condillac): "The *myself* cannot exist for itself without having the sentiment or the internal immediate apperception of the *coexistence of the body*: this indeed is the *primitive fact*."[73]

But what then happens, or what will happen, if the resistance to resistance—no longer only the contact between the chest and the hand (Condillac) or the hand with the other hand (Merleau-Ponty) but the hyperorganic as such, that is, the muscular capacity to auto-experience oneself—disappears in a "limit-experience"? Maine de Biran is a man of extremes—I have proclaimed this starting in the opening of the present essay, and we must not forget it: "Thinking does not depend on a *beautiful interiority* that would reunite the visible and the articulable," as I have mentioned, following Gilles Deleuze and referring to Michel Foucault as well as to Maurice Blanchot, "but occurs through the *intrusion of an outside* that eats into the interval and forces or dismembers the internal."[74] This exteriority or, rather, this *double foreignness*—the "foreignness outside myself" from a physiological point of view according to the hypothesis of an annihilated sense of effort (the paralyzed hand or the "spread body") and the "foreignness to myself" from a psychic point of view in a threatened "sentiment of the *myself*" (madness or the "extra-phenomenal")—will mean that these "limit-situations" come not to overthrow everything but to make visible "in counter-relief" a Biran that one might not have suspected.

Scarcely is the "primitive fact" defined as the "sentiment of the *myself*" on the basis of the "coexistence of the body" than Maine de Biran glimpses the *exception* to it, less as its negation than as the hidden face of a part of our humanity that we can no longer efface. There is first the subject "outside itself" that sinks into madness or that at the very least recognizes in itself an "organic unconscious" that is more determining

---

73. Maine de Biran, *Essai sur les fondements*, 382 (emphasis added).
74. Deleuze, *Foucault*, 87 (emphasis added). [Translation modified. –Trans.]

than any form of autoaffectivity (chapter 4) and then a foreign body "outside myself" or "foreign to myself" that means I will no longer have access to my body, as to my psyche (chapter 5): "Suppose that the hand on the whole surface of the body were *callous*, or that the external sensibility were *paralyzed*"; what would one then do to gain access to oneself once my own body becomes "foreign" to me? Thus questions the *Essai*, obliging us to continue. The "dead resistance" arises here that could make everything collapse, concerning which we will ask how far, physiologically (the spread body) and psychically (the extra-phenomenal), it can be taken:

> In the same state of *partial paralysis*, suppose that one hand were sensible, the other being sensible and mobile: the latter hand, placing itself on the former and not finding there the reply of sentiment, will perceive it first as a *foreign body* endowed with a *dead resistance*.[75]

---

75. Maine de Biran, *Essai sur les fondements*, 382–83 (emphasis partly in original).

4

A Counter-History of Madness

> But I know all the weakness of my means; I sense how disproportionate they are to the very goal of this essay. I *am leaving the port*; I am going *to sink into a subterranean sea*, but without hoping to touch its so-distant shores and to be able to cry out: *Italiam! Italiam!*
>
> MAINE DE BIRAN,
> *ESSAI SUR LES FONDEMENTS DE LA PSYCHOLOGIE*

Concrete Man in His Entirety

AFTER RESISTANCE (THE DOUBLE example of the hand and the statue), there now comes the descent into the depths (from madness to the alienated man). The reading that I have named a reading *in counter-relief* of Maine de Biran—as I also have a reading in counter-relief of the Condillacian statue by seeing in it a figure of trauma, or even of "lapidary existence" (§9c)—thus comes in full swing. It is not a matter of seeking something of the phenomenon, of the signified, or even of the autoaffected, but of questioning, following the thinker from Bergerac himself, and with him to accompany us, with regard to the "underpinnings" of man that it is indeed also a matter of probing. I have said that after the turn toward a certain form of "anthropological realism," starting in 1813 (*Rapports des sciences naturelles avec la psychologie*), there emerges little by little a discourse on limits or "alienation" (*Nouvelles considérations sur les rapports du physique et du moral de l'homme*, 1820). It is no longer the "primitive fact of the intimate sense" (phenomenal *myself*) or the "primitive fact of effort" (lived body) that takes priority but all that I cannot appropriate for myself and that I never will appropriate for myself. In the very work of the thinker from Bergerac, an extra-phenomenality from the psychic point of view (outside the phenomenon) and an extra-corporeality from the physical point of view (spread body) are produced or, rather, are deciphered, which cause everything that was once the rule, that is, the sentiment of the *myself* and the apperception of the lived body, to now become the exception. Or, rather, it is a matter, as one sinks into a "subterranean sea," of recognizing that there is also an "outside in man," this time in the sense of an "animality" that he cannot master, and that this, too, is part of his humanity.

If there is a counter-history of madness, as I will show through the distance from Michel Foucault's *History of Madness*, this is because Biran escapes, in a manner that is as exemplary as it is explicit, the inaccurate diagnostic on this point of a "great confinement" of the mad, or of madness in general, in the classical age to which Biran, however, belongs or on which he at the very least depends. Maine de Biran, certainly partly Cartesian in his return to a *cogitatio*, albeit in the mode of autoaffection rather than in the mode of reflection, is not Descartes. The "however, I have to consider that I am a man [and therefore not mad]" in the first *Meditation* will have no right to a place or, let us say, no right to preemption; I will return to this point. For "absurdity or madness" have just as much to teach us as "good sense or reason," even if this latter is "the best distributed thing in the world":[1] "Nothing is more instructive for the *waking man* than the *history of dreams*," masterfully specifies Biran in his speech at the Bergerac Medical Society on November 19, 1809, "just as nothing is more useful for the *reasonable man* than the *history of madness*."[2]

It is thus "the whole man" or, rather, "concrete man in his entirety" that we must envision. It is no longer a matter solely of what constitutes his humanity in the free act of a consciousness that gains access to itself (the spiritualist reading) or of the phenomenal *myself* and the lived body

---

1. Descartes, *Discourse on Method*, 1.
2. Maine de Biran, *Discours*, 105. This variant is in an appendix (appendix XV), 164: "Nothing is more instructive for the waking man than the history of dreams, just as nothing is more useful for the man enjoying reason and health than the knowledge of the history of madnesses and illnesses."

that would both have the particularity of autoaffecting themselves (the phenomenological reading) but of access to a humanity that this time will deny nothing of its animal, even bestial, underpinnings (the anthropological reading, if one takes this word *anthropology* in its etymological sense, that is, a "discourse" or "science of man" that is capable of embracing the whole of what we are). There will be no longer the psychic that raises up the physical or makes the physical ascend toward itself (spiritualism) nor the ontological that we must imperatively prefer to the ontic (phenomenology) but "meta-physics" as the "traversal of nature and of the human," as I have said (§1a), certainly to be transformed but never to be omitted or forgotten. Because philosophizing is also thinking, and because no one thinks or interprets an ancient text outside the culture or century in which he is placed—let us leave to the blind the lure of a *philosophia perennis* that has never existed—it is thus to psychiatric phenomenology that we must now refer.

There was the "backlash of theology on phenomenology" (*Crossing the Rubicon*), then the "backlash of psychoanalysis on phenomenology" (*Nothing to It*). Now comes the "backlash of spiritualism on phenomenology"; this time, however, deepening it in light of the advances of psychoanalysis (Freud), psychiatric phenomenology (Maldiney), and even of existential philosophy (Gabriel Marcel). A "true body" or a "carnal hermeneutics" that makes visible the "inverse paradox"—namely, as I have signaled in light of Paul Ricœur's *Oneself as Another*, "not what it means that a *body is my body*, that is, *flesh*, but that the *flesh* is also a *body among bodies*"[3] (§8a)—that is what we must now seek, so long as the "body" here signifies all thickness or all solidity (physical, certainly, but also psychic in a chaos that never stops invading me), as incompressible as it is irreducible: "Incarnation—the central given of metaphysic," noted Gabriel Marcel in his *Metaphysical Journal* on the date of November 10, 1928:

> Incarnation is the situation of a being who appears to himself as *bound to a body*. This given is *not transparent to itself*: opposition to the *cogito*. Of this body, I can neither say that it is me, nor that it is not me, nor that it is *for* me (object). The opposition of subject and object is found to be transcended from the start.[4]

---

3. Ricœur, *Oneself as Another*, 326 (emphasis added).
4. Marcel, *Being and Having*, 11–12 (emphasis partly in original).

For it is here a question not only of *phenomenology* but of *philosophy*—also in the sense of spiritualism, existentialism, and even quite simply of metaphysics. We must finally open or "reopen the valves," a thing Paul Ricœur practiced so well in his time—even though it is, in my view, a matter, in such an enterprise, less of *conciliating* than of *deciding*. We will certainly use the phenomenological method and will never abandon it. For interrogating our lived experiences—be they experiences of oneself (*Erlebnis*) or traversals of the world (*Erfahrung*)—is not confining ourselves to the infancy of philosophy but is philosophy's very essence. The false pretensions of a supposed return to some "realism," even if it is called "phenomenological," do not make sense, at least in my view. For saying that "the world exists independently of myself," while I "can nevertheless know it" (Wright, Romano . . .),[5] or affirming, following Aristotle in his *Metaphysics* (book Z), that "even if we had never seen the stars they would nonetheless, I take it, have been eternal substances beyond the ones we knew"[6] is certainly self-evident, and no one has ever denied it, including within the framework of phenomenology. The "reduction" (Husserl's *epoché*) brackets the world not to destroy or deny it (Descartes's doubt) but only to interrogate the "things themselves," that is, the world insofar as it concerns *me* or refers to *my subjective lived experiences* and not to the aforementioned "objective reality." The "resistance to the reduction" is not the "outside the reduction" but is what is opposed to it once it has been effected. The irreducible is not given in itself but is won against the reducible. This, rather than realism, is the veritable sense of the *res* insofar as it resists me.[7]

Interrogating the "outside in myself"—including in Maine de Biran and, contrary to the reading, this time purely phenomenological, "via the inside," that has always been carried out—is therefore not calling on the "outside" as such in the sense of a reality "outside myself" but that does not make sense (or even non-sense) for myself. Extra-phenomenality demands not any objective position of reality (old or new realism) but the irreducible of a "never-finished" reduction

---

5. See Romano, *Les Repères éblouissants*, 107: "What is realism? According to Crispin Wright's excellent definition, it is the 'fusion' of a modest thesis and a more presumptuous thesis: the modest thesis is that the world exists independently of our spirit. . . . the presumptuous thesis is that the world exists independently of us, but we can nevertheless know it" (the reference is to Wright, *Truth and Objectivity*, 1–2).

6. Aristotle, *Metaphysics* 1040b–1041a.

7. Concerning this debate, I refer to my contribution "Réalisme et phénoménologie."

(Merleau-Ponty). It is to the "brute," the "wild," and the "barbarous" that Maine de Biran is now going to lead us, as a thinker "at the edges of phenomenality," and not toward a supposed constituted "real" that certainly exists but that does not concern my existentiality. Anthropology refers to "man in his entirety," and not as a human science given alongside psychology, sociology, and many other sciences as well—in a *false* or at least *too exclusive* distinction between the ontic and the ontological. But it is indeed a matter, etymologically, of the "science of man" (anthropology), with all his contents and all his joints, which fully justifies the "Biranian" title of the work by François Azouvi.[8] In other words, it is an approach to "man in his entirety" that wishes to forget or efface nothing of his "below" in the descent into his animality, nor, however, of his "above" in his abandonment to divinity, to which I will return at the end of this work at the moment of concluding our traversal.

The project of founding a "philosophical society of anthropology" was thus born on the date of March 13, 1819, in Maine de Biran's *Journal*—as he also founded, more than ten years earlier, the Bergerac Medical Society (whose opening discourse was on February 15, 1807). Although the "philosophical society of anthropology" never saw the light of day, the program was launched, which refers here to the study of man in his entirety, or of "concrete man in his entirety," which, once again, is not far from according with the metaphysical project of Gabriel Marcel (*Essai de philosophie concrète* [*Essay in Concrete Philosophy*]) and of French spiritualism as a whole (from Lachelier to Bergson by way of Lagneau or Ravaisson): "Project for a philosophical society: division of tasks," notes the *Journal*.

> Instead of the abstract soul, since the society will take *concrete man in his entirety* as the object of its studies, we will have a division of anthropology that is exactly parallel to and corresponds to Bacon's division: 1) a science of man that studies the concrete phenomena of life and thought, that is, the facts of the soul and of the organic body, considered in their mutual

---

8. Azouvi, *Maine de Biran: La science de l'homme* [*Maine de Biran: The Science of Man*], 9: "The problem to which Maine de Biran devotes his whole work is the very problem that Barthez, Cabanis, or Dumas pose. The question of the *science of man* is the question by which he begins in philosophical reflections and the question with which his final works come to a halt. . . . But, contrary to them, Biran knows that the science of man will be accomplished only if one makes oneself capable of proposing, in place of the traditional juxtaposition of the disciplines, a real *theory of their connecting joint*" (emphasis added).

relations as an object that can fall under two experiences, one internal, the other external [*anthropology*]; 2) the science of the faculties grounded in the internal experience [that] constitutes psychology [*psychology*]; 3) the science of the object and use of man's faculties [*morality* and *philosophy*].[9]

§11. Maine de Biran's Psychiatric Phenomenology

Just as there was "Maine de Biran's spiritualism" (§1), "Maine de Biran's phenomenology" (§4), and "Maine de Biran's hermeneutics," there now comes "Maine de Biran's psychiatric phenomenology" (§11). Certainly, this is less commonplace and less well known regarding the thinker of Grateloup, and that is the least one can say. But reading Maine de Biran *in counter-relief* means going toward the extremes and touching the extremes—be it a matter of what he names the "physical" or the "moral" in man: that is, what I translate in terms of corporeality (the spread body) or psyche (the extra-phenomenal). It is now a question of drawing the deputy of Dordogne toward "limit-situations" or, rather, of discovering him in them, since he never left them. Karl Jaspers's program, set forth in his *Philosophical Autobiography* (1957), as a psychiatrist and philosopher, could just as well have been Maine de Biran's more than a century earlier as he was working on founding his philosophical society of anthropology: "It is first in *limit-situations* that man becomes conscious of his being. This is why, from my youth, I sought to *not hide the worst from myself.*"[10]

a) At the Confines

Maine de Biran is indeed first a man of the "confines" (*cum-finis*) [*confins*], understood here in the triple sense, in French, of the *extremity* or the reaching of the end by which we must also think (illness or madness, for example); of the *confinement* within the isolation of our intimacy (the "primitive *myself*") and of our corporeality (the "lived body"); and

---

9. J. II, 215 (entry dated March 13, 1819). This project of an "anthropology" is perfectly set in motion in the *Nouveaux essais d'anthropologie* (1823–24), in particular the "three divisions of the science of man" (*Dernière philosophie*, 25: "I will form *three divisions of the science of man*. . . . The first will comprise the phenomena of *animal life*. . . . The second division will encompass the facts related to the *life that is proper to man*. . . . The third division, the most important one of all . . . is, it is true, above the senses but is not foreign to the *spirit that knows God and itself* [*spiritual life*]" (emphasis added).

10. Jaspers, *Autobiographie philosophique*, 193 (emphasis added).

of the *proximity* of the disciplines or of their connection that means that we can no longer dissociate them (physiology and psychology, for example). This is an attitude that certainly does not fail to recall the attempt to think "at the edges of [*aux confins de*] phenomenality" or the attempt that requires "traversing the borders" between disciplines without only erecting "barriers."[11]

The "Mémoire sur les perceptions obscures" ["Treatise on Obscure Perceptions"] read by Maine de Biran on November 15, 1807, before the Bergerac Medical Society, of which he was both the founder and the president, testifies to this. Far from remaining enclosed within his own thought as well as far from remaining only within the purity of the "primitive fact" that, by dint of centering itself on autoaffectivity, forgets all our organicity, the philosopher, having made the trip from Grateloup to the dispensary of the pharmacist Gardet in the Bergerac city center (scarcely ten kilometers), there meets every one of the doctors, surgeons, and health officers from that "high society" who can teach him many things and let themselves be transformed. Immediately, he places himself *at the confines* or *at the limits* of the disciplines that also touch the limit. Not remaining within his domain, he wants to dialogue, to question, and above all to learn from the exception (illness or madness) what can contravene or modify his rule (the "sentiment of the *myself*" or the "lived body").

> Gentlemen, . . . the particular subject about which I propose to talk to you today is located, as it were, *at the confines* of the two sciences that embrace the whole of man; it belongs equally to *physiology*, which considers this mixed being as simply living and sensible, and to *psychology*, which considers him also as intelligent and thinking. I have chosen such a subject with the express intention of bringing to light the *points of contact* of our ideas, our works, and our views, as much as in order to *obtain from you*, gentlemen, the data that I lack, to enlighten myself by your experience, and to lean on your strength.[12]

11. Here I refer successively to two subtitles: that of *The Extra-Phenomenal* on the one hand (*Essay at the Edges of Phenomenality*) and that of *Crossing the Rubicon* on the other (*The Borderlands of Philosophy and Theology*).

12. Maine de Biran, *Discours*, 10–11 (emphasis added). The mention of "confines" both as a "meeting of the disciplines" (*Crossing the Rubicon*) and a "search for the limit" (*The Extra-Phenomenal*) is highlighted by Azouvi, *Maine de Biran*, 140, as well as by Rohrbach, "Maine de Biran," 476–77: "If the body of effort is indeed this *organic resistance* (that is, capable of being mobilized in a differentiated and coordinated manner), the *body of passivity is foreseen* [*pressenti*] *at the confines of the* myself; it has its own

b) At the Limit

Setting himself, therefore, "at the confines" of physiology and psychology as well as not wanting to stick only to the "spirit" to cross from it to the "organic"—hence the other project, albeit abortive this time, of a philosophical society of anthropology at the end of his life—Biran then interrogates the *limit* or, rather, the *limits*. As with "psychiatric phenomenology" today, from Binswanger through Henri Maldiney, he will examine "cases" (as has been done in our day for the "case" of Suzanne Urban) in order to renew and advance thought. Rather than reflecting only on the basis of the ordinary, we seek what departs from what is common (the extra-phenomenal) but not the extraordinary (the supra-phenomenal). For what matters is not what overwhelms us (but which we can still think) but what breaks or shakes (because that departs from the frameworks of our thought).

Maine de Biran's first notes (1794), found very late, after his death, in what is named his "old notebook," testify to this. It is even a matter of establishing not only a program of study but also a program for life: "I would like," hopes the thinker from Bergerac, perhaps also to treat himself, or at least to take care of himself, "for psychology joined to physiology to give us a theory about the different *illnesses of the spirit* and about their *remedies*, for *more of the physical* than we think enters into our moral state."[13]

It is indeed *of himself* that Biran is first speaking, to such an extent that there has rarely been forged such a unity between a man and his thought in the history of philosophy. He is not only overwhelmed (the supra-phenomenal) but *annihilated* by the fluctuation of his passions (the extra-phenomenal). The organic in him, that is, the famous movements of the "fibers of his brain"—Biran is a pioneer of neurobiology, as I will show, but cannot be reduced to that (§14b)—renders him *passive* and even radically and absolutely *only passive*. He witnesses the spectacle of himself, seeing images or ideas file past like so many phantoms or pictures projected by a sort of "magic lantern" (the ancestor of our projecting devices)—which comes to objectivate them without it being

---

climate, its mood; and one witnesses a sort of *refraction* of the passive and living body onto consciousness and its intrinsic activity" (emphasis added).

13. Maine de Biran, *Écrits de jeunesse*, 162 (emphasis added). The "side B" passage of the "old notebook" is not reproduced in its entirety in the edition of the *Journal* put together by Henri Gouhier (J. III, 20–25).

possible to recognize what has produced them or to know where they will end up going (what I have, for my part, named the "expansion of the psyche"):[14]

> Never, despite all my efforts and my prior resolutions, am I able to possess myself and maintain my composure: all the *fibers of my brain* are so mobile that they yield to the impression of objects without my being able to arrest their movement; dragged in various contrary directions, I am *only passive*; my reason *becomes null*; . . . when I come back into my study, if I want to occupy myself, what I have seen, what I have heard, presents itself to my imagination: so many *pictures* succeed each other and pass *before my eyes*, like those of the magic lantern, my capacity for attention is *destroyed*, and I remain for a long time without being able to apply myself to anything.[15]

Better, and this time appealing to his peers, Biran calls for such an experimenting *on oneself* concerning the "limit" to become also an experimenting *on* others and *by* others. One never speaks as well of something as when one has *oneself passed* [*passé*] through it—in the double sense of "suffering" [*pâtir*] and "crossing" [*passage*]. Experience, including in Biran, is not, in this sense, mere internal or autoaffected lived experience (*Erlebnis*) but is also what traverses me, even what befalls me (*Erfahrung*).[16] *Ex-per-ire* as the "traversal of oneself outside oneself," *Erfahrung* from *Gefahr* (danger)—it is not by remaining "closed" on oneself that one begins to think but by personally *being engulfed* [*s'abîmant*] (both as a "descent into the abyss" and an "attack on one's own integrity")[17] in a life, including an organic or at the very least physiological life, concerning which we know that it also makes us philosophers, or makes philosophy. *Der Leib philosophiert*, "it is the body that philosophizes," as I have already emphasized, following Nietzsche, in this regard the worthy successor of Maine de Biran:

> I would like for these profound *psychologists* who devote their time, their lives, to penetrating the phenomena of the

---

14. See *Hors phénomène*, 221–98.

15. J. III, 17 (entries dated 1794 or 1795, emphasis added).

16. On this distinction, see Gadamer, *Truth and Method*, 53–55 (for the first concept of experience), 56–61, 340–55 (for the second concept of experience). With my commentary in *Book of Experience*, 1–11.

17. [*S'abîmer* can mean "to sink" or "to be ruined" (or, literally, "to ruin oneself"). –Trans.]

human spirit, or those clever *physiologists* who seek to measure, to determine the diverse modes of sensibility—I would like, I say, for men such as Haller, Bonnet, Lecat, Malacarne, Barthez, Fontana, to also commit to *conducting on themselves experiments* rather like (albeit in a different genre) the one that Spalanzani had the courage to repeat, *at his own risk*, by *swallowing varied materials* to verify the manner in which digestion operated. I would like for these sagacious contemplators of themselves (for it is only *based on oneself* that one can judge in these matters) to make varied *attempts*, to subject themselves to different *dietary regimes*, . . . to sometimes be *excessive* in drinking and eating, sometimes *abstinent*, . . . to carefully *examine themselves* in the varied *states* in which these different dietary regimes would place the machine. . . . I believe that from *these experiments* there would result a few *lights* on subjects that are highly obscure unto this day.[18]

One does not know what to say, or even what to think. Could it be that our timid and sickly thinker of Grateloup demands going "to the margins," not solely to think "in the margins" (Derrida) but to go or to be "on the margins"—"marginal" [*marginal*], in short, as we would say in French, or *borderline* to refer to the word that is still more famous in English.[19] Let us be clear here, however. For the stakes are not first medical and experimental but rather philosophical and experiential. There is no question here of reaching a "limit" that would be only fleeting, like an illness or an indigestion from which one would indeed end up recovering. For it is now a matter not solely of the organic (the physical) but also of the psychic (the moral). And their unity, including with the world, is such that everything depends not on myself alone but also on this "environment" that also constitutes my life, even in the famous "primitive fact" of the sentiment of the *myself*. Thus the subprefect of Bergerac (1806), become deputy of Dordogne (1817), experienced and experimented with, for his whole life, and from the beginning of his life onward, these "illnesses of the spirit" and this moral state into which "more of the physical than we think" enters. That he was for himself and in himself *melancholic, hypochondriacal*, or even affected by what was called "black bile" no one can doubt. But he himself knows this and struggles his whole life long to think it. And this is what constitutes his originality.

18. J. III, 17–18 (entries dated 1794 or 1795, emphasis added).
19. [*Borderline* is in English in the original. –Trans.]

The *Journal* is packed with this "melancholy"—understood here not only as the "return toward oneself" or the "sweet sadness" that he also claims, in the manner of Dürer's *Melancholia* (1514), as a muse and creative inspiration,[20] but on the contrary as a "flight outside" or "outside oneself" in the impossibility of finding oneself or of "finding oneself again." In reality, everything, for Maine de Biran, if we put forth the hypothesis of a rereading of his *Journal* in the light of the Heideggerian existentials, flows from the "surrounding world" (*Umwelt*), from the "fundamental affective tonality" (*Grundstimmung*) by which I am determined in my everydayness (*Alltäglichkeit*).[21] Not, however, reducing affectivity to corporeality alone (by refusing both Condillac's sensualism and Cabanis's physiological reductionism), Maine de Biran will progressively forge for himself a sort of "climatology of the passions," according to which we depend, more than we think, on the rhythm of the seasons.

Everything, for the resident of Grateloup, indeed arises largely from the climate, the rain, the wind, the sky, nature, the seasons, and their contrasts. What is "little" (the "changing of the weather" deep in his Dordogne) becomes "everything" (the "outside" in this flight forward of occupations and diversions) but also the impossibility of mastering oneself and even of experiencing oneself "as oneself" in a veritable "sentiment of oneself." The striking entry dated May 30, 1817, in the *Journal* testifies to it thus, as a diagnosis of an incurable malady:

> From the 26 through the 30, rain and a cold east wind. Again this year we are going through the most beautiful of months without enjoying it; the sky is constantly foggy; nature is like a young, beautiful woman who is sad and in mourning. . . . These

20. A (positive) perspective on melancholy as that which, on the contrary, brings me back "to myself" is also present in Maine de Biran, which, however, makes us here depart from that sentiment of escaping oneself (also attested to through the word "melancholy" in Maine de Biran), which refers at the same time to the modern sense of "melancholy," in psychiatric phenomenology for example (Binswanger, Maldiney . . .). On this "positive" (and not only "negative") sense of melancholy, see Devarieux's accurate analysis, *Maine de Biran*, 396–99 ("La rêverie et la mélancolie de Biran"): "This amounts to saying that melancholy is an excursion *outside oneself*, but by which I am *not absolutely outside myself*" (emphasis added). This is supported by Maine de Biran's *Journal* (J. 1, 247–48, entry dated December 15, 1816): "The sentiment of the soul that I call sadness or melancholy differs essentially, *tota natura*, from the affection of malaise or the worry that is linked to a bad state of the nerves or to certain organic dispositions. The sentiment is as desirable as the affection is disagreeable."

21. This phenomenological perspective of a rereading of Maine de Biran's *Journal* in light of the Heideggerian existentials is suggested by Bégout, *Maine de Biran*, 3–37, esp. 20–25. See, in addition, Bégout, *Le Concept d'ambiance*.

contrasts are painful. One is grieved by the bad weather, and above all by the rain in this season, as by a calamity. I experience my *habitual melancholy* . . . it is *not a sweet sadness that brings me back to myself*; it is rather, on the contrary, a series of *disagreeable impressions* that make existence painful to me, are opposed to any regular and consistent exercise of my faculties, give me the sentiment of my *incapacity* and my *weakness*, and make me feel need to *disperse myself outwardly*, finding myself ill at ease at home [*chez moi*] or *with myself*.²²

The "limit of illness," be it a passing state (indigestion), a permanent or nearly permanent mode of being (melancholy), or an almost-definitive affection of the body (paralysis) or the spirit (madness) indeed has this particularity, in Maine de Biran's view, of marking less a difference in kind than a difference in degree between "what we are" (we, the beings said to be normal) and "what they are" (they, the beings designated as sick). For a long time indeed, for Maine de Biran, "patients" [*patients*], as they are called in French, have truly been *patient* ones [*patients*] who suffer [*pâtissent*] more than they expect: that is, those who "suffer" [*souffrent*] (*pathos*) like us all but who make it visible to such a degree that one cannot, or can no longer, reduce oneself to or satisfy oneself with thought alone. There is no longer a difference in kind between the "sick one" and the "healthy one," and it is for this reason, as I have said, following Biran, that "nothing is more instructive for the *waking man* than the history of dreams, just as nothing is more useful for the *man enjoying reason and health* than the knowledge of the *history of madnesses and illnesses*."²³

This time anticipating Canguilhem—decidedly, Biran was, unbeknownst to himself, the author of a great many anticipations (spiritualism, phenomenology, carnal hermeneutics, psychiatric phenomenology, and now epistemology)—there will, therefore, no longer be the "normal" on the one hand and the "pathological" on the other, the "sane person" on the one hand and the "madman" on the other, the "healthy" on the one hand and the "sick" on the other. Quite the contrary: the "sane person" will require the "insane person" in order to know himself, and the "healthy" man will require the "sick" man as another modality, for himself also, of existing. In short, and to say it with Georges Canguilhem in *The Normal and*

---

22. J. II, 46 (entry dated May 22–26, 1817, emphasis added). On this point, one should read Victor Emma-Adamah's highly instructive contribution "The Experience of Weakness and Power in Maine de Biran."

23. Maine de Biran, *Discours*, 105 (emphasis added).

the Pathological (1943): "There is no fact which is normal or pathological in itself. An anomaly or a mutation is not in itself pathological. These two express *other possible norms of life*."[24]

But it is above all in light of Michel Foucault that Maine de Biran proposes, as it were, a "counter-history of madness." Perhaps Biran indeed escapes, as I have foreshadowed, the accusation of the "great confinement" in the *History of Madness* (1972). "After defusing its violence, the Renaissance had liberated the voices of Madness. The age of reason, in a strange takeover, was then to reduce it to silence."[25] Here is a diagnosis and a "muzzling of madness" that certainly applies to Descartes inasmuch as "madness can no longer concern him"[26]—and this in spite of the lively opposition that Derrida addressed to his friend Foucault, and concerning which I think, for my part, that it is more a question of a problem of "corporeality" than of "rationality."[27] It remains that Biran cannot be accused either of this occultation of madness (for "unreason" is rich with teachings) nor of this loss of the thickness of corporeality (for there is no "flesh" without "body"). He will even totally escape this double reproach, since the extremes, or the limit, are in reality that on the basis of which he comes to think.

c) Outside Himself

Biran's writing indeed appears as the polar opposite precisely of Descartes's. Whereas the author of the first *Meditation* (1641) *excludes madness* from his reasoning or opens the door (or rather closes it) for the "great confinement"—"But such people are mad [the insane who steadfastly insist they are kings when they are utter paupers, or that they are arrayed in purple robes when they are naked, or that they are gourds, or that they are made of glass], and I would be no less mad, were I to take

24. Canguilhem, *Normal and the Pathological*, 144 (emphasis added). This is a Maine de Biran who is, moreover, cited and studied to a great extent by Georges Canguilhem himself, especially with regard to "anthropology" and not only "psychology," in his *Écrits d'histoire des sciences*, 771: "In Kant, and in Maine de Biran, psychology was situated in an anthropology, that is to say, despite the ambiguity, which is so fashionable today, of this term, in a philosophy."

25. Foucault, *History of Madness*, 44. [Translation modified. –Trans.]

26. Foucault, *History of Madness*, 46. [Translation modified. –Trans.]

27. See Derrida, "Cogito and the History of Madness." See also my viewpoint concerning this debate, which moves it from the question of "rationality" to that of "corporeality," in "The Discarnate Madman."

their behavior as an example for myself. I have, however, to consider that I am a man [and therefore not mad]"²⁸—Biran *reestablishes it* or, rather, *establishes it*, at the precise moment when he defines "the primitive fact of the intimate sense" (*Essai sur les fondements de la psychologie*), like Descartes on the verge of discovering the *cogito* (second *Meditation*). The most surprising thing is indeed that Descartes rejects what Biran accepts. Rather than excluding the hypothesis (of madness) with an outright dismissal—"I have to consider that I am a man"—the thinker from Bergerac claims it as exemplary, at least inasmuch as it enlightens us all, whether or not one is called "mad" or "insane":

> Without resorting to those extreme aberrations [mania, delirium, drunkenness, sleepwalking, sudden and vehement passions, such that the individual is "outside all knowledge" because he is "outside himself" and finds himself "excluded from the class of moral, intelligent beings" (*sic*)], it is a matter of experience that the more deeply affected we are, the less we perceive and know.²⁹

And this other state, opposed to the state of the "being" that is "conscious" (*conscium*) or "master of itself" (*compos sui*), is then, properly speaking, named the state of the "being that is outside itself," as I have insisted, powerfully and at length, in the opening of the present work in order to define this time "an outside" at the heart of interiority: "The first condition required for knowing is to be in that state called *conscium* or *compos sui*, in which one is *oneself*, or is *in oneself*, opposed to that other state that common language itself distinguishes very well with this phrase: *being outside* [beside] *oneself*."³⁰

Maine de Biran thus saw perfectly, in my view, in this famous passage, already studied, from the introduction to the *Essai sur les fondements de la psychologie* in which the "fact of the intimate sense" is determined (see §2 and §10), the "extra-phenomenal" or the total absence of this "intimate sense," of this "phenomenal *myself*," and even of this "lived body" in exceptional experiences that are capable of breaking

---

28. Descartes, *Meditations*, 60 (AT IX, 14). [Translation modified. –Trans.]

29. Maine de Biran, *Essai sur les fondements*, 17–18: "In the states of mania, delirium, drunkenness, sleepwalking, as in sudden and vehement passions, the individual, *outside all knowledge* because he is indeed *outside himself*, finds himself excluded from the class of moral, intelligent beings; thus human laws no longer reach him. But, without resorting to these extreme aberrations, it is a matter of experience that the more deeply we are affected, the less we perceive and know" (emphasis added).

30. Maine de Biran, *Essai sur les fondements*, 17 (emphasis in original). [On the French expression *être hors de soi*, see note 4 in the opening. –Trans.]

both the phenomenalizing subject and the phenomenalized horizon. What the common language says in French, "common" understood here as what is almost ordinary today—saying of someone, to take up Maine de Biran's examples, that he is "outside himself" when he becomes angry (sudden and vehement passion), when he has drunk too much (drunkenness), or when he talks absurdly (delirium)—is precisely what I, for my part, am looking for, not to oppose it to autoaffection ("the primitive fact of the intimate sense" and the "primitive fact of effort") but to not forget this other regime or this other state that I here name "outside affection" or "outside the phenomenon" (being outside oneself to the point of becoming "foreign to oneself").

Certainly, and Biran mentions this perfectly in the previously cited text, "it is a matter of experience that the more deeply we are affected, the less we perceive and know." But affected does not mean autoaffected; quite the contrary. For it is indeed, in the cases of madness, drunkenness, delirium, and mania, but also of sleep, sleepwalking, dreaming, and paralysis—so many cases precisely studied in multiple manuscripts by the thinker of Grateloup that have been found again—a matter of being heteroaffected, as if the *oneself* (*auto*) were "as another" (*hetero*), no longer in the sense of recognition (Ricœur) but in the sense of the most complete ignorance (my perspective). "The more we are affected, the less we know" because the less we know ourselves—being distanced from the "primitive fact of the intimate sense" (the phenomenal *myself*) or the "primitive fact of effort" (lived body) with a force equal to the life, thought, and writing that were necessary to say it and discover it. Not only does one "know less" through such an affection that overwhelms us from the inside as if it came from the outside (one would then call it a "saturated phenomenon," in a difference of degree), but one "no longer knows" and even "no longer knows at all" (which leads, then, to what I name the "extra-phenomenal," in a difference in kind). "Whence we can validly infer," concludes Biran, in a logical consequence given these "extreme aberrations" that are "mania," "delirium," "drunkenness," "sleepwalking," or "sudden and vehement passions" cited here, "that there is *no knowledge of any sort* for a purely sensitive being, such as a number of animals probably are," and even "the fetus within his mother or immediately after birth, etc."[31]

---

31. Maine de Biran, *Essai sur les fondements*, 18 (emphasis added).

d) The Problem of Passivity

The animal, according to Biran, suffers by a difference in kind, and not only in degree, from man, inasmuch as a gulf emerges between the *free and active sensibility* (the feeling of the hand in which the lived body experiences itself giving birth at the same time to the primitive self) and the *passive sensibility that is subject to necessity*. The *active* and/or the *passive*: this is what determines the dichotomy of the readings of the thinker from Bergerac—whether on the side of interiority (the activity of the "flesh" or the internal hyperorganic resistance) or on the side of exteriority, or at the very least of what I am subjected to rather than acting (the passivity of the "body" of the purely instinctive and animal life). *Active impressions* and *passive impressions* do not go together; hence the "problem of passivity": "When I experience pain or a pleasant sensation in some internal part of the body, or in general a sentiment of well-being or malaise, when I am hot or cold, when an agreeable or disagreeable odor follows me," already notes Maine de Biran as early as the introduction to *The Influence of Habit on the Faculty of Thinking*, "I say that I sense, that I am modified in a certain way; it is evident to me that I exercise *no power* on my modification, that I have *no available means* to interrupt or change it; I say, therefore, once more that I am or that I sense myself to be in a *passive state*.... But this purely internal game is executed *in me without me*."[32]

"A game that is executed in me without me"—such is extra-phenomenality or the pure outside of a subject that is "off*side*," which is certainly still experienced if it is endurable ("pleasant sensation" or "sentiment of well-being or malaise"), but outside any affection when it breaks the capacity to experience (sleep, paralysis, or delirium, as I will show). *Activity* and *passivity* do not intersect in Biran; they designate two totally different and incommunicable states—without, nevertheless, falling into an apologia for passivity and the purely organic, which the philosopher and doctor Georges Cabanis, a revolutionary and contemporary of Biran, did indeed profess:[33] "I sense that I am *nothing*; my activity is *null*," confides

---

32. Maine de Biran, *Influence of Habit*, 54–55 (emphasis added). [Translation modified. –Trans.]

33. See Cabanis, *Rapport du physique et du moral de l'homme*, to which Maine de Biran responds in his *Nouvelles considérations sur les rapports du physique et du moral de l'homme*, 1–83. One should note that Georges Cabanis is in this sense the inventor and the promoter of the aforementioned "science of man" or "anthropology," even though he essentially reduces it to the "knowledge of *physical human nature*" alone. See Voutsinas, "Maine de Biran," 70–71: "In place of 'psychology,' Cabanis uses the term

the thinker from Bergerac on the date of May 27, 1794, one of the first notes in his hand in his old notebook that was found late; "I am *absolutely passive* in my sentiments; I am almost always what I do not want to be, and almost never what I aspire to be."[34]

We will therefore not conflate here the "passivity" of autoaffection that we have hitherto encountered (the phenomenal self and the lived body) and the passivity of heteroaffection, or even of outside-affection when the affection is extreme (outside oneself to the point of no longer feeling oneself or escaping the "sentiment of the *myself*"). In the one case, everything is "interiority"—of which I have "had my fill," as I have affirmed, without turning back, from the opening of the present essay, to the point of "no longer being able to swallow anything" (p. xxiii)—in the other case, everything is "exteriority," certainly in the foreign outside myself when something comes to resist me (the cast-iron cannonball, as we have seen, or the paralyzed hand or hands, as I will show), but also and above all in the foreign *to* me in the case in which I become other or "alienated" (*alienus*) for myself and to myself. As Pierre Montebello highlights with considerable accuracy:

> No one more than Maine de Biran has had to such an extent the sentiment that our conscious life cannot totally shelter itself from the backwash of animal life, from those subterranean and impersonal affects that traverse the animal body. . . . He is the first to describe the ordeal of a *powerlessness to be* and *to exist* that comes to us from the affective whirlwinds of animal life.[35]

§12. The Outside

a) Of the Outside

One then understands why this type of "passivity" (purely animal)—stated as a "problem," a "contradiction," even a "critique" of Maine de Biran—should then be eliminated as null and void by Michel Henry in his work *Philosophy and Phenomenology of the Body* in his last chapter: "A Critique of the Thought of Maine de Biran: The Problem of

---

anthropology, which he imports from Germany by translating it as 'science of man,' a vast ensemble resting on 'the knowledge of physical human nature.'"

34. J. III, 5 ("old notebook," May 27, 1794, emphasis added).
35. Montebello, "Maine de Biran," 567 (emphasis added).

Passivity."³⁶ For with this passivity—certainly covering the melancholic affections produced in me from the outside and even my own paralysis (§15) but also that form of alienation that dreams, madness, and drugs can produce for me and in me, a point to which I will return (§17)—it is no longer only a question of the "phenomenal *myself*" (phenomenology or, in Biran's terms, psychology) but of the "real *myself*" (philosophy or anthropology), no longer of the "lived or proper body" (flesh) but of the "improper or non-appropriable body" (spread body).

This in reality results from man's "mixed nature"—it is no longer only a matter of unity, homogeneity, and autoaffection but, on the contrary, of plurality, heterogeneity, heteroaffection, and even of outside-affection—in short, of the "outside *in* me," as the opening of the present essay stated. There is certainly something of Nietzsche if one reads Maine de Biran well, according to Gilbert Romeyer-Dherbey, inasmuch as, far from reducing concrete man to the "immediate givens of his consciousness," like a Bergson, for example, the thinker of Grateloup denounces, for his part also and certainly in other words, the illusions of the "*myself* of consciousness" (*Ich*) alone, if it is not counterbalanced by the "great self of the body" (*Selbst*).³⁷ But there is also something of Deleuze in Biran or, rather, something of Biran in Deleuze in the famous last text that Deleuze published in September 1995 (in the journal *Philosophie*) before killing himself on November 4, 1995, "Immanence: A Life":

---

36. Henry, *Philosophy and Phenomenology*, 154–82.

37. Romeyer-Dherbey, *Maine de Biran*, 89: "This theory of the organic unconscious, which we can rapidly evoke here, shows us at least that *Biran would be in perfect agreement with the Nietzschean analysis* that denounces the *possible illusions of the immediate givens of consciousness*. For Nietzsche, a content of consciousness sometimes signifies something wholly other than that for which it is given to the subject that experiences it" (emphasis added). Let this be the occasion to insist here on the originality of this work and its author in his approach to Maine de Biran—via "Deleuzian immanence" (the plane of immanence) rather than "Henryan immanence" (the immanence of the subject as autoaffection). It is an introduction to Maine de Biran on which Ricœur relies in *Oneself as Another*, 321n26: "G. Romeyer-Dherbey, in *Maine de Biran ou le Penseur de l'immanence radicale* (Paris: Seghers, 1974), presents a synthetic view of the revolution in thought made by Maine de Biran." Things are wholly otherwise with Henry, who for his part referred, just after the war (*Philosophy and Phenomenology of the Body*, the writing of which was finished in 1948), to the *Œuvres choisies de Maine de Biran* by Henri Gouhier, relying on texts oriented solely toward a "psychology" of Cartesian appearance—especially the *Essai sur les fondements de la psychologie*—and not at all toward "anthropology" (except for the "life of the spirit"). As for the opposition between the "*myself* of consciousness" and the "self of the body" in Nietzsche, see *Thus Spoke Zarathustra*, 22–24.

Did Maine de Biran not go through something similar in his "last philosophy" (the one he was too tired to bring to fruition) when he discovered, beneath the transcendence of effort, an absolute immanent life? The transcendental field is defined by a plane of immanence, and the plane of immanence by a life.[38]

But there is also—and here we are going from one surprise to another—something of Bataille in Biran, that is, something of the radically "foreign" or the "heterogeneous elements" that are impossible to assimilate and homogenize: "the reality of *heterogeneous* elements," writes Bataille—but one would think one was reading Biran, at least when the exception (the "outside" or the "outside oneself" in oneself) confirms the rule (the "inside" or the "pure sentiment of oneself")—"is not of the same order as that of *homogeneous* elements. *Homogeneous* reality presents itself with the abstract and neutral aspect of strictly defined and identified objects (basically, it is the specific reality of solid objects). *Heterogeneous* reality is that of a force or shock.... It is identical to the structure of the *unconscious*."[39]

b) The Heterogeneous

Yet the "heterogeneous"—the word but also the concept—is also exactly what traverses Maine de Biran's whole oeuvre, and this as early as the *Essai sur les fondements de la psychologie*; it is what Michel Henry, precisely because he did see it, rejects as foolish in the last chapter of his *Philosophy and Phenomenology of the Body*: "To the extent that man is twofold, that his nature is a 'mixed nature,'" emphasizes the phenomenologist, but while regretting it and accusing Biran of a post-Cartesian "dualism," "the science of man cannot be completely identified with a transcendental phenomenology, because there is need to make place, alongside it, for a 'mixed psychology' which no longer moves in the sphere of pure subjectivity, but 'admits the mixture and the complexity of *heterogeneous elements*.'"[40]

Instead of accusing or regretting the "heterogeneous" or the "science of the mixed," it is on the contrary a matter, in my view, of praising it, of recognizing in it the ontological thickness of "concrete man in his

---

38. Deleuze, *Pure Immanence*, 28.
39. Bataille, *Visions of Excess*, 143 (emphasis in original).
40. Henry, *Philosophy and Phenomenology*, 156 (emphasis added).

entirety" and of not too immediately making uniform the whole of Biranian thought in a pure phenomenology become totally indifferent to its "anthropological" orientation. Here also, and necessarily, is produced what I have named the backlash of spiritualism on phenomenology, if one understands by "spiritualism" not the "soul" or the "spirit" opposed to the "body" but the "unity of the soul and the body" also stretched toward an elsewhere (§1c). It is thus in an intentional, formal, and even disciplinary way that Biran makes the "heterogeneous" the matter of another, absolutely new science named, no longer "pure psychology" but "mixed psychology," no longer the "science of the spirit and the *myself*" but the "moral and physical science of man," later called "anthropology."

Better, this science said to be "of the mixed" that is based on the heterogeneous (sleep, madness, sleepwalking, but also mania, drunkenness, delirium . . .) certainly loses in certainty but gains in concreteness through a positive and recognized obscurity, whereas the science of the "pure," which sticks to the homogeneous, certainly possesses an absolute certainty (the sentiment of the *myself*) but at the same time aims only at the pure transparency of a being stuck to itself: "I add that, as there is a *pure mathematical science* and one that is *mixed*," Biran masterfully indicates in the *Essai sur les fondements de la psychologie* at the moment of defining, in the introduction, the "criterion of truth in psychology,"

> of which the former [pure mathematics] enjoys a degree of certainty or patency relative to the simplicity of its object, . . . and of which the second [mixed mathematics] admits diverse *heterogeneous elements* and loses in certainty what it gains in a sort of clarity relative to the sensible phenomena to which it applies, so too is there a *pure psychology*, that is, the science of the spirit or of the *myself*, of that which is proper to and inherent in it, and a *mixed psychology*, that is, the moral and physical science of man.[41]

And Biran insists, for those who might not have seen that the "portion of the obscure" already lay within him from the beginning:

> *Pure psychology* is that of which I have spoken expressly under the name of science of the faculties, considered in themselves as primitive facts that carry with them all the activity inherent in the *myself*. . . . *Mixed psychology* admits *the mixture and the complication of heterogeneous elements*. . . . This mixed psychology, which offers more attractions to curiosity, more food for

---

41. Maine de Biran, *Essai sur les fondements*, 81 (emphasis partly in original).

the imagination, is nonetheless the more uncertain one, the more obscure one.[42]

c) The Obscure

That it is necessary to acknowledge the portion of, and "claim our portion" of, "obscurity" in us: this is Biran's great originality, supposing that he is read "in counter-relief," and no longer "in relief," and that he makes us exit from a notorious "overhanging transcendence" from which a certain form of contemporary phenomenology might still suffer. One can now better understand the interpretation of Maine de Biran that Maurice Merleau-Ponty delivers in that famous course published as *The Incarnate Subject: Malebranche, Biran, and Bergson on the Union of Body and Soul*—the lessons on Biran, as I have said (p. 18), were given in the department of letters of Lyon and at the École Normale Supérieure de Paris in 1948 (the date when Biran was for the first time featured on the program of the *agrégation*), and they orient, in my view, the whole of his thought that was to come. Although it is only sketched out, the thesis is clear, and the thesis is there, in counter-relief, giving a prominent place to (at least preliminary) "obscurity" and (essential) "facticity"—even though, for Merleau-Ponty here, both remain oriented toward phenomenalization. It is the "fact" and not the "consciousness" that matters in what the thinker from Bergerac names a "fact of consciousness," thus drawing the whole of Biranian thought toward that "science of man" or that "real" that "resists the reduction" or "makes a complete reduction impossible," as I have repeatedly emphasized:

> It is this notion [of "fact"], and not immediately consciousness, that Biran takes for his point of departure. Consciousness is an "existence For Itself" (a notion that Biran rediscovers free from any Hegelian influence). Biran does not begin with a being which exhausts itself in the consciousness that it has of itself, but with a being which is *in the process of becoming conscious that it exists, struggling for this consciousness against a pre-existing opaqueness*, with a being which seeks to "become self." . . . It

---

42. Maine de Biran, *Essai sur les fondements*, 81 (emphasis added). For the whole of the "science of the mixed," see the accurate exposition by Azouvi, *Maine de Biran*, 139–206 (on the double life—*homo duplex*—and the heterogeneous, see esp. 139–43).

[the word "fact"] denotes *essential "facticity"* of consciousness, a synthesis of interiority and exteriority.[43]

There is, then, *one* of the most exemplary phrases of Maine de Biran himself, drawn from the *Mémoire sur la décomposition de la pensée*, that, as it were, turns away from Michel Henry's Biranian interpretation to show an interpretation that could be Merleau-Ponty's—and also mine, though more radicalized inasmuch as it is not always certain that we can expect and hope for phenomenality in the *extra-phenomenal*: "By marking out the contours of the *shadow*, let us prepare ourselves to distinguish the point where the *light* begins."[44] This "portion of shadow" whose "contours" it is a matter of tracing or of "circling around," as with the "troumatism" of the extra-phenomenal into which we could sink by "descending" too much "into the hole,"[45] certainly refers, then, according to Biran, to *instinct* but also to a form of "blind power," which has earned him, for numerous commentators (Gouhier, Henry, Romeyer-Dherbey), the title of the inventor of the "organic unconscious."

d) Out of Area

Could Maine de Biran then have anticipated Freud—after having inspired, or been the source for, Henry, Merleau-Ponty, Ricœur, Deleuze, Tournier, Bataille, Maldiney, and even Canguilhem, as I have shown? Better, could Freud himself have encountered Maine de Biran's work here and there or, at the very least, have scented his importance, since we might have, besides, "the proof that S. Freud had read Maine de Biran's *Considérations sur le sommeil et sur les songes* [*Considerations on Sleep and Dreams*]"? The hypothesis has sometimes been advanced, to the point of elevating the thinker from Bergerac to the title of "founder of

---

43. Merleau-Ponty, *Incarnate Subject*, 67 (emphasis added).

44. Maine de Biran, *Mémoire sur la décomposition*, 382 (emphasis in original).

45. See Falque, *Hors phénomène*, 334–35 (the word "troumatism" to state the "troumatism" is here from Lacan—the seminar of February 19, 1974). [See note 22 in the opening. –Trans.]

French psychology,"[46] or even "founder of psychoanalysis."[47] It remains that it is probably saying *too much* and *too little* to thus bring Biranian "passivity" back to the Freudian "unconscious." It is "too much" in that, including in Biran, the "little perceptions" or "obscure perceptions," to which I will return (§15b) remain essentially of the order of the physical and not of the psychic; and it is "too little" in that it indeed properly belongs to Freud to have always maintained, as a psychiatric doctor, that there was a possible and necessary "organic underpinning" of the psychic unconscious (contrary to his followers) and that in this way he therefore remains Biranian or is fully in line with Maine de Biran.

"But I know all the weakness of my means," confesses the subprefect of Bergerac with such great profundity in his *Essai sur les fondements de la psychologie* at the moment of completing the summary and the outline of the work to enter into the heart of the matter; "I sense how disproportionate they are to the very goal of this essay. I *am leaving the port*; I am going *to sink into a subterranean sea,* but without hoping to touch its so-distant shores and to be able to cry out: *Italiam! Italiam!*"[48] Recognizing that he will never touch land and will therefore sink ever deeper into a "subterranean sea," Biran is not that conquering Napoleon that he knows, associates with, and admires—albeit with moderation. *Italiam! Italiam!*—that suits the emperor who contemplates from the Col de Tende the Piedmont plains that are to be vanquished and invaded. But in Bergerac, and even in Paris, Maine de Biran embarks on new conquests that are the philosophical, and not solely political, conquests of interiority (the primitive *myself*) but also of the outside in oneself (passive affections). The side, this side, that is very accurately said to be "out of area" by Henri Gouhier at

---

46. See Voutsinas, "Maine de Biran," 88n E: "We have the proof that S. Freud had encountered the *Considérations sur le sommeil et sur les songes* in which Maine de Biran says: 'Nothing is more instructive for the waking man than the history of dreams.'" But unfortunately no argument is developed either in the text or in the footnote to support this explicit connection between Freud and Maine de Biran.

47. Lemay, "Maine de Biran, fondateur de la psychanalyse," 362, quoted in Romeyer-Dherbey, *Maine de Biran,* 79n4: "One will recognize the first notions of psychoanalysis [in the theory of passive affections in Maine de Biran]." This is cited, to be rejected as too quick an identification, by Romeyer-Dherbey, *Maine de Biran,* 79n4: "This hypothesis of an *unconscious with an organic source* is *radically distinct* from the Freudian conception of an unconscious psychism.... That there is in Biran one of the first conceptions of what will be named the unconscious seems to me beyond doubt, but affirming the existence of an unconscious is not *ipso facto* subscribing to the interior of Freudian psychoanalysis" (emphasis added).

48. Maine de Biran, *Essai sur les fondements,* 109 (emphasis added).

the threshold of his anthology on Maine de Biran (1942) cannot be forgotten—at the risk, conversely, of melting only into the subjectivity that, however, escapes it, or of being engulfed in an autoaffection that is not only heteroaffection but "outside-affection" (or "extra-phenomenality"): "What we call 'unconscious' is here a notion that is perfectly defined: it corresponds to a purely passive psychic life that is *outside the area* in which there is this *I* that is sensed in effort."[49]

§13. The Organic Unconscious

a) A Foreign Cause

Anyone who says "organic unconscious" or, rather, non-conscious, also rooted in drives, must then refer to a sort of resistance that is "outside causes" or, rather, is a (psychic) "foreign cause" and to a force of "drives" or "instincts" that can never leave us and that, from the origin or "from the first age of human life," is already in us as if inserted or rather incarnate. As I have said (§11d), what distinguishes Biran's anthropology from Cabanis's is that his "science of man" is not grounded solely in the "physical" but also seeks to connect it with the "moral," although there is never any moral (including in the primitive *myself*) that is disconnected from the physical—even if one does have the faculty of grasping oneself as a lived body independently of any object taken in hand or in the hand (the purely internal intramuscular effort). The unconscious will in this sense be "organic" in that it stumbles over a foreign cause (unconscious or non-conscious) and refers to a blind power of an (organic) instinctual sort.

The same applies to "causality" as to "resistance" and "force" understood as "ef-fort," as I will show (§16). Biran does not seek to produce "new wine," and well he knows it, already living in Grateloup in the midst of vineyards where a very good Pécharmant is still produced (the wine of Bergerac).[50] But he knows how to make "new wine" with old vines, just as water is transformed into the wedding wine of Cana (John 2:1–11), including in philosophy. *Cause, resistance,* and *force* are

---

49. Gouhier, *Œuvres choisies*, 31 (emphasis added). On this point, see Romeyer-Dherbey's highly enlightening chapter, *Maine de Biran*, 80–90: "Le corps organique et l'inconscient."

50. See the Terre-Vieille chateau on the former domain of the Grateloup chateau, which has a special vintage of "Maine de Biran" Pécharmant that is much appreciated: https://www.chateauterre-vieille.com.

thus reworked metaphysical concepts that, far from making us leave the field of "classical" or "spiritualist" philosophy, which has wrongly been called "ontotheological," oblige us on the contrary to interrogate it again in order to rework it.

Causality is "the foundational notion of all true philosophy." Maine de Biran ceaselessly repeats this and insists on it even in his "late philosophy" and his *Nouveaux essais d'anthropologie*.[51] But it imposes itself because it is the other side, or the other face, of reality. There is indeed a "science," as there is pure mathematics and pure psychology (see *supra*) that causes one to know or at the very least to know *oneself*. "In this sense," indicates the author of the *Note sur l'idée de l'existence*, which is contemporaneous with this late period (on the eve of his death in 1824), "it is true to say that we have no idea or knowledge of *any force other than that of the* myself, which is immediately manifest to consciousness thanks to a special sense that I will soon characterize more specifically [the lived body]."[52] But he immediately adds—and it is here that the concession turns into a rule or that a reading "in counter-relief" of Maine de Biran becomes possible:

> *This does not prevent* us from affirming, with an intimate *confidence*, the *real existence* of the efficient cause of all movement that begins in *space* or *time*, including those movements that are brought about *in us* or in our organization *without us* or *without the sentiment of our own force*.[53]

Everything, or many things, are thus "brought about in us without us": our passions, certainly, whether they are joyful or painful, but also the instinctual movements of our bodies to displace us in space, even thoughts and images that we cannot master, especially in dreams. It is not that this does not exist—Maine de Biran is far from reducing everything to consciousness or knowledge alone—but that it does exist because I know—or, rather, "I believe," since I adhere to it without knowing its whys and wherefores, that this passes or happens—that I measure its effects (the involuntary movements of my body under the influence of habit, or the images of dreams that still have effects *on me* while I am awake). One

---

51. Maine de Biran, *Dernière philosophie*, 40: "This notion of 'causality', *the foundation of all true philosophy*, revolves, as it were, around two fixed *poles*: the one, first in the analytic order of facts, is the *myself*. The other, first in the synthetic order, is God" (emphasis partly in original).

52. Maine de Biran, *Dernière philosophie*, 229 (emphasis added).

53. Maine de Biran, *Dernière philosophie*, 229 (emphasis partly in original).

indeed finds here the trace of an "unconscious" or, better, of an "organic unconsciousness," for everything comes from a *corporeal and animal passivity* that I cannot tame, such that the true life is made not only of *knowledge* (the apperception of myself by myself) but of *belief* (the effect that I myself and things have on me without my ever being able to know them): "Belief and science being thus distinguished," continues the *Note sur l'idée de l'existence*, "there are always grounds, in truth, for asking whether they are indivisible or primitively bound to each other."[54]

b) A Mysterious Agent

It is thus the task of the *Mémoire sur la décomposition de la pensée* to name this (organic) "unconscious," of which the thinker from Bergerac does not yet have the name, although he perfectly discovers the notion. There indeed exists a "mysterious agent"—lacking the name of the vintage (under "whatever name," emphasizes Biran), at least we have the contents of the flagon—that certainly guides the "myself" but that could just as well steer the "non-myself." In other words, if it was indeed necessary to posit the hypothesis of a "mysterious property (or "force") underlying the whole analysis of Condillac's statue according to Biran, whereby it says, "I am rose-odor" and not "it will therefore be rose-odor" (§9a), it is now necessary for this same "*mysterious property*"—thus named in the letter to Destutt de Tracy (p. 104) of April 30, 1804, to recognize, at its side or in itself, a "*mysterious agent*" (unconscious and no longer the primitive *myself*), thus designated in the *Mémoire sur la décomposition de la pensée*, written in the same year, and whose effect is such that it acts in me without me, such that I know its effect without ever being able to determine its cause: "If, rejecting the testimony of the intimate sense," Biran dares to write in a reading *ab absurdo* of the primitive fact of effort,

> I grant to some *mysterious agent that is different from myself, under whatever name*, the actual efficacious power of acts or movements of which I sense myself as the cause, I can indeed, with far more reason and to draw closer to systematic unity, attribute to the *same agent* these obscure, vital movements that, never coming to my knowledge, are outside the limit of my powers, whether real or illusory.[55]

---

54. Maine de Biran, *Dernière philosophie*, 229.
55. Maine de Biran, *Mémoire sur la décomposition*, 311 (emphasis added).

"Obscure, vital movements that never come to my knowledge," that "are outside the limit of my powers," not only "real" but also "illusory." There is no better way to say it to designate here, as if in advance, the hypothesis of the unconscious understood as, or named, a "mysterious agent"—that is to say, "whatever name," for lack of another appellation. Positing that causality (in this sense) is "the foundational notion of all true philosophy" could go so far as to imply, with Dimitri Voutsinas, that Maine de Biran is the founder of (French) psychology or even of psychoanalysis in general: "From this [causality], *foreign causality* will be deduced, whose foundation is found in the second term of the primitive relation: the *resistance* or *Not-myself-cause*. The *foreign cause* (*outside the Myself, although internal*) is not *sensed* like our own causation but is *believed*."[56]

c) ORGANIC BASE

That there is first and always an "organic base" in the unconscious—as for Freud, moreover, as I have said—this is what clearly emerges from Biran's discussion with Dr. Gall concerning the "organic divisions of the brain considered as seats of different intellectual and moral faculties." We will indeed see, in this sense, the figure of the thinker of Grateloup as the precursor of what today we name *neurobiology*, concerning which we know to what an extent this sort of "organic physiology of the brain" already had the wind in its sails at the beginning of the nineteenth century (a speech given at the Bergerac Medical Society on November 13, 1808). What matters, however, in Biran's remarks about this organic base of the unconscious is seeing well, and noting well, that he categorically refuses to reduce this pure passivity in me, or this unconscious, to the influence of an organ or a precise topos of an organ, inasmuch as there are certainly "localizable affections"—"hunger, thirst, pain from colic or a stomachache"—but also and above all "affections that cannot be localized directly" or "affections that are not localizable": "affections, for example, of hilarity or sadness, calm or anxiety, courage or timidity, confidence in or distrust of one's strength."[57]

And these latter affections (hilarity, sadness, calm, anxiety, courage, timidity)—that is, a "fundamental affection" (*Befindlichkeit*) in

---

56. Voutsinas, "Maine de Biran," 83 (emphasis added).
57. Maine de Biran, *Discours*, 75–76.

its declensions as so many "tonalities" (*Stimmungen*) in Martin Heidegger[58]—have the particularity on the one hand of remaining incarnate in our corporeality or organicity (to a greater extent than *Being and Time* mentions) and on the other hand of determining the "general sentiment of our existence" (this time as in *Being and Time*). They are not "non-organic" but "non-organically localizable," which is not the same thing. It is my body *as a whole*—and we know the influence of climate and the seasons on the moral and physical life of Maine de Biran (p. 136)—that experiences without knowing *where* it experiences, and certainly not in a specific organ, not even an organic division of the brain. In other words, and to translate it today, Maine de Biran, with the "non-localizable affections" as sorts of unconscious forces that I am subjected to in my body as in my spirit, sets in advance a rampart against the pure physiological reductionism of neurobiology and saves, as it were, what remains of the benefit and even the propriety of psychology, even of psychoanalysis:

> What is proper to the affections [*passive and not localized*] in question is that they directly influence the *general sentiment of our existence*, make us immediately happy or unhappy *without our knowing* the internal cause of the happiness or unhappiness and *without our being able to say* what makes us suffer or rejoice, which *part of ourselves* is affected for good or ill.[59]

d) A Blind Power

Thus there is an "agent" in us, including in our organicity, though not reducible to it or its "organs"—named "mysterious," as I have said—on which we also depend and that escapes our "primitive *myself*": not an unconscious of which we have no consciousness (temporary ignorance) but that we will never reach (definitive ignorance). But it remains necessary, for approaching or "touching the shores" of this "outside the area" of which Henri Gouhier spoke (p. 149), that the agent not be too defined. It is not a question of "someone"—an evil genius or a demon—that would amuse itself by *passively* determining me, while I humanly

---

58. Heidegger, *Being and Time*, 129 (s. 136): "Attunement [*Befindlilchkeit*] is so far from being reflected upon that it precisely assails Da-sein in the unreflected falling prey to the 'world' of its heedfulness. Mood [*Stimmung*] assails. It comes neither from 'without' nor from 'within,' but rises from being-in-the-world itself as a mode of that being."

59. Maine de Biran, *Discours*, 76 (emphasis added). This passage is accurately and pertinently taken up and commented on by Romeyer-Dherbey, *Maine de Biran*, 82–84.

exist only by *actively* experiencing myself in myself (the lived body in the pure effort of the hand without any grasp on an object, for example). It is rather a question of a "blind" and even "neutral and drive-based" force, to again join with psychoanalysis here, that is alone capable of always and ever remaining this "foreign cause" that is "to be believed" but never "known" or "cognized."

Of an instinctual nature, this force that we experience in a purely passive way will never be eradicated—expressing itself "from the earliest ages of life" and taking root in our "animal organicity" that can never be overcome. Let us be careful here, however. The instinct or this "blind power" cannot be reduced either to early childhood (to be overcome) or to the purely animal (to be humanized). The late Biran has too keen a knowledge of anthropology or the "science of man" to not see on the one hand that we are determined all throughout our existence by such passions and drives and to not recognize on the other hand that there is animality in man and that this, too, belongs to "concrete man in his entirety." Descartes's famous words in the *Discourse on Method* (1637)— "We were all children before being men"[60]—are certainly also true for Biran, but only to the degree that *we never cease to be children*, not in the pure innocence of an endlessly rehashed gratuity but according to an "instinct" and a "blind power" in counter-relief that can never be totally taken from us: "The totality of the determinations that we are justified in thus understanding under the name of *instinct*," we read in a perfectly composed phrase of the *Mémoire sur la décomposition de la pensée* with a view to describing the "immediate constitutive affections of the organic temperament," "is not restricted to the *earliest age of human life*. The sphere in which this *blind power* continues to be exercised, far from being circumscribed, on the contrary takes on more extension by joining, at several points, with the power of our habits."[61]

We will therefore understand this. Man may indeed be "outside himself" in every sense of the term: recognizing that there is a terminus outside (the cast-iron cannonball) and no longer holding together in himself (madness, illness, sudden and vehement passions, deliriums, drunkenness, etc.). The subject that is "offside", that is, both "outside itself" and "out of play," will therefore not be only an invention of extra-phenomenality.

60. Descartes, *Discourse on Method*, 8 (AT VI, 13).

61. Maine de Biran, *Mémoire sur la décomposition*, 382 (emphasis added). As for the importance, and the sense, of "animality" in my own work, and its distinction from "bestiality," I refer to *Wedding Feast of the Lamb*, 63–99, 177–98.

There are found in Maine de Biran the presages and the confirmation of exactly what is being looked for—from the "lived or proper body" to the "improper body" ("Toward an Ethics of the Spread Body") and from the "myself" to the "foreign to myself" (*The Extra-Phenomenal*). Thus the path that is yet to be carried out is traced, at least on the map, a path that will this time render us close to extreme "psychiatric cases," in which the blockage is such that neither the body nor the spirit can "experience" anything any longer, in an impossible "transpassibility," to say it in the language of Henri Maldiney. Neither "transpossible" nor "transpassible," that is, no longer having an open horizon (transpossible) nor the capacity to suffer from it (transpassible)—that is what constitutes psychosis in Maldiney's view in *Penser l'homme et la folie* [*Thinking Man and Madness*] (2007), of which Maine de Biran is in the end also one of the pioneers, initiating in his own right a "psychiatric phenomenology" of psychoses—where the exception proves the rule and makes us radically "other" or "foreign" *to* ourselves: "As for the schizophrenic," we read at the heart of the famous Maldineyan text entitled "De la transpassibilité" ["On Transpassibility"], "he is the one who has led us to the gulf in which every event is swallowed up in advance. In schizophrenia, *there is no longer any event save the unique, non-transformed one of which his existence is a constant rehashing and that ceaselessly multiplies itself.*"[62]

---

62. Maldiney, *Penser l'homme et la folie*, 308 (emphasis added).

5

The Foreign Body

> Nothing is more instructive for the waking man than the history of dreams, just as nothing is more useful for the reasonable man than the history of madness.
>
> MAINE DE BIRAN,
> *DISCOURS À LA SOCIÉTÉ MÉDICALE DE BERGERAC*

The Double Absolute

THINKING *IN THE EXTREME* or standing *on the extremes*: this is now Maine de Biran's final voyage. Thus all his philosophy becomes a *search for the absolute*, but in both senses of the term this time: the *absolute*—from *absolvere* that signifies both the act of "detaching from" and of "finishing"—understood etymologically as "the separated, outside myself" and also as that which "absorbs the *myself*." Thus the "absolute" reaches or rejoins the extremes, and highlighting this is not the least of originalities. Rather than reducing the whole of Maine de Biran's thought to the "phenomenal *myself*" [*moi phénoménal*] and the "lived body" [*corps propre*] (two terms duly used in French by Maine de Biran himself, as I have shown), it is in reality the "outside" and even the "foreign" that constitutes his greatest specificity, for there stands the *concrete man in his entirety* that we cannot avoid (chapter 4). It is therefore a matter of reaching both ends and of holding all the ends together. The act of absorbing oneself in, or of being absorbed, can occur both from below in the chaos of our animality and from above in the abandonment to divinity. This is what we must here name the "double absolute"—or the two ways for the *myself* to be separated from itself to forget itself, even to alienate itself (positively also) in another: "The identification also occurs in the opposite sense: *with God*; consciousness will disappear no less than when it is absorbed in *animal life*."[1]

Maine de Biran testifies himself to this double absorption or double absoluteness—at the end of his life, this time, in one of his last *Fragments* dated 1823-18 24, precisely where the whole *descent from below* toward animality (catabasis) rejoins the ascent *from above* toward divinity (anabasis), but only by virtue of an *assumption* by God of our humanity (kenosis):

> Man is intermediate between God and nature. He is attached *to God by his spirit* and *to nature by his senses*. He can *identify himself with the latter* by letting his *myself*, his *personality*, and his *freedom* be absorbed by it and by *abandoning himself* to all the appetites, to all the impulses of the *flesh*. He can also, up to a certain point, *identify himself with God* by absorbing his *myself* through the exercise of a superior faculty.[2]

Thus a sort of "loss of the *myself*" or "disappearance of the *myself*" can take place—"alienation" certainly being negative in the case of trauma (the pure reduction to animality) but positive in identification with divinity (in a direct line from the manner in which Michel Henry rereads the prologue of John's Gospel in light of, but nevertheless without saying so, Maine de Biran's "Nouvelles notes sur l'Évangile de saint Jean" [New notes on St. John's Gospel]).[3] When resistance is lost, as I will show, existence,

---

1. Azouvi, "Conscience, identification et articulation," 470 (emphasis added). The duality of the absolute is perfectly noted by Umbelino, *Somatologia subjectiva*, 361–69 (esp. 363–64).

2. Maine de Biran, *Dernière philosophie*, 322 (emphasis partly in original).

3. See Maine de Biran, "Nouvelles notes sur l'Évangile de saint Jean" (classified and published under this title by Ernest Naville). Reprinted in J. II, 412-17. There is a (not stated) proximity between this line-by-line commentary on John's prologue (John 1:1-18) by Maine de Biran and the commentary that Michel Henry gives on it in *I Am the Truth*, but without referring to it, which certainly gives cause for surprise. See Henry, *I Am the Truth*, 69-93 (esp. 81-83): commentary on John 1:14 ("The Word became flesh and made his dwelling among us. We have seen his glory"), John 1:18 ("No one has ever seen God, but the Son the One and Only, who is in the Father's bosom, has made him known"), and 1 John 1:1 ("That which was from the beginning, which we have heard, which we have seen with our eyes, which we have looked at and our hands have touched"). Here I will refer to Devarieux's excellent chapter (which in

or at the very least the state that is "conscious" (*conscium*) and "master of itself" (*compos sui*) that, according to Biran, verbatim, "is man's natural state" in the development of his moral force and the struggle against "disordered appetites," is lost. But in the case of the fall into animality or elevation toward divinity, life will then become "effortless" in the literal sense of the term—that is, without that *resistance of oneself in oneself* (the hand that senses itself in its intramuscular force from the inside without grasping anything on the outside, not even itself by touching its chest) which causes me to "sense" myself "existing."

I have said this from the opening to this book onward: there can take place in man, according to Biran in the *Relationship Between the Physical and the Moral in Man*, an "obscuration" or a "total eclipse of the sentiment of the *myself*" (p. xxiv), which I, moreover, name the "subject that is offside" or extra-phenomenality, in normal (sleep) or paranormal (mental alteration) phenomena. It is there that "effort" is lost in the suspension of the *sentiment of the* myself when a foreign experience comes, if not to destroy it, at least to alienate it and render it inaccessible for myself to myself:

> I shall point out with respect to this successive invasion of the phenomena of *sleep* how *delirium* or *mental alteration* are, as it were, only a degree or circumstance of the same *essential condition* on which this state depends, namely the *progressive suspension of the exercise of will and of effort*, and as a direct result *the obscuration and total eclipse of the sentiment of the* myself, and of all that is strictly intellectual, etc.[4]

When *nothing resists (me)* any longer, I sense that *nothing exists any longer*, not even myself (§15a). Without resistance, and therefore *without effort*, I am disoriented or abandoned in myself, below myself in animality or above myself stretched toward divinity. There is no judgment here, including for Maine de Biran. For the "physical" and the "moral" are not and never will be contained in norms. If the work of the thinker from Bergerac always remains close to what will later be called "phenomenology" and even "psychiatric phenomenology," this is at least because it is content to describe phenomena and no longer sets up borders or barriers

---

my view deserves an entire book), *L'Intériorité réciproque*, 285–305: "Trinité biranienne et trinité henryenne." [The translations of Scripture in this footnote follow those given in Henry, *I am the Truth*. –Trans.]

4. Maine de Biran, *Relationship Between the Physical and the Moral*, 124 (emphasis added). [Translation modified. –Trans.]

between the normal on the one hand and the pathological on the other (chapter 4). Whether "by animalizing itself," therefore, or "by divinizing itself," the subject abandons or forgets itself in the other than itself—be it the other of trauma (the extra-phenomenal) or the other of the wholly other (God extra-phenomenal):

> *Above* and *below* this state [the proper natural state of the man who is "conscious," *conscium*, and "master of himself," *compos sui*], there is *no longer any* struggle, any effort, or any resistance, and consequently *no longer any* myself, but this is sometimes by divinizing himself, sometimes by animalizing himself.[5]

The "foreign body" (chapter 5) after the "constitution of the *myself*" (chapter 1) and the "resistance of the body" (chapter 2), the "search for the flesh" (chapter 3), and the "counter-history of madness" (chapter 4) will thus signify the "foreign *outside* myself" from the point of view of corporeality; and the "effortless life" (chapter 6) will point to the "foreign *to* myself," but this time from the point of view of the psychism. Whereas the former ("The foreign *outside* myself" [§15]) joins with the "spread body" (or the "physical," according to Biran's term) inasmuch as there is always something of the body, including my body, "that remains," from "sleep" to the "paralyzed hand," the second ("the foreign *to* myself" [§17]) states "spread thought" (or the "moral" in Biranian terminology), since the psychic this time is what can be traumatized in "dreams," "drunkenness," "sleepwalking," or "idiocy" (dementedness). In each case, it is indeed the foreign, or the *alienus*, that is given, and not turning away from it is accepting that to "so much exception" (paralysis, madness, dementedness, drunkenness) there corresponds "so much modification" (the leitmotif of *The Extra-Phenomenal*)[6]—becoming not only "another oneself" (*alter ego*), an "other than oneself" (*ego alter*), "oneself as another" (Ricœur), but an "other *to* oneself": "I am *modified in my whole existence*, physical, moral, intellectual, in an absolutely different way from when in Grateloup," confides Biran in his *Journal* on the date of December 6, 1822, when he had already reached Paris over

---

5. Maine de Biran, *Dernière philosophie*, 323 (emphasis added). On "God extra-phenomenal" (from above) who responds to the "extra-phenomenal" (from below), see Falque, *La Chair de Dieu*, 123–58; "God Extra-Phenomenal."

6. See Falque, *Hors phénomène*, 299–307: "Autant d'exception, autant de modification" ("So much exception, so much modification"). This takes the baton from "so much appearance, so much being" (Heidegger) and "so much reduction, so much givenness" (Marion).

two weeks earlier (November 21) and could not take any more of the capital. "It is almost *another myself*. There is a difference in system, a need for agitation and society, an impossibility of remaining in place, of giving oneself over to the inner life that has charms for me elsewhere than here."[7]

§14. Alienated Man

There is no philosophy, therefore, for Maine de Biran, as I have said, without crossing and traversing borders. No one can think without letting himself be transformed by disciplines and practices that constitute alterity. Thus he encounters, during the summer of 1820, the doctor Antoine Royer-Collard, the director of the "asylum for the alienated" at Charenton (since 1806), inspector general of the university (1808–1823), and professor of legal medicine at the École de médecine (1816). Preparing a course on "mental pathology" to be given in Paris (starting in 1819), Royer-Collard consulted Biran, drawing him still more toward the banks of the "outside oneself" and making him leave the "cozy island" of only the "sentiment of the *myself*." Thus we read, "1820, end of August" in the *Journal*, with a Maine de Biran fully devoted to tackling this new task:

> I have spent this whole month and the end of the previous month in serious occupations of my choice. I have revised my treatise for the Copenhagen Academy with the intention of transmitting it to Dr. Royer-Collard, who consulted me about a course that he proposes to give at Charenton on the subject of mental alienation.[8]

This revision of the *Relationship Between the Physical and the Moral in Man* [*Rapports du physique et du moral de l'homme*] (the 1811 Copenhagen treatise) would later result in the *Nouvelles considérations sur les rapports du physique et du moral de l'homme* (1820), an exemplary model not only of the "alienated" (even if he preserves a few "cases," Biran leaves that privilege to Royer-Collard) but of *alienation* itself. From pathological medicine (the alienated), we cross to philosophy (the concept of

---

7. J. II, 366 (entry dated December 6, 1822, emphasis added).

8. J. II, 287 (entry dated the end of August 1820). As for Royer-Collard's relation to Biran, see Baertschi's notice in Maine de Biran, *Nouvelles considérations*, viiin8, as well as the reprinting of the account of their discussion, appendix XIII, 257–58.

alienation) as a companion or even a counterpoint, at least in an experience of the extreme, to the sentiment of the *myself*.

a) *ALIENUS*

Anyone who says *alienus* (foreign) is not saying only *alterus* (other). Better, the *alienus* is the rejected *alterus*—that is, the "foreign," the refusal of "alterity." In other words, just as "bestiality" makes us sink below "animality,"[9] so too the "foreign" or, rather, "foreignerness" comes about when "alterity" is lacking. There is something of the foreign (*alienus*) not only when there is no longer a self (*ipse*) but also and still more when there is no longer an other (*alter*) in whom to recognize myself—neither "another myself" (*alter ego*), as I have said, nor an "other than myself" (*ego alter*), nor "myself as another" (Ricœur), but "other *to* myself."[10] Foreign to myself (the breaking of the phenomenalizing subject), I become foreign to the other or to the world (the breaking of the phenomenal horizon), such that nothing remains any longer except a traumatized "myself" or, rather, a traumatized "there is." Reduced to its purest neutrality, the subject is no longer declined in the nominative (I), in the vocative (here I am!), in the accusative (me), in the dative (to me), even in the ablative (for me), but in the neuter of the *it* (*Es* in German)—like "it rains" or "there is" [*il y a*], to here follow Levinas (taking up Blanchot, besides) in the preface to the second edition of *Existence and Existents* (1981):

> The notion of the *there is* developed in this book that is thirty years old (1947) seems to me to be its *pièce de résistance*. It is a negation that wants to be absolute, denying every existent: . . . an incessant "upheaval," to take up a metaphor from Blanchot, an impersonal there is [*il y a*], like an "it rains" [*il pleut*] or "it is night" [*il fait nuit*]. The term is fundamentally distinct from the Heideggerian "*es gibt*." It was never the translation or the

---

9. See Falque, *Wedding Feast*, 70–78.
10. See Falque, *Hors phénomène*, 254–97: "No longer 'other *myself*' (*alter ego*), 'other *than* myself' (*ego alter*), but 'other *to* myself' (*alterum quidem*)—such is the extreme of extra-phenomenality and of the expansion of the psyche. It is a matter of an 'other someone' [*quelqu'un autre*] (*alterum quidem*), radically foreign to oneself as to the other, and not a 'someone else' [*quelqu'un d'autre*] by whom we would 'still' belong to a common humanity and could 'still' recognize ourselves in our identity. Illness, or all other extra-phenomenality, does not only make us lose 'what we are' or our 'identity,' as if it had become difficult to recognize oneself and to also be recognized by others, but leads to there no longer being anything or anyone to answer *for* 'what one was' or *for* what one 'believed oneself to be'" (258).

cut-price version of the German expression and its connotations of abundance and generosity.[11]

b) Mental Alienations

A new perspective is thus opened in relief in Maine de Biran starting in 1820 (in the *Nouvelles considérations sur les rapports du physique et du moral de l'homme*), whereas "life at the extremes" had been envisioned only in counter-relief in 1812 (in the *Essai sur les fondements de la psychologie*). The being "at the limit" of illness (the melancholic or the hypochondriac) or "outside oneself" (the insane one or the madman) in the *Essai* had indeed reached the edges [*confins*] of phenomenality (§11). But the prolegomena of the *Nouvelles considérations* open this time onto a definition of alienation (§14) and of the forms of physical (§15) or mental (§17) alienation that constitute, properly speaking, the originality of this "other reading" of Maine de Biran that the present essay here wishes to carve out.[12]

As with the *Essai*, therefore, but in a still more decisive fashion in the *Nouvelles considérations*, it is again *the exception that proves the rule*. It is certainly fitting first of all to define what "existing" signifies for man— that is, appearing in his "phenomenal *myself*" (apperception) and feeling himself in his "lived body" (flesh):

> Existing, for man, as a thinking, active, and free subject means having the consciousness, the possession, of oneself. Enjoying one's good sense or one's reason, one's free activity, being able to say *me* and to recognize oneself as *myself*—that is the ground of human existence and the point of departure, the first given, the primitive *fact* of any science of *ourselves*.[13]

But I have proclaimed this since the opening, without, however, analyzing it: everything changes, or, rather, everything turns the moment that, in the case of trauma, this "consciousness of oneself," this "possession of oneself," this "power of saying and recognizing oneself as myself"—in short, the "primitive *fact*" or the "first given" of ourselves—disappears. In

---

11. Levinas, *De l'existence à l'existant*, 10. [The preface to the second edition is not included in the English translation. –Trans.]

12. As a pioneer on this way (for spotting Maine de Biran's texts), as I have emphasized, and whom I pay homage to anew, in particular for our rich meeting at Coimbra in Portugal (in May 2022), see Umbelino, *Somatologia subjectiva*, 359–472.

13. Maine de Biran, *Nouvelles considérations*, 5 (emphasis in original).

the case of mental alienations (all the forms of psychoses also interpreted in the era as physiological), indicates Biran verbatim in his discussion with the pathologist-doctor Royer-Collard, there remains, for a "being of our species," only the "external forms of man," "who, however, does not know himself or possess himself, does not exist for himself." This phrase from the prolegomena to the *Nouvelles considérations*, which is central to my study, thus deserves to be cited in full again:

> Thus it is very justly said in common language that in such a state [when a being of our species, having the external form of a man, neither knows nor possesses himself and does not exist for himself] man is *outside himself* and *foreign to himself* (*alienus*), whence the very fittingly coined word *alienation*, to which can be attributed a greater degree of generalization than it has in the ordinary sense of biologists and doctors. This term [*alienation*] would indeed be very well suited to all the states particular to [or the irregular states of, *sic*] the soul and the organized body that carry with them a *complete absence*, momentary or permanent, *of the sentiment of the* myself, although the vital and sensitive functions experience no interruption.[14]

One could then certainly believe and think that the alienated man is therefore no longer a man and that it would then be necessary to exclude madness from the human, in the manner that I have shown while relying on Descartes (and the interpretation of madness): "However, I have to consider that I am a man [and therefore not mad]" (first *Meditation*). But it is not a question of a "history of madness in the classical age" in Maine de Biran, as I have illustrated at length (chapter 4) inasmuch as madness, like the organic unconscious, far from being expelled from humanity, on the contrary again finds itself in its central place as an "exception to the human" that nonetheless tells us in what the human consists. The *outside* as an external edge of our humanity—be it a matter of the absolute from below of animality or of the absolute from above of divinity—tells of that "foreign" that will either make me sink into an untamable bestiality (the absolute from below) or will draw me toward a complete and other alterity (the absolute from above). For, even though we are not all *traumatized* (or alienated), we are at least all, without exception, *traumatizable* (or alienatable). It is not solely "what we are" that counts but also "what lies in wait for us"—this time not reducing our being to the "ought-to-be"

---

14. Maine de Biran, *Nouvelles considérations*, 5 (emphasis partly in original).

(according to established norms) but to the "able-to-be" (in the possibility of falling as also of elevating ourselves).

In such cases of "mental alienations"—to which we could, however, add, including according to Biran himself, illness, deliriums, drunkennesses, sudden and vehement passions, drugs, etc.—man is then said to be "*outside himself,*" as I have repeatedly emphasized: "outside himself" on the one hand in the sense that the subject no longer controls himself when anger invades him and "outside himself" on the other hand in the sense that he exits from himself, enters into what psychoanalysis will later name a "split" with himself. The subject that is declared to be "off*side*" no longer has access to himself—that is, properly speaking, when he has "become other" or "alienated," in other words, "foreign to himself": "Man is *outside himself* and *foreign to himself* (*alienus*), whence the very fittingly coined word *alienation*."[15] "Alienated man"—this is probably what characterizes Maine de Biran read "in counter-relief," whom we will turn inside-out like a glove to make visible "in relief" what had not yet been suspected there. The thinker of Grateloup did not only, as if in advance, invent *phenomenology* in its very terms (the "phenomenal *myself*" and the "lived or proper body") but he also saw its limit, less to contest it than to attest that a veritable "science of man" must also embrace the whole of our concrete existence, in particular when it is confronted with illness— "alienations" (psychoses and other secondary effects of drugs) or the "improper body" (the paralyzed hand, hemiplegia, etc.). It is by touching the "extremes" that one becomes a "thinker of the extreme." This is what the subprefect of Bergerac perfectly realized, albeit under the cover of a "society life" that he took upon himself. We all live with our own "tempest in a skull" (Victor Hugo)—but there are those who admit it (to themselves) and those who constantly hide it (from themselves). The real philosopher will always belong to the former and never to the latter.[16]

We will follow precisely, then, the etymological thread from the *alienus* or the "foreign" to reach those "extremes" and to think, with Maine de Biran, precisely what is in question here. For there is no question, for Biran, of speaking here of "alienation" in the Hegelian sense of a process of "transformation or estrangement" of the *myself* in view of its subjectivity (*Phenomenology of Spirit*),[17] any more than in the Laca-

15. Maine de Biran, *Nouvelles considérations*, 5 (emphasis added).

16. On this point, I refer to my contribution (which concerns myself as well): "Une tempête sous une crâne."

17. See Hegel, *Phenomenology of Spirit*, 244: "His true original nature and substance

nian sense of "separation or division" of the other in oneself through the impossibility of the radically other outside myself (*Seminar XI*).[18] It is rather to "psychiatric phenomenology" that we must here direct ourselves, as I have said (§11), after having shown the proximity of psychoanalysis to the "organic unconscious" (§13): "When a schizophrenic answers the question 'where' by saying, '*I am here, but for me that means nothing*,'" Maldiney indicates in his text "De la transpassibilité" (*Penser l'homme et la folie*), here perfectly illustrating the Biranian "foreign" or *alienus*, "he declares that he is *not from there*, that *here* in this place that is perfectly identifiable by him he is *not in the world*. . . . He cannot encounter *anyone*, [nor] can he be *in contact* with things; beings are not *at his hand*. . . . A *body without limit* lends itself to non-discrimination between one's own space and foreign space."[19]

The alienation with which Biran deals here is certainly that of Royer-Collard's "alienated ones," as with Binswanger's case of Suzanne Urban for Maldiney. But, like Maldiney, he extends the study from psychopathology alone to philosophy in general: "One could attribute [to the very fittingly coined word *alienation*] a greater degree of generalization than it has in the ordinary sense of biologists and doctors." The "outside man"—*infra*-human (animality) or *supra*-human (divinity) also tells something of man for Biran, as for Maldiney. Neither the *madman* [*fou*] (demented) nor the *fool* [*fol*] (in Christ) deny humanity. Or, rather, they are its negation and not its privation, inasmuch as they certainly reveal the process of blockage but also and above all of mutation or even

---

are now comprised in this spirit of the *estrangement* [*Entfremdung*] of his natural being. This process of *abnegation* [that leads him out of his natural self] is thus as much the *purpose* as the *being-there* of the individual; it's also a *means*, the *transition* of a thought-sustained substance into actual reality, and on the other hand a form of resolute individuality in transition to something of essential import" (emphasis added). [Translation modified to more closely follow the French translation that Falque cites. –Trans.] Whatever may be the terms for translating these declensions of "alienation" in German (*Äuserrung, Entäusserung, Entfremdung*), this word will always designate a "movement" or a "crossing" in a process of finalized dialectical transformation—which is not the case for the "foreign *to* oneself" in Maine de Biran (or in *The Extra-Phenomenal*). See Haber, "Terme 'aliénation' (*Entfremdung*)."

18. Lacan, *Four Fundamental Concepts*, 210: "Alienation consists in this *vel*, which—if you do not object to the word *condemns*, I will use it—*condemns* the subject to appearing *only in that division* which, it seems to me, I have just articulated sufficiently by saying that, if it appears on one side as meaning, produced by the signifier, it appears on the other as *aphanisis*" (emphasis partly in original). The phrase is certainly complex and can be clarified with the following commentary: Poli, "Concept d'aliénation."

19. Maldiney, *Penser l'homme et la folie*, 297 (emphasis added).

of "complete metamorphosis," in which we sometimes find ourselves involved, without realizing it.

c) So Much Exception, So Much Modification

"So much exception, so much modification," and no longer solely "so much appearance, so much being" (Heidegger) or "so much reduction, so much givenness" (Marion)—such is the *alienus* or the "foreign" for Maine de Biran first.[20] When the "alienation" is radical, it does not suffice, according to the thinker from Bergerac, coming to the aid of his friend Royer-Collard for his course on mental pathology given at the Charenton hospital, to say that the "alienated one" or the "madman" has simply *lost* a prior state of which he is supposedly deprived and that a good practice of medicine or a good treatment will help him to find again. The real alienation by which the subject notes himself as doubly foreign—both *to himself* (the phenomenalizing horizon) and *to the world* (the phenomenalized horizon)—does not lead to "finding" oneself "again" but to "finding" oneself or to discovering oneself as totally other and different, even as projected into another. The "offside"—outside the I (myself) and out of play (the world)—is radical. There remains only the *myself* in its survival and its "vital and sensitive functions [*sic*]," whereby it is worse to be a "living dead one" (the extra-phenomenal) than a "living one who is not yet dead" (the anguish of death)—precisely because, not being dead, everything in me that constituted my humanity, or at the very least my specificity and my appropriation, nonetheless becomes dead in me. Neither the "sentiment of the *myself*" nor the "primitive fact of effort" nor the "phenomenal *myself*" nor the "lived body"—so many determinations that have previously been studied (chapters 1 and 3)—nothing remains any longer but the neuter of a *there is*, of which one will scarcely say "me," and the outside in me, or even for me, of a spread body that is forever impossible to appropriate for myself: "This term [*alienation*] would indeed be very well suited *to all the states particular* to the soul and the organized body that carry with them a *complete absence*, momentary or permanent, *of the sentiment of the* myself, although the *vital and sensitive functions* experience no interruption."[21]

---

20. See Falque, *Hors phénomène*, 299–307.
21. Maine de Biran, *Nouvelles considérations*, 5 (emphasis added).

d) Alienation

"Alienation," or noting oneself as "being foreign to oneself" ("other to oneself" will thus first, and etymologically, be extended as a "ceding" or even a "sale of oneself" in the sense that one finds oneself totally disappropriated of any "right of property" (*alienus*, that which belongs to another, foreign)—as with "property alienation," the dispossession of a good that is transferred to another (here, animality or divinity) for free or subject to payment. Something remains, certainly, in Biran's view, but it is only myself encumbered by myself, no longer having any dwelling to inhabit—"*ich bin/bauen*"[22]—and therefore carried away by that "foreign cause" or that "blind power" that causes there to no longer be any "me" when I say "me" or, rather, when I can no longer say either "I" or "me" (in the "complete absence, temporary or permanent," of the "sentiment of the *myself*").[23]

At times madness comes and one senses it coming, advises the thinker from Bergerac in his dialogue with van Helmont this time (a doctor, chemist, and theologian from the early eighteenth century). But at times also it invades us to such an extent that nothing can any longer warn of it or protect us from it. The "foreign cause" becomes a "foreign force" more than a mere "mysterious agent" that cannot be named (§13). Alienation becomes total, to the point that an "other being" comes to substitute itself *for me* and *for the myself* "in myself," which is therefore no longer me, other *to* myself or "foreign to myself," *alienus* (foreign), concerning which nothing stipulates that one day it will recover any sort of *ego ipsum* (oneself). It is a "foreign force" that certainly comes "in place of me" (deposition or replacing) but also and above all "into my place" (invasion by a "filled-up of chaos" that has become unexchangeable). The *foreignerness* (*alienus*) of myself become other here replaces the *ipseity* (*ipse*) of the oneself as another (Ricœur), as its greatest "exception" and therefore also "modification."

This is, finally, what the *alienus* will result in—just as much in the "foreign *outside* myself" in corporeality and the paralyzed hand (§15) as in the "foreign *to* myself" at the heart of the psyche, invaded with

---

22. Heidegger, *Poetry, Language, Thought*, 145: "What then does *ich bin* mean? The old word *bauen*, to which the *bin* belongs, answers: *ich bin, du bist* mean: I dwell, you dwell. The way in which you are and I am, the manner in which we humans *are* on the earth, is *Bauen*, dwelling. To be a human being means to be on the earth as a mortal. It means to dwell" (emphasis in original).

23. Maine de Biran, *Nouvelles considérations*, 5.

dreams, deliriums, and manias (§17): "In any passion that is beginning, that does not yet go so far as to absorb the *myself*," Biran therefore warns, addressing van Helmont,

> the individual senses internally something like a *force foreign to himself* that *creeps in little by little* and that tends to *take hold of him* or to put itself *in* his place. It is thus that, in attacks of madness or rage, the unfortunate one, still in his right mind, foresees the attack, senses it coming, even dictates the precautions to be taken, not against him as he is at present, but against *another being that is going to replace his self*, against which his foresight offers him no means of protecting himself, but that he senses as if it were necessary.[24]

§15. The Foreign Outside Myself

There is, therefore, something of the *foreign in me* (*alienus*)—and this is what is an exception, surprisingly in Maine de Biran, to the autochthony of the "sentiment of the *myself*" and the "primitive fact of effort." This foreignness or, rather, "foreignerness" will then be considered from the physical point of view (the spread body) or the psychic point of view (the extra-phenomenal): either the "foreign outside myself" if it is a question of corporeality, which responds to the "resistance of the body" (chapter 2) and to the "search for the flesh" (chapter 3) or the "foreign *to* me" (§17) if it is a matter of affects that it is impossible for me to appropriate for myself, which refers back to the "constitution of the *myself*" (chapter 1) and to the "counter-history of madness" (chapter 4). In the former case—corporeality or the foreign *outside* oneself—there is resistance, force, and the paralyzed hand; and in the second case—the psyche or the foreign *to* me—there are dreams, drunkenness, sleepwalking, and idiocy. Saying what *resistance* is to the point, in certain limit-experiences, of recognizing that one "can no longer resist" and going from *force* to *effort* to recognize that at times we sink into an "effortless life"—this is the way opened by a Maine de Biran who is kept at the extremes or in contact with the extremes. After "causality" (§13)—as I proclaimed regarding the possibility of making "new wine" with old vineyards on the Grateloup estate (Pécharmant)—there now comes "resistance" (§15) and "force" (§16), as *metaphysical* concepts

---

24. Maine de Biran, *Nouvelles considérations*, 223 (emphasis added).

that are also valid and necessary. The conflict between *spiritualism* and *phenomenology* "will no longer take place"—I have made this the heart or, rather, the aim of the present work—inasmuch as it is in their "encounter" and their "backlash" that a new fruitfulness for thought will play out.

a) "Resist, Prove That You Exist"

Since the paradigmatic example of the marble statue, "resistance" is first: we know this for Condillac since the hand collides with the chest *from the outside* (chapter 2), and we also know this for Biran in the feeling of intramuscular effort in the hand (chapter 3). "Resisting" is *at the origin* and remains *from the origin onward*, with such a constancy in our protagonists that we cannot, in their era at the very least, derive it from the "given." Not solely a barricading of oneself (blockage), resistance is first constitutive of oneself (the primitive fact of effort). Better, it is precisely, and inversely, the moment that there is no longer any "resisting" that the ego no longer recognizes itself, sinks, and falls, for lack of being able to lean on anything—externally in *its body* to say "me" (Condillac: "It will therefore be rose-odor," "It's me, it's me again!") or internally in its *flesh* to say "I" (Biran: "I am rose-odor"). Cathedrals live by their buttresses, and *Jacob Wrestling with the Angel* painted by Delacroix displays a barehanded seizing of bodies, which makes the bodies exist.[25]

Resisting "first of all," not to be "first," but because there lies our "primacy" of being man, whereby we sense, but also know, that we exist. And that is what is essential—in Biran's view, certainly ("I am my body"), but also in Condillac's ("It's me again"). While one would be wrong to believe that there is no resistance save as an answer to givenness, we will recognize now that no one could exist without resisting, at least via oneself leaning on oneself (Maine de Biran) or even via the buttressing of oneself against or on the other (Condillac). To the famous "gift of the present" that has been endlessly rehashed, we should oppose the "resistance of presence" that makes us exist: "Indeed, we ordinarily think resistance as an 'opposition' to a force external to it," as I have already noted elsewhere (*The Extra-Phenomenal*), "and therefore to a given that supposedly precedes it. All resistance would then derive from a gift or from another

---

25. See Chrétien, "How to Wrestle." See also my commentary, "Wrestling with the Angel."

presence that would make it possible: the main dish of the meal, certainly (*pièce de résistance*), the electrical flow (the resistance of the coil), war (armed resistance), healing (resistance to care or overcoming resistance), etc. But this fails to take into account that which, in reality, is first. *For 'resisting' is not opposing but existing.*"[26]

Resist, prove that you exist. This is the refrain of one of France Gall's songs that is well-known to the French.[27] Nothing is more accurate, in view of these eighteenth and nineteenth centuries that have been so eclipsed by the overdetermination of the concepts of the gift and of vulnerability at the end of the twentieth century and the beginning of the twenty-first. We have lost sight of the fact that "resistance" is first because we now make it derive from *Gegebenheit* as a pre-given—as if the light were always "already there," and as if the screen [*écran*] of the subject were only the case [*écrin*] or the venue for an *es gibt* wrongly interpreted as "it gives," as we have seen, relying on Levinas, and not as the pure and simple "there is." Condillac and Maine de Biran did not understand it in this manner, seeing first, for their part, *resistance* as initial and originary in the case of the marble statue that we have studied at length, be it a matter of the resistance of my own body on myself (the hand that touches my chest [§7c]) or the resistance that I feel in myself (the internal muscular effort in my hand [§10c]).[28]

This is, therefore, a wholly other interpretation that opens up here—less on the basis of "giving" than of "resisting," less as givenness or Archi-Revelation than as an organic or inner hyperorganic force (§13) that is as "irresistible," to say the least, as it is incompressible. "It is therefore necessary to grant that the status of the body in Biran *cannot*

---

26. See Falque, *Hors phénomène*, 109–50 (cit. 111–12).

27. See France Gall, "Résiste," album *Tout pour la musique*, 1981: "Resist / Prove that you exist / Seek your happiness everywhere, go / Refuse this egotistical world / Resist / Follow your heart that insists / This world is not yours, come / Fight, sign, and persist / Resist." ("*Résiste / Prouve que tu existes / Cherche ton bonheur partout, va / Refuse ce monde égoiste / Résiste / Suis ton cœur qui insiste / Ce monde n'est pas le tien, viens / Bats-toi, signe et persiste / Résiste.*")

28. Regarding this possibility of thinking my concept of "resistance" in *Hors phénomène* (chapter 2: "Résistance de la présence") in light of the debate between Maine de Biran and Condillac, and therefore of also orienting my work in the pathway of "spiritualism," I refer to Sackin-Poll, "Michel Henry," esp. 870–79. I wish here to thank its author for having indicated to me the possible link between the concept of "resistance" as I developed it at a talk given at Cambridge in February 2019 (and translated by Andrew Sackin-Poll) and "resistance" as it is envisioned by Maine de Biran. See my contribution "The Resistance of Presence."

be reduced to pure immanence," writes Pierre Montebello, severely but with justification, in conclusion to *La Décomposition de la pensée* [*The decomposition of thought*].²⁹ And "it goes without saying that effort *is not*, for Biran, an 'autoaffection,'" corroborates Anne Devarieux, in a manner that is no less abrupt but nevertheless pertinent, again faithful in this regard to the text of Maine de Biran himself. Because he always interprets the Biranian *cogito* as a "*living* ego," continues the author of *L'Interiorité réciproque* [*Reciprocal interiority*], the "mode of givenness proper to the ego" is named "revelation," which "presupposes the identification of the thing given to itself and auto-givenness itself": "Digging upstream of Biranian effort, from the *ego* to the *Before-the-ego*," as we must remember, according to an already-cited phrase, "Henry transforms an active inner experience into a passive test [*épreuve*] of oneself."³⁰

In short, if there is *pathos* in Maine de Biran, its belonging to an *originary life* is in no way self-evident. There is no "archi-" to be found in Biranian thought, be it Archi-Life or Archi-Revelation, since nothing is given outside the resistance that is first and presupposes not only the "lived body" (the flesh as the pure lived experience of oneself by oneself—*Leib*) but also of the organic (muscular and therefore belonging to the domain of the body—*Körper*). In the thinker from Bergerac precisely, albeit in limit-experiences, as I have declared, my body at times arises no longer as "lived" or "proper" but as "improper," no longer as "mine" but as "other." This is true first of the *organicity of the sleep of the body* against the *waking of the flesh* and then of the hypothesis of the *paralyzed hand* that renders impossible, partly at least, the famous "primitive fact of effort" by which I sense myself existing.

b) The Organicity of Sleep

Let us consider first the organicity of sleep. A passage from *Of Immediate Apperception* (1807) suffices to make clear the double yielding of the "sentiment of the *myself*" and the "primitive fact of effort," not exactly by resisting, but by abandoning all resistance. If "existing is resisting" (§15a), it could indeed be the case that not or no longer resisting (in one's body through sleep, even through one's psyche in dreams, a point to which I will return) is a manner of annihilating oneself or of no longer existing.

---

29. Montebello, *La Décomposition*, 271 (emphasis added).
30. Devarieux, "Michel Henry et Maine de Biran," 129–30 (emphasis added).

For, far from being unable to distinguish "sleep" from "wakefulness" and therefore making sleep an indication or even a proof of a doubt about my very existence (Descartes), Biran indubitably knows and senses, on the contrary, that my body awakens only by winning out over sleep—as with light over shadow, the diurnal over the nocturnal—and not the reverse. While one could wrongly believe that the passive is only the retreat of the active—whether this latter is consciousness (spiritualism) or the lived body (phenomenology)—one sees and one reads, on the contrary, in counter-relief in Maine de Biran, an obscurity at the origin (§12), out of which we strive each day to pull ourselves. We are not a wakefulness, forgetting ourselves in sleep; we are on the contrary a sleep from which we extricate ourselves by wakefulness. The *continuum of the flesh's existing* (sensing myself as existing) is resolved only in its *inner opposition to the body* (my hyperorganic that I must indeed find again and rediscover each morning as mine): "The fundamental mode of individual personality, periodically *suspended in the sleep of the myself and of thought*," emphasizes, very precisely, the thinker from Bergerac, "is always *reborn* the same: it is always the same relation of force to resistance, the same immediate apperception, the same self."[31]

This could not be any clearer. The immediate apperception of oneself by oneself, lived in relief when it is a matter of the "sentiment of the *myself*" (chapter 1) or the "lived body" (chapter 3), struggles against the disappearance, or at the very least the obscurity, of oneself to oneself (chapter 5). That the individual personality has to be "always reborn the same" in the concomitant relation to oneself of the (lived) body and of (the intimate) consciousness (of oneself) is indeed the sign *in relief* of a continuity of the *myself* but also *in counter-relief* of a subject that wrecks itself each night or that loses itself in the "always different." It is indeed a matter, each day, of being "reborn" in wakefulness because one forgets oneself each night in sleep. "Everything was effaced, everything disappeared," Biran writes perfectly, "transcribing" the one whom he names "the immortal Buffon" [sic] in his speech at the Bergerac Medical Society entitled "Nouvelles considérations sur le sommeil, les songes et le somnambulisme" ["New Considerations on Sleep, Dreams, and Sleepwalking"]: "The thread of my thoughts was interrupted; I lost the

---

31. Maine de Biran, *Of Immediate Apperception*, 117 (emphasis added).

sentiment of my existence. This sleep was deep. My awakening was but a second birth; *I sensed only that I had ceased to be*."[32]

"There can be no partial sleep, as there is no partial *myself*," the thinker from Bergerac then comments.[33] Either I sleep or I wake. But there is no guaranteed continuity, as for Leibniz who still sees a link, even an organic and necessary one, between the "*myself* who sleeps" and the "*myself* who wakes," since the little perceptions teach me that "we never sleep so soundly that we do not have some feeble and confused sensation; and the loudest noise in the world would never waken us if we did not have some perception of its start that is sensed."[34] We will not move too quickly in this direction to identify Leibniz's "little perceptions" with Biran's "obscure perceptions," to which he also devotes a speech addressed to the Bergerac Medical Society.[35] Continuity here is not unilaterally accepted. And even though obscurity is still waiting for light, nothing says or proves that there is any *continuum*, at least an organic one, between wakefulness and sleep.[36]

"Sleeping is being absent from,"[37] as Anne Devarieux comments from within the gap, in my view, between Biran's "obscure perceptions" and Leibniz's "little perceptions." For if the former (obscure perceptions) are certainly still waiting for light, as sleep waits for rebirth in wakefulness, they do not remain always present like the latter (little perceptions). Sleep, according to Biran, produces a radical, even organic, rupture in the double loss of the sentiment of oneself (experiencing oneself by oneself) and the primitive fact of effort (sensing oneself, including muscularly, by oneself). He is thus all the more distant from Leibniz in his search for continuity as the act of sleeping, if not that of falling asleep, is in itself an annihilation—"plunged into sleep"—a break, alienation, a complete change of state and not the conservation of a prior state.

And this is what is extraordinarily profound, and also extraordinarily contemporary—not solely in view of psychoanalysis (which will always look still more for a continuity between wakefulness and sleeping via dreaming) but also in view of philosophy, for which sleep has always

32. Maine de Biran, *Discours*, 83 (emphasis added).
33. Maine de Biran, *Discours*, 84–85.
34. Leibniz, *New Essays*, 6. [Translation modified. –Trans.]
35. Maine de Biran, *Discours*, 10–43.
36. On this analysis of "sleep" in Maine de Biran, one should refer to the excellent pages that Devarieux has devoted to it in *Maine de Biran*, 382–91.
37. Devarieux, *Maine de Biran*, 382–91.

been identified as a form of "death." The abyss is there that, at every sunset, opens for me and holds itself out, without knowing if ever, one day, I will leave it again and see the light anew. I would sometimes like to not sink into it, but I can and must only let myself go—at the risk, conversely, of never forgetting myself and of dying by virtue of remaining awake. "Falling" from sleep[38] is not enough; it remains necessary to "sink" into it and to let oneself fall into it in an abandonment that is not only detachment but is also and first loss and nothingization: "By falling asleep," writes Jean-Luc Nancy, remarkably and as a near-Biranian in *Tombe de sommeil* [*The Fall of Sleep*] (2007),

> I fall inside myself: from my exhaustion, from my boredom, from my exhausted pleasure or from my exhausting pain. I fall inside my own satiety as well as my own vacuity: I myself become the abyss and the plunge, the density of deep water and the descent of the drowned body sinking backward. . . . I sleep and this *I* that sleeps can no more say it sleeps than it could say that it is dead. So it is *another* who sleeps in my place. But so exactly, so perfectly in this, my own place, that he occupies it wholly without overlooking or overflowing even the slightest portion. It is not a part of me, or an aspect, or a function that is sleeping. It is *that entire other who I am* as soon as I am removed from all aspects of me and from all my functions except the function of sleeping, which perhaps is not a function, or else functions only to suspend all functioning.[39]

In light of this double "falling" [*tombée*] or even "tomb" [*tombe*] of sleep—"sensing only that I had ceased to be" (Biran) or "another who sleeps in my place" (Nancy)—the Parmenidian of the "sentiment of oneself" and the "primitive fact of effort" struggles, including in Biran, against the Heraclitean of a relation of force "of oneself in oneself" that is named resistance—whereby the *cosmos* (order and beauty) sinks into *chaos* (the filled-up or an opening ready to close again), or being, including organic being, into nothingness. Certainly, the "phenomenal *myself*" remains, in particular in that in-between of sleep and wakefulness, either at the moment of falling asleep or in the abandonment to

---

38. [The French expression *tomber de sommeil*, literally "to fall from sleep," means "to be extremely tired." "Dropping from exhaustion" is a reasonable equivalent in English but does not contain the word "sleep," which is essential in this context. Because the concepts of falling and of sleep are both essential to Falque's meaning, I have chosen to translate the phrase literally. –Trans.]

39. Nancy, *Fall of Sleep*, 5–6 (emphasis added).

relaxation. Such is the existential of the "in-between" remarkably described again in *Of Immediate Apperception*, from the moment that all the sensations of things are as if "suspended" and "reduced" to reach only, to say it in Biran's language, "all the internal impressions reduced to the natural tone of organic life" in a veritable phenomenological experiment or variation: "all the voluntary muscles contracted in the immobility of the body, eyes open in the shadows, hearing tensed (*acuta*) in the silence of nature, the ambient air at rest and the external temperature in balance with that of the surface of the body."[40] In such situations of immobile rest—which Jean-Yves Lacoste would perhaps name the "phenomenon of ease" in the simple fact, for example, of "well-being-there" to have a cup of tea[41]—"*effort alone remains,*" writes Maine de Biran verbatim, "and with it, the pure *phenomenal* myself, reduced to its immediate internal apperception."[42]

But all this applies only—and it is here that the "exception proves the rule" and that it is necessary to read Maine de Biran "in counter-relief" (in an outside that is internal to oneself) and no longer "in relief" (in a pure presence in oneself)—to the degree that I am there apperceiving myself or, rather, autoaffecting myself by myself, that is, in the awakening, including the muscular or, rather, intramuscular awakening, of my own body: "*For as long as this invariable mode persists, that is, for as long as the wakefulness of the* myself *lasts,*" we read verbatim in this panegyric to "immediate apperception," "sensory and accidental impressions coinciding with it can participate according to diverse laws or conditions in its reproductive activity and in the light of consciousness that springs from this source."[43]

But what will happen, or what would happen, if this "invariable mode" of the sentiment of effort in me that constitutes the *continuum* of

40. Maine de Biran, *Of Immediate Apperception*, 118.

41. Lacoste, *Monde*, 20–21: "*Ease simply introduces*—and this is assuredly not a small thing—*a third logic of the relation to place.* . . . The third logic that is attested in the experience of *well-being there* is apparently a logic of concession (doubtless excusable) to frivolity. . . . *Ease* tames the world without giving itself over to the enchantments of the earth." He gives the famous example of the moment of the "cup of tea" (near the cat and in the company of books) to illustrate this "phenomenon of ease": "*Ease* [*aise*] is conquered from a malaise [*malaise*] that is more radical than ease: closing my door to *have tea* in the company of my *books* and my *cat* will not prevent me from wondering what exactly I am doing 'here'" (20, emphasis added).

42. Maine de Biran, *Of Immediate Apperception*, 118.

43. Maine de Biran, *Of Immediate Apperception*, 118 (emphasis added). [Translation modified. –Trans.]

my existing did not last? What would happen if "the wakefulness of the *myself*" were suddenly transformed into a "deep sleep," which we have already named "complete sleep" and "cases of malfunction," relying on the *Essai sur les fondements de la psychologie* (§3d)? Maine de Biran states this, but again "in counter-relief" and not "in relief." In "sleep, sleepwalking, dreams, madness, or the effects of drugs" (Biran)—as also in "illness, separation, the death of a child, a natural disaster, or a pandemic" (*The Extra-Phenomenal*)—what was the rule, namely "the wakefulness of the *myself*," according to Maine de Biran's terminology, could well become the exception. There is a form of *permanent insomnia in man*, even if it is only for living and for remaining in wakefulness, since it is necessary to be "always *reborn* the same" in wakefulness, writes the thinker from Bergerac, from the moment that the ego is "*suspended* in the sleep of the *myself* and of thought"—and this even before Emmanuel Levinas made *insomnia* the recurring theme of the "impossible retreat" and of the irremissible fact of being "cornered into oneself."[44]

It is *extraction* from sleep that constitutes the living one—from the child who sleeps to the old man who dozes off. In the meantime, and in time, there stands only this waking in a struggle against fatigue, which constitutes us as such. The "myself" is never truly "mine," even in the sentiment of oneself, and the "lived or proper body" is never "proper" to me, since the sense of effort is forgotten and as if stunned for a considerable part of my life. Sleep as the "foreign outside myself," that is, as outside this body that I no longer experience as "proper" and that nonetheless determines me, makes it a swelling that is impossible to reduce, for life is only negatively a manner of not sleeping. What is true of "organic sleep" will be still truer of the "paralyzed hand." For it is precisely there that the inner muscular effort is as though blocked (the example of the statue feeling itself in a hand with no object or grasp) and is therefore neither experienced nor autoaffected to say "I am" (rose-odor).

c) The Paralyzed Hand

After the flight into sleep, the example of the "paralyzed hand" is then what makes clear, again, to what an extent the primitive fact of effort is also the primitive fact of an "organic resistance," even an internal one, and

44. Levinas, *Time and the Other*, 48: "Insomnia is constituted by the consciousness that it will never finish—that is, that there is no longer any way of withdrawing from the vigilance to which one is held."

not simply a lived experience of the flesh (in a pure sentiment of myself for myself). From the treatise *Of Immediate Apperception* for sleep (1807), we will return to the *Mémoire sur la décomposition de la pensée* for the example of the paralyzed hand—precisely where the "reply of resistance" (the body) takes the baton from the "reply of sentiment" (consciousness) in the "extension of the lived body" that "is manifest internally and is circumscribed" (§4a). Here again, and according to a method that is progressively becoming the rule [*la règle*], or becoming mandatory [*de règle*], the host of Grateloup gives us an argument *ab absurdo* by which effort is measured only when it can disappear. In other words, man is the one who "has the *sense of effort*"—according to the double meaning of his "signification" and his "will" in French[45]—especially if, in certain cases, he seems to live or, rather, to survive "effortlessly" [*sans effort*] (deep sleep, as we have seen, but also the man with the paralyzed hand).

"Effortless life" [*La vie sans effort*], as a dream for those who do not, or no longer, want to work, in reality marks, for Maine de Biran, the worst nightmare. For *without effort* [*sans effort*], that is, without that "virtual force" in us by which we live and feel, there is no longer any life [*vie*] but only "survival" [*survie*]. Although effort is certainly not the will to arrive at or to attain a goal, the will as consciousness of oneself (*conscium*), even mastery of oneself (*compos sui*) is, however, born from this free act by which I gain access to the "I" by feeling and saying that it is indeed "me" who feels myself from the inside: "*I am* rose-odor" (§10) and not "it will therefore be rose-odor" (§7). Since the lived body or the "inner extension" is precisely that whereby the "intimate sentiment of the *myself*" concomitantly arises, a "philosophy of the limits" must thus interrogate the *suppression* of the "lived body" or, rather, the *access* to the lived body in the possibility, or not, of being born to subjectivity.

After sleep, therefore, as the total suspension of the *myself* (*Of Immediate Apperception*), let us now imagine "*two hands paralyzed* with regard to external sentiment, without being paralyzed for *movement* or *voluntary locomotion*" (*Mémoire sur la décomposition de la pensée*).[46] We are not far here from the Husserlian "touching-touched" taken up by Merleau-Ponty, but with this additional difficulty that the touched (the right hand) will not necessarily respond to the touching (the left hand), such that the "reversibility of the flesh" (no longer knowing which is

---

45. [The French *sens*, like the English *sense*, can refer to meaning or to the senses or sensation. –Trans.]

46. Maine de Biran, *Mémoire sur la décomposition*, 438n (emphasis added).

the touching hand and which the touched hand) will not necessarily be able to take place. What would then happen "if I moved one hand against the other,"[47] writes Maine de Biran, *stricto sensu*? Decidedly, as with the "phenomenal *myself*" or the "lived body," the touching-touched is not, again, a pure invention of modern phenomenology but already of Condillacian or Biranian thought.

As with the phantom limb in Maurice Merleau-Ponty—which causes the legless person to feel, surprisingly and nearly organically, the limb that he does not have (his leg) to constitute the space that is his (§15)—Maine de Biran will spare one exit, such that the *flesh* or the "lived body" (the extension felt from the inside) can complete what is lacking in the *body* or in the organic. Just as *wakefulness* is won from *sleep* to struggle against the forgetting of oneself in the night, so too is the *flesh* conquered from the *body* in the case of the "legless person" or of the paralyzed hand. We are all, at the origin and from the origin onward, plunged into the black night (sleep) and are as though handicapped (the paralyzed hand). Like the child awakening to life, with all the Biranian discussions about the "fetus" as a possible self-consciousness or not,[48] we feel from within that we are living and that this is what we call "life" or even the "sentiment of one's own existence."

This must be said and said again. Michel Henry is right to see in Maine de Biran the root of Archi-Life and of the First Living One. But, contrary to what he ceaselessly repeats, this root is not discovered *immediately* (in an already-given pure proximity) but *is conquered in the struggle against a radical obscurity*, even a *paralysis of the body*, which means that the "foreign outside myself" is indeed what is first—not objectivity but opacity, not light but the black night. The resistance of the body constitutes the body not solely through the feeling of internal effort (the flesh or the "lived body"—the intramuscular feeling of the hand and the sentiment of the *myself*) but through what resists it at the origin in an organicity whose entropy also never ceases to drag me away (the "spread body"—lethargy in sleep, the paralyzed hand, even eternal sleep in death). The "outside," the "heterogeneous," the "obscure," the "out of area," as I have insisted at length (§12) acquires its patent of nobility in Maine de

---

47. Maine de Biran, *Mémoire sur la décomposition*, 438n.

48. Maine de Biran, *Essai sur les fondements*, 18: "Hence we have excellent grounds to conclude that there is no knowledge of any sort for a purely sensitive being, such as a number of *animals* probably are, such as the *fetus* within its mother or immediately after birth, etc." (emphasis added).

Biran for whoever knows how to read him well or read him otherwise, *in counter-relief* and no longer *in relief*. Not forgetting this is giving consistency to our humanity, which could well suffer from too much light in a well-respected apophatism: it is not, or no longer, the "more than luminous shadow of silence" (Pseudo-Dionysius) but the "shadow of the other night," forgetful even of the very idea of day (Blanchot).

This is what occurs when, to return to the Biranian analysis *ab absurdo*, the paralyzed hand that "no longer senses" and "no longer senses *itself*" from the inside can still move itself on the outside. It will certainly encounter the other hand, but in the manner of a pure "obstacle"—as we experience, for example, upon returning from the dentist with a still-anesthetized jaw. This obstacle of the left hand for the right hand in the touching-touched, if the left hand is designated as the paralyzed hand, or, better, if the "two hands" are paralyzed in the extreme hypothesis conducted here by Maine de Biran, certainly entails that I will not be able to experience *myself* or feel *myself* in either the left hand or the right hand, which a footnote in the *Mémoire sur la décomposition de la pensée* names a "reply of the sensation of contact"[49] (a third reply, therefore, in addition to the reply of sentiment and the reply of resistance). With the right hand not sensing the left hand (simple paralysis), and the two hands not sensing each other (double paralysis), there is certainly no longer any sensing or any sensed. Two paralyzed hands do not sense and do not sense *each other*. And since they do not sense *each other*, one could then believe or think—which would be Condillac's exact hypothesis in the example of the statue and of the hand touching its chest (§7)—that they could never say "I" (and barely "me") and therefore never gain access to the continuous sentiment of existing. In short, if the paralyzed hand were a "case of malfunction," it would mean that I would no longer have any means of reaching any sort of subjectivity. Since I am no longer able to "feel myself in my touch"—which is the transcendental condition of any self-knowledge via exteriority (Condillac) or interiority (Biran)—it is therefore the metaphysical access to the subject that seems to be definitively barred.

But where Biran certainly goes farther than Condillac, inasmuch as the latter's sensualism is restricted to the parts of organs (if my hands do not sense each other, I do not sense myself at all), is that the "reply of resistance," which doubles the "reply of sentiment," contained in affect, at the level of the body, always remains, even if the "reply of the sensation of

---

49. Maine de Biran, *Mémoire sur la décomposition*, 438n.

contact" does not occur or, rather, is absent or suppressed. The *paralytic's hand* certainly neither senses nor senses itself, but the resistance that it brings about (the reply of resistance) without sensation (the reply of contact) means that it will act on the whole body as *mine*. There is no need, as Condillac claimed in what I have named the "exception of touch" (§7), for the hand to touch or caress all the parts of the body *partes extra partes* for someone, albeit in a certain neutrality, to still be able to exclaim, "It's me, it's me again!" Indeed, for Biran it is not absolutely necessary—in an "extension of the lived body," concerning which we have seen that it is *interiorized*, therefore leaving the Cartesian schema of the geometrized extension (§4)—to *successively* "touch oneself" or "sense oneself" to know *who* one is and *what* one is. For the "reply of resistance" in the case of the statue, as I have shown for the "search for the flesh" (chapter 3), does not come from outside but solely from the inside for the thinker of Grateloup. It is indeed necessary that I sense *myself* already in myself, be it in a muscular and organic way, to sense something outside myself, and not the reverse. "*Because I sense myself* (the carnal *cogito*), I *sense* (sensation, then perception)": this is the carnal Biranian subjectivism according to which I touch *myself* in myself in a nearly transcendental fashion to then be able to touch (chapter 3). And it is not "*because I sense* (sensation, then perception)" that "*I sense myself* (the carnal *cogito*)": that would be the Condillacian sensualism that receives touch, including its own, *only* from the outside (chapter 2).

My two hands, whether or not they are paralyzed, according to Biran, indeed are already "part of this same body that is mine" and do not belong to "two different bodies," as Maine de Biran very precisely writes, surprisingly anticipating the constitution of space by the lived body in Merleau-Ponty's phenomenology of perception.[50] "For I indeed essentially appropriate for myself *all the parts of this whole*," continues, and remarkably explains, the next part of the already-cited footnote from the *Mémoire sur la décomposition de la pensée*, "which, obeying the *same will*, makes me *continuously* experience the sentiment of organic resistance."[51] Here the matter is as clear as it is essential. The "sentiment of organic resistance"— and we now see to what an extent the two replies "of sentiment" (affect) and "of resistance" (organic) henceforth make only one to constitute the

---

50. Merleau-Ponty, *Phenomenology of Perception*, 141: "I am not in space and in time, nor do I think space and time; rather, I am *of* space and *of* time; my body fits itself to them and embraces them" (emphasis added).

51. Maine de Biran, *Mémoire sur la décomposition*, 439n (emphasis added).

"lived body"—becomes the sentiment of an *internal continuum* rather than of an external shock. There is no need to "touch oneself," except in a pure interiority devoid of any object or any grasp, to know that one exists. The proof of this is, concludes Maine de Biran in his footnote, that if only *one* of the two hands were paralyzed (and not both), the "two resistances" would then again be opposed in the "simultaneous sentiment of the effort of which they are the terminus": "*The foreignness would disappear*, and *this case would be the same as the previous one.*"[52]

But will such a "foreignness"—the word thus appears anew here as the *alienus* or the body outside myself—of this paralyzed hand (the exception) disappear or be effaced so easily by "being the same as the previous case," which is that of the "touching-touched"? Nothing is less certain, for Biran is a man of radicality. Limit-situations, as I have proclaimed, must be analyzed, for it is there that extra-phenomenality plays out. And the "spread body," that is, the body that is objectivated for itself and is as if "outside itself," in the experience of palliative care for example ("Toward an Ethics of the Spread Body"), is already reached by Biran in experiences that precisely are medicalized.

There is indeed something worse than having a paralyzed hand, or even two paralyzed hands, namely, having *half the body* be paralyzed. One will then ask, in the extreme case of the *hemiplegic*, to still follow Maine de Biran, whether the lived body, or the flesh, to complete what is lacking in the internal test of the (muscular or organic) body, will suffice for feeling and therefore for accessing the "I." Better, there will be something even worse than the *hemiplegic* (who feels only half his body), namely the *paralytic from birth* (who does not feel his body and who therefore should not access himself, for lack of a lived body). Here we are probably standing at "confines" from beyond which we can no longer return. If everything depends on the sense of effort, and if organically and pathologically an "effortless life" sometimes becomes possible, we will then reach limits of the human when his vital functions are altered and he at times comes close to pure and simple animality or even to the state of minerality without being able any longer to experience anything, even becoming "like a stone" (§9c).

---

52. Maine de Biran, *Mémoire sur la décomposition*, 439n (emphasis added).

d) The Hemiplegic

Maine de Biran then refers, several times in *Of Immediate Apperception* but also in the *Mémoire sur la décomposition de la pensée*, to an account from Dr. Rey Regis, a doctor of the Montpellier faculty, concerning one of his sick people who, he said, "seemed paralysed in *half the body*, after a recent attack of apoplexy."[53] Without having the word for it, or at least without using it, the Montpellier doctor indeed faces a case of hemiplegia, the examination of which is unfolded in his *Histoire naturelle et raisonnée de l'âme* (1789), a "little-known" work according to Maine de Biran himself, which is evidence that he sought books everywhere to nourish his Grateloup library, as also his thought.

The doctor here asks himself the question that will later be the very question of Maine de Biran: "I was curious to know if he had any remaining feeling [*sentiment*] and any movement in the parts affected."[54] Then comes the experiment or, rather, the medical exam with an eye to diagnosis and even to the right treatment. It is not only phenomenology, with its imaginative variations, that can fertilize thought (the example of the "marble statue"), but also medicine, which deals this time with true reality, understood here as a patient who is indeed struck by an illness that it is necessary to diagnose. Rey Regis continues: "For that, I put my hand under the cover of the bed and pressed one of his fingers hard, which made him give out a cry."[55] The conclusion should therefore be clear, at least within the framework of the touching-touched of the other's hand, that is, here, the doctor's hand and the patient's hand. With the hand or, rather, the fingers being pressed, the partially paralyzed man nevertheless senses, and what he senses he feels, and therefore he can say "me" or, rather, "I" in the "primitive fact of effort" that is first experienced intramuscularly while at the same time providing the "sentiment of the *myself*."

But in reality that is not the case, or, rather, the case is otherwise. For the hand that is touched or, rather, pressed by the doctor was grasped on the patient's paralyzed side. This is therefore surprising, which only the Biranian analysis of the lived body is able to realize, and also only that analysis is able to make progress in the diagnosis—for philosophical

---

53. Maine de Biran, *Of Immediate Apperception*, 108n33 (emphasis added). [Translation modified. –Trans.]

54. Maine de Biran, *Of Immediate Apperception*, 108n33.

55. Maine de Biran, *Of Immediate Apperception*, 108n33.

thought, certainly, but also for what we today name "neuropsychology." For the sick person "feels [*ressent*] without sensing," or, to say it in Biran's previously developed terminology, he experiences a "reply of effort" that gives access to a "reply of sentiment" without a reply of contact: "In doing the same to each finger, he sensed each time a very sharp pain, but *without relating it anywhere*."[56] Here, therefore, is the paradox: there is a pain in the hand without a hand or, rather, a pain in the whole entire body (not related "anywhere"), for lack of localizing it and feeling it in an organ where it would precisely be experienced.

Aside from the learning process to which the patient will submit to regain his motility, there is here for Biran the proof of a "lived body" and therefore of a *flesh* that is capable of constituting us. It is exactly the same for Maine de Biran's hemiplegic in *Of Immediate Apperception* as for Maurice Merleau-Ponty's phantom limb in *The Phenomenology of Perception*. The "lived body"—with the usage of the same term by the thinker of Grateloup and the phenomenologist—has this in common in our two protagonists: it accesses the *flesh* (*Leib*) not "without a body" but through a mutilated body that is not an obstacle for subjectivity. The "lived body" or the *flesh* is indeed, in both cases, that sort of "internal extension" of which Maine de Biran spoke (§4), such that I live "what I *do not feel*" (my fingers in the case of the hemiplegic) or "what I *do not have*" (the leg in the case of the legless person) *as if* I felt it or *as if* I had it: "Consciousness of the phantom limb therefore remains equivocal," writes Merleau-Ponty this time, so close in this regard to Maine de Biran and Dr. Rey Regis's account.

> *The amputee senses his leg,* as I can sense vividly the existence of a friend who is, nevertheless, not here before my eyes. *He has not lost his leg because he continues to allow for it.* . . . The phantom arm is not a representation of the arm, but rather the *ambivalent presence* of an arm. . . . To have a phantom limb is to *remain open* to all of the actions of which the arm alone is capable and *to stay within the practical field that one had prior to the mutilation.*[57]

The homology here is surprising, and the filiation obvious, between the Biranian lived body and the Merleau-Pontyan lived body—even though the former feels only an "internal extension" (Biran), while the

---

56. Maine de Biran, *Of Immediate Apperception*, 108n33 (emphasis added). [Translation modified. –Trans.]

57. Merleau-Ponty, *Phenomenology of Perception*, 84 (emphasis added).

latter sees in it the constitution of an "external space" (Merleau-Ponty). But it does not suffice to stop there. For if there is no "flesh without body," it indeed seems that it is always a question of "saving the flesh" (a carnal feeling in itself) and not of defying the body (an incompressible mass is as if outside oneself). Responding to the "turn of the flesh," as I have shown elsewhere—and this is my thesis—amounts, on the contrary, to envisioning "the reversal of the phantom limb" of Merleau-Ponty. It is no longer "feeling the body that I do not have" (the phantom limb) but "not feeling the body that I have" (anesthesia)—and this is what constitutes what I call, properly speaking, the "spread body":

> There is indeed [in my view] much worse and more existential than *being the body one does not have* (the phantom limb), namely *not being the body that one does have* (bodily numbness or illness).... In the first case—*"feeling what I do not have"* (the phantom limb)—one constitutes or continues to constitute oneself and the world on the basis of the "flesh" or the lived body, even though it is missing a limb, or what is closest to one and oneself, for the constitution.... In the second case—*"not feeling what I have"* (anaesthesia or a tumour)—the object is not constituted for it is in one way or another unconstitutable. *There is* a limb, *there is* flesh, *there is* a tumour, *there is* a lump, *there is* a wound; but it is absolutely impossible to relate these to an ego capable of appropriating them.[58]

Is fleeing or, rather, overturning Merleau-Ponty joining with Sartre? In other words, and still relying on a divergent double interpretation of Maine de Biran, is no longer being centered solely on the "lived or proper body" or the body-subject (phenomenology) then sacrificing everything to the "improper body" or the body-object (existentialism)? Michel Henry, certainly, but also Maurice Merleau-Ponty and Paul Ricœur, as I have shown, have "made their Maine de Biran." But Jean-Paul Sartre, for his part, is not to be outdone. Better, it is precisely at the moment of opening his chapter on "the body" (that he will not name flesh) in *Being and Nothingness* (1943) that he mentions the thinker from Bergerac or, better, castigates him as the first initiator of the "sensation of oneself" who supposedly forgot all about the "sensation of things." And Sartre here (a) is wrong, but he is also (b) partly right.

---

58. See my contribution "Turn of the Flesh," 245–46 (emphasis partly in original). [Translation modified. –Trans.]

(a) We must indeed recognize that his failing is probably opposing or even cleaving everything. Speaking of the objectivation of my body amounts, according to him, to denying its transcendental function and therefore its capacity for subjectivation: "*Either* it [my body, my eye, my hand] is a thing among things, *or* it is that through which things are disclosed to me. But it cannot be *both at the same time*."[59] The opposition requires, then, that the "classic" Maine de Biran, the one who has always been seen as the founder of the "lived body" and therefore of the body-subject, can only be rejected and even accused of every ill. According to the Parisian existentialist philosopher, what the thinker of Grateloup says or, better, "seeks" *is not*. "Seeing" one's hand does not amount to "knowing" it or sensing it from the inside, since it is not for me an object among objects—(my) hand or (this) inkwell, it matters little: "Similarly, I can see my hand touching objects, but I do not *know* it, in its act of touching them. *That is the reason why, necessarily, Maine de Biran's famous 'sensation of effort' does not really exist.*"[60]

The accusation "misfires" because the whole of the "body-subject" cannot be reduced to the "body-object." What is the exception (aiming at one's own body as an object) is not, for me or for Maine de Biran, the rule (experiencing oneself as a body-subject). "So much exception, so much modification," as I have shown (§14). It is *not always* or *all the time* that my body appears to me as objectivated. This plays out, in my own view, only in the limit-experiences of spread thought (illness, separation, death of a child, etc.) or of the spread body (swelling, tumor, anesthesia, etc.). Inversely, and as a general rule, my body "for me" as a lived or proper body is not the same as my body "for the other" who aims at it only as improper. There is indeed the body-subject that is not the body-object, even though their "in-between" (the spread body) makes it necessary to bind them together or at least to relate them. In palliative care as in any other medical situation ("Toward an Ethics of the Spread Body"), we can therefore follow no further this passage by Jean-Paul Sartre that, rejecting Maine de Biran's lived body, makes the improper body the rule of all intercorporeality:

> In this way, I see *my hand* no differently from the way I see *this inkwell*. . . . When a doctor takes my bad leg and examines it, while I, semi-upright in my bed, watch him do this, there is *no*

---

59. Sartre, *Being and Nothingness*, 410 (emphasis added).
60. Sartre, *Being and Nothingness*, 410 (emphasis partly in original).

difference of kind between the visual perception that I have of the doctor's body and the one I have of my own leg.[61]

(b) Sartre, however, is *also* right, including as regards what would be an accurate commentary on Maine de Biran, which, however, he rejects. For in stating, as a justification of the fact of my own body's exteriority for me, that "my hand reveals to me the resistance of objects, their hardness or their softness, but it does not reveal *itself*,"[62] he in reality only finds again the interpretation "in counter-relief" of Maine de Biran—not the interpretation that bets everything on the lived or proper body but the interpretation that is constructed on the basis of the deterrent or even the terror of the improper body and the pure objectivation of myself for myself. Objects have their "foreignness" and their "foreignerness" in Sartre (as also in Biran)—let it suffice, to show this, to remember the "root's absurdity" in the garden of Bouville for Antoine Roquentin in *Nausea*:

> The roots of the chestnut tree were sunk in the ground just under my bench. I couldn't remember it was a root anymore. The words had vanished and with them the significance of things, their methods of use, and the feeble points of reference which men have traced on their surface.[63]

What is true of things is indeed true, then, but *only sometimes*, in my view, and not always, of my own body—without signification or explanation in the extreme case of illness and, of course, here in Maine de Biran, of paralysis. There is not, or no longer, any access to myself for myself via the muscular interiority of the sensation of my own hand once it no longer "feels" what it "senses" or should sense. My own body "becomes other" or alienated (*alienus*) once it is or becomes paralyzed—whereby the thinker from Bergerac, in this foreignness of my own body to myself, could now be the precursor not only of spiritualism, phenomenology, and hermeneutics but also of existentialism. Relying, therefore, on Sartre, but only when it comes to an "exception" that proves the rule, we will then radicalize Maine de Biran's thought even more, this time to reach the "totally alienated" or paralyzed body. If we fall constitutively into sleep to the point of forgetting light, such that awakening is only a conquest from shadow, if we fall accidentally into illnesses that can cause paralyses in us (the paralyzed hand, hemiplegia), what would then

61. Sartre, *Being and Nothingness*, 410 (emphasis added).
62. Sartre, *Being and Nothingness*, 410 (emphasis in original).
63. Sartre, *Nausea*, 126–27.

happen in the "extreme case" of a "paralytic from birth," as there are, for that matter, people blind from birth? Here we touch the utmost end of "limit-situations," to say it with Karl Jaspers—since Maine de Biran never recoils before an obstacle, including before the hypothesis of a sense of effort that has become totally absent or, rather, that was never present. That is, a "sentiment of the *myself*" is rendered impossible, the lived body having lost all feeling and therefore all "internal extension," to be only a "mass" that it is impossible to subjectivate.

e) The Paralytic from Birth

The hypothesis of the "(complete) paralytic from birth" arises, then, at the opening of the *Essai sur les fondements de la psychologie* ("Analyse des faits primitifs du sens intime" [Analysis of the primitive facts of the intimate sense]). Again it is the method *ab absurdo*, Biranian par excellence, which consists in passing through the exceptions to prove the rule. Having just designated the "sense of effort" as "that which is most intimate in or closest to us or, rather, because it *is* ourselves [*sic*],"[64] Biran then proposes to us what he calls a "more detailed analysis," entering then into the "summary" of a descriptive analysis, which is certainly difficult to envision, of a *total paralysis from birth*—still more probably what we today would call not hemiplegia but quadriplegia (in which the paralysis of the limbs could hypothetically prevent sensing and even sensing *oneself* or feeling—and therefore saying "I").

In those centuries of medical research, of medicine, and of encyclopedias, people liked pursuing such hypotheses—and perhaps Biran's *paralytic from birth* is the response to Molyneux's *man blind from birth* (who has to distinguish, when gaining sight, the sphere and the cube that he had hitherto differentiated only by touch), cited by Locke, taken up by Diderot, Condillac, and many others as well.[65] It remains that the case is extreme and even radical, since the paralytic from birth will never know sensation, contrary to the man blind from birth who suddenly, at least in Molyneux's hypothesis, gains sight. In reality, it is not the muscles that are threatened (we would then remain confined to a neurological diagnosis) but the access to the "myself" or, rather, to the "I" (whereby it is really a matter of a philosophical analysis). If I cannot say "I am my body," like "I

---

64. Maine de Biran, *Essai sur les fondements*, 179–80 (emphasis added).
65. See note 51 in chapter 2.

am rose-odor" (§10) (and not "it will therefore be rose-odor" like Condillac [§6]) via my lived body that also first experiences itself intramuscularly in the primitive fact of effort, the total absence of internal muscular tension would cause to disappear any "phenomenal *myself*," that is, any "intimate sentiment of the *myself*." Without at least "feeling myself" via sensation (the lived body), I cannot "feel myself" via autoaffection (the phenomenal *myself*). The access to myself is not blocked but suppressed, and denying this would mean losing corporeality or the "extension in myself," to make thought a separate substance.

In short, nothing of myself—the "lived body" and the "sentiment of the myself"—can then take place, from the moment that the "primitive fact of effort" (including but not only organic effort) is suppressed. Worse yet, the paralytic from birth will not be able to access intelligence itself, since without such a "sentiment of the *myself*" conquered by the "lived body," the entirety of the world is forbidden to me, since it can be only transcendentally on the basis of such a *carnal subjectivity* that it is impossible to surpass: "If there were, for example, some *paralytic from birth*," writes Biran verbatim, going to the farthest degree of alienation or of the foreign outside myself (§15), "who had never acted voluntarily to move his limbs or to move foreign bodies, supposing that this being could have the slightest degree of intelligence, which seems impossible to me, there would *no more be any way to make him understand with words what effort is* than there would be *to explain to a man born blind what colors are and what the sense of sight is.*"[66]

The "case" is therefore clear, until the blade falls. A "(complete) paralytic from birth," *medically diagnosed* as unable to move any limb or to feel any muscle by means of which, therefore, to "sense himself by himself" in his lived body, becomes *philosophically unfit* for any subjectivity and even for all the modes of intelligence that must derive from it. As Henri Gouhier perfectly emphasizes in the introduction to his anthology on Maine de Biran, thereby indicating, moreover, that the case of the "paralytic from birth" cannot be omitted simply because he was probably not born thus:

> Let us imagine a *complete paralytic from birth* who was never able to act on his muscles: explaining Biranism to him would be the same as speaking of color to a man born blind; he would lack the fundamental experience that would render him capable

---

66. Maine de Biran, *Essai sur les fondements*, 180 (emphasis added).

of giving the words a sense. Let us go farther: for a Biranian, the hypothesis is absurd: whereas a blind person can be very intelligent, such a paralytic could not even raise himself to the level of self-consciousness.[67]

The "foreign outside myself" or the "foreign body" is total here—for the *myself* itself is wholly alienated, even annihilated, in the complete impossibility of experiencing his body. What applies to the paralytic from birth in Maine de Biran applies also, although to a different degree and in other circumstances, to Charlotte Delbo's account upon leaving Auschwitz in *None of Us Will Return*. The "will to resist" that is so dear to Biran has definitively disappeared, and there remains only the "cold skeleton," like the paralytic from birth or the Condillacian marble statue before it has even experienced anything whatsoever. Life has become "effortless," not in the sense of a laziness or a negligence that could be excused—but in the sense of an asthenia that means I am able only to notice myself as (still) there, according to a mode of survival that imposes so much on me that I should no longer exist either. There is no longer any lived or proper body but a "disappropriated body" (the spread body); there is no longer any "I" but only a being that is "still there," annihilated and cornered—that is, totally "off*side*" (the extra-phenomenal): "I am standing amid my comrades and I think to myself that if I ever return," we read from the pen of Charlotte Delbo, grippingly indeed, and like a confession,

> and will want to explain the inexplicable, I shall say: "I was saying to myself: you must stay standing through roll call. You must get through one more day. It is because you got through today that you will return one day, if you ever return." *And this will be false*. Actually I said *nothing* to myself. I thought of *nothing*. The *will to resist* was doubtlessly buried in some deep, hidden spring which is now broken, I will never know. And if the women who died had required those who returned to account for what had taken place, they would be unable to do so. I thought of *nothing*. I looked at *nothing*. I felt *nothing*. I was a *cold skeleton*, with cold blowing through all the crevices in between a skeleton's ribs.[68]

---

67. Gouhier, *Œuvres choisies*, 31 (emphasis added).

68. Delbo, *Auschwitz and After*, 64 (emphasis added). [Translation modified. – Trans.] For an analysis of this experience (of the impossible experience) in Charlotte Delbo's work, I refer to my contribution "Mal et finitude," esp. 426–29.

"Resist, prove that you exist" (§15a): the *organicity of sleep*, the *paralyzed hand*, the *hemiplegic*, and the (complete) *paralytic from birth* are, if not the proof of this, at least the sign of it. In these "limit-cases" or these extreme hypotheses, there stands what I have elsewhere defined as the "spread body" caught between the extended body (Descartes) and the lived body [*le corps vécu*] (Husserl). Rarely has a descriptive analysis (Biran's, that is) so greatly confirmed that which, besides, I have never stopped and will not stop seeking. Let it suffice here to say this again:

> It is in fact a body—perhaps we should describe it as "*intermediate*," or a *frontier zone*? And this residue is between the *subjective flesh* of the phenomenologist and the *objective body* of the scientist. It is that of the organic matter to deal with or operate on, which is not totally objective because it cannot be reduced to a geometric form. Nor is it totally subjective, because it does not fully correspond to the ego when we examine it in terms of consciousness. We can take as an example the body under anesthetic, something most of us have experienced ourselves and seen in others, both animals and human beings. . . . Extended, the anesthetized body is, as it were, spread out onto the operating table; it is fleshly matter that has often been offered and given and over which the doctor would be able, in the absence of regulation, to exercise an unlimited power.[69]

---

69. Falque, *Wedding Feast*, 13 (emphasis partly in original).

6

Effortless Life

> The successive periods of drunkenness, brought about by opium and wine, . . . show that the *capacity for effort* has diminished, that the will is uncertain, the limbs intractable, to the point that, finally, this power being totally suspended in its exercise, there is *no more effort, no more movement, no more "myself."*
>
> MAINE DE BIRAN,
> *DISCOURS À LA SOCIÉTÉ MÉDICALE DE BERGERAC*

The Method *ab Absurdo*

THUS WE MUST NOW enter into what Biran himself means by the "sense of effort," already defined above as "that which is most intimate in or closest to us or, rather, because it *is* us [sic]"[1]—the "sense of effort" understood in French both as a definition (*what effort is*) but also as a natural tendency (*having the sense of effort*). For effortless life, as I have just shown, is not in resistance but rather in the absence or even the complete loss of all resistance. One no longer makes any "effort(s)," not because one no longer resists—as is well known and experienced by each and every one of us—but because, on the contrary, one no longer has the strength [*force*] to resist. *The Extra-Phenomenal* has shown this. There

---

1. Maine de Biran, *Essai sur les fondements*, 179–80 (emphasis added).

lies the "fall of the body" that most often falls with its full weight to the point of losing its strength [*forces*] and therefore thought, supposing that the "break of fatigue" is always at the same time the break of the psyche. Certainly not all "traumatized," we are all potentially "traumatizable." Whether one calls it *burnout* or *breakdown*,[2] with English words that at least perfectly have the merit of signifying it, extra-phenomenality is there, and we can no longer deny it.

From the negative, then, we will come back to the positive, or from the *ab absurdo* we will reascend toward the *in senso*. The extremes (drunkenness, drugs, paralysis, madness, dementedness, etc.) make visible the norm, if there is one, and the exceptions make visible the rule. "Effortless life" thus requires coming back to the "sense of effort," and the "loss of strength [*forces*]" to the "internal exercise of force [*force*]." For the foreign outside myself is not only that of my body lived as an "outside" (with a total loss of the sentiment of the *myself* in sleep or in complete paralysis) but is also that of an exteriority that resists me without which also I could not exist, and still less could I experience. Biran *does not lose the world*, contrary to the interpretation that Michel Henry was able to give of him. The "world is at my fingertips" [*au bout de mes doigts*], even though I am never "at the end of myself" [*au bout de moi*], a point to which I am coming. "Virtual force," in a discussion with Leibniz this time to define in what the "primitive fact of effort" consists—as there was a discussion with Descartes and the impossible crossing from the *cogito* to the *res cogitans* to determine the "primitive fact of the sentiment of the *myself*" (§3)—will thus serve as a spearhead for this determination of the *effort in me* that, however, also stumbles on the *outside myself*, without which I could no longer exist, and still less could I say "me" or "I" in this lived body or this "internal extension" that constitutes my specificity.

§16. The Sense of Effort

a) Resistance at Its Terminus

To the *resistance of oneself to oneself* (the primitive fact of effort) alone we must therefore also oppose the *resistance of oneself to the world* (the resisting terminus), or at least we must differentiate the latter from the former: "We know that resistance can be either organic, as when, for

---

2. [*Burnout* and *breakdown* are in English in the French text. –Trans.]

example, the subject moves a muscle," emphasizes Bernard Baertschi, very accurately, in *L'Ontologie de Maine de Biran*, "or external, as when the hand closes on a ball or the individual wills to lift a weight. There are therefore two types of resistances."[3] Let us be careful here, however. There is no question here, for Maine de Biran, of constituting the "myself" or constituting "oneself" on the basis of the body or the world considered as an object for me (Condillac's sensualism), but it is only a matter of recognizing that the movement by which I experience myself (the lived body) must also be the movement by which I experience the world (the reiteration or reply of my lived body in my relation to the world): "But if the body is a subjective being, it is also an objective being, and this *from the same point of view, from within* the primitive fact."[4]

I already have precisely emphasized this with regard to the always-resisting "cannonball" taken in the hand (§8d). It is not in reality the "terminus" itself (things or the world) that Maine de Biran suspends or "brackets" in a generalized *epoché* according to which only the pure autoaffected *myself* would remain. It is the *movement toward this terminus* that he reverses, including for the body: it is no longer from the body-object (sensed) to the body-subject (sensing) but from the body-subject (sensing) to the body-object (sensed). In other words, in phenomenological terms this time, it is from the "flesh" (*Leib*) to the "body" (*Körper*) and no longer from the "body" to the "flesh." But thus going from the carnal (*leiblich*) to the corporeal (*körperlich*) is not suppressing all bodies; far from it. The thinker from Bergerac spells this out plainly in a footnote in the *Mémoire sur la décomposition de la pensée*, indicating in his debate with Condillac, in a conscious and perfectly mastered way, that his intention was never to say or make anyone believe that nothing exists outside us (in the sense of the external) and that everything plays out only in us (in the intimate) but only that effort (in us) can certainly be applied to ourselves and to our own bodies (the lived body) but also to the external world (the foreign body). In other words, the Husserlian distinction between "flesh" (*Leib*) and "body" (*Körper*) in Maine de Biran is conceptualized perfectly, but we must never, in his view and in my own, think a "flesh without body," at the risk of forgetting the world by wanting to too much forget ourselves or be engulfed in ourselves.[5]

3. Baertschi, *L'Ontologie de Maine de Biran*, 77. See also Baertschi, *L'Ontologie de Maine de Biran*, 77–131.

4. Baertschi, *L'Ontologie de Maine de Biran*, 88.

5. It is impossible, therefore, to apply to Maine de Biran the critique that I have

b) Ef-fort

It is because effort is certainly applied "either to the lived body" or also—and this is the crucial point—"to the foreign body" that resistance is double, according to the philosopher of Grateloup, even though resistance could never be sensed [*senti*] (outside) without first being felt [*ressenti*] (inside)—hence the importance of the "reply," be it the "reply of sentiment (consciousness or affect), the "reply of effort" (the lived body from myself to myself), or even the "reply of sensation and contact" (the foreign body experienced in myself). We will not conflate "foreign resistance" or the soul projected "outside myself" with no access to itself, in the rose-odor, for example (Condillac), and the "foreign body" that is different from the "lived body" and that means that "something" resists me also, and sometimes from the outside, for me to sense myself. The "resistance" is internal, but the "resisting body" can be experienced either *without* the object (the muscular tension of the hand) or *through* the object (the cast-iron cannonball). There is therefore no pure autoaffection in Maine de Biran, nor is there any "transcendental flesh" below the "organic body" and the "objective body" (§10d). *Effort* or the autoaffection of oneself by oneself (the hyperorganic) is also a heteroaffection of oneself by the other (the resisting terminus)—definitively barring the way for any subjectivity that would deny all foreign bodies: "I have *substituted*," Biran firmly emphasizes, facing Condillac, but without denying the "foreign body," "*organic inertia or resistance* for *foreign resistance*, and I have seen the faculties originarily constituted, not *exclusively* in that constrained movement that teaches us that there exists something *outside ourselves*, but more generally in the effort that is essentially relative to some term, be it applied *to the lived body* or *the foreign body*."[6]

There are, certainly, the "tractable life" and terminus, the life that belongs to me, that clings to me like it clings to my skin. Even if it involves suffering and not just enjoying, it is always, in its *pathos*, a life of oneself with oneself (autoaffection). But there is also the "intractable life" and terminus, the life that I can never tame, that resists me and forbids me any pure coincidence with myself. In this irreducible residue, that which is not me and which can never be wholly referred back to myself (the foreign outside myself) is also said. As Anne Devarieux

---

addressed to Michel Henry. See chapter 5 in *Loving Struggle*, 143–73, "Is There a Flesh Without Body? Michel Henry."

6. Maine de Biran, *Mémoire sur la décomposition*, 164n (emphasis added).

emphasizes with great accuracy, with the Henryan interpretation of Maine de Biran in her sights:

> Iteration (or the reply) has a basis, but only on the condition of thinking *the movement* and *its terminus* (the world and things) as a *resisting terminus*. . . . The analysis therefore presupposes the wholly Biranian distinction between the *two termini* of my effort: the *relative and tractable* terminus of the resistance of my body and the *intractable* terminus of the absolute resistance of external things. Though the world is at my fingertips [*au bout de mes doigts*], I am never at the end of myself [*au bout de moi*].[7]

Saying that "the world is at my fingertips," to do justice to this accurate, well-tempered phrase, thus means first that there is a world and that the world for me (internal) is also faced with and in contact with a world that resists me (external). There is no negation of the world for Biran but rather a constitution of the world on the basis of myself, in my lived body and its internal effort, but also on the basis of the resisting terminus that resists it. And adding that "this world is at my fingertips" ought to make me recognize that "I am never at the end of myself" and requires thinking, and positing, that it never suffices to go from myself to myself in an effort that is only interiorized, but rather the veritable "end of myself" is also outside myself in a resistance, even an external resistance, that I cannot suppress. Let us remember the "cast-iron cannonball" as a "solid" or a "body as a mass"—whether it is perceived or imagined: if "this object is placed on his hand that he wills to close[,] at a certain moment, the *movement of his fingers will be stopped*, even if he makes a very great effort" (§8d).

Thus the *sense of effort* must be well understood, both for what it signifies and for what it produces. Let it suffice indeed to come back to the term "effort" that is so central in Maine de Biran's thought—the "effort of oneself in oneself" in the lived body, certainly (the primitive fact), but also the "effort outside oneself" that is as if felt in contact with the lived body (the resisting terminus)—to recognize that it never etymologically signified the mere entrance into oneself (*cogito*) but also the internal tension toward the outside-oneself: *ex-fortis* or "ef-fort," an exit from oneself by force, or crossing "at any cost [*à toute force*]." "Below representation," Pierre Montebello perfectly emphasizes, rightly recognizing "the foreign outside oneself" in the sense of effort properly understood, "thought is

---

7. Devarieux, "Michel Henry et Maine de Biran," 126 (emphasis added).

already a certain way of being *outside oneself*, as the word 'effort' says. What good is *making an effort* [*s'efforcer*] if one possesses *oneself* entirely?"[8]

Saying and understanding that "making an effort"—inasmuch as the "sense of effort" indicates in French not only what it signifies ("what is effort?") but what it produces ("having the sense of effort")—will thus certainly refer back to this form of *force* or *internal resistance* that I sense in myself, but also to it inasmuch as it collides with an *external resistance* outside myself. After having lost the world (like the *cogito* in Descartes's second *Meditation*), we must find it again (as in the sixth *Meditation*) or, rather, understand that we have never left it. It is only if one remains confined to the autoaffection of oneself by oneself and if one reduces *Biranian force* to *Leibnizian force* that one encloses "ef-fort" or force in the soul's monad alone and does not see that there is also a resistance to force outside oneself. While force exerts itself "in the absence of the world" (Henry) or in "a single world" contained in the monad (Leibniz), it is a question of defining an outside-oneself or a world "outside its sole world" (closer in this regard to Merleau-Ponty) such that the whole of the *myself* is not reduced to the "myself" alone. There is a *power of force*, including in Biran (in the manner of Nietzsche, perhaps), which is all the more "virtual" as it refers less to imagined possibles than to real effects or modifications that are at least engendered in oneself.

c) Virtual Force

Maine de Biran thus brings about with regard to "Leibnizian force" exactly what he had carried out with regard to the Cartesian *cogito* (§2): namely, a "desubstantialization," such that force will no longer be designated as a substance in an in-itself, even a dynamic one (Leibniz), any more than one could or should pass from the *cogito* to the *res cogitans* (Descartes). As Henri Gouhier emphasizes in a cutting but nevertheless justified fashion in *Les Conversions de Maine de Biran*—a work published in 1948, the very year, that is, in which the thinker from Bergerac was for the first time placed on the program for the *agrégation* in philosophy in France (with the renewal that this produced as much on Michel Henry's side as on Maurice Merleau-Ponty's): "The definition of the soul as a *virtual force* must be located on the same plane as the theory of belief in soul-substance. But it represents [and here Gouhier firmly opposes Vancourt's

8. Montebello, *Décomposition*, 273 (emphasis added).

interpretation in *La Théorie de la connaissance chez Maine de Biran* (*The Theory of Knowledge in Maine de Biran*), 1930] an attempt to escape soul-substance rather than a prefiguration of substance."⁹

A force that is not a thing (as in Leibniz) and that does not set up only a sort of center of drives (like the Freudian libido as a unified pole oriented within the first topography)¹⁰—that is what the "virtual force" fundamentally brings about here. Freeing force from any reification, in itself as outside itself, it sets up what Nietzsche will later name "pure force," not only because Maine de Biran no longer separates force from what it can do but because it is no longer a "simple potentiality [*puissance*]" (stretched toward an act as in scholasticism) or a "pure dynamism" (an activity without rest founded on a multiplicity of substantial spontaneities contained in the monad in Leibniz). An *other* and *new dynamic*: that is what Maine de Biran wants to initiate—namely, a thought of force in itself and on the basis of itself to constitute the *myself* (named effort) but not without resistance, confronting Leibniz in particular with regard to force (chapter 5), as he was confronting Descartes with regard to the "sentiment of oneself" (chapter 1) or Condillac with regard to the "lived body" (chapter 2).

We know this, since we have said it and have even explicitly been surprised by it (p. 4): the thinker of Grateloup published in his lifetime only his treatise *The Influence of Habit on the Faculty of Thinking* (1802), a short essay entitled *Examen des leçons de philosophie de M. Laromiguière* [*Examination of Mr. Laromiguière's Philosophy Lessons*] (1817), and an article on the "Exposition de la doctrine philosophique de Leibniz" ["Exposition of Leibniz's Philosophical Doctrine"] in Michaud's *Biographie universelle* [*Universal Biography*] (1819). Certainly, that is little, even very little—specifically, hardly more than three hundred pages out of the seven million pages found after his death (eighteen volumes today), not counting the fifteen hundred pages of the *Journal*. I will not retrace again the story already told in the introduction, but it is important again here because only his monograph on Leibniz, among the numerous authors on whom he commented—there are three volumes of *Commentaires et marginalia* [*Commentaries and Marginalia*] in volume 11 of the *Œuvres de Maine de Biran* published by Vrin: *XVIIe siècle* [*Seventeenth*

---

9. Gouhier, *Conversions de Maine de Biran*, 232.

10. Falque, *Nothing to It*, 21: "By passing from the first to the second topography, Freud progressively gave up on the original ideal of the Enlightenment (*Aufklärung*), the paradigm of a controlled scientificity, with its duly demarcated borders."

Century] (11.1), *XVIIIe siècle* [*Eighteenth Century*] (11.2), and *XIXe siècle* [*Nineteenth Century*] (11.3)—received the honor of "going to publication." One could say and believe that this was the work of chance or of a strange lucidity. That, however, is not the case, since his "Exposition de la doctrine de Leibniz" was intentionally written for the *Biographie universelle*, as the *Journal* entry on the date of May 15, 1819, testifies: "I have begun seeing to the Leibniz article, for which I am insistently being asked for the *Biographie. The foundational idea* of Leibnizian philosophy is the idea of activity, of *force*."[11] And we know, by the way, that force will also constitute a "key notion" for me in order to say the "force of the resurrection"[12] or the "power of transubstantiation."[13]

Reading, then, this famous "Exposition de la doctrine de Leibniz," today reprinted in the *Commentaires et marginalia* on the seventeenth century, one sees in it a Maine de Biran who first pays his tribute to the author of the *Principles of Nature and Grace Based on Reason* (1714), in which one finds, from the opening, this definition of substance by force (and no longer in its beingness or in the relation of potentiality to act): "*Substance* is a being capable of action."[14] And Biran comments, relying this time nearly word for word on the Leibnizian opuscule "On the Correction of Metaphysics and the Concept of Substance" (1694)—but bringing about a sort of "subjectivization of force," since force is deployed less in the world (constituted by monads) than in the subject acting and experiencing itself (in the intramuscular effort felt in the hand):

> Yet, to clarify the notion of *substance*, we must go back to the notion of *force* or *energy*, the explication of which is the object of a particular science called "dynamic." The *active or acting force* is not the *naked potentiality* of Scholasticism; we must not indeed understand it, as the Scholastics did, as a mere *faculty* or possibility of acting that, to be *effected* or reduced to the *act*, would

---

11. J. II, 225 (emphasis in orignal).

12. See Falque, *Metamorphosis of Finitude*, 79: "The Holy Spirit, as metamorphosis of the Son by the Father, and of mankind in him, thus paradoxically connects with what Nietzsche despaired of finding in Christianity—the non-separation '*of strength from what it can do*'" (emphasis in original). [Translation modified. –Trans.]

13. See Falque, *Wedding Feast*, 111: "The true weakness of the Christian comes not from a renunciation of force (the force of his body, in particular)—in the misinterpretation that is the paralogism of force of which Nietzsche wrongly accused him. Rather, it comes from entrusting his force to another (the Holy Spirit in him)." [Translation modified. –Trans.] On transubstantiation as an "acting force," see *Wedding Feast*, 200–205. On this "turn of force" taken in my work, see Falque and Costa, "Turning Point?"

14. Leibniz, "Principles of Nature and Grace," 636 (emphasis in original).

need an excitation from the outside, like a foreign *stimulus*. The veritable *active force* includes the action in itself; it is *entelechy*, the *middle power* between the mere faculty of acting and the determined or effected act: this energy contains or envelops the effort (*conatum involvit*) and inclines itself of itself to act, without any external provocation.[15]

The Biranian summary of the Leibnizian position is perfect here. Reading it, one really is delighted that Maine de Biran was able to frequently organize "philosophical Fridays" in Paris (at which François Naville, the Protestant pastor who saved his manuscripts from being forgotten, was an established listener), so pertinent is his reading of authors, and so greatly does he let himself be transformed by precisely that which, through books, is addressed to him. For Leibniz, therefore, force is no longer potentiality in its relation to act, as with the naked potentiality of the Scholastics. Such a *passive potentiality*, which sets itself in motion only because it is drawn by the act, exists only for itself and does not depart from itself. The *active* (or acting) *force*, on the contrary, applies by itself or for itself, as will be the case for Biranian effort, and instead of constituting a point of departure or a unique center, it is the intermediary itself or, rather, the "link" (*vinculum*) between a faculty of acting in oneself (a substance-force) and the act itself (the expression of the substance).

d) The Exerted Force

One could, then, and one even should, be satisfied with this new notion of substance as "force," that is, as a "Being capable of Action." This, however, is what Maine de Biran does not want, or is the point starting from which he does not follow or no longer follows Leibniz, and this for at least two reasons. Every "force" must be immediately exercised, for the thinker from Bergerac, and it would be nonsensical to posit a "reserve of forces" as if life were capable of being stored up, as likewise to separate force from what it can do (the paralogism of force), which would then lose its continuous character.

1. The first reason, therefore, is that "if Leibniz's merit [in Maine de Biran's view] is to have associated the notions of force and substance,

---

15. Maine de Biran, *Commentaires et marginalia: XVIIe siècle*, 143–44 (emphasis partly in original). One can, then, profitably compare it with Leibniz, "On the Correction of Metaphysics" (esp. 433).

his error is to have dissociated the activity of the soul from that of the *myself*."[16] Force indeed is meaningful in itself for Leibniz. It is sufficient for a monad to have or, rather, to be a "soul" to "be a force" qua substance-force. Whether the force is exercised or not, or even whether it "binds" (*vinculum*) or not, matters little. All that counts is that it *is* capable of action (substance) and not that it *exercises* an action (the sentiment of its effort or its effectuation). In Maine de Biran's eyes, Leibniz has, as it were, reversed the copy and the model. Instead of first seeing *force in myself* insofar as *I* exercise it and feel it, since it constitutes me in my specificity [*en propre*] (and as a lived or proper body), to then possibly think it as constitutive of animated beings, he first thinks and sees force *in itself*, always ready (or not) to exercise itself. In short, and to say it in Aristotle's terminology, Leibnizian force still remains in the order of *poiesis* (being able to deploy a transitive effect outside itself, albeit in the monad) and is not a *praxis* (a pure immanent force in itself that is meaningful only when it is exerting itself): "Placing the foundation of the primitive notion of cause or of potentiality in a wholly internal activity," indicates the thinker from Bergerac, this time in his *Mémoire sur la décomposition de la pensée*, in a barely veiled critique of Leibniz, "one can still realize this virtual activity *outside the sentiment of its exercise*, by affirming it of a subject taken *in abstracto*, which is indeed *putting the copy before the model*."[17] Independently of the technical aspect of the debate, force is no longer the force of the monad or of the universe, in Maine de Biran, but is my force insofar as I force *myself* [*m'efforce*][18]—myself qua subject that senses *itself* and inclines *toward itself*, in the exercise of the double reply of sentiment and of effort, albeit in the resistance of a terminus external to myself: a thing or the world.

2. Hence the second reason for the difference from Leibniz, namely that force can no longer be enclosed in the monad alone, and therefore be solipsistically cloistered in a form of autoaffection. Like the "resistance at its terminus," the virtual force (Biran), and no longer the active or acting force (Leibniz), extends beyond itself and senses that a residue is opposed

16. I am here following Parmentier's accurate interpretation in "Maine de Biran," 4.

17. Maine de Biran, *Mémoire sur la décomposition*, 124–25.

18. [*S'efforcer* means *to strive*, *to make an effort*, or *to struggle* (to do something). It does not necessarily refer to making oneself do something that one does not want to do, as *to force oneself* typically does in English, but I have here translated *je m'efforce* as *I force myself* in order to preserve both the play on "force" and the reflexivity of the verb. *I effort myself* would be better if it were a possible formulation in English, but it is not. –Trans.]

outside itself and renders impossible the complete reduction of oneself to oneself. The Berlin treatise, *Of Immediate Apperception*, insists on this. It is not by remaining within oneself that force is exercised but by exiting from oneself or by opposing oneself to the "outside-oneself," as "effort" (*ex-fortis*) never stops signifying: "In Leibniz's system, the soul is indeed endowed with *force* or, rather, is itself merely an acting force, but its activity does not extend beyond its own domain, and consists *only* in *appetites*, *desires* or tendencies to a change of state."[19]

Whence, then, the fact that force is called "virtual" in Maine de Biran, and not only "acting" as in Leibniz? It is not virtual in the sense of possible but in the sense of power [*puissance*] or virtue in the etymological sense (*virtus*), constituting the subject in its specificity and constituting its specificity: "In this relation to the *subject*," specifies the thinker from Bergerac in *Le Système de Leibniz* [*Leibniz's System*], "the tendency, *even the virtual tendency*, or the non-exercised, non-determined force (energy, the *middle power* between *the mere faculty and the act*), is what constitutes *the proper ground of our being*, that which remains when everything changes or passes."[20] There is, therefore, in Biran neither a force enclosed in itself (monadology or autoaffection) nor a simple link between terms via force (*vinculum*) but a ground of our virtual being in the sense of a force that is always exercised in me as being me and defining the *myself*. The "reply of resistance" through the body (effort) and the "reply of sentiment" through consciousness (affect) are but one in this force that is exercised in me for me to experience myself and whose exteriority or bodies outside me oppose a terminus through which I also sense myself. The "outside oneself" (that which resists a self closed upon itself) is certainly not identical to the "foreign in oneself" (that which destroys me, this time psychically, in extreme situations), but it carries out a considerable step toward a "thought of the outside in me," which entails that we are confined neither to the moist gastric intimacy of the *myself* (autoaffection) nor to projection outside oneself (existentialism or phenomenology of being-in-the-world). Desubstantialized because it no longer belongs to the already-given soul-substance, but making the always-modified *myself*, force in its exercise or its *virtus* never ceases to constitute me, and it is therefore by being "without force," or having lost any "sense of effort" in the double sense of the term (signification

---

19. Maine de Biran, *Of Immediate Apperception*, 86–87 (emphasis partly in original).

20. Maine de Biran, *Commentaires et marginalia: XVIIe siècle*, 150 (emphasis partly in original).

and will) that the outside oneself, like the "foreign to oneself," will now come to interpose itself.

§17. The Foreign to Myself

The *alienus*, or man "outside himself and foreign to himself," has thus not ceased to be a topic of discussion, supposing that we proceed from the "foreign *outside* oneself" (the *organic resistance* that is annihilated in sleep and paralysis [§15] and the *resistance at its terminus* that is also necessary as a stop [*butée*] on effort [§16]) to the "foreign *to* oneself" (the *psyche* this time, and no longer only the body, become at times if not annihilated then at least blocked or totally transformed). From the "spread body" (in sleep, the paralyzed hand, the hemiplegic or the paralytic from birth), we cross to "spread thought" or the "extra-phenomenal" (in dreams, states of drunkenness, sleepwalking, and dementedness). Indeed, there at times occurs in man, to return here to the Biranian definition of alienation in his prolegomena to the *Nouvelles considérations sur les rapports du physique et du moral de l'homme*, a "*complete absence, temporary or permanent*, of the *sentiment of the* myself, although the *vital and sensitive functions* experience no interruption" (§14a).[21] It is thus the "complete absence, temporary or permanent, of the sentiment of the *myself*" that guides, from the beginning, this reading and "my" reading of Maine de Biran, less by the inside than by the "outside in oneself," less by the rule (the "sentiment of the *myself*" and the "primitive fact of effort") than by the exception (the double "alienation" of egoity and corporeality), less by autoaffection than by extra-phenomenality.

The "Nouvelles considérations sur le sommeil, les songes et le somnambulisme," that is, that famous speech delivered by Maine de Biran before the Bergerac Medical Society on November 19, 1809 (and on which I have already relied to develop the "organic" dimension of sleep [§15b]), will here serve us as a guide. A treatise on medicine, psychology, and philosophy—everything is found in it, or at least everything we are looking for (the "spread body" and the "extra-phenomenal"), all disciplines that Biran has already linked with the expressions the "physical" and the "moral" in man.[22] The thinker from Bergerac, as we have, therefore, now understood, despite his melancholia, has no other

---

21. Maine de Biran, *Nouvelles considérations*, 5 (emphasis added).
22. See Maine de Biran, *Discours*, 82–123.

ambition, as the "Columbus of Metaphysics" (opening), than to venture forth, wherever the wind takes him, in wildernesses that cannot be untangled or to reach those unsuspected, or at least rarely approached, shores: "If we could be surprised by the phenomena that habit has made most familiar to us," he confides in the introduction to his speech to his "contemporaries" who have, rather, become his "colleagues" (doctors, surgeons, and health officers),

> how could we not experience a *surprise mingled with terror* when reflecting on *such a prodigious difference* between *two alternate modes of existence*, in *one* of which we live, sense, and act with the consciousness or intimate sentiment of our existence . . . whereas in the *other* we often live, sense, and act through the *same organs*, and apparently in the *same manner, without consciousness, without self, without memory*, and while remaining as if *foreign*, in one of these states or modes of existence, to all that we experienced, sensed, imagined, and did in the other?[23]

a) DREAMS

The already-studied *organicity* of sleep (§15b) and the *psychic* aspect of sleep that we now encounter (§17a) have in common that one must "sink," even be "annihilated"—at least in a sleep in which the "sentiment of the *myself*" and the "primitive fact of effort" are, at least for a time, eclipsed. There is, however, as Maine de Biran recognizes, "probably no sleep without dreams."[24] Thus *one always dreams*—which does not mean that one "always thinks" in the manner of Descartes, for whom there is thought only in wakefulness (§3)—and the activity of what I have called the "organic unconscious," following a Biran who is nearly a precursor of Freud (§13), indeed remains the foundation of the psyche. Like my *animal* but purely passive *body*, which always remains in activity during organic sleep, even though the "I" (in the sentiment of oneself) and the lived body (in the primitive fact of effort) are totally suspended, even annihilated, *psychic life* still exercises a certain continuity while sleeping, but of a wholly other order—a mysterious agent, a blind or unconscious power (§13)—inasmuch as the dreamer here descends into a "subterranean sea" from which it is not certain that he will be able to return: "I *am leaving the port*; I am going *to sink into a subterranean sea*, but without

23. Maine de Biran, *Discours*, 82–83 (emphasis added).
24. Maine de Biran, *Discours*, 99.

hoping to touch its so-distant shores and to be able to cry out: *Italiam! Italiam!*" as I have already related, echoing the gripping cry from the *Essai sur les fondements de la psychologie*.[25]

But that one always dreams and that an activity of the psyche therefore remains, albeit of a wholly other type, is not what is essential, at least for the thinker from Bergerac. For the real, gnawing question remains, without interruption, that of this "myself" that is not "myself," that is no longer "myself," and that I will never be able to recognize as "myself," so much do the images produced in dreams, which I sometimes remember, make me de facto *alienus*, that is, "foreign *to* myself." There is no question, for Biran, of a "non-myself" that would explain or open onto the "myself," like a sort of unconscious that would prepare and justify conscious life. In the foreignness or, rather, the foreignerness, of oneself to oneself in dreams, I am indeed confronted with "eccentricity," even "bizarreness." Better, it is the transcendental conditions of space and time that are annihilated here—exactly as in the case, elsewhere studied at length, of Kant's cinnabar that is "now red, now black," "now light, now heavy" or of the man transformed "now . . . into this animal shape, now into that one," or, finally, of the earth covered "now with fruits, now with ice and snow."[26]

Belonging to *extra-phenomenality* (coming from myself as if from the "outside in myself") and not *infra-phenomenality* (like a dream that would prepare for or explain wakefulness) or *supra-phenomenality* (like images in which I could certainly still recognize myself but that overwhelm me): this is, very precisely, the nature of dreams for Maine de Biran. "So much exception, so much transformation": thus we are become "other *to* ourselves" in phantasms in which we would have great difficulty recognizing ourselves: "I will say first, indeed, that dreams *exclude any active exercise* of the faculty of attention," the president of the Bergerac Medical Society affirms straightaway to contemporaries who will not be afraid to descend with him into the abysses of our depths.

---

25. Maine de Biran, *Essai sur les fondements*, 109.

26. Kant, *Critique of Pure Reason*, 229 (A100–101): "If cinnabar were now red, now black, now light, now heavy, if a human being were now changed into this animal shape, now into that one, if on the longest day the land were covered now with fruits, now with ice and snow, then my empirical imagination would never even get the opportunity to think of heavy cinnabar on the occasion of the representation of the color red." See also my commentary in *Hors phénomène*, 207–18.

> The proof of this fact is obviously deduced from the *eccentricity* of most of our dreams, the *contradictions* and *bizarrenesses* that they present: it indeed happens that we *conflate* as we dream times and places that are separated by considerable intervals; in the course of one and the same dream, the same object is represented to our imagination as existing in different parts of the world; we converse with dead people, without considering that they are dead, even if their recent loss has strongly affected us, etc.[27]

Thus it is not the content of the dream that interests Biran, even though his descriptions would provide food for thought for many psychoanalysists and dream specialists—I have noted that Freud perhaps read these "new considerations" (on sleep, dreams, and sleepwalking)[28]—but rather the effect that dreams have on us or, better, the absence of ourselves from ourselves in our own dreams. For the true strangeness, for Biran, entirely accurately, moreover, from the point of view of psychoanalysis and its theory of repression, is not that we do not remember our dreams but, on the contrary, that we can sometimes recollect them: "We must therefore ask, no longer *why we do not preserve* the memory of all our dreams, but rather how it happens *that we sometimes recall* a few of them."[29]

Sleep is always sleep for Maine de Biran, that is, the total absence of oneself or the extinction of oneself for oneself—an "annihilation" by which one "falls from sleep"[30] (§15). Even though it still remains an activity of the organic, or even of the psychic, it does not concern us, or no longer concerns us, and perhaps it has never concerned us. And that is why, according to the thinker of Grateloup—concerning whom we will wonder, besides, whether he sometimes slept, so much did he write in addition to his numerous intellectual and political activities—*deep sleep*, that is, the sleep without memory, the sleep in which one does not recall one's dreams, and in which one does not even know if one dreamed, is perfect sleep. To the question, "Why do we not preserve the memory of all our dreams, but only of a few of them?" the thinker, and even the physiologist and psychologist, from Bergerac responds that in the cases

---

27. Maine de Biran, *Discours*, 97 (emphasis added).

28. See Voutsinas, "Maine de Biran," 88nE: "We have the proof that S. Freud had encountered the *Considérations sur le sommeil et sur les songes* in which Maine de Biran says: 'Nothing is more instructive for the waking man than the history of dreams.'"

29. Maine de Biran, *Discours*, 99 (emphasis added).

30. [See note 38 in chapter 5. –Trans.]

where one remembers one's dream, or this or that dream, it is because one was not really sleeping—in a sleep that today we would name "paradoxical" (in which, moreover, we dream more) and not "deep": "I answer with the previous observation that in a *complete sleep*, there is *no memory*, and that where there is *memory*, the sleep *was not perfect*."[31]

At the dawn of this nineteenth century, analyses of sleep were indeed developing apace—and Biran cites numerous "physiologists" (Bichat and Barthez, to whom he refers several times) who "do not seem to have grasped or sufficiently noted the essential character of this periodic function."[32] Hence his own answer, which is that there is a total *forgetting of oneself* or "eclipse of the *myself*" in sleep, just as much from a psychic point of view as from a somatic one. Just as there is no "sense of effort" (or internal sensation of oneself) in organic sleep, without which one would not be sleeping, so too is there no "sentiment of the *myself*" (through an autoaffection) in dreams or psychic sleep, or else one would not be sleeping either. Dreaming is still autoaffecting oneself and perhaps is autoaffecting oneself more than ever without any "resistance to the object" either in oneself or outside oneself. But this is what Biran definitively rejects in the subject that is "outside itself" or "foreign to itself." Sleeping well is really sleeping. Nothing remains of "myself" or of the "to myself" in dreaming; hence the fact that dreaming is the site of the greatest "distance" from oneself to oneself—certainly according to a "defense mechanism," as psychoanalysts would say, but whose pure nothingness of oneself as "non-myself" (Biran) is easier to think than the neuter of the "id" that always constitutes me (Freud).

There is thus a great distance, to tell the truth, between Biran and Freud, if we must still believe that the "blind power" of the organic unconscious (§13) or this "mysterious agent" (§13b) can concern us and enlighten us for living and surviving: "This hypothesis of an unconscious with an *organic* source is *radically distinct* from the Freudian conception of an unconscious *psychism*."[33] The "extra-phenomenal," which in this sense separates itself, as if in advance with Maine de Biran, from psychoanalysis, requires a radical cut between *obscurity* (which waits for or feeds on light) and the *black night* (which has forgotten everything, unto the very idea of light). Despite the accusation that the organic, even psychic, unconscious explains nothing of "physical" or "moral" life, which

31. Maine de Biran, *Discours*, 99–100 (emphasis added).
32. Maine de Biran, *Discours*, 83.
33. Romeyer-Dherbey, *Maine de Biran*, 79n4 (emphasis partly in original).

could certainly be legitimately addressed to the author of the "Nouvelles considérations sur le sommeil," we will nonetheless recognize that the thinker from Bergerac has the merit of having truly descended here into a "psychology of the depths," if by "psychology" we here mean the study of the "myself" or of the soul (*Essai sur les fondements de la psychologie*) and not only that of the psychic unconscious (as in Freud's *Five Lectures on Psychoanalysis*, 1910).

A century separates Biranian psychology and Freudian psychoanalysis. This century of *distance* is also the site of a *difference*. We will not prefer the one (the Biranian absolute nothingness) to the other (the Freudian underpinnings), but we will recognize that extra-phenomenality, "radical strangeness," or the "outside oneself" is well illustrated in this surprisingly modern analysis of dreams: "*Sleep* is nothing else than the *temporary suspension of the will or power of effort*," writes the philosopher in the opening of his speech, in a definition that will remain famous, "and all the phenomena that accompany it can be explained by this principle *alone*."[34]

b) Drunkenness

With drunkenness there occurs an additional step, or rather another step, relative to dreams and sleep. This is first because the state is provoked by a substance or by substances (vinicultural or medicinal) and second because they produce images that are closer to hallucinations than to dreams, up to the point of a complete sleep in which one forgets oneself, including one's own body: "The successive periods of *drunkenness*, occasioned by *opium* or *wine*," indicates Biran, again to his contemporaries of the Bergerac Medical Society, "put us in a position to follow the progression of this sort of *enslavement of the power of the will and of effort* from the first states of exaltation of the brain that cause *images* and *lively intuitions* to spring forth from it . . . to the moment when the organs of locomotion begin to *stagger*, to *hesitate* . . . the body, no longer being sustained by that power whose exercise constitutes the waking state, then obeys, like any ordinary mass, the *mechanical force of gravity*, and already everything is *asleep*."[35]

In drunkenness, or through drunkenness, in a state initiated either by the "drug" cited many times by the thinker from Bergerac (here,

34. Maine de Biran, *Discours*, 83 (emphasis added).
35. Maine de Biran, *Discours*, 88 (emphasis added).

opium) or by alcohol (here, wine), it is "concrete man in his entirety" that is struck. It is a matter not solely of the physical, nor only of the psychic or the moral in man, but of this "point of junction" of the psychosomatic, which is certainly localized in the "brain," and whose consequences are not exclusively a modification of the biological but can go so far as the loss of what man as such is, supposing that he is borne and moved by his "phenomenal *myself*" immediately conjoined with his "lived body" or "internal extension." For what counts, because Biran is a philosopher and not only a physiologist, is the philosophical or, rather, anthropological displacement produced by this possible modification of our being in its entirety.

It is indeed the "sense of effort" that falls, such that the drunkard or, rather, the one who voluntarily places himself in a state of drunkenness (including under the effect of drugs) not only no longer *masters* himself but *is* no longer himself. The two essential features of self-consciousness (*conscium*) and self-mastery (*compos sui*) that constitute *the primitive fact of the intimate sense* precisely are exhausted and fall through what he also calls "narcotics," "certain poisons and contagious miasmas," or "fermented liquors." Life becomes *effortless* in the literal sense of the word, not only in the sense in which the individual no longer has the courage to advance or continue (tiredness, laziness, delirium, or drunkenness), but in the sense that the very idea of effort has disappeared, that is, that "resistance of myself to myself" that, from the inside and even in my flesh, makes me exist. Biran here formulates this explicitly, such that drunkenness (joined to opium and wine), which could be only one example of the loss of the *myself*, here becomes its paradigm, for it is through myself that I fall from myself (the more or less explicit intention to drink or to drug myself) to the point of forgetting myself. It is most often, but not always, because life *tout court*, made of effort, is too heavy to bear that one prefers to give way to the resistance of the living thing rather than to continue confronting it in order to exist (well):

> All the external signs [at the moment when the organs of locomotion begin to stagger] show that the *capacity for effort* has diminished, that the will is *uncertain*, the limbs *intractable*, to the point that finally, this power having been *totally suspended in its exercise*, there is no more *effort, no more will, no more* "myself."[36]

---

36. Maine de Biran, *Discours*, 88 (emphasis added).

Rarely has a text—cited as an epigraph to the present chapter—been more explicit for justifying my interpretation *in counter-relief* of Maine de Biran, on the basis no longer of the "inside" ("the primitive fact of the intimate sense" and the "primitive fact of effort") but of the "outside in me" (no longer any "myself," and no longer any "effort"). *Effortless life* reaches its peak—not only through a weariness of living but still more by a refusal of life: that is, the loss of the resistance that constitutes existence (§15a). The subject, precisely in such a state and under such effects (of drugs or drinks) becomes "outside itself" in the already-mentioned double sense: certainly as an exceeding of himself by himself (sudden and vehement passions) but above all as a loss of himself outside himself, no longer having access either to the "I" or to the "me" that, however, constituted the unity of his body and his thought.

To the "fall [*tombée*] of sleep" there responds, then, the "fall of the body." Or, rather, when sleep digs its own "tomb" [*tombe*] by sinking into it at least for the night, drunkenness also causes one to enter into the "tomb of a body" so shaky and numb that it too ends up reaching, albeit accidentally this time, this state and this site of a total forgetting of oneself. "Falling with one's whole body" certainly applies to the fault and to sin, and probably alcohol and drugs are "drifts" away from the inner sentiment and the primitive fact of effort that makes us exist, but it also applies to the "heaviness" or the "weight" of my body that reels and reminds me of, or brings me back to, the earth from which I was drawn.[37] The *flesh* gives way to the *body*, or the *Leib* to the *Körper*, such that the "spread body," caught between Descartes's extended body and Husserl's lived body [*corps vécu*], becomes this point and this site par excellence whereby I myself weigh on myself: my lived or proper body that has become "improper," for example in the case of illness—bearing a "myself" that can no longer even say "myself" or gain access "to the *myself*."

Oneri mihi sum, "I am a weight for myself," said St. Augustine.[38] But this time, and in the case of drunkenness, this weight for me, otherwise named "finitude" by Martin Heidegger, is lived "without me" or "without the *myself*." Far from any horizon of death in a future that certainly spills

---

37. I refer here to Philippe Richard's very beautiful book, *Tomber de tout son corps*: "*I fall, therefore I am*. That is the novelist's essential conviction" (11).

38. Augustine, *Confessions*, 262 (10.28.39): "Anyone whom you fill you also uplift, but I am not full of you, and so I am a burden to myself [*oneri mihi sum*]." See also my commentary (and the rupture that Martin Heidegger brings about in his reading of St. Augustine through finitude rather than sin): "Après la métaphysique?" (esp. 115–19).

over into the present (living, not yet dead), it is here rather a matter of a life as if one were already dead (living dead)—rejoining all bodies in their "weight" and their *lapidary existence* (stone or statue) whereby I sink, as I have cited (p. 207–8), by the "mechanical force of gravity" alone that draws me toward the tomb, having wholly forgotten the "vital force of internal effort" that would draw me toward life or, rather, that was life: "The body, no longer being sustained by that power [effort] whose exercise constitutes the waking state, then obeys, like any ordinary mass, the *mechanical force of gravity*, and already everything is *asleep*."[39]

c) Sleepwalking

Sleepwalking, for its part, does not belong to the domain of dreams or of drunkenness, yet it is in relation to them that we must think it to also classify it as a particular mode of *effortless life*. But we must complete one more step, proving thereby that the march forward of the "outside in oneself" is not yet finished. For what first constitutes, for Biran, the specificity of the sleepwalker—and in this regard he is neither the dreamer nor the drunk or drugged person—is the "deception" to which he leads. The sleepwalker is the one who mimes, even in his body, which we would be wrong to here call a "lived body," the trappings of life. He simulates wakefulness while he remains in sleep, a proof, if one were needed, not only that we must "doubt" because of the impossible distinction between sleep and wakefulness (Descartes) but also that at times, and paradoxically, sleep *is* wakefulness, or at the very least takes on its garb. *Outside himself*, the sleepwalker deceives his world and deceives himself. Outside any sentiment of oneself, he gives the impression of a "phenomenal *myself*" without, however, referring it to the primitive fact of effort. He gives the impression of a "lived body," but, in reality, his (visible) "outside" certainly comes from an (invisible) "inside," yet without the (invisible) "inside" having any other characteristic than that of being taken for a (visible) "outside."

The sleepwalker is outside himself not only because he escapes himself (like in dreams or drunkenness) but because he gives the appearance of a *himself* when there is not, or no longer, any self to be referred to.

39. Maine de Biran, *Discours*, 88 (emphasis added). We will relate this phrase here to Philippe Richard's book, in which the "fall" is understood not solely from a theological point of view (sin) but also from an anthropological one (vertigo): *Tomber de tout son corps*, esp. 80–87: "The fall into silence, vertigo from the very fact of living."

Closed to the "external senses," one could believe that everything comes from the "internal sense," but the internal here is no longer that of feeling but of the image that is imposed on him as in madness: "Everything deceives in the sleepwalker," Biran writes perfectly on the basis of Dr. Pigatti's studies and also the observations of Mr. Delpit, who resides "in this town" (Bergerac):

> [The *sleepwalker*] is the living proof that it is often necessary to *beware of initial appearances* and above all to not always judge the absolute identity of causes by the *likeness* of the sensible effects. One would say that in this singular state the individual behaves, *as when he is awake*, based on the perception of present objects, and yet these real objects are nothing for him; the external senses are closed to their impressions, and all their fictitious value relates to the *imaginary tableau* that represents them first and foremost accidentally and independently of any impression received from the outside.[40]

In reality, the sleepwalker sleeps, as one also sleeps in sleep. But whereas the sleeper *falls into nothingness*, the sleepwalker also remains there, according to Biran, but *while giving the impression of being and of being there*. Such an illusion, not only outside oneself (others seeing the sleepwalker) but also for oneself even though there is no longer any "oneself" for gaining access to oneself (the sleepwalker who does not know he is a sleepwalker), is then produced through images in oneself, like dreams, even though this time they say nothing about oneself or about the self (phantasms) but mime and even carry out a relation to the world (through the external senses). The deception here is double. From the point of view of his *psyche* first, whereby it is also a question of images in oneself and of objects outside oneself, the sleepwalker causes it to be believed, or lets himself believe, that he is affected when he is not. He gives the illusion of an "intimate sense of oneself" inasmuch as he can react to an external given (it is said that one must not surprise a sleepwalker, lest one make him fall or succumb), while in reality such a sense is not intimate but "extimate" (like Tournier's "extimate" journal,

---

40. Maine de Biran, *Discours*, 120 (emphasis added) (with the mention of Dr. Pigatti, a contributor to the article "Somnambules" ["Sleepwalkers"] in Sigaud de Lafond's *Dictionnaire des merveilles de la nature*, as well as of the note on "Somnambulisme" ["Sleepwalking"] and the "Observations sur des somnambules" ["Observations on Sleepwalkers"] conducted by Delpit, 155–59). On this question of sleepwalking, among others, and also of this "interiority that is not the interiority of effort" (333), see Devarieux, *Maine de Biran*, 320–52.

p. xxii), to the degree that he does not relate to himself while giving the illusion of himself:

> Sleepwalking is distinct from the other sorts of dreams of which I have spoken because of two essential circumstances: first, because the one who is affected *has* or *seems to have* the intuition of the objects that are currently present to the external senses, although these senses seem wholly or partially *closed*.[41]

Second, from the point of view of his *body*, the sleepwalker gives the impression, without realizing it, that he is present to his surrounding world through his external senses—leaving his bed, taking food, opening cupboards, etc.—while they are in reality totally disconnected from any internal sense, be it a matter of the "phenomenal *myself*" or the "lived body." *Effortless life* mimes *effortful life*, and that is indeed what is most deceptive. For, believing that there is *someone*, or at the very least a body inhabited by an "I" capable of answering it and answering for it, there is in reality *no one*—that is, the pure *neutrality* of Condillac's statue upstream of all sensation (§6), but this time giving the impression of sensation. For what matters, in Maine de Biran's view at the very least, is not that the sleepwalker, like the statue, senses or does not sense the rose but that the statue *senses itself* sensing the rose.[42] Yet, even if the sleepwalker left at night for the garden to sense a rose, he would never sense *himself* sensing the rose, for sleep is "total" or is not sleep, as we have seen, and therefore he would produce kinestheses or movements of the body that would give the appearance of freely directing himself toward the rose, while it was only automatically, machinally, even by instinct, that he tended toward it and moved himself. The inner will of the lived body, on which I have insisted so as not to lose the activity of the *myself* that is the characteristic mark of our humanity (§4a), is here radically absent, while one could believe it was present, at least because of the external modalities of the body's movements (sensing the rose) miming a free inner activity (willing to sense the rose) that in reality *is* not:

> The second reason [for which sleepwalking is distinct from the other sorts of dreams of which I have spoken] is that the sleepwalker carries out the whole series of movements or acts

---

41. Maine de Biran, *Discours*, 88 (emphasis added).

42. [When reading this passage, it is useful to bear in mind that *sentir* can mean "to sense" or "to smell." In most contexts *sentir la rose* would be translated simply as "smelling the rose"; here, the sentence naturally implies both these meanings of *sentir*. –Trans.]

of locomotion that are necessary to go toward objects, to push them aside or to grasp them, to appropriate them for his use, and will behave with regard to them *as he might do* in the most complete state of wakefulness.[43]

What is most surprising, then—and it is here that *instinct*, or a "blind power," still more than the illusion of the *affection of the psyche* and the *miming of an inhabited body*, enters into consideration—is that the movements of the body that are accomplished in the state of sleepwalking are better directed and more perfect than they would be during wakefulness. It is certainly necessary first to emphasize that the body's automatism is always surer than any free will that would will to move it, at least if it is a matter of most perfectly suiting the means to the end: "One would indeed say that the sleepwalker carries out all the acts of locomotion in the *same manner* and by the *same principle* as when he is awake," Biran perfectly analyzes. "His movements are *just as coordinated*; they even have *more precision* and *dexterity*: they are just as well suited to a goal and tend toward it with a superior assurance or a sort of impassibility."[44]

But it is not only in the "reliability of automatism," even according to the thinker from Bergerac, that we ought to trust. This is also an acknowledgement, precisely through the reference to sleepwalking, that "no one, it is true, has determined *what the body can do*," to take up this time the famous phrase from Spinoza's *Ethics* (1677).[45] And the philosopher from Amsterdam explains, indeed with this very example of "sleepwalkers," which the philosopher from Bergerac could not have been unaware of (even though he does not cite him on this point), indicating very exactly that "*sleepwalkers* do many actions in their sleep that they would not dare while awake." And this is what "is all good evidence," concludes the scholium of the famous Proposition II of the third part of the *Ethics* ("Of *the Origin and Nature* of the Emotions") "that merely by the laws of its own nature a body can do many things by itself that strike its soul with surprise."[46]

Certainly, this is far from a unilateral identification of the *power of the body* assigned to nature alone in Spinoza (*conatus*) with the *blind*

43. Maine de Biran, *Discours*, 113 (emphasis added).
44. Maine de Biran, *Discours*, 120 (emphasis added).
45. Spinoza, *Ethics*, 97 (Third Part, Prop. 2, Scholium) (emphasis added). [Translation modified to more closely follow the French translation that Falque cites. –Trans.]
46. Spinoza, *Ethics*, 97 (Third Part, Prop. 2, Scholium). [Translation modified to more closely follow the French translation that Falque cites. –Trans.]

force discovered in *our* nature when the intimate sense of the *myself* gives way in Biran (§13b). The former is oriented and finalized (it is indeed the body that coordinates with the soul to guide our affections), while the latter is, as it were, "outside affection" and does nothing but mime a corporeality that in reality is emptied of all intentionality, including of the intentionality of nature itself (a sort of instinct or organic unconscious in oneself, as I have shown in §13). Once the thing has started up—that is, this "outside oneself" in me that seems to autonomize itself—my whole entire being is confided to my animality alone. It is not that my being cannot survive—far from it (for the animal is often more assured through its instinct in dangerous situations)—but that the internal effort that constitutes the human as the sentiment of oneself capable of saying "I" has totally disappeared. Instinct is paradoxically what grants the movements of the sleepwalker's body their automatic nature, losing everything of the man but telling everything about the animal. If, for Biran, the sleepwalker is not to be envied, his exemplarity at least has the merit of making clear that the greatest fraud—"everything deceives in the sleepwalker" is also that which best and most greatly simulates the truth, whence the most regulated movements:

> But this latter circumstance [coordinated movements that have even more precision and dexterity, being suited to a goal and tending toward it with a greater assurance or a sort of impassibility] is itself a *proof* that the movement is determined by a *blind principle* that does not have the faculty of suspending, stopping, or modifying the impulsion once it is given but that continues it as it first impresses that impulsion with all the necessity of automation.[47]

We will then, understand the point. The sleepwalker adds to the drunkard or to the man or woman who is under the effect of drugs that he is nearly their opposite, but each time in a same forgetting of oneself, the one in the "disordered body" (drunkenness), and the other in the "ordered body" (sleepwalking). Thus we will not judge by appearances, but we will know that appearances themselves can deceive, since the sleepwalker at the very least gives the impression of an *effortful life*, whereas he suffers from the evil of an *effortless life,* that is, a life without internal resistance, whereby he cannot inhabit himself. The sleepwalker is in every way what we could here name a "disaffected man" [*homme*

---

47. Maine de Biran, *Discours*, 120 (emphasis added).

désaffecté]—in the double sense of a being empty of itself (like an *abandoned building* [*bâtiment désaffecté*]) and who does not feel himself or no longer feels himself (to the point of *disaffection* as the loss of all the attachments that he could once have experienced). The sleepwalker is also "outside himself," but through an "outside in himself" that mimes and gives the impression of a life "from the inside."

d) Idiocy

Idiocy or "dementedness," after dreams, drunkenness, and sleepwalking, becomes the ultimate, and probably the most radical, manner of saying or reaching this "foreign *to* myself" from the point of view of the *psyche* (the extra-phenomenal), overdetermining the "foreign *outside* myself" from the point of view of the *body* (the spread body): the organicity of sleep, the paralyzed hand, hemiplegia, and the paralytic from birth (§15). The point is known, at least according to the psychiatric nomenclature of Maine de Biran's era: the pathology of "idiocy" is not "dementedness" [*démence*], the former designating a sort of absence of affect or speech, and the latter a production of disordered images bordering on madness.

Idiocy, taken from the Greek *idios* (proper, particular) designates that wholly singular psychic state that has also historically been named "imbecility" whereby the subject experiences himself as "foreign *to* himself." To say it with Pinel, a contemporary of Maine de Biran and a psychopathologist doctor at Bicêtre (with Royer-Collard), any patient is afflicted with *idiocy* whose trauma is such that it "*takes speech from the man* and leads him *to mutism*."[48] Here we are referred very exactly to what I have elsewhere named "the extra-phenomenal"—or to the "case of Suzanne Urban" as it would later be analyzed by Binswanger and Maldiney within the framework of psychiatric phenomenology. Thus we see, from the patient's pen, how far trauma can lead, to the point of blocking speech (mutism) when her husband's cancer is announced—indeed, what was once named, following Pinel, "idiocy":

> I was going with my husband to the doctor and waited in the adjoining room. I heard, trembling and crying, his horrible groanings. The doctor told him that he had a small wound in the bladder, but he looked at *me* while turning his back to him,

---

48. Cited by Bonald, *Législation primitive*, 274: "Dr. Pinel, a doctor at the Bicêtre hospital, in a work on mental alienation" (emphasis added).

with a look *so terrifying and devoid of hope* that *I remained frozen, my mouth open with terror*, to such an extent that the doctor grasped my hand strongly to indicate to me that I must not *show any* of my emotions.[49]

Without returning at length to this "case" (Suzanne Urban), having already discussed it elsewhere, inasmuch as it has led to considerable debate within the framework of psychiatric phenomenology, let us note only that Henry Maldiney interprets this case precisely as "psychosis" or "closure to the event":

> What is most remarkable in psychosis is the *closure to the event*. One day, an event took place that was never assumed and that, not overcome, *obstructs* a man's horizon. . . . This holds true for Ludwig Binswanger's *Le Cas Suzanne Urban* [*The case of Suzanne Urban*]. There, the triggering event was the doctor's frightful pantomime, announcing to this woman, immediately, without a word, while theatrically signaling to her to keep silent, her husband's cancer and the abandonment of all hope.[50]

Whether "psychosis" or "idiocy" are simply matters of a *blockage* of a horizon given according to an *a priori* of an always-presupposed openness (Maldiney's thesis), or whether one finds in them rather the site of the *creation* of a radically other horizon, following the adage "so much exception, so much modification" (my thesis, relying rather on Binswanger) is a point that I will not develop here.[51] It remains that Maine de Biran, discussing Pinel's argument in the *Mémoire sur la décomposition de la pensée*, sees in idiocy, as also in dementedness, moreover (which today we would call two forms of psychosis), precisely a state of man in which consciousness is absent from itself to be closed to any humanized opening (*Dasein*) and confined to a pure animality—one would think one was reading Henry Maldiney: "Whatever the cause that suspends the *perceptive* function in its conditions or its proper motive," writes Biran, interpreting "the purely affective state in cases of mental alienation," "impressions can be received, the animal can be affected and can move in consequence, but *the myself is not there, consciousness is blanketed*, and so long as such a state lasts, it is *impossible to mark in it*

---

49. Binswanger, *Cas Suzanne Urban*, 26 (emphasis added).
50. Maldiney, *Penser l'homme et la folie*, 230–31 (emphasis added).
51. See Falque, *Hors phénomène*, 328–34, as well as my contribution "Henri Maldiney et le hors phénomène."

any of those characteristics that constitute for us the intelligent being, endowed with apperception, will, and thought."[52]

There is no "intelligence" (apperception, will, or thought) for the alienated one according to Biran, as there is no "opening" (*Erschlossenheit*) for the psychotic according to Maldiney. Certainly, the diagnosis is severe, but in the two cases it is a matter of the same assessment, which is entirely accurate and which thus constitutes this extreme type, or limit-case, of the foreign *to* oneself from the psychic point of view: "the *myself* is not there," to take up Maine de Biran's well-turned and finely chiseled phrase—which is another manner of saying the subject that is "off*side*," both "outside himself" and "out of play."

In this "absence of myself from myself" or this "absence of myself for myself," the difference between *idiocy* and *dementedness* is articulated. Whereas the former (the idiot) "lives and senses . . . but beyond this sphere there is no longer anything" (according to phrases that are here surprisingly modern), the latter (the demented one) "spontaneously produces images that are sometimes connected, more often disjointed, while thought is dormant or from time to time casts a few fleeting lights."[53] Although the typology of psychoses is not yet strictly fixed (melancholia for the past, mania for the present, and schizophrenia for the future), one sees here Maine de Biran's considerable effort in attempting to define, within the framework of a nomenclature of mental illnesses, a subject that is certainly still affected (in an animal way) but absolutely not, or no longer, autoaffected (in a human way). The "outside in myself" has taken the place of the "intimate sense of the *myself*," inasmuch as the very idea of "the *myself*" or of "a *myself*" has disappeared.

We will, then, think "Biran *versus* Pinel," to return this time to the debate initiated in the *Nouvelles considérations sur les rapports du physique et du moral de l'homme*. For, surprisingly, the philosopher from Bergerac is more radical here than the Parisian psychopathologist. Whereas Pinel sees a few "actively exercised mental faculties" (memory, attention, imagination) still at work in the alienated, Biran discovers in them on the contrary such a radical passivity that the patient becomes, as it were dehumanized, reduced to nothing—that is, a "dis-affected" being, or a being in the mode of "lapidary existence" (§8): "Dr. Pinel, in his *Traité sur l'aliénation mentale* [*Treatise on Mental Alienation*],"

---

52. Maine de Biran, *Mémoire sur la décomposition*, 387 (emphasis partly in original).
53. Maine de Biran, *Mémoire sur la décomposition*, 387–88.

specifies Biran in a severe discussion with the Bicêtre doctor (whom he seems to hold in less esteem than his friend Royer-Collard), "says he has observed that such and such alienated one exercises by turns and in isolation a particular intellectual faculty such as attention, judgment, meditation, etc., while other faculties such as perception, memory, etc. seem wholly obliterated."[54]

Indeed, dividing the faculties in man and daring to believe or think that some are destroyed (perception, memory) and others safeguarded (attention, judgment) means not seeing, according to Biran, that in the case of madness, as in the case of sleep, it is "all or nothing." Either I sleep (and I do not dream), or I do not sleep or I fall asleep in a light sleep (and then I dream). Either I sink into *idiocy* and I "live and sense, but beyond this sphere there is no longer anything" (the case of Suzanne Urban who was later totally "openmouthed" under the blow of trauma before, years later, she could begin to write a journal on the subject), or I "produce disjointed images" in *dementedness* while, however, "thought is dormant" or, at the very most, "casts from time to time a few fleeting lights." But in both cases, the *alienated one* is or becomes really alienated from the moment that all his faculties are destroyed or are impossible to exercise, just as the sleeper is really a sleeper in the annihilation of himself in organic sleep (in "effortless" life or life "without resistance") and in the absence of any dream as likewise of images or psychic activity (in the total eclipse of the "sentiment of the *myself*").[55]

Biran is a man of "all or nothing" and not of "compromise." Thus he knows how to *think*, as likewise to *decide*. His goal is not to deny humanity, and he cannot be accused of that, so greatly does the reading *in relief* of his work make visible in the "lived body" and the "sentiment of the *myself*" that which constitutes the specificity of the human. But it is now and also a matter of recognizing, in his reading *in counter-relief*, an "outside oneself" or, rather, an "outside in oneself" in which the "spread body" is stretched out (the organicity of sleep, the paralyzed hand, the hemiplegic, and the paralytic from birth) and where extra-phenomenality stands (dreams, drunkenness, sleepwalking, idiocy),

---

54. Maine de Biran, *Nouvelles considérations*, 32.

55. On this difference between Biran and Pinel, see Umbelino's accurate analysis in *Somatologia subjectiva*, 390–98, as well as Carvalho, "Biran et le traitement moral," as well as, by the same Umbelino, "Le regard qui ment" (in connection with the work of Marc Richir). This is an original reading of the thinker from Bergerac, in light of a contemporary corpus of texts that also have much to inspire us.

like so many pathologies that are certainly to be treated but also and first recognized and inhabited.

Appearance does not give being (Heidegger), and the reduction does not deliver givenness (Marion), but the *exception* produces *transformation*—which is why crossing via such "limit-experiences" frees us both from the presupposition of health and illness as likewise from the presupposition of openness and closing. With Biran, it is a matter of "creating" and reaching the "edges of phenomenality." At this price, and only at this price, will we discover a *neuter* or an "organic unconscious" that could indeed also constitute me and of which I cannot so easily rid myself. From sleep to paralysis (the spread body) or from drunkenness to sleepwalking (extra-phenomenality), the margin becomes the norm of an existence that is assuredly undone but that is also otherwise constituted. Far from only the "privation" of a normalized being, it could indeed happen that the "negation" of all normality might cause to appear an "outside-of-the-body"—the improper body—like an "outside-of-thought"—the subject that is off*side*—that no one had yet suspected.

The "Columbus of metaphysics" did not reach the shore, not even of that continent "outside everything," including oneself, for by "leaving the port" he did indeed "sink into a subterranean sea" (*Italiam! Italiam!*) whose shores are in reality only ever rounded but never landed on. *In counter-relief*, man will no longer be, in order to sink into the absolute or the below of the animal, recognizing thereby what he should be *in relief*, human and even divine, but what in reality he is not always, or does not always become, under the blow of trauma as likewise of alienation. A phrase drawn from the *Nouvelles considérations sur les rapports du physique et du moral de l'homme* suffices to summarize this and brings to their acme these reflections on "spiritualism" and "phenomenology" that the "case" of Maine de Biran has produced and even initiated: "In truth, the *alienated one*, so long as he *does not have the sentiment of the* myself and *does not know himself*, finds himself *struck* from the list of intelligent beings and moral persons: he *does not perceive*, for perceiving is *distinguishing oneself* from every object of external intuition and representation."[56]

---

56. Maine de Biran, *Nouvelles considérations*, 32 (emphasis added).

Conclusion

Three Lives in One

By how many *lives* Maine de Biran has then crossed, and what lives! No one could say or determine this. There is the life of the defender in the royal guard of Louis XVI during the Revolution, certainly, the life of the subprefect of Bergerac during the Empire under Napoleon (1806), the life of the councilor of State and the deputy of Dordogne twice during the Restoration under Louis XVIII (1816). But there is also the life of the founder of the Bergerac Medical Society (1806–1810), the life of the one who wanted to start an anthropological society (1820), and the life of the one who returned, in a last "conversion," toward Christianity as the highest of truths (1823–1824)[1]—like Michel Henry, finally, who followed this same pathway from the beginning to the end: from the "fact of the intimate sense" or autoaffection to "abandonment in God" or detachment.

The "double absolute": this, as I have said (pp. 156–57) is the ultimate point of Biran's thought and life. For, though he certainly has several lives, it is by raising himself *toward what is above* (divine life) and not only by discovering or observing himself *through what is below* (animal life) that man must also exert himself and test himself. Hence the "three lives," summarized thus by Maine de Biran in his *Nouveaux essais d'anthropologie* (1823–1824)—and which I can only point out, at the risk of opening here onto a new work, this time a theological one— "animal life" (affectability and motility), the "life of man" (the thinking and willing subject), and the "life of the spirit" (the receptive faculties

---

1. See Gouhier, *Conversions*, 411–22.

that are in relation only with an invisible world).² These are certainly three lives but above all are "three lives in one." For, as with the "science of the mixed," in Biran we cannot separate everything, even if some wrongly accuse him of a "metaphysical dualism," when in reality it is a matter only of an anthropological, psychological, and mystical duality or even triplicity: animal life, human life, spiritual life.

A "conversion" or even "conversions" come about over the course of Maine de Biran's existence; this is known. And if some have said that the last, "religious" conversion is marked by "doubts" and "hesitations" (Gouhier),³ I will say, for my part, that it is more and explicitly "Christian" and "certain," so obvious is its imprint at least in the evening of his life (in a strange similarity, therefore, with the itinerary of Michel Henry, who also returned to Christianity in his last decade and to close his work). Certainly, recognizes the solitary man of Grateloup in an entry in his *Journal* on the date of June 6–7, 1818, "it is said that if men become religious or devout as they advance in age, it is because they are afraid of death and of what must follow it in another life."⁴ But he himself will not stop there. For it is not *negatively*, by virtue of the fear of death, that he will turn toward this other absolute that is God himself, but *positively* through a profound and inner "experience of the intimate sense of God" (the sense of God), as there was also for him a profound and inner "experience of the intimate sense of oneself" (the primitive fact of intimate sense). No "terror like" that of death (or even that of illness), decrees Biran verbatim in this same entry, or this same avowal, in the *Journal*, but only the aspiration to be converted *toward God* rather than only believing *in God*:

> Then God, the sovereign good, emerges as if from the clouds [sic]: our souls *sense* him, *see* him, by *turning* toward him, the source of all light, because *even as one escapes into the sensible world*, phenomenal existence no longer being sustained by external and internal impressions, one senses the need to rely on something that remains and no longer deceives, on a reality, on an eternal, absolute truth.⁵

2. Maine de Biran, *Dernière philosophie*, 329–31.

3. Gouhier, *Les Conversions*, 412: "All the historians of Maine de Biran have noted his hesitations concerning the scope of *religious experience*. . . . What should be emphasized is that they do not appear only at the beginning of his *religious itinerary*: they *persist* in the last months of his life" (emphasis added).

4. J. II, 127 (entry dated June 6–7, 1818).

5. J. II, 127–28.

The fear of death as the negative disappearance of oneself in one's body is therefore superseded, at the very end of the life of the thinker of Grateloup, by positive attachment to God as the unique *source* of phenomenality. Since as he ages man is ever more bent in a diminishing of "force in itself" as much from the point of view of the body (the primitive fact of effort) as of affect (the sentiment of the *myself*), it is by attaching himself to God himself, and no longer only to "external and internal impressions" that Maine de Biran will be converted: that is, the "spiritual life" (the spirit that knows God himself) that is added to, but that perhaps also assumes and transforms, "animal life" (the organic) and the "life that is proper to man" (the sensing and thinking being).

Will we then follow Henri Gouhier in *Les Conversions de Maine de Biran* (published in 1948, the very year in which Maine de Biran was for the first time put on the program of the *agrégation* in philosophy in France) in affirming that "Maine de Biran advances *beyond Platonism* without going *all the way to the end of Christianity*"?[6] The phrase—lined with suspicion of the "Christian temptation" [sic] of a thinker who, however, "adhered to the Catholic communion" at the very end of his life—is severe, and that is the least one can say. Perhaps in reality it signifies only saving the figure of an "exclusively philosophical" Biran well after Church and State had separated in France (1905), based this time on a "hostile" or "neutral" secularism rather than a "tolerant" one (§1b). Better, if such a judgment had to turn out to be a correct designation of the final position of the thinker of Grateloup—the position of an unfinished Christianity, or a Christianity that did not "go all the way to the end"—it would probably then apply to the figure of his most faithful successor—in phenomenology, that is: Michel Henry himself. But this is not the case, in my view, for neither of them remained at the "threshold" of Christianity. The attachment to the figure of Christ as the "Word made flesh" cannot be denied, even if it is inspired by the *French spirituality of abandonment to God* for the one (Bossuet, so often recopied word for word in Maine de Biran's last notes) and by *detachment* for the other (Meister Eckhart, cited by Michel Henry as early as *The Essence of Manifestation*).

It is not "Christianity" that did not "go all the way to the end" to remain confined to a certain form of "Platonism," but it is a "streamlined Christianity," free of any exteriority, that we must call on here—to

---

6. Gouhier, *Conversions*, 366: "By welcoming, in his late philosophy, an incarnate Word as the guide of the third life, Maine de Biran advances *beyond Platonism* without going *all the way to the end of Christianity*" (emphasis added).

remain only within the space of intimacy and interiority: "It is a matter of making in one's soul *a solitude that the world cannot penetrate*.... May *our inside* become a temple worthy of God!" avows Maine de Biran, this time as a spiritualist or, rather, as a "spiritual man," shortly before dying on July 20, 1824 (entries dated December 6 and 20, 1823).[7] This is a double phrase that Michel Henry also would not hesitate to sign with his eyes closed, to such an extent is the space of phenomenology not, or no longer, that of the world or of society—in order to set himself totally in search of interiority: "According to the phenomenology of life, there exist two fundamental and irreducible modes of appearing: that *of the world*, and *that of life*."[8]

Among these *three lives*, "spiritual life" (where "the wind blows where it will") will then take the "baton" from "animal life" (made of instincts and appetites) and from "human life" (in the sentiment of oneself). The *third life* is not another life but another "way of living the same life." There is indeed something of the "proper" in the Spirit, as there was in the lived or proper body or in the sentiment of oneself. And if the improper is to be fled, as I have ceaselessly shown in a reading *in counter-relief* of Maine de Biran, it is because nothing is more to be feared than being "outside oneself"—which happens sometimes, even often. God keeps me *in myself* and inhabits *in me* in order to not leave me "outside myself." Only thus will I also be *in him*, he who alone, and uniquely, is capable of reaching the "original solitude" in which I am held, even imprisoned:

> It is *even often* when the body is *struck down*, when all its functions languish, when the machine falls into ruin, and when the animal has lost all vivacity, all *vital* energy, that the *light of the spirit* casts the most radiance and that the *soul* lives most completely in *the life of that spirit*, that it enjoys it with the most love.... *The spirit blows* where it will (John 4:8); sometimes it withdraws; the soul falls into languor and dryness.[9]

The *confession*, even the *conversion*, with regard to Christianity is therefore evident in Maine de Biran, who does not remain "at the edge [*bord*]" of faith in a supposed form of "Platonism" or only just "beyond" Platonism. The *personal encounter* (or what can be interpreted as such) with this Spirit that "blows where it will" in the "Word made flesh"

---

7. J. II, 417 (entry dated December 6, 1823), 419 (entry dated December 20, 1823).
8. Henry, *Incarnation*, 94 (emphasis added).
9. J. III, 411 (entry dated November 1823, emphasis partly in original).

mentioned in John's prologue is related by Maine de Biran's own pen for those who know how to read it and also to decipher it. The "spiritualist" of Grateloup also had his own *Memorial*. On the date of November 23, 1823, when Biran says he had only just "arrived in Paris"—like a certain Blaise Pascal, also in Paris (Monsieur-le-Prince street) during the "night of fire" of November 23–24 in the year of grace 1654, St. Clement's day[10]—the solitary man, scarcely disembarked from his "dear Dordogne" notes in the aforementioned "green notebook" (a notebook also found late and posthumously, as was the case for the Pascalian *Memorial* discovered by his valet in the lining of his coat) that his trip was occupied with "meditations during the journey on the life of the spirit."[11] There then follows a long series of annotations written by Biran himself in his own copy of John's Gospel—a sort of *marginalia* to the prologue, as spiritual as they are perfectly phrased—and published for the first time by Ernest Naville under the title "Nouvelles notes sur l'Évangile de saint Jean" ["New Notes on St. John's Gospel"].[12]

Thus we read, as a commentary on verse 14 of the prologue—"and the Word became flesh and dwelt among us ... full of grace and truth" (John 1:14):

> The *Word*, the spirit, or the spiritual *myself has put on a form of flesh* without, nevertheless, identifying itself with the flesh.... Jesus Christ was thus the *truest manifestation* of the Father of lights.... Jesus Christ merited being called the *only son* of God because he has no *brother equal* in virtue or in spirit, but he has for *a relative*, of the *same family, from the same lineage*, every man who lives from the spiritual life and who has merited

---

10. See Pascal, "Memorial," 178 (L. 913), with my commentary (on the *Memorial*), "Blaise Pascal."

11. J. II, 410 (entry dated November 30, 1823).

12. J. II, 412–17. This is a long series of handwritten notes on the "three lives" taken from Maine de Biran's copy of the Gospel According to St. John and initially published by Naville under the title "Nouvelles notes sur l'Évangile de saint Jean," in *Œuvres inédites de Maine de Biran*, 314–20. As for the parallel to be established, and these notes (or at the very least the memory of them) as a possible source for the writing of the works *I Am the Truth, Incarnation,* and also *Words of Christ* by Michel Henry, see the comparison of these texts established by Anne Devarieux—while distancing these two authors, including as regards their commentary on John's Gospel: *L'Intériorité réciproque*, 285–305 ("Trinité biranienne et trinité henryenne), esp. 295–302 ("Notes sur l'Évangile de Jean"), 302–5 ("La parole johannique selon Henry").

being in *possession* of grace and truth without being able to be *full* of them like the mediator.¹³

"The *Word*, the spirit, or the spiritual *myself has put on a form of flesh* without, nevertheless, identifying itself with the flesh," "Jesus Christ was thus the *truest manifestation* of the Father of lights," "he has for *a relative*, of the *same family, from the same lineage*, every man who lives from the spiritual life" .... What of Maine de Biran, once again, did Michel Henry read in his own commentary on John's Gospel in *I Am the Truth*? Or what of Michel Henry did Maine de Biran read in his *marginalia* to his own copy of the Gospel? No one knows—at the very least because Michel Henry himself never indicated it. But, bringing them together, the line of descent cannot be denied, with regard to form (a commentary on John's prologue) as to the content (a flesh for appearing, the Son as a manifestation, man engendered like the Son and through the Son, etc.). The work, which is not only philosophical but also theological and exegetical, certainly remains to be undertaken, although it has already begun—albeit within a gap that is to be noted between Henry and Biran, including as regards the third life: "In his last book, *Words of Christ*," Anne Devarieux rightly indicates in the last chapter of her work *L'Intériorité réciproque: L'hérésie biranienne de Michel Henry*, "Henry emphasizes, on the contrary, the *decomposition* of bonds between men and the *substitution* of the divine genealogy for the natural relation between father and son."¹⁴

It remains that, beyond these texts and their comparison—and even Maine de Biran's *relevance* [*actualité*] for today not only in the sense of his "modernization" but of his possible "realization" [*actualisation*] or "potentialization"—Michel Henry himself, like the thinker from Bergerac, also had *his* third life, "spiritual" this time, which gave us his *trilogy* (as I have also, for my part, composed a *Philosophical Triduum*).¹⁵ This is a fortunate thing, and that is the least one can say—all the more so as *Spiritualism and Phenomenology: The "Case" of Maine de Biran* (the present work) responds, as it were, less to object to it than to trace out another path, to *Philosophy and Phenomenology of the Body: An Essay*

13. J. II, 415–16 (emphasis partly in original).

14. Devarieux, *L'Intériorité réciproque*, 302.

15. Thus one can compare, if not in its content, then at least in its movement, the Henryan trilogy (*I Am the Truth*; *Incarnation*; *Words of Christ*) to the *philosophical triduum* such as I composed it (*Guide to Gethsemane*; *Metamorphosis of Finitude*; *Wedding Feast of the Lamb*), with *La Chair de Dieu* as a link or "hinge" between the three panels of the triptych.

on Biranian Ontology (Henry).¹⁶ The absolute from "below" (animal life) and the absolute from "above" (divine life) perhaps also meet in the mixed life that is the life of man, this time inhabited by a "God extraphenomenal" who has come to join us in the depths of our trauma, less to draw us out of it than to abide in it "with us."¹⁷ Whether one remains in the intimacy of oneself (phenomenology), goes into ecstasies in a God outside oneself (spiritualism), or recognizes the blended and obscure life of a God in oneself ("between" spiritualism and phenomenology), one will, then, not cease exclaiming, with Royer-Collard as he left the funeral of his friend Maine de Biran in the Saint-Thomas-d'Aquin church in Paris: "He was the master of us all!"¹⁸

---

16. [See note 2 in chapter 3. –Trans.]
17. See Falque, *Chair de Dieu*, 151–58.
18. Gouhier, *Maine de Biran*, 8.

Bibliography

Aristotle. *De anima*. Translated by Christopher Shields. Oxford: Clarendon, 2016.
———. *Metaphysics*. Translated by C. D. C. Reeve. Indianapolis: Hackett, 2016.
———. *On the Parts of Animals*. Translated by James G. Lennox. Oxford: Clarendon, 2016.
Armand, Guilhem. "Quand le conte nous fait croire en la science: le cas de Boureau-Deslandes." *Féeries* 10 (2013) 181–93.
Augustine. *Confessions*. Translated by Maria Boulding. Hyde Park, NY: New City, 1997.
Azouvi, François. "Conscience, identification et articulation chez Maine de Biran." *Revue de métaphysique et de morale* 88.4 (1983) 465–84.
———. "Genèse du corps propre chez Malebranche, Condillac, Lelarge de Lignac et Maine de Biran." *Archives de philosophie* 45.1 (1982) 85–107.
———. *Maine de Biran, la science de l'homme*. Paris: Vrin, 1995.
Baertschi, Bernard. "L'idéologie subjective de Maine de Biran et la phénoménologie." *Revue de théologie et de philosophie* 113.2 (1981) 109–22.
———. *L'Ontologie de Maine de Biran*. Freiburg: Éditions universitaires de Fribourg, 1982.
———. "La statue de Condillac, image du réel ou fiction logique?" *Revue philosophique de Louvain* 82.55 (1984) 335–64.
Barbaras, Renaud. *Le Tournant de l'expérience*. Paris: Vrin, 1998.
Bataille, Georges. "The Psychological Structure of Fascism." In *Visions of Excess: Selected Writings, 1927–1939*, edited and translated by Allan Stoekl et al., 137–60. Minneapolis: University of Minnesota Press, 1985.
Bégout, Bruce. *Le Concept d'ambiance: Essai d'éco-phénoménologie*. Paris: Seuil, 2020.
———, ed. *Maine de Biran: La vie intérieure*. Paris: Petite Bibliothèque Payot, 1995.
———. *Le Sauvetage*. Paris: Fayard, 2018.
Bergson, Henri. *The Two Sources of Morality and Religion*. Translated by R. Ashley Audra et al. Notre Dame, IN: University of Notre Dame Press, 1977.
Bianco, Giuseppe. *Après Bergson. Portrait de groupe avec philosopho*. Paris: Presses Universitaires de France, 2015.
Binswanger, Ludwig. *Le Cas Suzanne Urban: Étude sur la schizophrénie*. Translated by Jacqueline Verdeaux. Paris: Allia, 2019.

Blanchot, Maurice. *The Space of Literature.* 1955. Translated by Ann Smock. Lincoln, NE: University of Nebraska Press, 1982.
Bonald, Louis de. *Législation primitive.* Vol. 1. Paris: Le Clere, 1802.
Bouillot, Bénédicte. *Le noyau de l'âme selon Edith Stein: De l'épochè phénoménologique à la nuit obscure.* Paris: Hermann, 2015.
Cabanis, Georges. *Rapport du physique et du moral de l'homme.* 2 vols. Paris: Crapart, Caille et Ravier, 1802.
Canguilhem, Georges. *The Normal and the Pathological.* Translated by Carolyn R. Fawcett with Robert S. Cohen. New York: Zone, 1989.
Canullo, Carla. *Coscienza e libertà: Itinerario tra Maine de Biran.* Rome: Scientifiche Italiane, 2001.
Carraud, Vincent. *L'Invention du moi.* Paris: Presses Universitaires de France, 2010.
Carvalho, Cláudio Alexandre S. "Biran et le traitement moral de la subjectivité mélancolique." In *Corps ému: Essais de philosophie biranienne,* edited by Luís António Umbelino, 95–121. Coimbra: Coimbra University Press, 2021.
Chrétien, Jean-Louis. *The Call and the Response.* New York: Fordham University Press, 2004.
———. *Hand to Hand: Listening to the Work of Art.* Translated by Stephen E. Lewis. New York: Fordham University Press, 2003.
Condillac, Étienne Bonnot de. *Traité des animaux.* Edited by Michel Malherbe. Paris: Vrin, 2000.
———. *A Treatise on the Sensations.* In *Philosophical Writings of Étienne Bonnot, Abbé de Condillac,* 153–422. Translated by Franklin Philip with Harlan Lane. 1982. Reprint, New York: Psychology, 2014.
Courtine, Jean-François. *Heidegger et la phénoménologie.* Paris: Presses Universitaires de France, 1990.
Decout, Maxime. "Maurice Blanchot: 'Je' ou comment s'en débarrasser." In *Maurice Blanchot entre roman et récit,* edited by Alain Milon, 111–23. Paris: Presses Universitaires de Paris-Nanterre, 2013.
Delbo, Charlotte. *Auschwitz and After.* Translated by Rosette C. Lamont. 2nd ed. New Haven, CT: Yale University Press, 2014.
Deleuze, Gilles. *Foucault.* Translated by Seán Hand. Minneapolis: University of Minnesota Press, 1988.
———. *Pure Immanence: Essays on a Life.* Translated by Anne Boyman. New York: Zone, 2001.
Deleuze, Gilles, and Félix Guattari. *A Thousand Plateaus: Capitalism and Schizophrenia.* Translated by Brian Massumi. Minneapolis: University of Minnesota Press, 1987.
Derrida, Jacques. *Writing and Difference.* Translated by Alan Bass. Chicago: University of Chicago Press, 1978.
Descartes, René. *Discourse on Method.* In *Discourse on Method and Meditations on First Philosophy,* 1–44. Translated by Donald A. Cress. 4th ed. Indianapolis: Hackett, 1998.
———. *Meditations on First Philosophy.* In *Discourse on Method and Meditations on First Philosophy,* 47–103. Translated by Donald A. Cress. 4th ed. Indianapolis: Hackett, 1998.
Devarieux, Anne. "Au principe du spiritualisme? Maine de Biran." In *Le Supplément d'âme ou le Renouveau du spiritualisme,* edited by Jean-Louis Vieillard-Baron, 55–71. Paris: Hermann, 2016.

———. *L'Intériorité réciproque: L'hérésie biranienne de Michel Henry*. Grenoble: Millon, 2018.

———. "Maine de Biran et l'invention du corps propre." In *Corps ému: Essai de philosophie biranienne*, edited by Luís António Umbelino, 27–59. Coimbra, Portugal: Universidade de Coimbra, 2021.

———. *Maine de Biran: L'Individualité persévérante*. Grenoble: Jérôme Millon, 2004.

———. "Michel Henry et Maine de Biran: phénoménologie de la mémoire et réminiscence personnelle." *Cahiers philosophiques de Strasbourg* 30 (2011) 121–41.

Emma-Adamah, Victor. "The Experience of Weakness and Power in Maine de Biran." *Journal for Continental Philosophy of Religion* 7.1 (2025) 114–43.

Falque, Emmanuel. "Blaise Pascal and the Anxiety of Faith." Translated by Jacob Benjamins. *Louvain Studies* 42 (2019) 151–74.

———. *The Book of Experience: From Anselm of Canterbury to Bernard of Clairvaux*. Translated by George Hughes. London: Bloomsbury, 2024.

———. *La Chair de Dieu*. Paris: Cerf, 2023.

———. *Crossing the Rubicon: The Borderlands of Philosophy and Theology*. Translated by Reuben Shank. New York: Fordham University Press, 2016.

———. "The Discarnate Madman." Translated by Sarah Horton. *Journal for Continental Philosophy of Religion* 1.1 (2019) 90–117.

———. "Edith Stein: L'empathie comme problème. Phénoménologie et personnalisme." In *Penser avec Edith Stein: de la phénoménologie à la métaphysique*, edited by Jean-François Lavigne, 83–107. Paris: Hermann, 2022.

———. "God Extra-Phenomenal: For a Phenomenology of Holy Saturday." Translated by Jan Juhani Steinmann. *Journal for Continental Philosophy of Religion* 4.2 (2022) 190–297.

———. *God, the Flesh, and the Other: From Irenaeus to Duns Scotus*. Translated by William Christian Hackett. Evanston, IL: Northwestern University Press, 2015.

———. "Henri Maldiney et le hors phénomène: *A priori* de l'apérité et présupposé du pathique." *Le Cercle herméneutique* 38–39 (2022) 213–28.

———. *Hors phénomène, Essai aux confins de la phénoménalité*. Paris: Hermann, 2021.

———. *The Loving Struggle: Phenomenological and Theological Debates*. Translated by Bradley B. Onishi and Lucas McCracken. London: Rowman and Littlefield, 2018.

———. "Mal et finitude: Dialogue avec Ricœur et Levinas." *Études théologiques et religieuses* 92.2 (2017) 413–31.

———. "Mémorandum: dix thèses pour *Hors phénomène*." *Transversalités* 166.3 (2023) 123–27.

———. *The Metamorphosis of Finitude: An Essay on Birth and Resurrection*. Translated by George Hughes. New York: Fordham University Press, 2012.

———. *Nothing to It: Reading Freud as a Philosopher*. Translated by Robert Vallier and William L. Connelly. Leuven: Leuven University Press, 2020.

———. "Réalisme et phénoménologie: Pour une phénoménologie *a minima*." *Revista Portuguesa de Filosofia* (forthcoming).

———. "The Resistance of Presence." Translated by Andrew Sackin-Poll. *Continental Philosophy Review* 56.1 (2023) 113–43.

———. "The Turn of the Flesh." In *The Emmanuel Falque Reader: Key Writings in Phenomenology and Continental Philosophy of Religion*, edited and translated by Nikolaas Cassidy-Deketelaere, 235–62. London: Bloomsbury, 2024.

———. "Une tempête sous une crâne." *Revista Filosófica de Coimbra* 31.62 (2022) 265–78.

———. *The Wedding Feast of the Lamb: Eros, the Body, and the Eucharist*. Translated by George Hughes. New York: Fordham University Press, 2016.

———. "Wrestling with the Angel." Translated by Madeleine Chalmers. In *Fragility and Transcendence: Essays on the Thought of Jean-Louis Chrétien*, edited by Jeffrey Bloechl, 63–81. New York: Rowman and Littlefield, 2023.

Falque, Emmanuel, and João Paulo Costa. "A Turning Point? Interview with Emmanuel Falque." Translated by Pablo Irizar and Donald N. Boyce. *Journal for Continental Philosophy of Religion* 5.2 (2023) 217–28.

Foucault, Michel. *History of Madness*. Edited by Jean Khalfa. Translated by Jonathan Murphy and Jean Khalfa. London: Routledge, 2006.

Franck, Didier. *Flesh and Body: On the Phenomenology of Husserl*. Translated by Joseph Rivera and Scott Davidson. London: Bloomsbury, 2014.

Freud, Sigmund. "Beyond the Pleasure Principle (1920)." In *The Standard Edition of the Complete Psychological Works of Sigmund Freud*, edited and translated by James Strachey, 18:7–64. London: Hogarth, 1991.

———. "The 'Uncanny.'" In *Collected Papers*, edited by Ernest Jones, 4:368–407. Translated by Alix Strachey. London: Hogarth, 1950.

Gadamer, Hans-Georg. *Truth and Method*. 2nd rev. ed. Translation revised by Joel Weinsheimer and Donald G. Marshall. New York: Continuum, 1994.

Gall, France. "Résiste." 5. *Tout pour la musique*. 1981. Vinyl.

Gouhier, Henri. *Les Conversions de Maine de Biran*. Paris: Vrin, 1948.

———, ed. *Maine de Biran: Œuvres choisies*. Paris: Aubier-Montaigne, 1942.

———. *Maine de Biran par lui-même*. Paris: Seuil, 1970.

Haber, Stéphane. "Le terme 'aliénation' (*Entfremdung*) et ses dérivés au début de la section B du chapitre 6 de *La Phénoménologie de l'esprit* de Hegel." *Annales littéraires de l'université de Franche-Comté* 8 (2005) 5–36.

Hegel, G. W. F. *The Phenomenology of Spirit*. Translated by Peter Fuss and John Dobbins. Notre Dame, IN: Notre Dame University Press, 2019.

Heidegger, Martin. *Being and Time*. Translated by Joan Stambaugh. Albany, NY: State University of New York Press, 1996.

———. "Building Dwelling Thinking." In *Poetry, Language, Thought*, 141–59. Translated by Albert Hofstader. 1975. Reprint, New York: Perenniel, 2001.

Henry, Michel. *The Essence of Manifestation*. Translated by Girard Etzkorn. The Hague: Nijhoff, 1973.

———. *The Genealogy of Psychoanalysis*. Translated by Douglas Brick. Stanford, CA: Stanford University Press, 1993.

———. *I Am the Truth: Toward a Philosophy of Christianity*. Translated by Susan Emanuel. Stanford, CA: Stanford University Press, 2003.

———. *Incarnation: A Philosophy of Flesh*. Translated by Karl Hefty. Evanston, IL: Northwestern University Press, 2015.

———. *Philosophy and Phenomenology of the Body*. Translated by Girard Etzkorn. The Hague: Nijhoff, 1975.

———. *Words of Christ*. Translated by Christina M. Gschwandtner. Grand Rapids: Eerdmans, 2012.

Husserl, Edmund. *Cartesian Meditations: An Introduction to Phenomenology*. Translated by Dorion Cairns. 1950. Reprint, Dordrecht: Kluwer Academic, 1999.

———. *Zur Phänomenologie der Intersubjektivität. Texte aus dem Nachlass, Zweiter Teil: 1921–1928*. Vol. 14 of *Husserliana*. Edited by Kern Iso. The Hague: Martinus Nijhoff, 1973.
Irenaeus. *Against Heresies*. Translated by Alexander Roberts and William Rambaut. Revised by Kevin Knight. New Advent. http://www.newadvent.org/fathers/0103.htm.
Jaspers, Karl. *Autobiographie philosophique*. Translated by Pierre Boudot. Paris: Aubier, 1963.
Kant, Immanuel. *Critique of Pure Reason*. Edited and translated by Paul Guyer and Allen W. Wood. Cambridge: Cambridge University Press, 1999.
Kearney, Richard. *Touch: Recovering Our Most Vital Sense*. New York: Columbia University Press, 2021.
———. "The Wager of Carnal Hermeneutics." In *Carnal Hermeneutics*, edited by Richard Kearney and Brian Treanor, 15–56. New York: Fordham University Press, 2015.
Kearney, Richard, and Brian Treanor, eds. *Carnal Hermeneutics*. New York: Fordham University Press, 2015.
Lacan, Jacques. *The Four Fundamental Concepts of Psychoanalysis*. Edited by Jacques-Alain Miller. Translated by Alan Sheridan. Seminar of Jacques Lacan 11. 1978. Reprint, New York: Norton and Company, 1998.
Lacoste, Jean-Yves. *Le Monde et l'Absence d'œuvre*. Paris: Presses Universitaires de France, 2000.
Lafargue, Paul. "Reminiscences of Karl Marx." In *Marx and Engels Through the Eyes of Their Contemporaries*, 28–50. Moscow: Progress, 1972.
Leibniz, G. W. *New Essays on Human Understanding*. Edited and translated by Peter Remnant and Jonathan Bennett. Cambridge: Cambridge University Press, 1996.
———. "On the Correction of Metaphysics and the Concept of Substance, 1694." In *Philosophical Papers and Letters*, edited and translated by Leroy E. Loemker, 432–34. 2nd ed. Dordrecht: Kluwer Academic, 1989.
———. "The Principles of Nature and Grace, Based on Reason, 1714." In *Philosophical Papers and Letters*, edited and translated by Leroy E. Loemker, 636–42. 2nd ed. Dordrecht: Kluwer Academic, 1989.
Lelarge de Lignac, Joseph-Adrien. *Éléments de métaphysique tirés de l'expérience*. Paris: Desain et Saillant, 1753.
Lemay, Pierre. "Maine de Biran, fondateur de la psychanalyse." *Courrier médical* 85 (1935).
Léna, Marguerite, ed. *Honneur aux maîtres*. Paris: Centurion, 1993.
Le Roy, Édouard. *Une philosophie nouvelle: Henri Bergson*. 1912. Reprint, Paris: Alcan, 1922.
Levinas, Emmanuel. *De l'existence à l'existant*. 2nd ed. Paris: Vrin, 1998.
———. *Time and the Other*. Translated by Richard Cohen. Pittsburgh: Duquesne University Press, 1987.
———. *Totality and Infinity*. Translated by Alphonso Lingis. Pittsburgh: Duquesne University Press, 1969.
Locke, John. *An Essay Concerning Human Understanding*. Edited by Peter H. Nidditch. Oxford: Clarendon, 1975.

Maine de Biran, Pierre-Gontier de. *Commentaires et marginalia: XVIIe siècle*. Vol. 11.1 of *Œuvres de Maine de Biran*. Edited by Christiane Frémont. Directed by François Azouvi. Paris: Vrin, 1990.

———. *Commentaires et marginalia: XIXe siècle*. Vol. 11.3 of *Œuvres de Maine de Biran*. Edited by Joël Ganault. Directed by François Azouvi. Paris: Vrin, 1990.

———. *Correspondance philosophique: 1766-1804*. Vol. 13.2 of *Œuvres de Maine de Biran*. Edited by André Robinet and Nelly Bruyère. Directed by François Azouvi. Paris: Vrin, 1996.

———. *De l'existence*. Edited by Henri Gouhier. Paris: Vrin, 1966.

———. *Dernière philosophie: Existence et anthropologie*. Vol. 10.2 of *Œuvres de Maine de Biran*. Edited by Bernard Baertschi. Directed by François Azouvi. Paris: Vrin, 1989.

———. *Discours à la Société médicale de Bergerac*. Vol. 5 of *Œuvres de Maine de Biran*. Edited by François Azouvi. Directed by François Azouvi. Paris: Vrin, 1984.

———. *Écrits de jeunesse: 1792-1798*. Vol. 1 of *Œuvres de Maine de Biran*. Edited by Bernard Baertschi. Directed by François Azouvi. Paris: Vrin, 1998.

———. *Essai sur les fondements de la psychologie*. Vol. 7 of *Œuvres de Maine de Biran*. Edited by F. C. T. Moore. Directed by François Azouvi. Paris: Vrin, 1984.

———. *Essai sur les fondements de la psychologie*. Vols. 8-9 of *Œuvres de Maine de Biran*. Edited by Pierre Tisserand. Paris: Alcan, 1932.

———. *Influence de l'habitude sur la faculté de penser*. Vol. 2 of *Œuvres de Maine de Biran*. Edited by Gilbert Romeyer-Dherbey. Directed by François Azouvi. Paris: Vrin, 1987.

———. *The Influence of Habit on the Faculty of Thinking*. Translated by Margaret Donaldson Boehm. Westport, CT: Greenwood, 1929.

———. *Journal*. Edited by Henri Gouhier. 3 vols. Neuchâtel, Switzerland: La Baconnière, 1954-1957.

———. *Mémoire sur la décomposition de la pensée*. Vol. 3 of *Œuvres de Maine de Biran*. Edited by François Azouvi. Directed by François Azouvi. Paris: Vrin, 1988.

———. *Nouvelles considérations sur les rapports du physique et du moral de l'homme*. Vol. 9 of *Œuvres de Maine de Biran*. Edited by Bernard Baertschi. Directed by François Azouvi. Paris: Vrin, 1990.

———. *Of Immediate Apperception*. Edited by Alessandra Aloisi et al. Translated by Mark Sinclair. London: Bloomsbury, 2020.

———. *Œuvres inédites de Maine de Biran*. Edited by Ernest Naville. Vol. 3. Paris: Dezobry, Magdeleine et Compagnie, 1859.

———. *The Relationship Between the Physical and the Moral in Man*. Edited and translated by Darian Meacham and Joseph Spadola. London: Bloomsbury, 2016.

Maldiney, Henri. *Penser l'homme et la folie*. 1991. Reprint, Grenoble: Jérôme Millon, 2007.

Marcel, Gabriel. *Being and Having*. Translated by Katharine Farrar. Glasgow: Glasgow University Press, 1949.

———. *Creative Fidelity*. Translated by Robert Rosthal. New York: Fordham University Press, 2002.

Marion, Jean-Luc. *On Descartes' Metaphysical Prism: The Constitution and the Limits of Onto-theo-logy in Cartesian Thought*. Translated by Jeffrey L. Kosky. Chicago: University of Chicago Press, 1999.

———. *Reduction and Givenness: Investigations of Husserl, Heidegger, and Phenomenology*. Translated by Thomas A. Carlson. Evanston, IL: Northwestern University Press, 1998.
Markovits-Pessel, Francine. *La Statue de Condillac: Les cinq sens en quête de moi*. Paris: Hermann, 2028.
Merleau-Ponty, Maurice. *The Incarnate Subject: Malebranche, Biran, and Bergson on the Union of Body and Soul*. Edited by Andrew G. Bjelland Jr. and Patrick Burke. Translated by Paul B. Milan. Amherst, MA: Humanity, 2001.
———. *Phenomenology of Perception*. Translated by Donald A. Landes. London: Routledge, 2012.
———. *Signs*. Translated by Richard McCleary. Evanston, IL: Northwestern University Press, 1964.
———. *L'Union de l'âme et du corps chez Malebranche, Biran et Bergson*. Paris: Vrin, 2002.
———. *The Visible and the Invisible*. Edited by Claude Lefort. Translated by Alphonso Lingis. Chicago: Northwestern University Press, 1968.
Montaigne, Michel de. *Essays*. Translated by J. M. Cohen. 1958. Reprint, New York: Penguin, 1993.
Montebello, Pierre. *La Décomposition de la pensée*. Grenoble: Millon, 1994.
———. "Maine de Biran et la vie animale." In *Corps ému: Essais de philosophie biranienne*, edited by Luís António Umbelino, 563–71. Coimbra, Portugal: Coimbra University Press, 2021.
Musil, Robert. *L'Homme sans qualités*. Vol. 1. Paris: Seuil, 1957.
Nancy, Jean-Luc. *Corpus*. Translated by Richard A. Rand. New York: Fordham University Press, 2008.
———. *The Fall of Sleep*. Translated by Charlotte Mandell. New York: Fordham University Press, 2009.
Nietzsche, Friedrich. *Thus Spoke Zarathustra*. Edited by Adrian Del Caro and Robert Pippin. Translated by Adrian Del Caro. Cambridge: Cambridge University Press, 2006.
———. *Unpublished Fragments from the Period of Thus Spoke Zarathustra (Summer 1882–Winter 1883/84)*. Translated by Paul S. Loeb and David F. Tinsley. Stanford, CA: Stanford University Press, 2019.
Parmentier, Marc. "Maine de Biran, Leibniz et le virtuel." *Méthodos* 16 (2016) 1–25.
Pascal, Blaise. "The Memorial." In *Pensées and Other Writings*, edited by Anthony Levi, 178. Translated by Honor Levi. Oxford: Oxford University Press, 1995.
Péguy, Charles. "Note conjointe sur M. Descartes." In *Œuvres en prose complètes*, edited by Robert Burac, 3:1439–40. Paris: Pléiade, 1992.
Plato. *Alcibiades*. Translated by D. S. Hutchinson. In *Plato: Complete Works*, edited by John M. Cooper, 557–95. Indianapolis: Hackett, 1997.
———. *Sophist*. Translated by Nicholas P. White. In *Plato: Complete Works*, edited by John M. Cooper, 235–93. Indianapolis: Hackett, 1997.
———. *Theaetetus*. Translated by M. J. Levett. Revised by Myles Burnyeat. In *Plato: Complete Works*, edited by John M. Cooper, 157–234. Indianapolis: Hackett, 1997.
———. *Timaeus*. Translated by Donald J. Zeyl. In *Plato: Complete Works*, edited by John M. Cooper, 1224–91. Indianapolis: Hackett, 1997.
Poli, Maria Cristina. "Le concept d'aliénation en psychanalyse." *Figures de la psychanalyse* 12.2 (2005) 45–68.

Ravaisson, Félix. *French Philosophy in the Nineteenth Century*. Translated by Mark Sinclair. Oxford: Oxford University Press, 2023.

Richard, Philippe. *Tomber de tout son corps: Philosophie de Bernanos*. Paris: Hermann, 2017.

Ricœur, Paul. *Fallible Man*. Translated by Charles A. Kelbley. New York: Fordham University Press, 1986.

———. "Intellectual Autobiography." Translated by Kathleen Blamey. In *The Philosophy of Paul Ricœur*, edited by Lewis Edwin Hahn, 1–53. Chicago: Open Court, 1995.

———. *Oneself as Another*. Translated by Kathleen Blamey. Chicago: University of Chicago Press, 1992.

Rohrbach, Philippe. "Maine de Biran au seuil de la pensée: Le fait primitif et l'absolu." In *Corps ému: Essais de philosophie biranienne*, edited by Luís António Umbelino, 469–513. Coimbra, Portugal: Coimbra University Press, 2021.

Romagnoli, Simone. "La décomposition de la 'sensation transformée': Maine de Biran lecteur de Condillac." *Revue de théologie et de philosophie* 134.4 (2002) 341–52.

Romano, Claude. *Les Repères éblouissants: Renouveler la phénoménologie*. Paris: Presses Universitaires de France, 2019.

Romeyer-Dherbey, Gilbert, ed. *Maine de Biran ou le Penseur de l'immanence radicale*. Paris: Seghers, 1974.

Sackin-Poll, Andrew. "Michel Henry and the Resistance of the Flesh." *Revista Portuguesa de Filosofia* 76.2–3 (2020) 857–80.

Sartre, Jean-Paul. *Being and Nothingness*. Translated by Sarah Richmond. London: Routledge, 2018.

———. "Intentionality: A Fundamental Idea of Husserl's Phenomenology." Translated by Joseph P. Fell. *Journal of the British Society for Phenomenology* 1.2 (1970) 4–5.

———. *Nausea*. Translated by Lloyd Alexander. 1959. Reprint, New York: New Directions, 2007.

Scheler, Max. *The Nature of Sympathy*. Translated by Peter Heath. 2008. Reprint, London: Routledge, 2017.

Spinoza, Baruch. *Ethics*. Edited by Matthew J. Kisner. Translated by Michael Silverthorne and Matthew J. Kisner. Cambridge: Cambridge University Press, 2018.

Stein, Edith. *On the Problem of Empathy*. Translated by Waltraut Stein. 3rd rev. ed. Washington, DC: ICS, 1989.

———. *Philosophy of Psychology and the Humanities*. Translated by Mary Catharine Baseheart and Marianne Sawicki. Washington, DC: ICS, 2000.

Tilliette, Xavier. "Nouvelles réflexions sur le Cogito biranien." *Revue de métaphysique et de morale* 88.4 (1983) 436–46.

Tournier, Michel. *Journal extime*. Paris: Folio, 2004.

Uexküll, Jakob von. *A Foray into the Worlds of Animals and Humans*. Translated by Joseph D. O'Neil. Minneapolis: University of Minnesota Press, 2010.

Umbelino, Luís António. *Somatologia subjectiva: Apercepção de si e Corpo em Maine de Biran*. Lisbon: Fundação Calouste Gulbenkian, 2010.

Vasseur, Clara-Élisabeth. "Penser le réel avec Marcel Jousse et Henri Bergson." *Transversalités* 2.157 (2021) 21–34.

Vieillard-Baron, Jean-Louis. *Le Spiritualisme français*. Paris: Cerf, 2021.

Voutsinas, Dimitri. "Maine de Biran, fondateur de la psychologie française." *Revue internationale de philosophie* 20.75 (1966) 69–89.

Wright, Crispin. *Truth and Objectivity*. Cambridge: Harvard University Press, 1994.

Books by Emmanuel Falque in English Translation
LISTED IN ORDER OF PUBLICATION

The Metamorphosis of Finitude: An Essay on Birth and Resurrection. Translated by George Hughes. New York: Fordham University Press, 2012.

God, the Flesh, and the Other: From Irenaeus to Duns Scotus. Translated by William Christian Hackett. Evanston, IL: Northwestern University Press, 2015.

Crossing the Rubicon: The Borderlands of Philosophy and Theology. Translated by Reuben Shank. New York: Fordham University Press, 2016.

The Wedding Feast of the Lamb: Eros, the Body and the Eucharist. Translated by George Hughes. New York: Fordham University Press, 2016.

The Loving Struggle: Phenomenological and Theological Debates. Translated by Bradley B. Onishi and Lucas McCracken. New York: Rowman and Littlefield, 2018.

Saint Bonaventure and the Entrance of God into Theology. Translated by Brian Lapsa. Revised by William C. Hackett. St Bonaventure, NY: Franciscan Institute, 2018.

The Guide to Gethsemane: Anxiety, Suffering, Death. Translated by George Hughes. New York: Fordham University Press, 2019.

Nothing to It: Reading Freud as a Philosopher. Translated by Robert Vallier and William L. Connelly. Leuven: Leuven University Press, 2020.

By Way of Obstacles: A Pathway Through a Work. Translated by Sarah Horton. Eugene, OR: Cascade, 2022.

The Book of Experience: From Anselm of Canterbury to Bernard of Clairvaux. Translated by Georges Hughes. London: Bloomsbury, 2024.

The Emmanuel Falque Reader. Edited by Nikolaas Cassidy-Deketelaere. London: Bloomsbury, 2024.

The Extra-Phenomenal: At the Limits of Phenomenality. Translated by Nikolaas Cassidy-Deketelaere. London: Bloomsbury, forthcoming.

The Flesh of God. Translated by Georges Hughes. New York: Fordham University Press, forthcoming.

Index

affectivity, 46–47, 98n19, 102, 107, 112, 135
 affect, xxv, 1, 34, 37–38, 50–51, 60, 83, 97, 102–3, 105–6, 111, 113, 178–79, 193, 200, 214, 221
 affection, xix, xxv, 34, 39, 47, 55, 60, 65, 98, 102, 105–7, 118, 120, 135n20, 136, 139–41, 148, 151, 212–13
alienation, alienated, alienatable, xvii–xviii, xviin6, xxv, 1, 21, 31, 96, 112, 125–26, 141–42, 156, 159–66, 164n17–18, 172, 185, 187–88, 201, 214n48, 215–18
 See also madness
animal, animality, xxi, xxv, 29, 56, 62, 73, 108, 115, 117, 126–27, 129, 130n9, 140–41, 150, 153, 153n61, 156–57, 160, 162, 164, 166, 180, 202–3, 213, 215–16, 218–22, 225
anthropology, xix, xxi, 4, 8, 25, 96n17, 127, 129–30, 132, 137n24, 140n33, 142, 142n37, 144, 148, 153
apperception, 34, 37n36, 38–39, 43–44, 51, 87, 116–17, 119, 123, 126, 150, 161, 171, 174, 216

Aristotle, 22, 55–59, 57n18, 58n20n23, 63, 78, 82, 115, 115n55n57, 128, 199
Armand, Guilhem, 61n27
Augustine, 79, 208
autoaffection, xvi, xix–xxi, xxiii, xxv, 14–15, 18–19, 28–30, 45–47, 51, 55, 65–66, 83, 93, 97–99, 103, 106–7, 121, 126, 139, 141–42, 142n37, 148, 170, 187, 193, 195, 199–201, 205, 219
Azouvi, François, xxin16, 53n9n11, 129, 131n12, 145n42, 156n1

Baertschi, Bernard, xxin17, 66, 91–92, 91n8, 97n18, 101n27, 117, 119–21, 159n8, 192, 192n4
Barbaras, Renaud, 74
Bataille, Georges, 143, 143n39, 146
Bégout, Bruce, 9n12, 34n30, 135n21
Bergson, Henri, xxiin17, 14, 17, 18n3, 23–24, 26–27, 29, 37, 58, 95–96, 115, 129, 142
Bianco, Giuseppe, 18n3, 41n45
Binswanger, Ludwig, 132, 135n20, 164, 214–15, 215n49
Blanchot, Maurice, xxiii–xxiv, 6, 10, 114, 123, 160, 178

INDEX

body, xviin6, xviii, xix, xxiii, xxvi, 17–18, 20–21, 25–31, 27n19, 36, 38, 40, 48–55, 58, 60–63, 62n31, 66, 68–70, 74–86, 88–93, 90n3, 95, 98–102, 108, 110, 113, 114–21, 123–24, 127, 129, 131n12, 133, 136–37, 140, 141–42, 144, 149, 152, 154, 158, 162, 164–65, 167–71, 173–86, 188–89, 191–94, 197n13, 200–202, 206, 208–9, 211–13, 221–22
  body-object, 66, 183–84, 192
  body-subject, 66, 81, 183–84, 192
  See also improper body, lived body, spread body
Bonald, Louis de, 214n48
Bouillot, Bénédicte, 95n15
Boureau-Deslandes, André-François, 61, 68
Buffon, comte de, 61, 62n29, 63, 63n34, 68, 171

Cabanis, Georges, 129n8, 135, 140, 148
Canguilhem, Georges, 136, 137n24, 146
Canullo, Carla, 24n14
carnal hermeneutics, 56, 89–90, 102, 127, 136
Carraud, Vincent, 52n4n5
Carvalho, Cláudio Alexandre S., 217n55
chaos, 73, 127, 156, 166, 173
Chrétien, Jean-Louis, xxvii, 55, 59, 78, 115, 168n25
cogito, 31, 33, 35, 40, 42, 44, 60, 67, 79, 91, 127, 138, 170, 179, 191, 194–95
Condillac, Étienne Bonnot de, xvi, 9, 12, 29, 31, 40, 42n45, 48–49, 51, 53n10, 54–57, 59–62, 61n28, 62n29, 63–72, 63n34, 69n41, 72n46, 74, 76–86, 88–89, 98–99, 101–116, 121–23, 135, 168–69, 178–79, 186–87, 192–93, 196
  See also statue (Condillac's)
consciousness, xxin17, xxiii, xxviin27, 14, 17, 20–21, 28–34, 37–43, 50, 65n38, 93, 101, 118, 126, 132n12, 142, 145–46, 149, 152, 156, 161, 171, 174, 175n44, 176–77, 182, 188–89, 193, 200, 202, 207, 215
corporeality, xix, 16, 102, 110, 119, 130, 135, 137, 152, 158, 166–67, 187, 201, 213
Courtine, Jean-François, 59n24
Cousin, Victor, 9, 11–14, 21, 24–26, 89
crisis, xxviin27, 74 n49

Decout, Maxime, 10n13
Delbo, Charlotte, 108, 188
Deleuze, Gilles, xvi, xviin4, xxiii, 123, 142, 143n38, 146
delirium, xxiv, 138–40, 144, 157, 207
dementedness, 75, 158, 191, 201, 214–17
Derrida, Jacques, 134, 137
Descartes, René, xxiii, 9, 12, 14, 23, 31–35, 36n35, 39, 41–47, 52n4, 53n10, 60, 66, 79, 83–85, 90–91, 104–5, 112, 118, 126, 126n1, 128, 137–38, 138n28, 153, 162, 171, 189, 191, 195–96, 202, 208–9
Devarieux, Anne, xxn14, 27, 50n2, 52n5, 53n10, 111, 118, 135n20, 156n3, 170, 172, 172n3, 193, 194n7, 210n40, 223n12, 224
Diderot, Denis, 60, 186
divinity, divine, 14, 21, 24, 26, 96, 129, 156–57, 162, 164, 166, 218–19, 224–25
dream, dreaming, xviii, 10, 10n13, 139, 172, 176, 203–5, 217
drugs, xviii, xxi, xxv, 15, 21, 30–31, 67, 75, 121, 142, 163, 175, 191, 207–8, 213
drunkenness, 60, 75, 138–39, 144, 153, 158, 167, 190–91, 201, 206–9, 213–14, 217–18
dualism, 98n19, 118, 143, 220

effort, xxiv, 18, 28–30, 35–36, 42n45, 48, 50–51, 50n2, 55, 57, 59–60, 82, 86, 92–93, 98–99, 101, 115–18, 121, 131n12, 143, 148, 153, 157–58, 167–70, 174–77, 182, 184, 187, 190–98, 200–1, 206–9, 210n40, 213, 216

INDEX

sense of effort, 116, 121, 123, 175–76, 180, 186, 190–91, 194–95, 200, 205, 207
sentiment of effort, xxn14, xxiii, 21, 120, 174, 180, 184, 199
See also primitive fact of effort (*under* primitive fact)
Emma-Adamah, Victor, 136n22
empiricism, xvi, 19, 74, 74n49, 76, 81, 104
exception, xviii, xxv, 1, 47, 67, 75, 89, 109n38, 111, 114, 118, 122–23, 126, 131, 143, 154, 158, 161–62, 165–67, 174–75, 179–80, 184–85, 201, 203, 215, 218
existentialism, xxiii, xxviin27, 128, 183, 185, 200
extended body, 120, 189, 208
exteriority, xvi, xvin3, xix, xxiii, xxvi, 15, 21, 48, 56, 65, 74, 79, 81, 83, 92, 98–100, 112–13, 121–23, 140–41, 146, 178, 185, 191, 200, 221
extra-phenomenal, extra-phenomenality, xvii–xx, xxiin17, xxiii–xxiv, xxviin27, 15–16, 23, 30, 37, 47–48, 67, 73–74, 74n49, 76–77, 88, 100, 114, 123–24, 126, 128, 130, 132, 138–40, 146, 148, 153, 157–58, 160n10, 165, 167, 180, 188, 191, 201, 203, 205–6, 214, 218
See also outside-the-phenomenon

flesh, xv, xxiii, xxvi, 14, 19, 26, 31, 36, 39–40, 48, 50–51, 53, 54n12, 55, 56n17, 60, 76, 83, 86–93, 95, 99, 102, 102n28, 110, 117–22, 127, 137, 140, 142, 156, 156n3, 161, 168, 170, 176–77, 179–80, 182–83, 189, 192–93, 207–8, 221–24
force, 27–29, 50, 98, 100–1, 103, 106, 116–18, 139, 143, 148–50, 153, 157, 166–69, 171, 173, 190–91, 194–200, 206, 209, 213, 221
virtual force, 121, 176, 191, 195–96, 199–200
foreign, foreignness, foreignerness, xv, xvii–xix, xxvn25, 23, 31, 38, 41n43, 47, 60, 67–68, 70, 76, 85–86, 97–98, 121, 123–24, 130n9, 139, 141, 143, 148, 151, 153–55, 157–58, 160, 162–67, 175, 177, 180, 185, 187–88, 191–94, 198, 200–3, 205, 214, 216
Foucault, Michel, xxiii, 123, 126, 137, 137n25n26
Franck, Didier, 48n56, 90n6
Freud, Sigmund, xvii, 109, 127, 146–47, 147n46, 151, 196n10, 202, 204–6

Gadamer, Hans-Georg, 133n16
Gall, France, 151, 169n27
God, 23, 25–26, 51, 94–96, 101, 109n40, 130n9, 149, 156, 156n3, 219–23, 225
God extra-phenomenal, 23, 158, 225
Gouhier, Henri, xxn14, 4, 4n5, 7, 11, 18, 89, 91, 96, 97n18, 132n13, 142n37, 146–47, 148n49, 152, 187, 188n67, 195, 196n9, 219n1, 220–21, 225n18

Haber, Stéphane, 164n17
hand, 48, 54–55, 57–59, 63, 78–86, 88, 99–101, 104, 107–8, 110, 113–18, 120–25, 140–41, 148, 153, 157–58, 163, 166–70, 175–82, 184–85, 189, 192–94, 197, 201, 214–15, 217
Hegel, G. W. F., 163n17
Heidegger, Martin, 22–23, 33, 33n28, 56, 59–60, 83, 94, 116, 116n58, 152n58, 158n6, 165, 166n22, 208, 218
hemiplegia, hemiplegic, 163, 180–82, 185–86, 189, 201, 214, 217
Henry, Michel, xxn14, xxi, xxiii, xxvi, xxviin27, 11, 14–15, 17–20, 22, 25, 28, 32, 40–41, 45–46, 47n54, 50n2, 51–54, 71, 83, 87, 89, 91–92, 96–99, 100–103, 105–7, 111–14, 116–22, 119n65, 120n68, 122n71, 141, 142n36n37, 143, 146, 156, 169n28, 170, 177, 183, 191, 193n5, 194n7, 195, 219–22, 223n12, 224–25

INDEX

hermeneutics, 89–90, 93, 102, 130, 185
  See also carnal hermeneutics
heteroaffection, 46, 65, 141–42, 148, 193
heterogeneous, heterogeneity, 15n20, 142–44, 145n42, 177
Holy Spirit, 21, 26, 197n12n13
human, humanity, xxii, xxv, 22, 24, 29–30, 32, 35n33, 38–39, 45, 52–54, 58, 73, 78, 85, 93–95, 108, 117–18, 119n65, 123, 126–27, 129, 134, 138n29, 140n33, 148, 153, 156, 160n10, 161–62, 164–65, 166n22, 178, 180, 189, 203n26, 211, 213, 216–18, 220, 222
hyperorganic, hyperorganicity, 50, 117–21, 123, 140, 169, 171, 193
Husserl, Edmund, xxi, xxviin27, 9n12, 33–35, 37, 39, 41–45, 48, 51, 53–54, 56–57, 69, 83, 90, 92–95, 101–2, 119, 128, 189, 208

idiocy, 158, 167, 214–17
idealism, xxin17, 27, 74n49, 93
illness, xviii, 47, 60, 67, 73–76, 80, 109, 114, 130–31, 134, 136, 153, 160n10, 161, 163, 175, 181, 183–85, 208, 218, 220
improper body, xvi, xvin2, xix, 21, 48, 91, 154, 163, 183–85, 218
immanence, xxiii, 19, 27, 120, 142n37, 143, 170
intentionality, xxvi, xxviin27, 34, 41–42, 98, 213
interiority, xix, xxii–xxiii, xxvi, 15, 17–18, 28, 76, 79, 81, 83, 91, 98–99, 102, 112, 122–23, 138, 140–41, 146–47, 178, 180, 185, 210n40, 222
Irenaeus, 25n16

Jaspers, Karl, 93, 130n10, 186
John, Gospel of, 15, 47n54, 148, 156, 156n3, 222–24, 223n12

Kant, Immanuel, 28n21, 41, 42n45, 94n14, 104, 137n24, 203n26
Kearney, Richard, 56n17, 90

Lacan, Jacques, xxivn22, 146n45, 164n18
Lachelier, Jules, 13–14, 24–26, 129
Lacoste, Jean-Yves, xxviin27, 174
Lafargue, Paul, 15
lapidary existence, 107–9, 114, 125, 209, 216
Leibniz, G. W., 9, 12, 21, 27–29, 38–39, 41, 42n45, 52n4, 53, 104, 172, 191, 195–200, 198n15
Lelarge de Lignac, Joseph-Adrien, 53
Lemay, Pierre, 147n47
Léna, Marguerite, 112n48
Le Roy, Édouard, 95n16
Levinas, Emmanuel, xxvn25, xxviin27, 25, 41, 53, 54n12, 56–57, 100, 102, 114, 160, 161n11, 169, 175
limit, limits, 51, 53n10, 81, 86, 90, 90n3, 96, 126, 131–34, 131n12, 136–37, 150–51, 161, 163–64, 176, 180, 189
  limit-experiences, 1, 31, 42, 48, 60, 65, 121, 123, 167, 170, 184, 218
  limit-situations, xviii, xix, 15, 30, 46, 76, 81, 108, 123, 130, 180, 186
lived body, xvi, xix–xx, 15, 21, 30, 43, 48–55, 53n10, 60, 63, 66, 70–71, 74, 76, 80, 83, 87, 90–91, 93, 97–98, 102, 105, 110–11, 113, 116–23, 126, 130–31, 138–42, 148–49, 153–55, 161, 163, 165, 170–71, 175–77, 179–89, 191–94, 196, 199, 202, 207–9, 211, 217, 222
Locke, John, xvi, 9, 12, 42n45, 52, 60, 68, 75n51, 104, 186

madness, mad, xviii, xxi, xxv, 15, 21, 30–31, 60, 66, 75, 121, 123, 125–26, 130–31, 136–39, 142, 144, 153, 155, 158, 162, 166–67, 175, 191, 210, 214, 217
  See also alienation
mania, 138–39, 144, 167, 216
Maine de Biran, Pierre-Gontier de
  as "Columbus of metaphysics," xv, xxii, xxv–xxvi, 79, 202, 218
  conversions of, 96, 220

INDEX   241

death of, 7, 11–13, 36, 96, 132, 149, 196
defender in royal guard, 2, 219
deputy of Dordogne, xi, xvi, xxi, 2, 5, 12, 33, 130, 134, 219
discovery of manuscripts of, 9–14
ennoblement of 2, 6
founder/president of Bergerac Medical Society, 47, 117, 121, 129, 131, 203, 219
Journal of, xv, xxii, 2–4, 6, 11–13, 15–16, 32–33, 97, 129, 135, 158–59, 196–97, 220
member of *Corps législatif d'État*, 2
quaestor, 2, 5
reading in counter-relief of, xxi–xxii, 15, 65, 107, 125, 130, 145, 149, 161, 163, 171, 178, 217, 222
royalist, 1, 24
son Félix, 11–13
subprefect of Bergerac, xi, 2, 5, 25, 134, 147, 163, 219
Malebranche, Nicolas, 61
Maldiney, Henri, 114, 127, 132, 135n20, 146, 154, 154n62, 164, 214–16
man-statue. *See* statue
Marcel, Gabriel, 8, 92–93, 112, 127, 129
Marion, Jean-Luc, xxviin27, 94n13, 114, 158n6, 165, 218
Markovits-Pessel, Francine, 64n37, 112n45
materialism, 21, 27
medicine, xix, 4, 89, 96, 159, 165, 181, 186, 201
melancholy, melancholia, 6, 135–36, 201, 216
Merleau-Ponty, Maurice, xxi, xxvi, 17–20, 18n1, 19n4, 22, 39, 40n42, 41, 51–57, 54n12, 74n49, 83, 87, 89, 92, 93–95, 98, 100, 102, 113, 122–23, 129, 145–46, 146n43, 176–77, 179, 182–83, 195
metaphysics, xix, 21–24, 32–33, 56–57, 71, 94–97, 94n13, 128
mixed, xxi, 131, 142–44, 145n42, 220, 225
modification, xviii, 37, 47, 67, 78, 86, 110, 113, 140, 158, 165–66, 184, 207, 215

See also transformation
Molyneux's problem, 60, 75, 186
Montaigne, Michel de, 16
Montebello, Pierre, 92, 141, 170, 194, 195n8
Morellet, André (Abbé), 32–33, 35
Musil, Robert, 75n50
myself, xxiv–xxv, xxviin27, 17, 31–33, 35–37, 41–45, 47, 50, 52, 53n10, 55, 60, 63–64, 65n38, 66, 73, 79, 81, 84–85, 87, 89, 92n10, 98–99, 105, 113–14, 117, 123, 131n12, 142, 144, 147–52, 149n51, 154–56, 158, 160, 163, 165–67, 171–77, 186, 188, 195–96, 199–200, 203, 205–8, 211, 213–16, 223–24
phenomenal myself, 15, 49, 51–52, 126, 138–39, 142, 155, 161, 163, 165, 173–74, 177, 187, 207, 209, 211
sentiment of (the) myself, xviii, xxiv–xxv, 1, 15, 18, 20–21, 23, 29, 31, 36–39, 44–45, 49–50, 52, 55, 67, 121, 123, 126, 131, 134, 141, 144, 157, 159–60, 162, 165–67, 170–71, 176–77, 181, 186–87, 191, 201–2, 205, 217–18, 221

Nancy, Jean-Luc, xxvi, xxviin27, 79, 80n57, 84, 173
Naville, Ernest, xxii, 9, 13, 156n3, 223
Naville, François, 8–9, 12–13, 198
Nietzsche, Friedrich, 7, 76, 110, 133, 142, 195–96, 197n12n13

objectivity, xvi, xxi, xxiii, 32–33, 42, 45, 56, 101, 113, 116, 177
offside, xxii, xxiv, xxviin27, 21, 48, 65–66, 72–73, 108, 111, 140, 153, 157, 163, 165, 188, 216, 218
organic, organicity, 7, 14, 21, 39, 65, 100, 117–21, 123, 129, 131, 131n12, 132–34, 135n20, 140, 142n37, 146–48, 147n47, 150–53, 162, 164, 169–70, 172–75, 177, 179–80, 187, 189, 191, 193, 201–2, 204–5, 213–14, 217–18, 221

INDEX

outside-the-phenomenon, 30, 75n50, 108, 114, 121, 126, 139
  See also extra-phenomenal

paralysis, paralytic, 60, 75, 117, 121, 124, 136, 139–40, 142, 158, 177–78, 180, 185–89, 191, 201, 214, 217–18
Parmentier, Marc, 199n16
Pascal, Blaise, 6, 36n35, 52, 223
passion, passions, 3, 132, 135, 138–39, 149, 153, 163, 167, 208
Péguy, Charles, 31
perception, 62n31, 99, 101, 103, 119, 172, 179, 185, 210, 217
  little perceptions, 38, 103–4, 147, 172
  obscure perceptions, 104, 147, 172
phenomenology, xix, xxiii–xxiv, xxvi, xxviin27, 14, 17–23, 25–26, 28–30, 33, 38, 41–42, 44–45, 50–52, 54, 57, 69, 74, 74n49, 83, 87–98, 100, 106, 113–14, 121, 127–28, 136, 142–45, 157, 163, 168, 171, 177, 179, 181, 183, 185, 200, 214, 218, 221–22, 225
  psychiatric phenomenology, 89, 127, 130, 135–36, 154, 157, 164, 214–15
physiology, 4, 131–32, 151
  physiologist, 204, 207
Plato, 16, 21, 26, 55, 58
  Platonism, 96n17, 221–22
Pinel, Philippe, 214–16, 217n55
Poli, Maria Cristina, 164n18
proper body. See lived body
psyche, xix, 6, 22, 25–26, 48, 60, 66, 124, 130, 133, 160n10, 166–67, 170, 191, 201–3, 210, 212, 214
psychiatry, 96
psychology, xix, xxi, 4, 7–8, 37, 94, 129–32, 137n24, 140n33, 142–44, 142n37, 147, 149, 151, 152, 201, 206
primitive fact, xxi, xxin17, 18n3, 19, 21, 23, 29, 31–32, 34–37, 41, 42n45, 43–44, 66, 87, 97–100, 110–11, 113, 121, 123, 126, 131, 134, 138–39, 144, 161, 175, 186, 191–92, 194, 207–8, 220
primitive fact of effort, 14, 17, 19–20, 28, 49–50, 67, 83, 92–93, 97, 105, 110–11, 113, 120–21, 126, 139, 150, 165, 167–68, 170, 172–73, 175, 181, 187, 191, 201–2, 208–9, 221
  See also effort

Ravaisson, Félix, 14, 24–26, 28, 129
reduction, xxi, xxiii, 32, 40–41, 43–45, 51, 61, 69, 72, 74, 76, 92–94, 96–100, 107, 116–17, 128, 145, 156, 158n6, 165, 200, 218
Regis, Rey, 181
religion, xix, 4, 24, 96
resistance, xv, xxiii, 21, 31, 36, 48–51, 54–55, 59, 65–66, 73, 77–79, 82–83, 86, 88–90, 92–98, 100–101, 116–18, 120–21, 123–25, 128, 131n12, 140, 148, 151, 156–58, 167–71, 173, 175, 177, 179, 185, 190–91, 193–96, 199, 201, 205, 207–8, 213, 217
  reply of resistance, 49–51, 60, 87, 176, 178–79, 200
Ricœur, Paul, 52–54, 90–93, 94n12, 95, 101–2, 102n28, 113, 127n3, 128, 139, 142n37, 146, 158, 160, 166, 183
Rohrbach, Philippe, 131n12
Romagnoli, Simone, 65
Romano, Claude, 128
Romeyer-Dherbey, Gilbert, 36n36, 38n39, 142, 146, 147n47, 148n49, 152n59, 205n33
Rousseau, Jean-Jacques, 61
Royer-Collard, Antoine-Athanase, 13, 159, 162, 164–65, 214, 217, 225

Sackin-Poll, Andrew, 169n28
Sartre, Jean-Paul, xxviin27, 183–85, 184n59n60
Scheler, Max, 69
secularism, 24–25, 221
self, xi, xviin7, xxn14, xxii, xxvi, 36–37, 38n39, 40–41, 45, 52, 76, 79,

INDEX

85, 116n58, 123, 140–42, 145, 160, 164n17, 167, 171, 200, 202, 209–10
  sentiment of the self, xxi, 36
  See also myself
sensation, xxv, 34, 39–40, 55, 60, 62, 65–66, 72–75, 77–79, 81–86, 100, 103–5, 108, 113, 118, 121, 140, 172, 176n45, 178–79, 183–87, 193, 205, 211
sensibility, 29, 98n19, 124, 134, 140
sensualism, xvi, 40, 48, 64–67, 76, 79, 81, 88, 104, 108–9, 121, 135, 178–79, 192
sentiment, xxv, xxviin27, 7–8, 33–37, 34n30, 40, 46–47, 51, 59–60, 62, 66, 83–84, 87, 97–98, 107, 111, 120–21, 123, 135n20, 136, 140–41, 149, 152, 172, 176–81, 199, 202, 208
  reply of sentiment, 49–50, 60, 87, 124, 176, 178, 182, 193, 199–200
  sentiment of oneself, xv, xviii, xxi, xxv, 36, 38, 40, 44, 47n54, 50, 93, 117, 135, 143, 172–73, 175, 196, 202, 209, 213, 222
  See also sentiment of effort (*under* effort), sentiment of (the) myself (*under* myself) *and* sentiment of the self (*under* self)
sleep, xviii, xxi, xxiv–xxv, 15, 21, 30–31, 46–47, 67, 75, 121, 139–40, 144, 157–58, 170–73, 175–77, 185, 189, 191, 201–2, 204–6, 208–12, 214, 217–18
sleepwalking, xviii, xxi, xxv, 15, 21, 30–31, 60, 75, 121, 138–39, 144, 158, 167, 175, 201, 204, 209, 210n40, 211–14, 217–18
solitude, 2, 16, 222
soul, xviii, xxvi, 7, 16, 22–23, 25–27, 29–32, 36, 47, 49–50, 55, 57–58, 59n25, 69, 78–79, 82, 84, 93–95, 103–4, 108, 111, 117–18, 120–21, 129, 135, 144, 162, 165, 193, 195, 199–200, 206, 212–13, 222

Spinoza, Baruch, 27–29, 50–51, 212, 212n45n46
spirit, xxvi, 5, 21–22, 25–30, 40, 68, 93, 97, 128n5, 130n9, 132, 134, 136, 142n37, 144, 152, 154, 156, 164n17, 197n12n13, 219, 221–24
spiritualism, xix, xxvi, 11, 14, 17, 20–30, 38, 52, 74n49, 89, 91–96, 98, 121, 127–30, 136, 144, 168, 169n28, 171, 185, 218, 225
spread body, xix–xx, xxiii, 15, 21, 30, 46, 66, 76–77, 102, 114, 120, 123–24, 126, 130, 142, 158, 165, 167, 177, 180, 183–84, 188–89, 201, 208, 214, 217–18
statue (Condillac's), 19, 39–40, 48–49, 51, 53n10, 56n17, 60–86, 72n47, 75n51, 88, 99–101, 103–16, 120, 122, 125, 150, 168–69, 175, 178–79, 181, 188, 209, 211
Stein, Edith, 69n43, 95
subject, subjectivity, xv–xvii, xix, xxii–xxv, xxviin27, 17, 19, 21, 23, 29, 31, 35, 38, 42–48, 52, 60, 63, 66, 71–73, 76, 84, 88, 91, 94, 100, 103–8, 110–12, 115–17, 122–23, 127, 139–40, 142n37, 143, 148, 153, 157–58, 160–61, 163, 164n18, 165, 169, 171, 176, 178, 182, 187, 192–93, 197, 199–200, 205, 208, 214, 216, 218

thought, xvi, xix–xxi, xxiii, xxv–xxvi, 1–2, 4, 8–9, 11, 13–16, 15n20, 20–22, 24, 26, 28–30, 34–36, 38, 40, 42–45, 47, 51, 55, 57, 59–61, 76–77, 81, 83–85, 88, 93–95, 97, 100, 103, 107, 111–12, 114, 117–18, 121, 129, 131–32, 136, 139, 142n37, 144–45, 155, 158, 168, 170–71, 175, 177, 181–82, 184–85, 187–88, 191, 194, 196, 200–2, 208, 216–19
Tilliette, Xavier, 41

touch, 19, 31, 40, 53n10, 54–57, 61, 63–66, 69–70, 75–79, 81–85, 97, 99–100, 104, 106–8, 110, 114–15, 122, 125, 131, 147, 178–80, 186, 203
    touching-touched, 19, 39, 48, 56n17, 63, 77–78, 81–83, 85, 88, 104, 116, 122, 176–78, 180–81
Tournier, Michel, xxii, 146
transcendence, xxiii, 22, 143, 145
transformation, xxviin27, 21, 64, 67, 163, 164n17, 203, 218
    see also *modification*
trauma, traumatized, traumatizable, xxiii, xxivn22, xxv–xxvi, xxviin27, 20, 23, 42, 47–48, 65–67, 73, 79, 88, 98, 108–9, 121, 125, 156, 158, 160–62, 191, 214, 217–18, 225

Uexküll, Jakob von, 56, 62, 63n33, 70, 73
Umbelino, Luís António, 54n13, 156, 161n12, 217n55
unconscious, 123, 142n37, 143, 146–48, 147n47, 150–52, 162, 164, 202–3, 205–6, 213, 218
Urban, Suzanne, 132, 164, 214–15, 217

Vasseur, Clara-Élisabeth, 95n16
Vieillard-Baron, Jean-Louis, 21, 22n8, 24, 26
Voutsinas, Dimitri, 140n33, 147n46, 151, 204n28

Wright, Crispin, 128, 128n5

www.ingramcontent.com/pod-product-compliance
Lightning Source LLC
Chambersburg PA
CBHW030822230426
43667CB00008B/1337